Managing
Fiscal
Stress

CHATHAM HOUSE SERIES ON CHANGE IN AMERICAN POLITICS

edited by Aaron Wildavsky
University of California, Berkeley

Managing
Fiscal Stress

The Crisis in the Public Sector

Edited by

C͏HARLES H. L͏EVINE
University of Maryland
College Park

C͏HATHAM H͏OUSE P͏UBLISHERS, I͏NC.
Chatham, New Jersey

MANAGING FISCAL STRESS:
The Crisis in the Public Sector

CHATHAM HOUSE PUBLISHERS, INC.
Post Office Box One
Chatham, New Jersey 07928

Publisher: Edward Artinian
Design: Quentin Fiore
Composition: Columbia Publishing Company, Inc.
Printing and Binding: Hamilton Printing Company

Library of Congress Cataloging in Publication Data

Main entry under title:

Managing fiscal stress.

    (Chatham House series on change in American politics)
    Includes bibliographical references.
    1. Finance, Public—United States—1933-
—Addresses, essays, lectures. 2. Government spending
policy—United States—Addresses, essays, lectures.
I. Levine, Charles H. II. Series.
HJ257.2.M36   352.1'0973   79-27266
ISBN 0–934540–02–1

Manufactured in the United States of America
10 9 8 7 6 5 4 3 2 1

Acknowledgments

The editor would like to thank the following authors, periodicals, and publishers for their kind permission to reprint copyrighted material:

Charles H. Levine, "Organizational Decline and Cutback Management." Reprinted from *Public Administration Review* ©1978 by The American Society for Public Administration, 1225 Connecticut Avenue, N.W., Washington, D.C. All rights reserved.

B. Guy Peters and Richard Rose, "The Growth of Government and the Political Consequences of Economic Overload," is a revised version of a paper prepared for delivery at the 1978 annual meeting of the Midwest Political Science Association, Pick-Congress Hotel, Chicago, Illinois, 20–22 April 1978.

Edward K. Hamilton, "On Nonconstitutional Management of a Constitutional Problem." Reprinted by permission of *Daedalus*, Journal of the American Academy of Arts and Sciences, Boston, Massachusetts. Winter 1978, *A New America?*

"New York City's Fiscal Crisis: The Politics of Inflation and Retrenchment" by Martin Shefter from *The Public Interest*, no. 48, Summer 1977, pp. 98–127. ©1977 by National Affairs, Inc. Reprinted by permission of the author and the publisher.

David T. Stanley, "Cities in Trouble." Reprinted by permission of the Academy for Contemporary Problems, Columbus, Ohio.

Richard L. Lucier, "Gauging the Strength and Meaning of the 1978 Tax Revolt." Reprinted from *Public Administration Review* ©1979 by The American Society for Public Administration, 1225 Connecticut Avenue, N.W., Washington, D.C. All rights reserved.

"Nonincremental Policy Making: Notes Toward an Alternative Paradigm" by Paul R. Schulman. From *The American Political Science Review*, vol. 69, no. 4, December 1975, pp. 1354–70. Copyright ©1975 by The American Political Science Association. Reprinted by permission of the author and the publisher.

Irene Rubin, "Universities in Stress: Decision Making Under Conditions of Reduced Resources." From *Social Science Quarterly*, Volume 58, no. 2 (September 1977), pp. 242–254. Reprinted by permission of The University of Texas Press.

Nancy S. Hayward, "The Productivity Challenge." Reprinted from *Public Administration Review* ©1976 by The American Society for Public Ad-

Contents

PART ONE

Introduction

CHARLES H. LEVINE

1. The New Crisis in the Public Sector

Economic growth is a powerful solvent for the problems that trouble governments. Each increment of real growth in national income can enhance the take-home pay of citizens or can be used to create new public programs without accelerating the rate of inflation or forcing politically divisive tradeoffs between old programs and new demands. Because economic growth allows government benefits to expand without depriving anyone, it helps solve the most fundamental political problem of democratic societies: it helps maintain national consensus by reinforcing citizens' beliefs that their system of government works to their advantage and that their taxes are being well spent by a government that is equitable, stable, and efficient.

Throughout the 1970s, the economic growth rates of Western industrial nations declined from the levels attained during the 1950s and '60s. These declining growth rates have forced Western governments to confront some politically sensitive tradeoffs that are inherent in mixed economic systems but are largely ignored during periods of rapid growth. These tradeoffs include (1) the choice between inflation or unsatisfied public demands for goods and services; (2) the choice between providing services through tax-supported bureaucracies or through market arrangements; (3) the choice between attempting to provide equal health, housing, and educational opportunities to all citizens or (in effect) rationing opportunities to those who can afford to pay for them; and (4) the choice between spending for national defense or spending to alleviate the hardship of the poor, the sick, and the underprivileged (i.e., the dilemma of "guns vs. butter").

These politically sensitive tradeoffs have always shaped national policy choices, but throughout most of the 1950s and '60s they were less obvious and less constraining than they are now—at least in the United States. Economic necessities and political realities are now colliding in many countries as political leaders are being forced to face up to these tradeoffs without the comfort of knowing that they can retain the support of the electorate while implementing austerity policies. Aside from wartime, there is no formula for success when elected officials are forced to ask their constituents to accept a lower standard of living or fewer public goods and services at the same time these officials are seeking support for reelection.

These large-scale national policy issues provide a context for the problems of lesser scope that are increasingly plaguing public managers—both elected and

3

appointed—in the United States. The combination of slow economic growth and double-digit inflation—"stagflation"—is causing some governmental units to stretch resources, ration services, cut back programs, make tradeoffs between programs and projects, close facilities, cancel projects, defer maintenance on public works and equipment, abolish positions, and lay off employees. Complicating these difficult management problems is the fact that they have to be solved in a political environment composed of clients and public employees who have come to expect and need *more* services, benefits, and wages from government, and who are not easily persuaded to lower their expectations or make some sacrifices.

This gap between the needs and expectations of citizens and government employees for government services and benefits and the inability of the economy to generate enough economic growth to expand (or even sustain, in some places) tax-supported programs without putting unacceptable demands on taxpayers' take-home pay defines *fiscal stress*. The symptoms of fiscal stress can be found almost everywhere in our govenmental system. For example, we have been told by the White House that a comprehensive national health insurance program is too expensive to undertake at this time. Some critics of the Social Security System have argued that we can no longer afford to expand social security benefits to keep up with inflation without bankrupting the system or further slowing economic growth. In the area of defense spending, a good part of the rationale behind the Strategic Arms Limitation Treaty (SALT II) is fiscal; neither the United States nor the Soviet Union can afford to expand rapidly changing high-technology weapons systems indefinitely without compromising social programs.

At the state and local government level, the legal requirement to balance budgets on a year-to-year basis has made the symptoms of fiscal stress more pronounced. Not only have we witnessed the economic and political chaos of New York City and Cleveland in bond default, but in the late 1970s we have also seen the negative response of taxpayers to rising taxes in the form of California's Proposition 13 and similar initiative movements that have developed in other states and localities.

These symptoms of an "era of limits" have created a number of stresses in government that require reexaminations of our revenue raising, spending, and management systems. These points of stress include (1) the methods used for setting priorities for government action and public programs, (2) the methods used for taxation and revenue generation, (3) the way public services are organized and public employees are compensated to produce services, and (4) the methods used for scaling down and terminating public programs that are no longer of high priority. These direct pressure points contain policies and procedures that are amenable to reform. As such, they provide an agenda for building management strategies for coping with fiscal stress that reflects new approaches to the formulation and implementation of public programs. Before proceeding with these management issues, it is important to reiterate that the struggle to alleviate fiscal stress is conditioned by four facts of political life:

1. Most taxpayers believe that government programs are wasteful. As inflation and recession cause them to experience increased personal financial stress, citizens are more inclined to demand that their taxes be lowered, that government productivity be improved, and that waste in government be eliminated.
2. Few citizens and public employees are willing to voluntarily surrender government services and benefits they have come to expect and depend on.
3. Public officials are forced to make changes within a structure of laws, rules, procedures, and regulations (e.g., merit systems, line-budget items, and special boards, commissions and authorities) that limit alternatives, rigidify decision making, and fragment authority. For the most part, these constraints were installed during periods of growth to control budget expansions and are limited tools for managing budget contractions.
4. Fine-tuning the finances and administration of public agencies and programs will not alone solve the larger problems of stimulating economic growth, but it may contribute—along with other government policies and private-sector initiatives—to restoring the economic growth rates of the 1950s and '60s.

These four facts of political life are both constraints and opportunities—constraints on the ability of public officials to fashion strategies to combat fiscal stress, and opportunities for them to take imaginative action to improve cost effectiveness in government.

Managing Fiscal Stress

In a world without politics, finding the optimal strategy for managing fiscal stress would be a straightforward task. First, one would take a long-range view of the causes of a government's fiscal problems by developing a multiyear forecast of its revenue-raising capacity and the demand for its services and benefits. Second, one would develop a list of priority rankings for all government programs, projects, services, and benefits so that high-priority items could be retained or augmented and low-priority items could be reduced or terminated. Finally, one would design an integrated strategy to generate new resources, improve productivity, and ration services so that both the revenue and expenditure sides of the budget could be neatly balanced. But, instead of an apolitical world that supports a comprehensive approach to the problem of maintaining fiscal solvency, most public management decisions—and especially those that involve cutting back services and benefits—are permeated by politics.

The involvement of interest groups in budgetary decisions usually produces a strategic response to fiscal stress composed of weakly coordinated short-run incremental tactics undertaken by financially pressed agencies at different places through the governmental system. This disjointed response to fiscal stress is usually predicated on the comfortable assumption that the resource shortfall will be temporary and that soon new resources will be found to restore, perhaps even to augment, previous program, service, and workforce levels. This approach is politically convenient because it avoids tradeoffs between programs and agencies and the political conflict that arises when one group or agency feels it is being singled out to make sacrifices while other groups and agencies are being spared. Among the short-run tactics used to "muddle through" fiscal stress, hiring and budget freezes, the absorption of attrition, across-the-board cuts, and the deferring of equipment replacement and maintenance schedules are the most popular because no one group or agency is targeted to make special sacrifices.

But even though this set of tactics is high in political expediency and acceptability, the assumption on which it rests—that the resource squeeze is temporary—may be invalid in a time of limited economic growth. Denying that fiscal stress may be a long-run situation may only put off the day when a real financial crisis will cause runaway inflation, force valuable employees to be laid off, property to be sold, and bonds and notes to be defaulted.

The possibility that fiscal stress is a long-run phenomenon—at least for some cities, regions, agencies, and sectors—suggests the need to develop a middle course for strategic planning that combines a managerial disposition to make government more cost effective with a realistic acceptance of the political forces that constrain comprehensive policy making. This approach should acknowledge, first, that there is no one best way to manage fiscal stress in government. The optimal strategy will differ from place to place and from time to time, depending on (1) the severity of the stress, (2) the size and power of the affected governmental units, (3) the power and alignment of interest groups, (4) the power and professionalism of public employees, and (5) the informal and formal power accumulated by political leaders.

Once fiscal stress is recognized, officials should do everything possible to clear away the underbrush of ambiguity and habit that stand in the way of making tough decisions and designing innovative solutions. Several questions are useful guides for organizing this task:

1. *What activities are mandated?* That is, what services and benefits are required by law? This question is intended to sort out activities that are "musts" from activities engaged in by habit or custom.
2. *What activities can be terminated?* This question focuses on activities that are nonmandated and may have low public support.
3. *What additional revenues can be raised?* Where can user charges and fees be instituted and raised? Where can uncollected taxes be collected? What services can be sold to other government units? What grants can be obtained from the federal government, the state, or private sources?
4. *What activities can be assigned to other service providers?* This question

helps identify services that can be shifted to other units of government, contracted out at lower cost, shared with other governments, provided by the private sector, or "co-produced" with client participation at lower cost.

5. *What things can be done more effectively?* This question addresses the broad area of productivity improvement. It should help generate alternative approaches to delivering existing services, changing organizations, and using technological improvements to reduce costs.

6. *Where can low-cost or no-cost labor be used?* Where can positions be reclassified and downgraded? Where can tasks be simplified, paramilitary jobs be manned by civilians, and paraprofessionals and volunteers be utilized?

7. *Where can capital investments be substituted for labor expenses?* At a time when labor expenses comprise 70 to 80 percent of many agencies' budgets, labor-saving technologies can yield substantial savings; this question seeks to identify opportunities for such savings.

8. *Where can information gathering methods be installed and improved?* Good information can improve financial forecasts and account for the direct and indirect costs and the benefits of service alternatives.

9. *Where can demand be reduced and services rationed?* Because many public services are free, they are often squandered. This question addresses the possibility of using fees and other means (e.g., eliminating low-usage hours in some public services and smoothing out peak hours in others) to reduce demand and pare down the availability of some services.

10. *What policies can help strengthen the economic base and promote economic development?* This question addresses the link between economic development and government policies. It suggests a careful look at the long-run payoffs of governmental policies and underscores the importance of private-sector investment decisions for public-sector fiscal solvency.

11. *What arrangements can be made to identify and strengthen the leadership of this process?* This final question underlies all others. Without able leadership the process of guiding a government through a fiscal squeeze may turn out to be haphazard and self-defeating. Decision-making structures that facilitate interest aggregation and build consensus are likely to reinforce leadership and help ease the adjustment to constrained budgets.

These eleven questions are a beginning for the development of broad management strategies for coping with fiscal stress. Together they provide the outline of a middle course between comprehensive planning and "muddling through" strategies while acknowledging the full importance of the basic mission of public management: balancing economic necessities with political realities.

About This Book

The selections in this book were chosen to help explore the political and economic problems, constraints, alternatives, and choices available to public managers wrestling with fiscal stress. This is a new field of inquiry. The literature, while growing, is not voluminous, but enough material is available to cover much of the subject with high-quality and useful research. As a whole, the readings here are intended to be both exploratory and suggestive—to explore the causes, constraints, and consequences of fiscal stress and to suggest alternatives for balancing fiscal solvency with adequate, equitable, and stable levels of public services and benefits. This book also contains a mix of descriptive case studies and prescriptive readings that underscore the choice and action components of public management roles. The services that public organizations deliver, the way services are organized and financed, and the way services are produced are not fixed and locked in place forever. Instead, they are amenable to managed change along lines suggested.

Situational Factors $\longrightarrow$	Managerial Factors $\longrightarrow$	Outcome Factors
1. Economic base	1. Decision-making methods	1. Fiscal solvency
2. Taxing capacity	2. Resource mix	2. Adequate, stable, and equitable services and benefits
3. Organization of taxing and spending authority	3. Productivity improvements	
4. Scope of governmental service responsibility	4. Cutbacks and terminations	
5. Citizen's service demands and expectations		
6. Interest-group and public-employee demands		

Figure 1.1. Managing Fiscal Stress: The Major Factors

This book is organized along the lines suggested in figure 1.1. Readings in the first two sections discuss situational factors that cause or contribute to fiscal stress. "Organizational Decline and Cutback Management" is intended to frame the study of managing fiscal stress by underscoring the ways in which declining resources force new constraints and decision-making procedures on public officials. The chapter by B. Guy Peters and Richard Rose, "The Growth of Government and the Political Consequences of Economic Overload," outlines the national economic and political forces that are overloading the governmental systems of some advanced industrial societies. Similarly, Edward K. Hamilton's "On Nonconstitutional Management of a Constitutional Problem" traces the economic problems of some state and local governments to issues of national economic development and their revenue-raising constraints. Hamilton argues that many fiscal problems of those governmental units are rooted in the way taxing authority and spending responsibility is organized in the United States. Economic-base erosion also underpins the fiscal plights of the cities. This factor and its consequences is discussed in David Stanley's "Cities in Trouble." But, as Martin Shefter's "New York City's Fiscal Crisis: The Politics of Inflation and Retrenchment" points out, economic-base erosion alone does not produce fiscal stress. Instead, the high demands and expectations of citizens for services and the unyielding demands of special-interest groups and public employees *combine* with lagging economic growth to produce fiscal stress. Finally, as Richard Lucier discusses in "Gauging the Strength and Meaning of the 1978 Tax Revolt," even where economic growth has been strong, citizens may constrain the taxing capacity of their governments with little consideration for the effects of constraints on the public provision of services and benefits. In combination, these chapters cover most of the forces causing fiscal stress at all levels of government. While some hint at means for resolving stress, they were selected primarily for their clear treatment of the causes of fiscal problems.

The remaining chapters suggest directions for managerial action—decision making, revenue generation, productivity improvement, and cutbacks and terminations. These managerial factors encompass the principal levers available to public officials for coping with fiscal stress on a year-to-year basis. (The causes of fiscal stress may also be amenable to change, but in most cases this would involve multiyear economic and political strategies requiring action beyond the authority of most public managers.)

The majority of the chapters deal with problems and alternatives confronting state and local governments. There are two reasons for this. First, fiscal stress has been felt most sharply at state and local levels. By law, most state and local governments must balance their budgets on a year-to-year basis, which causes any fiscal downturn to have almost immediate repercussions for their services. In contrast, a balanced federal budget is a rarity. Second, a number of federal agencies and private foundations have supported research on state and local government financial and service-delivery problems; many of the chapters in this book are by-products of this research commitment. Nevertheless, some authors have focused on the experiences of federal agencies and projects, and almost all the lessons the chapters teach are relevant to public managers at every level of government.

The decision-making chapters are both descriptive and analytic. Paul R. Schulman's "Nonincremental Policy Making: Notes Toward an Alternative Paradigm" is an analysis of decision making in the National Aeronautical and Space Administration (NASA) over the ten-year period of its growth and decline. Schulman's analysis points to the difficulties involved in trying to decide how to retrench public organizations gradually. Irene Rubin's "Universities in Stress: Decision Making Under Conditions of Reduced Resources" describes the decision-making strategies used by five state universities undergoing financial stress. Rubin's study underscores the importance of information and the uncertainty in decision making when administrations confront revenue shortfalls and difficult cutback decisions. David W. Singleton, Bruce A. Smith, and James R. Cleaveland's "Zero-Based Budgeting in Wilmington, Delaware," and Regina E. Herzlinger's "Zero-Base Budgeting in the Federal Government: A Case Study," are intended to illustrate the advantages and limits of zero-base budgeting in public-sector decision making. Singleton, Smith, and Cleaveland describe a successful application of ZBB in Wilmington, Delaware, a medium-size city, while Herzlinger analyzes a largely unsuccessful attempt to use ZBB in a huge, complex federal agency, the Public Health Service (PHS). Together, the decision-making chapters illustrate the difficulties involved in applying rational decision making to cutbacks and suggest areas where data analysis and decision-making aids can be useful in budgeting.

When a budget squeeze occurs, attention is immediately directed toward the revenue side of budgets, because increased revenues can eliminate the need to increase productivity or cut back services and workforces. The chapters on resources examine some directions and consequences of searching for new revenues. The primary source of such funds, is, of course, the federal government. But David B. Walker's "The New System of Intergovernmental Relations: More Fiscal Relief and More Government Intrusions" describes the growth of federal grants to state and local governments as a mixed blessing; fiscal stress may be alleviated, but local autonomy may be seriously compromised. Another approach to generating new revenues is discussed in Selma J. Mushkin and Charles L. Vehorn, "User Fees and Charges." The authors argue that instituting and hiking fees and charges for a wide range of services can generate additional resources and place the costs of public benefits directly on those who use them; such actions can also greatly improve the public allocation of resources. In certain cases fees and charges may be more fair than taxation. User charges, fees, and many other means for raising revenues and lowering costs are discussed in Charles A. Morrison's "Identifying Alternative Resources for Local Government." Morrison outlines strategies for seeking out nonlocal revenues from federal and state governments, private foundations, and local businesses and industries; developing local employees as resources; developing intergovernmental contracts and other interjurisdictional arrangements for sharing service-delivery burdens; utilizing volunteers and nongovernmental facilities; and finding nonservice alternatives to the actual delivery of services. Each of the strategies is intended to expand the range of possible revenue sources available to meet downward shifts in traditional revenue sources, as well as to help alleviate the pressures on the resource base caused by increased demands for public services.

One of the principal palliatives for alleviating the revenue-expenditure squeeze is to increase the productivity of public services. But "productivity" is an elusive concept and productivity improvement is easier to advocate than to achieve. The chapters in part 5 underscore this point, but they also direct attention to some examples where productivity improvement efforts can yield positive results. Nancy S. Hayward's "The Productivity Challenge" outlines some promising national trends and developments aimed at facilitating improved governmental productivity. In a similar vein, Harry Hatry's "Current State of the Art of State and Local Government Productivity Improvement — and Potential Federal Roles" assesses a number of productivity-improvement techniques and suggests some directions for federal action in promoting state and local productivity efforts. Finally, E. S. Savas's "Policy Analysis for Local Government: Public vs. Private Refuse Collection" analyzes the comparative efficiency of public and private organizational arrangements used for providing refuse collection. Savas argues that contracting out provides a mechanism for enhancing productivity that can be extended to a variety of municipal services. In combination, the three chapters in this part provide a backdrop for considering the feasibility of productivity improvement strategies as a means of maintaining service levels with lower revenues or for increasing services with constant levels of revenue.

When all else fails — when budgets cannot be balanced with projected levels of revenues and expenditures or when high-priority programs cannot be undertaken within projected levels of revenue — cutbacks are called for. Cutback management means making and implementing hard decisions about which employees will be laid off, which programs and agencies will be scaled down or terminated, and which clients will be asked to make sacrifices. These decisions are compounded by the legal constraints on government and the political power and activity of public employees and organized groups of constituents. Some of the problems, dilemmas, and paradoxes of managing cutbacks are included in "More on Cutback Management: Hard Questions for Hard Times." Of all the problems of cutback management, one of the hardest choices facing managers is the one between whether to reduce the size of an agency by absorbing attrition or by laying off employees. Leonard Greenhalgh and Robert B. McKersie's "Reduction in Force: Cost Effectiveness of Alternative Strategies" analyzes this problem through the use of cost-benefit analysis. Their methodology is useful for decision makers weighing similar choices in different circumstances. The final chapter in the book deals with what is perhaps the knottiest problem in public management — how to terminate a public policy within the rules of democratic government. Robert D. Behn's "How to Terminate a Public Policy: A Dozen Hints for the Would-Be Terminator" outlines the constraints that block termination efforts and outlines tactics that may help overcome political resistance and bureaucratic inertia. Cutbacks and terminations are growing phenomena in public management. The chapters in part 6 are intended to alert the reader to the pitfalls of presuming that reducing public programs can be straightforward and uncomplicated.

The "bottom line" for government managers in a time of austerity is finding a balance between fiscal solvency and levels of services and benefits that are adequate, equitable, and stable. *Adequacy* can be defined as a level of public goods and services capable of sustaining civil society and promoting individual well-being. This means adequate public goods and services ranging from national defense and law enforcement to housing and education. *Equity* can be defined as a system of service provision that guarantees citizens equal access and opportunities to use and benefit from public goods and services. Finally, *stability* refers to the maintenance of goods and services commensurate with the needs and expectations of citizens. Unstable service provision breeds uncertainty, cynicism, and alienation—all of which undermine consensus and support for government.

The "worst-case scenario" would be one in which fiscal solvency cannot be attained at or above a plateau; where public goods and services are no longer adequate, equitable, or stable. In this situation, either citizens' expectations must be lowered or they must be persuaded to make sacrifices in their personal disposable incomes to provide the additional revenues necessary to increase public services and benefits. This latter course is unlikely to win much public support, and so the task of managing fiscal stress will probably have to key on strategies for increasing the cost effectiveness of government programs and gradually lowering citizens' demands.

Even though this worst-case scenario is likely to be atypical, the problem of maintaining fiscal solvency at adequate, equitable, and stable service levels is common to almost all governments, and is becoming an even more difficult task as resources become more scarce. Indeed, it was the recognition that public officials are confronting an increasingly challenging task that inspired this book. It is dedicated to those public officials who must carry the heavy responsibility—and bear with the frustration—of managing fiscal stress in a democracy.

Charles H. Levine

2. Organizational Decline and Cutback Management

Government organizations are neither immortal nor unshrinkable.[1] Like growth, organizational decline and death, by erosion or plan, is a form of organizational change; but all the problems of managing organizational change are compounded by a scarcity of slack resources.[2] This feature of declining organizations—the diminution of the cushion of spare resources necessary for coping with uncertainty, risking innovation, and rewarding loyalty and cooperation—presents for government a problem that simultaneously challenges the underlying premises and feasibility of both contemporary management systems and the institutions of pluralist liberal democracy.[3]

Growth and decline are issues of a grand scale usually tackled by only the most brave or foolhardy of macro social theorists. The division of scholarly labor between social theorists and students of management is now so complete that the link between the great questions of political economy and the more earthly problems of managing public organizations is rarely forged. This bifurcation is more understandable when one acknowledges that managers and organization analysts have for decades (at least since the Roosevelt administration and the wide acceptance of Keynesian economics) been able to subsume their concern for societal level instability under broad assumptions of abundance and continuous and unlimited growth.[4] Indeed, almost all our public management strategies are predicated on assumptions of the continuing enlargement of public revenues and expenditures. These expansionist assumptions are particularly prevalent in public financial management systems that anticipate budgeting by incremental additions to a secure base.[5] Recent events and gloomy forecasts, however, have called into question the validity and generality of these assumptions, and have created a need to reopen inquiry into the effects of resource scarcity on public organizations and their management systems. These events and forecasts, ranging from taxpayer revolts like California's successful Proposition 13 campaign and financial crises like the near collapse into bankruptcy of New York City's government and the agonizing retrenchment of its bureaucracy, to the foreboding predictions of the "limits of growth" modelers, also relink issues of political economy of the most monumental significance to practices of public management.[6]

We know very little about the decline of public organizations and the management of cutbacks. This may be because even though some federal agencies, such as the Works Progress Administration, Economic Recovery Administration, Department of Defense, National Aeronautics and Space Administration, the Office of Economic Opportunity, and many state and local agencies have expanded and then contracted,[7] or even died, the public sector as a whole has expanded enormously over the last four decades. In this period of expansion and optimism among proponents of an active government, isolated incidents of zero growth and decline have been considered anomalous; and the difficulties faced by the management of declining agencies coping with retrenchment have been regarded as outside the mainstream of public management concerns. It is a sign of our times — labeled by Kenneth Boulding as the "Era of Slowdown" — that we are now reappraising cases of public organization decline and death as exemplars and forerunners in order to provide strategies for the design and management of *mainstream* public administration in a future dominated by resource scarcity.[8]

The decline and death of government organizations is a symptom, a problem, and a contingency. It is a symptom of resource scarcity at a societal, even global, level that is creating the necessity for governments to terminate some programs, lower the activity level of others, and confront tradeoffs between new demands and old programs rather than to expand whenever a new public problem arises. It is a problem for managers who must maintain organizational capacity by devising new managerial arrangements within prevailing structures that were designed under assumptions of growth. It is a contingency for public employees and clients; employees who must sustain their morale and productivity in the face of increasing control from above and shrinking opportunities for creativity and promotion while clients must find alternative sources for the services governments may no longer be able to provide.

Organizational Decline and Administrative Theory

Growth is a common denominator that links contemporary management theory to its historical antecedents and management practices with public policy choices. William Scott has observed that "...organization growth creates organizational abundance, or surplus, which is used by management to buy off internal consensus from the potentially conflicting interest group segments that compete for resources in organizations."[9] As a common denominator, growth has provided a criterion to gauge the acceptability of government policies and has defined many of the problems to be solved by management action and organizational research. So great is our enthusiasm for growth that even when an organizational decline seems inevitable and irreversible, it is nearly impossible to get elected officials, public managers, citizens, or management theorists to confront cutback and decremental planning situations as anything more than temporary slowdowns. Nevertheless, the reality of zero growth and absolute decline, at least in some sectors, regions, communities, and organizations, means that management and public policy theory must be expanded to incorporate nongrowth as an initial condition that applies in some cases. If Scott's assertions about the pervasiveness of a growth ideology in management are correct, our management and policy paradigms will have to be replaced or augmented by new frameworks to help identify critical questions and strategies for action. Put squarely, without growth, how do we manage public organizations?

We have no ready or comprehensive answers to this question, only hunches and shards of evidence to serve as points of departure. Under conditions and assumptions of decline, the ponderables, puzzles, and paradoxes of organizational management take on new complexities. For example, organizations cannot be cut back by merely reversing the sequence of activity and resource allocation by which their parts were originally assembled. Organizations are organic social wholes with emergent qualities which allow their parts to recombine into intricately interwoven semi-lattices when they are brought together. In his study of NASA's growth and drawdown, Paul Schulman has observed that viable public programs must attain "capture points" of public goal and resource commitments, and these organizational thresholds or "critical masses" are characterized by their indivisibility.[10] Therefore, to attempt to disaggregate and cut back on one element of such an intricate and delicate political and organization arrangement may jeopardize the functioning and equilibrium of an entire organization.

Moreover, retrenchment compounds the choice of management strategies with paradoxes. When slack resources abound, money for the development of management planning, control, information systems, and the conduct of policy analysis is plentiful even though these systems are relatively irrelevant to decision making.[11] Under conditions of abundance, habit, intuition, snap judgments, and other forms of informal analysis will suffice for most decisions because the costs of making mistakes can be easily absorbed without threatening the organization's survival.[12] In times of austerity, however, when these control and analytic tools are needed to help minimize the risk of making mistakes, the money for their development and implementation is unavailable.

Similarly, without slack resources to produce "win-win" consensus-building solutions and to provide side payments to overcome resistance to change, organizations will have difficulty innovating and maintaining flexibility. Yet, these are precisely the activities needed to maintain capacity while contracting, especially when the overriding imperative is to minimize the perturbations of adjusting to new organizational equilibriums at successively lower levels of funding and activity.[13]

Lack of growth also creates a number of serious personnel problems. For example, the need to reward managers for directing organizational contraction and termination is a problem because without growth there are few promotions and rewards available to motivate and retain successful and loyal managers — particularly when compared with job opportunities for talented managers outside the declining organization.[14] Also, without expansion, public organizations constrained by merit and career tenure systems are unable to attract and accommodate new young talent. Without an inflow of younger employees, the average age of employees is forced up, and the organization's skill pool becomes frozen at the very time younger, more flexible, more mobile, less expensive, and (some would argue) more creative employees are needed.[15]

Decline forces us to set some of our logic for rationally structuring organizations on end and upside down. For instance, under conditions of growth and abundance, one problem for managers and organizational designers is how to set up *exclusionary* mechanisms to prevent "free riders" (employees and clients who share in the consumption of the organization's collective benefits without sharing the burden that produced the benefit) from taking advantage of the enriched common pool of resources. In contrast, under conditions of decline and austerity, the problem for managers and organizational designers is how to set up *inclusionary* mechanisms to prevent organizational participants from avoiding the sharing of the "public bads" (increased burdens) that result from the depletion of the common pool of resources.[16] In other words, to maintain order and capacity when undergoing decline, organizations need mechanisms like long-term contracts with clauses that make pensions nonportable if broken at the employee's discretion. These mechanisms need to be carefully designed to penalize and constrain "free exiters" and cheap exits at the convenience of the employees while still allowing managers to cut and induce into retirement marginally performing and unneeded employees.

As a final example, inflation erodes steady states so that staying even actually requires extracting more resources from the organization's environment and effectuating greater internal economies. The irony of managing decline in the public sector is particularly compelling under conditions of recession or so-called "stagflation." During these periods of economic hardship and uncertainty, pressure is put on the federal government to follow Keynesian dictates and spend more through deficit financing; at the same time, critical public opinion and legal mandates require some individual agencies (and many state and local governments) to balance their budgets, and in some instances to spend less.

These characteristics of declining public organizations are like pieces of a subtle jigsaw puzzle whose parameters can only be guessed at and whose abstruseness deepens with each new attempt to fit its edges together. To overcome our tendency to regard decline in public organizations as anomalous, we need to develop a catalogue of what we already know about declining public organizations. A typology of *causes* of public organizational decline and corresponding sets of *tactics* and *decision rules* available for managing cutbacks will serve as a beginning.

The Causes of Public Organization Decline

Cutting back any organization is difficult, but a good deal of the problem of cutting back public organizations is compounded by their special status as authoritative, nonmarket extensions of the state.[17] Public organizations are used to deliver services that usually have no direct or easily measurable monetary value or when market arrangements fail to provide the necessary level of revenues to support the desired level or distribution of services. Since budgets depend on appropriations and not sales, the diminution or termination of public organizations and programs, or conversely their maintenance and survival, are political matters usually calling for the application of the most sophisticated attack or survival tactics in the arsenal of the skilled bureaucrat-politician.[18] These strategies are not universally propitious; they are conditioned by the causes for decline and the hoped-for results.

The causes of public organization decline can be categorized into a four-cell typology as shown in figure 2.1. The causes are divided along two dimensions: (1) whether they are primarily the result of conditions located either internal or external to the organization, or (2) whether they are principally a product of political or economic/technical conditions.[19] This is admittedly a crude scheme for lumping instances of decline, but it does cover most cases and allows for some abstraction.

	Internal	External
Political	Political Vulnerability	Problem Depletion
Economic/ Technical	Organizational Atrophy	Environmental Entropy

Figure 2.1. The Causes of Public Organization Decline

Of the four types. *problem depletion* is the most familiar. It covers government involvement in short-term crises like natural disasters such as floods and earthquakes, medium-length governmental interventions like war mobilization and countercyclical employment programs, and longer-term public programs like polio research and treatment and space exploration—all of which involve development cycles. These cycles are characterized by a political definition of a problem followed by the extensive commitment of resources to attain critical masses and then contractions after the problem has been solved, alleviated, or has evolved into a less troublesome stage or politically popular issue.[20]

Problem depletion is largely a product of forces beyond the control of the affected organization. Three special forms of problem depletion involve demographic shifts, problem redefinition, and policy termination. The impact of demographic shifts has been vividly demonstrated in the closing of schools in neighborhoods where the school-age population has shrunk. While the cause for most school closings is usually neighborhood aging—a factor outside the control of the school system—the decision to close a school is largely political. The effect of problem redefinition on public organizations is most easily illustrated by movements to *de*institutionalize the mentally ill. In these cases, the core bureaucracies responsible for treating these populations in institutions has shrunk as the rising per patient cost of hospitalization has combined with pharmaceutical advances in antidepressants and tranquilizers to cause public attitudes and professional doctrine to shift.[21]

Policy termination has both theoretical import and policy significance. Theoretically, it is the final phase of a public policy intervention cycle and can be defined as "the deliberate conclusion or cessation of specific government functions, programs, policies, or organizations."[22] Its policy relevance is underscored by recent experiments and proposals for sunset legislation which would require some programs to undergo extensive evaluations after a period of usually five years and be reauthorized or be terminated rather than be continued indefinitely.[23]

Environmental entropy occurs when the capacity of the environment to support the public organization at prevailing levels of activity erodes.[24] This kind of decline covers the now familiar phenomena of financially troubled cities and regions with declining economic bases. Included in this category are market and technological shifts, such as the decline in demand for domestic textiles and steel and its effect on the economies and quality of life in places like New England textile towns and steel cities like Gary, Indiana, Bethlehem, Pennsylvania, and Youngstown, Ohio;[25] transportation changes that have turned major railroad hubs and riverports of earlier decades into stagnating and declining economies; mineral depletion, which has crippled mining communities; and intrametropolitan shifts of economic activity from central cities to their suburbs.[26] In these cases, population declines often have paralleled general economic declines, which erode tax bases and force cities to cut services. One of the tragic side effects of environmental entropy is that it most severely affects those who cannot move.[27] Caught in the declining city and region are the immobile and dependent: the old, the poor, and the unemployable. For these communities, the forced choice of cutting services to an ever more dependent and needy population is the cruel outcome of decline.[28]

Environmental entropy also has a political dimension. As Proposition 13 makes clear, the capacity of a government is as much a function of the willingness of taxpayers to be taxed as it is of the economic base of the taxing region. Since the demand for services and the supply of funds to support them are usually relatively independent in the public sector, taxpayer resistance can produce diminished revenues which force service reductions even though the demand and *need* for services remains high.

The *political vulnerability* of public organizations is an internal property indicating a high level of fragility and precariousness that limits their capacity to resist budget decrements and demands to contract from their environment. Of the factors that contribute to vulnerability, some seem to be more responsible for decline and death than others. Small size, internal conflict, and changes in leadership, for example, seem less telling than the lack of a base of expertise or the absence of a positive self-image and history of excellence. However, an organization's age may be the most accurate predictor of bureaucratic vulnerability. Contrary to biological reasoning, aged organizations are more flexible than young organizations and therefore rarely die or even shrink very much. Herbert Kaufman argues that one of the advantages of organizations over solitary individuals is that they do provide longer institutional memories than a human lifetime, and this means that older organizations ought to have a broader range of adaptive skills, more capacity for learning, more friends and allies, and be more innovative because they have less to fear from making a wrong decision than a younger organization.[29]

Organizational atrophy is a common phenomenon in all organizations but government organizations are particularly vulnerable because they lack market-generated revenues to signal a malfunction and pinpoint responsibility. Internal atrophy and declining performance, which can lead to resource cutbacks or to a weakening of organizational capacity, come from a host of system and management failures almost too numerous to identify. A partial list would include inconsistent and perverse incentives, differentiation without integration, role confusion, decentralized authority with vague responsibility, too many inappropriate rules, weak oversight, stifled dissent and upward communication, rationalization of performance failure by "blaming the victim," lack of self-evaluating and self-correcting capacity, high turnover, continuous politicking for promotions and not for program resources, continuous reorganization, suspicion of outsiders, and obsolescence caused by routine adherence to past methods and technologies in the face of changing problems. No organization is likely to be afflicted by them all at once, but a heavy dose of some of these breakdowns in combination can contribute to an organization's decline and even death.

Identifying and differentiating among these four decline situations provides a start toward cataloging and estimating the appropriateness of strategies for managing decline and cutbacks. This activity is useful because when undergoing decline, organizations face three decision tasks: first, management must decide whether it will adopt a strategy to resist decline or smooth it (i.e., reduce the impact of fluctuations in the environment that cause interruptions in the flow of work and poor performance); second, given this choice of maneuvering strategies it will have to decide what tactics are most appropriate;[30] and third, if necessary, it will have to make decisions about how and where cuts will occur. Of course, the cause of a decline will greatly affect these choices.

Strategic Choices

Public organizations behave in response to a mix of motives — some aimed at serving national (or state or local) purposes, some aimed at goals for the *organization as a whole*, and others directed toward the particularistic goals of organizational subunits. Under conditions of growth, requests for more resources by subunits usually can be easily concerted with the goals of the organization as a whole and its larger social purposes. Under decline, however, subunits usually respond to requests to make cuts in terms of their particular long-term survival needs (usually defended in terms of the injury cutbacks would inflict on a program with lofty purposes or on a dependent clientele) irrespective of impacts on the performance of government or the organization as a whole.

The presence of powerful survival instincts in organizational subunits helps explain why the political leadership of public organizations can be trying to respond to legislative or executive directives to cut back at the same time that the career and program leadership of subunits will be taking action to resist cuts.[31] It also helps explain why growth can have the appearance of a rational administrative process complete with a hierarchy of objectives and broad consensus, while decline takes on the *appearance* of what James G. March has called a "garbage can problem"—arational, polycentral, fragmented, and dynamic.[32] Finally, it allows us to understand why the official rhetoric about cutbacks—whether it be to "cut the fat," "tighten our belts," "preserve future options," or "engage in a process of orderly and programmed termination"—is often at wide variance with the unofficial conduct of bureau chiefs who talk of "minimizing cutbacks to mitigate catastrophe" or "making token sacrifices until the heat's off."

Retrenchment politics dictate that organization will respond to decrements with a mix of espoused and operative strategies that are not necessarily consistent.[33] When there is a wide divergence between the official pronouncements about the necessity for cuts and the actual occurrence of cuts, skepticism, cynicism, distrust, and noncompliance will dominate the retrenchment process and cutback management will be an adversarial process pitting top and middle management against one another. In most cases, however, conflict will not be rancorous, and strategies for dealing with decline will be a mixed bag of tactics intended either to *resist* or *smooth* decline. The logic here is that no organization accedes to cuts with enthusiasm and will try to find a way to resist cuts; but resistance is risky. In addition to the possibility of being charged with nonfeasance, no responsible manager wants to be faced with the prospect of being unable to control where cuts will take place or confront quantum cuts with unpredictable consequences. Instead, managers will choose a less risky course and attempt to protect organizational capacity and procedures by smoothing decline and its effects on the organization.

An inventory of some of these cutback management tactics is presented in figure 2.2. They are arrayed according to the decline problem which they can be employed to solve. This collection of tactics by no means exhausts the possible organizational responses to decline situations, nor are all the tactics exclusively directed toward meeting a single contingency. They are categorized in order to show that many familiar coping tactics correspond, even if only roughly, to an underlying logic. In this way a great deal of information about organizational responses to decline can be aggregated without explicating each tactic in great detail.[34]

The tactics intended to remove or alleviate the external political and economic causes of decline are reasonably straightforward means to revitalize eroded economic bases, reduce environmental uncertainty, protect niches, retain flex-

Tactics to Resist Decline	Tactics to Smooth Decline
(Problem Depletion)	
External 1. Diversify programs, clients and	1. Make peace with competing
Political constituents	agencies
2. Improve legislative liaison	2. Cut low prestige programs
3. Educate the public about the	3. Cut programs to politically weak
agency's mission	clients
4. Mobilize dependent clients	4. Sell and lend expertise to other
5. Become "captured" by a powerful	agencies
interest group or legislator	5. Share problems with other
6. Threaten to cut vital or popular	agencies
programs	
7. Cut a visible and widespread	
service a little to demonstrate	
client dependence	
(Environmental Entropy)	
Economic/ 1. Find a wider and richer revenue	1. Improve targeting on problems
Technical base (e.g., metropolitan reor-	2. Plan with preservative objectives
ganization)	3. Cut losses by distinguishing
2. Develop incentives to prevent	between capital investments and
disinvestment	sunk costs
3. Seek foundation support	4. Yield concessions to taxpayers
4. Lure new public and private	and employers to retain them
sector investment	
5. Adopt user charges for services	
where possible	
(Political Vulnerability)	
Internal 1. Issue symbolic responses like form-	1. Change leadership at each stage
Political ing study commissions and task	in the decline process
forces	2. Reorganize at each stage
2. "Circle the wagons," i.e., develop	3. Cut programs run by weak
a siege mentality to retain esprit	subunits
de corps	4. Shift programs to another agency
3. Strengthen expertise	5. Get temporary exemptions from
	personnel and budgetary regula-
	tions which limit discretion
(Organizational Atrophy)	
Economic/ 1. Increase hierarchical control	1. Renegotiate long term contracts
Technical 2. Improve productivity	to regain flexibility
3. Experiment with less costly service	2. Install rational choice techniques
delivery systems	like zero-base budgeting and
4. Automate	evaluation research

Figure 2.2. Some Cutback Management Tactics

5. Stockpile and ration resources

3. Mortgage the future by deferring maintenance and downscaling personnel quality
4. Ask employees to make voluntary sacrifices like taking early retirements and deferring raises
5. Improve forecasting capacity to anticipate further cuts
6. Reassign surplus facilities to other users
7. Sell surplus property, lease back when needed
8. Exploit the exploitable

Figure 2.2. Some Cutback Management Tactics (continued)

ibility, or lessen dependence. The tactics for handling the internal causes of decline, however, tend to be more subtle means for strengthening organizations and managerial control. For instance, the management of decline *in the face of resistance* can be smoothed by changes in leadership. When hard unpopular decisions have to be made, new managers can be brought in to make the cuts, take the flak, and move on to another organization. By rotating managers into and out of the declining organization, interpersonal loyalties built up over the years will not interfere with the cutback process. This is especially useful in implementing a higher-level decision to terminate an organization where managers will make the necessary cuts knowing that their next assignments will not depend on their support in the organization to be terminated.

The "exploit the exploitable" tactic also calls for further explanation. Anyone familiar with the personnel practices of universities during the 1970s will recognize this tactic. It has been brought about by the glutted market for academic positions, which has made many unlucky recent Ph.Ds vulnerable and exploitable. This buyers' market has coincided neatly with the need of universities facing steady states and declining enrollments to avoid long-term tenure commitments to expensive faculties. The result is a marked increase in part-time and nontenure track positions, which are renewed on a semester-to-semester basis. So while retrenchment is smoothed and organization flexibility increased, it is attained at considerable cost to the careers and job security of the exploited teachers.

Cutback management is a two-crucible problem: besides selecting tactics for either resisting or smoothing decline, if necessary, management must also select who will be let go and what programs will be curtailed or terminated. Deciding where to make cuts is a test of managerial intelligence and courage because each choice involves tradeoffs and opportunity costs that cannot be erased through the generation of new resources accrued through growth.

As with most issues of public management involving the distribution of costs, the choice of decision rules to allocate cuts usually involves the tradeoff between equity and efficiency.[35] In this case, "equity" is meant to mean the distribution of cuts across the organization with an equal probability of hurting all units and employees irrespective of impacts on the long-term capacity of the organization. "Efficiency" is meant to mean the sorting, sifting, and assignment of cuts to those people and units in the organization so that for a given budget decrement, cuts are allocated to minimize the long-term loss in total benefits to the organization as a whole, irrespective of their distribution.

Making cuts on the basis of equity is easier for managers because it is socially acceptable, easier to justify, and involves few decision making costs. "Sharing the pain" is politically expedient because it appeals to commonsense ideals of justice. Further, simple equity decision making avoids costs from sorting, selecting, and negotiating cuts.[36] In contrast, efficiency cuts involve costly triage analysis because the distribution of pain and inconvenience requires that the value of people and subunits to the organization has to be weighed in terms of their expected *future* contributions. In the public sector, of course, things are never this clear-cut because a host of constraints like career status, veteran's preference, bumping rights, entitlements, and mandated programs limit managers from selecting optimal rules for making cuts. Nevertheless, the values of equity and efficiency are central to allocative decision making and provide useful criteria for judging the appropriateness of cutback rules. By applying these criteria to five of the most commonly used or proposed cutback methods—seniority, hiring freezes, even-percentage-cuts-across-the-board, productivity criteria, and zero base budgeting—we are able to make assessments of their efficacy as managerial tools.

Seniority is the most prevalent and most maligned of the five decision rules. Seniority guarantees have little to do with either equity or efficiency per se. Instead, they are directed at another value of public administration; that is, the need to provide secure career-long employment to neutrally competent civil servants.[37] Because seniority is likely to be spread about the organization unevenly, using seniority criteria for making cuts forces managers to implicitly surrender control over the impact of cuts on services and the capacity of subunits. Furthermore, since seniority usually dictates a "last-in-first-out" retention system, personnel cuts using this decision rule tend to inflict the greatest harm to minorities and women, who are recent entrants in most public agencies.

A *hiring freeze* is a convenient short-run strategy to buy time and preserve options. In the short run it hurts no one already employed by the organization because hiring freezes rely on "natural attrition" through resignations, retirements, and death to diminish the size of an organization's work force. In the long run, however, hiring freezes are hardly the most equitable or efficient way to scale down organizational size. First, even though natural and self-selection relieves the stress on managers, it also takes control over the decision of whom and where to cut away from management and thereby reduces the possibility of intelligent long-range cutback planning. Second, hiring freezes are more likely to harm minorities and women, who are more likely to be the next hired rather than the next retired. Third, attrition will likely occur at different rates among an organization's professional and technical specialities. Since resignations will most likely come from those employees with the most opportunities for employment elsewhere, during a long hiring freeze an organization may find itself short on some critically needed skills yet unable to hire people with these skills even though they may be available.

Even-percentage-cuts-across-the-board are expedient because they transfer decision-making costs lower in the organization, but they tend to be insensitive to the needs, production functions, and contributions of different units. The same percentage cut may call for hardly more than some mild belt tightening in some large unspecialized units but when translated into the elimination of one or two positions in a highly specialized, tightly integrated small unit, it may immobilize that unit.

Criticizing *productivity criteria* is more difficult but nevertheless appropriate, especially when the concept is applied to the practice of cutting low producing units and people based on their *marginal product* per increment of revenue. This method is insensitive to differences in clients served, unit capacity, effort, and need. A more appropriate criterion is one that cuts programs, organization units, and employees so that the *marginal utility* for a decrement of resources is equal across units, individuals, and programs thereby providing for *equal sacrifices* based on the *need* for resources. However, this criterion assumes organizations are fully rational actors, an assumption easily dismissed. More likely, cuts will be distributed by a mix of analysis and political bargaining.

Aggregating incompatible needs and preferences is a political problem, and this is why *zero base budgeting* gets such high marks as a method for making decisions about resource allocation under conditions of decline. First, ZBB is future directed; instead of relying on an "inviolate-base-plus-increment" calculus, it allows for the analysis of both existing and proposed new activities. Second, ZBB allows for tradeoffs between programs or units below their present funding levels. Third, ZBB allows a ranking of decision packages by political bargaining and negotiation so that attention is concentrated on those packages or activities most likely to be affected by cuts.[38] As a result, ZBB allows both analysis and politics to enter into cutback decision making and therefore can incorporate an expression of the *intensity of need* for resources by participating managers and clients while also accommodating estimates of how cuts will affect the *activity levels* of their units. Nevertheless, ZBB is not without problems. Its analytic component is likely to be expensive—especially so under conditions of austerity—and to be subject to all the limitations and pitfalls of cost-benefit analysis, while its political component is likely to be costly in political terms as units fight with one another and with central management over rankings, tradeoffs, and the assignment of decrements.[39]

These five decision rules illustrate how strategic choices about cutback management can be made with or without expediency, analysis, courage, consideration of the organization's long-term health, or the effect of cuts on the lives of employees and clients. Unfortunately, for some employees and clients, and the public interest, the choice will usually be made by managers to "go along" quietly with across-the-board cuts and exit as soon as possible. The alternative for those who would prefer more responsible and toughminded decision making *to facilitate long-run organizational survival* is to develop in managers and employees strong feelings of organizational loyalty and loyalty to clients, to provide disincentives to easy exit, and to encourage participation so that dissenting views on the location of cuts could emerge from the ranks of middle management, lower-level employees, and clients.[40]

Ponderables

The world of the future is uncertain, but scarcity and tradeoffs seem inevitable. Boulding has argued that "in a stationary society roughly half the society will be experiencing decline while the other half will be experiencing growth."[41] If we are entering an era of general slowdown, this means that the balance in the distribution between expanding and contracting sectors, regions, and organizations will be tipped toward decline. It means that we will need a governmental capacity for developing tradeoffs between growing and declining organizations and for intervening in regional and sectorial economies to avoid the potentially harmful effects of radical perturbations from unmanaged decline.

So far we have managed to get along without having to make conscious tradeoffs between sectors and regions. We have met declines on a "crisis-to-crisis" basis through emergency legislation and financial aid. This is a strategy that assumes declines are special cases of temporary disequilibrium, bounded in time and space, that are usually confined to a single organization, community, or region. A broad-scale long-run *societal-level* decline, however, is a problem of a different magnitude, and to resolve it, patchwork solutions will not suffice.

There seem to be two possible directions in which to seek a way out of immobility. First is the authoritarian possibility; what Robert L. Heilbroner has called the rise of "iron governments" with civil liberties diminished and resources allocated throughout society from the central government without appeal.[42] This is a possibility abhorrent to the democratic tradition, but it comprises a possible future—if not for the United States in the near future, at least for some other less affluent nations. So far we have had little experience with cutting back on rights, entitlements, and privileges; but scarcity may dictate "decoupling" dependent and less powerful clients and overcoming resistance through violent autocratic implementation methods.

The other possible future direction involves new images and assumptions about the nature of man, the state, and the ecosystem. It involves changes in values away from material consumption, a gradual withdrawal from our fascination with economic growth, and more efficient use of resources—especially raw materials. For this possibility to occur, we will have to have a confrontation with our propensity for wishful thinking that denies that some declines are permanent. Also required is a widespread acceptance of egalitarian norms and of anti-growth and no-growth ideologies, which are now only nascent, and the development of a political movement to promote their incorporation into policy making.[43] By backing away from our obsession with growth, we will also be able to diminish the "load" placed on central governments and allow for greater decentralization and the devolvement of functions.[44] In this way, we may be able to preserve democratic rights and processes while meeting a future of diminished resources.

Nevertheless, the preferable future might not be the most probable future. This prospect should trouble us deeply.

Notes

1. The intellectual foundations of this essay are too numerous to list. Three essays in particular sparked my thinking: Herbert Kaufman's *The Limits of Organizational Change* (University, Ala.: University of Alabama Press, 1971) and *Are Government Organizations Immortal?* (Washington, D.C.: Brookings Institution, 1976) and Herbert J. Gans, "Planning for Declining and Poor Cities," *Journal of the American Institute of Planners*, September 1975, pp. 305–7. The concept of "cutback planning" is introduced in the Gans article. My initial interest in this subject stemmed from my work with a panel of the National Academy of Public Administration on a NASA-sponsored project that produced *Report of the Ad Hoc Panel on Attracting New Staff and Retaining Capability During a Period of Declining Manpower Ceilings.*

2. For an explication of the concept of "organizational slack" see Richard M. Cyert and James G. March, *A Behavioral Theory of the Firm* (Englewood Cliffs, N.J.: Prentice-Hall, 1963), pp. 36–38. They argue that because of market imperfections between payments and demands "there is ordinarily a disparity between the resources available to the organization and the payments required to maintain the coalition. This difference between total resources and total necessary payments is what we have called *organizational slack.* Slack consists in payments to members of the coalition in excess of what is required to maintain the organization.... Many forms of slack typically exist: stockholders are paid dividends in excess of those required to keep stockholders (or banks) within the organization; prices are set lower than necessary to maintain adequate income from buyers; wages in excess of those required to maintain labor are paid; executives are provided with services and personal luxuries in excess of those required to keep them; subunits are permitted to grow without real concern for the relation between additional payments and additional revenue; public services are provided in excess of those required.... Slack operates to stabilize the system in two ways: (1) by absorbing excess resources, it retards upward adjustment of aspirations during relatively good times; (2) by providing a pool of emergency resources, it permits aspirations to be maintained (and achieved) during relatively bad times."

3. See William G. Scott, "The Management of Decline," *The Conference Board RECORD*, June 1976, pp. 56–59 and "Organization Theory: A Reassessment," *Academy of Management Journal*, June 1974, pp. 242–53; see also Rufus E. Miles, Jr., *Awakening from the American Dream: The Social and Political Limits to Growth* (New York: Universal Books, 1976).

4. See Daniel M. Fox, *The Discovery of Abundance: Simon N. Patten and the Transformation of Social Theory* (Ithaca, N.Y.: Cornell University Press, 1967).

5. See Andrew Glassberg's contribution to this symposium, "Organizational Responses to Municipal Budget Decreases," and Edward H. Potthoff, Jr., "Pre-planning for Budget Reductions," *Public Management*, March 1975, pp. 13–14.

6. See Donella H. Meadows, Dennis L. Meadows, Jorgen Randers, and William H. Behrens III, *The Limits to Growth* (New York: Universe Books, 1972); also Robert L. Heilbroner, *An Inquiry into the Human Prospect* (New York: Norton, 1975) and *Business Civilization in Decline* (New York: Norton, 1976).

7. See Advisory Commission on Intergovernmental Relations, *City Financial Emergencies: The Intergovernmental Dimension* (Washington, D.C.: U.S. Government Printing Office, 1973).

8. Kenneth E. Boulding, "The Management of Decline," *Change*, June 1975, pp. 8–9 and 64. For extensive analyses of cutback management in the same field that Boulding addresses, university administration, see: Frank M. Bowen and Lyman A. Glenny, *State Budgeting for Higher Education: State Fiscal Stringency and Public Higher Education* (Berkeley, Calif.: Center for Research and Development in Higher Education, 1976); Adam Yarmolinsky, "Institutional Paralysis," *Special Report on American Higher Education: Toward an Uncertain Future*, 2 vols., *Daedalus* 104 (Winter 1975): 61–67; Frederick E. Balderston, *Varieties of Financial Crisis* (Berkeley, Calif: Ford Foundation, 1972); The Carnegie Foundation for the Advancement of Teaching, *More Than Survival* (San Francisco: Jossey-Bass, 1975); Earl F. Cheit, *The New Depression in Higher Education* (New York: McGraw-Hill, 1973) and *The New Depression in Higher Education—Two Years Later* (Berkeley, Calif: Carnegie Commission on Higher Education, 1975); Lyman A. Glenny, "The Illusions of Steady States," *Change* 6 (December/January 1974–75): 24–28; and John D. Millett, "What Is Economic Health?" *Change* 8 (September 1976): 27.

9. Scott, "Organizational Theory: A Reassessment," p. 245.

10. Paul R. Schulman, "Nonincremental Policy Making: Notes Toward an Alternative Paradigm," *American Political Science Review*, December 1975, pp. 1354–70.

11. See Naomi Caiden and Aaron Wildavsky, *Planning Budgeting in Poor Countries* (New York: Wiley, 1974).

12. See James W. Vaupel, "Muddling Through Analytically," in Willis D. Hawley and David Rogers, eds., *Improving Urban Management* (Beverly Hills, Calif.: Sage Publications, 1976), pp. 124–46.

13. See Richard M. Cyert's contribution to this symposium, "The Management of Universities of Constant or Decreasing Size."

14. See National Academy of Public Administration *Report* and Glassberg, "Organizational Response to Municipal Budget Decreases."

15. See NAPA *Report* and *Cancelled Careers: The Impact of Reduction-In-Force Policies on Middle-Aged Federal Employees*, A Report to the Special Committee on Aging, United States Senate (Washington, D.C.: U.S. Government Printing Office, 1972).

16. See Albert O. Hirschman, *Exit, Voice and Loyalty: Responses to Decline in Firms, Organizations and States* (Cambridge, Mass.: Harvard University Press, 1970); also Mancur Oldon, *The Logic of Collective Action* (Cambridge, Mass.: Harvard University Press, 1965).

17. The distinctive features of public organizations are discussed at greater length in Hal G. Rainey, Robert W. Backoff, and Charles H. Levine, "Comparing Public and Private Organization," *Public Administration Review*, March/April 1976, pp. 223–44.

18. See Robert Behn's contribution to this symposium, "Closing a Government Facility," Barry Mitnick's "Deregulation as a Process of Organizational Reduction," and

Herbert A. Simon, Donald W. Smithburg, and Victor A. Thompson, *Public Administration* (New York: Knopf, 1950) for discussions of the survival tactics of threatened bureacrats.

19. This scheme is similar to those presented in Daniel Katz and Robert L. Kahn, *The Social Psychology of Organizations* (New York: Wiley, 1966), p. 166; and Gary L. Wamsley and Mayer N. Zald, *Political Economy of Public Organizations: A Critique and Approach to the Study of Public Administration* (Lexington, Mass.: Heath, 1973), p. 20.

20. See Schulman, "Nonincremental Policy Making," and Charles O. Jones, "Speculative Augmentation in Federal Air Pollution Policy-Making," *Journal of Politics*, May 1974, pp. 438–64.

21. See Robert Behn, "Closing the Massachusetts Public Training Schools," *Policy Sciences*, June 1976, pp. 151–72; Valarie J. Bradley, "Policy Termination in Mental Health: The Hidden Agenda," *Policy Sciences*, June 1976, pp. 215–24; and David J. Rothman, "Prisons, Asylums and Other Decaying Institutions," *The Public Interest*, Winter 1972, pp. 3–17. A similar phenomenon is occurring in some of the fields of regulation policy where deregulation is being made more politically feasible by a combination of technical and economic changes. See Mitnick, "Deregulation as a Process of Organizational Reduction."

22. Peter deLeon, "Public Policy Termination: An End and a Beginning" (essay prepared at the request of the Congressional Research Service as background for the Sunset Act of 1977).

23. There are many variations on the theme of Sunset. Gary Brewer's contribution to this symposium, "Termination: Hard Choices–Harder Questions" identifies a number of problems central to most sunset proposals.

24. For two treatments of the phenomenon in the literature of organization theory see Barry M. Staw and Eugene Szwajkowski, "The Scarcity-Munificence Component of Organizational Environments and the Commission of Illegal Acts," *Administrative Science Quarterly*, September 1975, pp. 345–54; and Barry Bozeman and E. Allen Slusher, "The Future of Public Organizations Under Assumptions of Environmental Stress" (paper presented at the Annual Meeting of the American Society for Public Administration, Phoenix, Arizona, April 9–12, 1978).

25. See Thomas Muller, *Growing and Declining Urban Areas: A Fiscal Comparison* (Washington, D.C.: Urban Institute, 1975).

26. See Richard P. Nathan and Charles Adams, "Understanding Central City Hardship," *Political Science Quarterly*, Spring 1976, pp. 47–62; Terry Nichols Clark, Irene Sharp Rubin, Lynne C. Pettler, and Erwin Zimmerman, "How Many New Yorks? The New York Fiscal Crisis in Comparative Perspective" (Report No. 72 of Comparative Study of Community Decision-Making, University of Chicago, April 1976); and David T. Stanley, "The Most Troubled Cities" (discussion draft prepared for a meeting of the National Urban Policy Roundtable, Academy for Contemporary Problems, Summer 1976).

27. See Richard Child Hill, "Fiscal Collapse and Political Struggle in Decaying Central Cities in the United States," in William K. Tabb and Larry Sawers, eds., *Marxism and The Metropolis* (New York: Oxford University Press, 1978); and H. Paul Friesema, "Black Control of Central Cities: The Hollow Prize," *Journal of the American Institute of Planners*, March 1969, pp. 75–79.

28. See David T. Stanley, "The Most Troubled Cities" and "The Survival of Troubled Cities" (paper prepared for delivery at the 1977 Annual Meeting of the American Political Science Association, The Washington Hilton Hotel, Washington, D.C., September 1–4, 1977); and Martin Shefter, "New York City's Fiscal Crisis: The Politics of Inflation and Retrenchment," *The Public Interest*, Summer 1977, pp. 98–127.

29. See Kaufman, *Are Government Organizations Immortal?* and "The Natural History of Human Organizations," *Administration and Society*, August 1975, pp. 131–48; I have been working on this question for some time in collaboration with Ross Clayton. Our partially completed manuscript is entitled "Organization Aging: Progression or Degeneration." See also Edith Tilton Penrose, "Biological Analogies in the Theory of the Firm," *American Economic Review*, December 1952, pp. 804–19; and Mason Haire, "Biological Models and Empirical Histories of the Growth of Organizations," in Mason Haire, ed., *Modern Organization Theory* (New York: Wiley, 1959), pp. 272–306.
30. For a fuller explanation of "smoothing" or "leveling," see James O. Thompson, *Organizations in Action* (New York: McGraw-Hill, 1967), pp. 19–24.
31. For recent analyses of related phenomena see Joel D. Aberbach and Bert A. Rockman, "Clashing Beliefs Within the Executive Branch: The Nixon Administration Bureaucracy," *American Political Science Review*, June 1976, pp. 456–68; and Hugh Heclo, *A Government of Strangers: Executive Politics in Washington* (Washington, D.C.: Brookings Institution, 1977).
32. See James G. March and Johan P. Olsen, *Ambiguity and Choice in Organizations* (Bergen, Norway: Universitetsforlaget, 1976); and Michael D. Cohen, James G. March, and Johan P. Olsen, "A Garbage Can Model of Organizational Choice," *Administrative Science Quarterly*, March 1972, pp. 1–25.
33. See Charles Perrow, *Organizational Analysis: A Sociological View* (Belmont, Calif.: Wadsworth, 1970); and Chris Argyris and Donald A. Schon, *Theory in Practice: Increasing Professional Effectiveness* (San Francisco, Calif.: Jossey-Bass, 1974) for discussions of the distinction between espoused and operative (i.e., "theory-in-use") strategies.
34. For extensive treatments of the tactics of bureaucrats, some of which are listed here, see Francis E. Rourke, *Bureaucracy, Politics, and Public Policy* (2nd ed.; Boston: Little, Brown, 1976); Aaron Wildavsky, *The Politics of the Budgetary Process* (2nd ed.; Boston: Little, Brown, 1974); Eugene Lewis, *American Politics in a Bureaucratic Age* (Cambridge, Mass.: Winthrop, 1977); and Simon, Smithburg, and Thompson, *Public Administration*.
35. See Arthur M. Oken, *Equity and Efficiency: The Big Tradeoff* (Washington, D.C.: Brookings Institution, 1975).
36. For a discussion of the costs of interactive decision making, see Charles R. Adrian and Charles Press, "Decision Costs in Coalition Formation," *American Political Science Review*, June 1968, pp. 556–63.
37. See Herbert Kaufman, "Emerging Conflicts in the Doctrine of Public Administration," *American Political Science Review*, December 1956, pp. 1057–73; and Frederick C. Mosher, *Democracy and the Public Service* (New York: Oxford University Press, 1968). Seniority criteria also have roots in the widespread belief that organizations ought to recognize people who invest heavily in them by protecting long-time employees when layoffs become necessary.
38. See Peter A. Pyhrr, "The Zero-Base Approach to Government Budgeting," *Public Administrative Review*, January/February 1977, pp. 1–8; Graeme M. Taylor, "Introduction to Zero-base Budgeting," *The Bureaucrat*, Spring 1977, pp. 33–55.
39. See Brewer, "Termination: Hard Choices — Harder Questions"; Allen Schick, "Zero-base Budgeting and Sunset: Redundancy or Symbiosis?" *The Bureaucrat*, Spring 1977, pp. 12–32 and "The Road From ZBB," *Public Administration Review*, March/April 1978, pp. 177–80; and Aaron Wildavsky, "The Political Economy of Efficiency," *Public Administration Review*, December 1966, pp. 292–310.
40. See Hirschman, *Exit, Voice and Loyalty*, especially chap. 7, "A Theory of Loyalty," pp. 76–105. Despite the attractiveness of "responsible and toughminded decision

making" the constraints on managerial discretion in contraction decisions should not be underestimated. At the local level, for example, managers often have little influence on what federally funded programs will be cut back or terminated. They are often informed after funding cuts have been made in Washington and they are expected to make appropriate adjustments in their local work forces. These downward adjustments often are also outside of a manager's control because in many cities with merit systems, veteran's preference, and strong unions, elaborate rules dictate who will be dismissed and the timing of dismissals.

41. Boulding, "The Management of Decline," p. 8.
42. See Heilbroner, *An Inquiry into the Human Prospect*; also Michael Harrington, *The Twilight of Capitalism* (New York: Simon & Schuster, 1976).
43. For a discussion of anti-growth politics, see Harvey Molotch, "The City as a Growth Machine," *American Journal of Sociology*, September 1976, pp. 309–32.
44. Richard Rose has made a penetrating argument about the potential of governments to become "overloaded" in "Comment: What Can Ungovernability Mean?" *Futures*, April 1977, pp. 92–94. For a more detailed presentation, see his "On the Priorities of Government: A Developmental Analysis of Public Policies," *European Journal of Political Research*, September 1976, pp. 247–90. This theme is also developed by Rose in collaboration with B. Guy Peters in *Can Government Go Bankrupt?* (New York: Basic Books, 1978).

PART TWO

Causes of
Fiscal Stress

B. Guy Peters and Richard Rose*

3. The Growth of Government and the Political Consequences of Economic Overload

> To restore confidence is perhaps the most important though least tangible facet of the tasks facing government.
>
> The McCracken Report to OECD,
> *Towards Full Employment and Price Stability* (1977)

Is there fire behind the smoke? Are certain problems of major Western nations simply one more proof that there is no such thing as a free lunch, a lesson every budget director has known since time immemorial? Or do today's problems of political economy also threaten something else: a challenge to the political authority of government as we have known it in the contemporary mixed-economy welfare state? To deny any possibility of economic difficulties disturbing or disrupting the political system is to assume that, whatever the state of the nation's political economy, government can operate on a "business as usual" basis. But to assume that economic troubles can lead to political difficulties, big or small, does not tell us what form these difficulties might take.

One of the principal problems that has arisen in the contemporary mixed-economy welfare state is a significant shift in the mixture of the mixed economy. Government—measured as levels of taxation, spending, employment, regulation, or however—has been growing relative to the size of the total resources in society. This growing sphere of governmental activity has been cited as producing a number of problems in the economies of Western nations, but this chapter is directed more toward an understanding of the political consequences of the "overloading" by government of many Western economies and societies.

In this chapter we present a dynamic model of the political consequences of the current overloading of the political economies of major Western nations. The

*We are grateful to the United States-United Kingdom Fulbright Educational Commission for enabling the first-named author to spend a year at the University of Strathclyde, thus making our collaboration possible. The work reported herein is being extended at Strathclyde in a project on Overloaded Government financed by the Volkswagen Foundation.

dependent variable in the model is political authority, for it is the polity rather than the economy that we are most concerned with. Under certain circumstances specified in the model, a government could be politically bankrupt in terms of authority. Political bankruptcy is not inevitable; in the model we also identify other logically possible outcomes and paths to achieve something better or, conceivably, something worse.

Political bankruptcy is an intermediate form of authority. It occurs when a government's overloading of the economy is no longer confined to an issue of effectiveness, to be resolved within conventional electoral and administrative institutions. It sets off "double trouble," undermining consent while making citizens increasingly indifferent to authority. A politically bankrupt government has not made citizens dissenters or rebels by actively antagonizing them. Its ineffectuality limits the antagonism it can engender. Citizens withdraw their support from established authority without having confidence that any other regime would be better. Such a "broken backed regime" has its authority crippled rather than destroyed. Citizens may prefer the weakness of a bankrupt regime to the power of a coercive regime, but those who live under fully legitimate authority undoubtedly prefer government as they have known it to a political system in which government is ineffectual and *incivisme* the individual norm.

The discussion is divided into three parts. The first part presents a simple dynamic model of the way in which governments allocate national resources and how this has led to the overloading of political economies in the 1970s. In the second section two strategies are considered that governments have invoked in an effort to buy time—inflation and pseudo-corporatist controls. The final section describes the mechanism that forces a government to effectively reduce its overloading and considers the alternative choices it might make. For the sake of clarity, this chapter concentrates on the logic of the argument. Full empirical evidence and discussion of many germane points not covered herein can be found elsewhere.[1] Our study emphasizes the extent to which nominally similar "postindustrial" societies faced with the common problem of resource allocation have responded differently, and thus differ greatly in their potential vulnerability to political bankruptcy.

The Dynamics of the Contemporary Political Economy

Every major Western nation today is a mixed economy, albeit with different mixtures from country to country. In a mixed economy, both political choices and market forces are important, and the interaction of the two is of the greatest importance. As Lindbeck has demonstrated, in the contemporary political economy politicians must be treated as endogenous rather than exogenous variables. A government cannot control completely an economy that is open to influence by market forces as well as political choices, but it can certainly have an effect on the economy—for better or worse.[2]

Our model of the political economy is intentionally simple in order to concentrate on what is causing government so much trouble today. There are three components: the national product, the costs of public policy, and workers' take-home pay.

The National Product

The total output of goods and services (measured in monetary terms) a society produces annually for consumption by its citizens is not paid entirely into the public coffers. It is nonetheless of great concern to government. First, as these outputs are that part of the work for which money is spent, they result in money incomes, and money is fungible (i.e., can be spent to purchase many different kinds of goods and services). Second, government needs money to finance many of its activities, and cannot tax income and production that do not exist. Thus the size of the total national product limits government's potential tax revenue in real terms. Third, the growth of the national product affects the material prosperity of individual citizens, and these citizens are voters, who may judge the record of the current government at the next election on the basis of their individual economic situations.

The Costs of Public Policy

To write about public policy rather than public spending is to emphasize the purposes of government. The money government raises in tax revenues is spent for policies intended to benefit citizens, collectively and individually. While money is not the measure of all political values, nearly every activity of contemporary government has some cash cost, and the principal policies of the welfare state—pensions, education, and health—are among its most costly policies. Thus, any question of public policy also involves a question of political economy and the cost of the policy. Governments like to do everything they can to aid citizens, but are constrained by the necessity of choosing how to use scarce resources.

The costs of public policy reflect not only the current choices of the government of the day but also past decisions. They reflect commitments embodied in laws authorizing and requiring government to spend money annually for stated purposes.[3] Because the costs are established with the force of law, any newly elected government is immediately committed to them unless it wishes to risk the political odium of repealing benefits that millions of citizens have come to expect. The estimates of the effectively "uncontrollable" element in a government's budget can approach or even exceed 100 percent of the previous year's spending.[4]

There are several important inertia reasons for a steady increase in the costs of public policy. One is the relative price effect, reflecting the fact that public-sector costs tend to rise faster than those in the private sector.[5] Even with no changes in the volume of public goods and services produced, their costs as a proportion of the national product will rise. In Britain, this has added an estimated 0.6 percent per annum to the proportion of national product devoted to public policy, and estimates for some programs in the United States are for a 1.2 percent per annum increase.[6] In addition to the relative price effect, the shifting demographic structure of most Western democracies has made a larger proportion of the population eligible for pensions and has increased the use of medical-care programs.

Take-Home Pay

Individual affluence, as distinct from national affluence, is reflected in take-home pay; this is money that an individual considers his or hers as a right. An individual's gross earnings differ substantially from take-home pay, for income tax and compulsory social security taxes, the dues of citizenship, subtract a significant portion.

In a mixed economy, both government and the individual have a claim to a part of earnings. Whereas the benefits that an individual derives from public policy are determined by collective political choices, take-home pay is preeminently a private good, to be spent as each individual wishes. To note this is not to argue that individual choice is invariably superior to collective choice, but simply to emphasize that it is different.

Together, these terms describing what society produces and consumes result in a very simple identity:

National Product = Public Policy + Take-Home Pay

In contemporary mixed economies, the government is responsible for the size of the national product as well as how it is divided between public policies and take-home pay. In theory, economic growth can resolve potential conflicts between the claims of zublic policy and take-home pay and/or among competing public policies by providing something for almost everybody. Government is not equally effective in influencing each side of this question, however. The world recession of the 1970s has demonstrated that Keynesian demand-management does not guarantee a country steady economic growth, and that high levels of public spending and big public deficits are consistent with the twin evils of "stagflation" rather than necessarily producing full employment and economic growth.[7]

As government has the legal power to control how the national product is allocated, citizens consume what government allocates. The taxing powers of government today are the equivalent of the *droit de seigneur* of medieval times. The government's claim on national resources takes the first slice of the national product. Individual take-home pay constitutes whatever is left over *after* government has taken the revenue it requires. For example, the British government in its 1976 forward-spending projections assumed a relatively constant rate of increase of public spending, however high or low the country's economic growth. Any risk of the economy's failing to meet optimistic expectations is borne by the take-home pay of individual citizens.[8]

Managing the political economy of a modern state is a continuing process that cannot easily be summarized in an annual budget or a single year's national income accounts. At any one point in time, a government can face one of three situations: a fiscal dividend, no dividend, or overloaded government.

A Fiscal Dividend

If the national product is growing faster than inertia claims of public policy, then government enjoys a fiscal dividend that can be distributed according to political tastes and pressures. Western governments enjoyed a fiscal dividend of growth consistently throughout the 1950s and '60s, two decades of historically unprecedented economic prosperity. The fiscal dividend of growth was used to sustain treble affluence, for both take-home pay and spending on public policy rose along with the national product.

In a period of treble affluence, government does not need to choose between raising taxes to spend more on public policies or keeping taxes down to protect take-home pay, at the cost of inadequate public services. There can be something for everybody. Daniel Bell has summarized the political consequences thus:

> Economic growth has been a political solvent. While growth invariably raises expectations, the means of financing social welfare expenditures and defense without reallocating income (always a politically difficult matter) or burdening the poor (which has become an equally difficult affair) has come essentially from economic growth.[9]

No Dividend

In theory, the national product, inertia commitments to public policies, and take-home pay might each grow at such a rate that politicians would find that claims upon the national product matched what was there to be spent. This is unlikely to happen in the real world except by accident, for the performance of the economy can turn down or up unexpectedly, and the larger public budgets become, the harder it is to fine-tune the political economy to reach a "no dividend" point.

A government with no fiscal dividend in hand must decide whether to endorse established claims on the national product, or do one of two things: expand public policy or take-home pay, one at the cost of the other. As established commitments have organized groups to defend them, the easiest thing to do politically is to leave things as they are and hope that the national product will turn up in the following year.

Overloaded Government

When the national product grows more slowly than inertia commitments to public policy and take-home pay, the political economy is overloaded. Government does not have enough revenue in hand to meet its established claims and maintain take-home pay at its previous level. Because raising and spending money is a continuing process, there will always be some periods when a government is temporarily overloaded, whether from an excess of spending zeal directed at winning an election or because an unexpected downturn in the economy leads to a shortfall of revenue and an increase in spending on unemployment benefits and other income-maintenance programs. But no government can resolve its political problems by indefinitely spending more than its country produces.

The era of treble affluence has made the risks of overloading government greater and greater. In every major Western country, the costs of public policy have been growing faster than the national product (see table 3.1). In Italy the growth rate

TABLE 3.1. THE RELATIVE GROWTH IN PUBLIC POLICY COSTS AND TAKE-HOME PAY, 1951–77

	Public Policy	Take-Home Pay
America	211%	88%
Britain	207%	63%
France	270%	89%
Germany	162%	83%
Italy	387%	74%
Sweden	299%	51%

NOTE: Index numbers (1951 = 100) of Public Policy and Take-Home Pay, each as percentages of Gross Domestic Product.

SOURCES: Public Policy derives from table 7, "Income and Outlay Transactions of General Government," OECD, *National Accounts of OECD Countries, 1976* (Paris: OECD, 1978), vol. 2. Take-Home Pay calculated from Gross Domestic Product at market prices taking into account the effect of direct and indirect taxes. OECD, *National Accounts of OECD Countries, 1976* (1978), vol. 1. 1977 figures from preliminary OECD figures for Gross Domestic Product and taxation.

of public policy costs has been more than three times that of the national product; in America, Sweden, and France, it has been more than twice the rate of the national product.[10] When public policy took only a small fraction of the national product, then a large growth in percentage terms was not necessarily large in absolute terms; for example, an increase of one-half when public policy took 10 percent of the national product would only raise its proportionate share to 15 percent. But when at least 40 percent of the national product goes on public policy, as is now the case in Italy, Sweden, Britain, and France, an increase of one-half would raise its take to more than 60 percent of the national product.

When public policy grows faster than the national product, then take-home pay must inevitably grow more slowly. Table 3.1 shows how much the increase in take-home pay has lagged behind the growth of public policy. In Germany, take-home pay has risen relatively fast—but only half as fast as public policy. In Italy, by contrast, public policy costs, starting from a very low base in 1951, have grown more than five times faster than take-home pay. The relative decline in the growth of take-home pay is nonetheless consistent with a steady increase in its absolute value. For the moment, at least, these different national experiences are all consistent with an era of treble affluence.

But the logical implication of public policy costs rising faster than the national product is clear. If these trends continue, then sooner or later take-home pay must fall in absolute as well as relative terms. The larger the share of the national product taken by public policies, the quicker any percentage increase is likely to consume the whole of the fiscal dividend of economic growth. In this sense, economists and politicians who express anxieties about the growing proportion of national product devoted to public spending have seized upon a half-truth. There is no magic line at which an economy runs into trouble by devoting 25 or 50 or 60 percent of its national product to public policies.[11] A government is squeezed only as and when spending on public policy threatens to consume the whole of the fiscal dividend and then some, forcing a real and not just a relative cut in the take-home pay of individual citizens.

The world recession of the 1970s has made this theoretical point of immediate practical concern. Growth rates have fallen in every major Western nation, and simultaneously, the costs of public policy have grown at an accelerating rate, in part because of so-called countercyclical spending policies. Governments have not consciously sought to reduce the take-home pay of individual citizens, but they have succeeded in doing so in one or more years of the 1970s in every major Western country except France. But rather than choosing to do this, or reducing commitments to spend on public policies, politicians have preferred to temporize, in the hopes that the squeeze may not last.

The Costs of Buying Time

When commitments to the growth of public policy and take-home pay cannot be met by a slowly growing national product, the logical thing for governors to do is to remove the causes of an overloaded economy and cut one or the other or both. But doing this goes against the grain of most contemporary politicians, who are more interested in providing benefits and activity (often for its own sake) than in a reputation for fiscal caution. Politicians can adopt a variety of strategies, each of which has the immediate political advantage of buying time. These strategies postpone the moment at which government may have to deal with the causes of its difficulties, but do nothing to remove the underlying causes.

A Micawber Policy

Mr. Micawber appreciated what happened to anyone who was committed to spend more than he earned: "result, misery." But he also had a strategy for dealing with the progressive accumulation of commitments in excess of earnings: he pronounced "a hope of something turning up." A politician wishing to avoid choice when all choices are unpalatable can act like Mr. Micawber. A Micawberish economic policy is unsatisfying in a rational age, for it offers no theory to explain why conditions should get better rather than worse. To rely solely on luck (or unknown and exogenous events) to remove the problems of an overloaded economy runs the risk that, sooner or later, luck will run out. But in the words of the British Chancellor of the Exchequer, Denis Healey, "If I worried about all the problems I have to face I would have died within a month of taking office."[12]

Solace without Solution

When all choices open to government are unpleasant, the most immediately comforting thing for a politician to do is to seek a placebo. For example, "planning" provides a symbol of power and control to the tidy-minded, even though planning does not create any additional resources for a country to consume. "Increased efficiency" is a perennial nostrum; but the more it is repeated, the more this emphasizes the resistance of institutions to reform.[13] Changing the party or the men in office does not alter the loads on government; a former Conservative Chancellor of the Exchequer described the position of the succeeding Labour government thus: "They inherited our problems and our solutions."[14] More generally, the spending patterns of Left and Right governments in Europe have varied little. Even changing the ownership of the means of production does not increase the national product; it simply transfers profits (or losses) from private to governmental hands. Placebo politics offer reform without change. The economy remains overloaded; only those taking the placebos feel better.

Logically, the most attractive solution would be to *increase* the growth of the national product, thus leading to treble affluence by increasing the fiscal dividend of economic growth. But this is to solve a problem by stipulating the conditions that will solve it. Governments do not need to be told what to do, but *how* to do it. Governments that have failed to produce a big or big enough rate of economic growth cannot simply be told: "Don't fail again." This is especially true as resource constraints and shattered confidence limit the growth rates of contemporary economies.

In only one of the six major Western nations—Britain—can the overloading of government be said to result from a low rate of economic growth. British governments have been relatively successful in keeping public policy from growing rapidly; it has increased at an average rate of only 4.3 percent since 1951, the least in our universe of analysis. But the economy itself has grown even more slowly; its 2.8 percent average growth rate is the lowest among the nearly two dozen nations for which OECD tabulates data. At the other extreme, a high rate of economic growth has not prevented the Italian economy from becoming overloaded, because the costs of public policy have been increasing at a rate of 9.4 percent per year since 1951. Even if the optimistic forecasts of growth for the period 1974 to 1980 were realized, this would only delay rather than prevent Germany from reaching the point at which governments become economically overloaded, for on past trends, the costs of public policy would still be growing even faster.[15] And as the McCracken Report notes, growth scenarios "should in no way be interpreted as representing either national or OECD forecasts of what is likely to happen."[16]

Inflation

Everywhere in the Western world, overloaded governments have resorted to the money illusion generated by *inflation* to avoid the appearance of cutting take-home pay or cutting public policies. Inflation is thus a symptom and not a cause of an overloaded economy. It is easy for a government to adopt, because government literally does have the power to print money, expand credit, or use its international credit to borrow money from abroad. As the commitments of society have increased, so rates of inflation have increased, and were doing so before the oil crisis of 1973. In the late 1970s, inflation has been greater in every major Western nation than in the whole of the decade of the 1960s. Every major Western nation except Germany has experienced double-digit inflation in at least one year of the 1970s. In the course of time, double-digit inflation cumulatively produces treble-digit inflation, for an annual inflation rate of 15 percent compounds into a doubling of the price index within five years, and would quadruple prices if sustained over ten years. Britain and Italy saw inflation double the cost of living from 1970 to 1976, and have had their double-digit inflation recur.

The effects of inflation are gross and pervasive throughout society. Because of this, even those who may be net beneficiaries from inflation feel like losers. The change in the money value of prices and the drop in the purchasing power of money is disturbing, because no reliance can be placed upon a familiar and recognized standard for evaluating the worth of many goods and services in society. The rise in the cost of living immediately squeezes every family by reducing the real purchasing power of their earnings. Although individuals win large increases in earnings, they may fail to maintain the status quo ante. Even groups who are ahead in the race for higher living standards may feel that they are among the losers, insofar as the impact of an increased cost of living is subjectively greater than that of an equal increase in take-home pay.

Inflation effectively redistributes money between government and individuals in three ways. First, tax revenue rises disproportionately in relation to real economic growth because of a disproportionate increase in taxation caused by fiscal drag. This is the tendency of inflation to force individuals into paying a higher proportion of their income in taxes as they are pushed into higher tax brackets. Second, as the nation's largest debtor, government benefits most when rates of interest become negative. As long as inflation rates are higher than the interest that government pays on its borrowing, then the value of money it repays is less than the value of the money it borrows. The lenders (i.e., the citizens, among others) are the losers. In addition, the relative price of government goods and services, which is rising in any event, tends to rise faster. Independently of changes in the content of public policies, inflation threatens to squeeze the real purchasing power of the take-home pay of the average citizen.

Getting Organized

As the disturbing effects of inflation accumulate, the immediate problem of an overloaded economy is redefined. Instead of being too little growth, it is too much inflation, and governors are pressed to do something about it. The characteristic response of governors is to treat the symptoms: rapidly rising prices and wages. At a maximum, a government may hope to control inflationary wage-and-price increases with the cooperation of leaders of business and labor. At a minimum, it may hope to share the blame for the difficulties of the mixed economy by implicating other institutions through public consultations and participation in quasi-corporatist institutions.

As long as there is a fiscal dividend of growth sufficient to meet the claims of public policies and take-home pay (including profits and investment for business), then the leaders of these organizations are primarily concerned with the happy task of distributing benefits. But, by definition, in an overloaded economy there is not a fiscal dividend and, in 1975, every major nation but Sweden actually suffered a fall in its national product.

In effect, wage-and-price controls are an attempt to take the politics out of economics, by substituting imposed standards of what is a "just" wage and a "fair" profit in place of sums of money arrived at by conventional industrial bargaining. But there is no normative agreement about standards of fairness.[17] Moreover, the pressures to increase prices and wages arise from forces outside the control of contemporary Western governments. In open economies importing a quarter or more of the goods that constitute the national product, internal prices are influenced by international decisions or by alterations in currency exchange rates. If businesses do not pass on these increased costs in higher prices, they are threatened with a loss of funds for investment, a cash-flow squeeze, and finally commercial bankruptcy. If increased prices are passed on, then workers will demand higher wages to prevent their real standard of living from falling. Wage increases in turn imply higher prices, for they increase the cost of producing good and services. It is precisely this inflationary spiral that governments wish to break.

Wage-and-price controls risk failure through success under Western-style representative institutions.[18] If government secures the temporary assent of business and labor to keep prices and wages relatively steady in money terms, this will lead to a fall in the value of wages and profits in real terms, because of inflationary pressures that are not controlled. In the short run, emergency economic difficulties can lead to agreement to accept such cuts because of a common interest in avoiding greater economic difficulties (e.g., a runaway inflation or a balance-of-payments crisis). But the longer such a policy is in effect in an overloaded economy, the greater the cumulative losses it inflicts. At some point, intense pressures from below on leaders of peak business and union organizations will push for "something" to be done. Controls, rather than inflation, will then be defined as the problem.

The operation of wage-and-price policies in countries as diverse as America, Britain, and Sweden demonstrates that such policies may hold wages and prices down for a year or two in an emergency — even longer in good times, as in Sweden — but that they will break down under strong market pressures arising from the overloading of the political economy.[19] Leaders of businesses and unions can detach themselves from government and return to the articulation of interest-group demands, or they can persist in collaborating with government at the risk of losing their limited authority to shop leaders or competing union factions, or in business, at the risk of seeing individual firms make decisions according to market pressures rather than government directives. The former course maintains consent for business and union representatives, albeit in ways that challenge the effectiveness of government policy. The latter risks consent, with the loss of consent by economic leaders also affecting consent for an overloaded government.

Forced Choice

In analyzing the dynamics of an increasingly overloaded political economy, the difficult thing to do is to identify a point at which governments are forced to make the choices they have tried to avoid. In the literal sense of the term, no modern state can go bankrupt, as a nineteenth-century Afro-Asian country might put itself under alien rulers to control its finances or maintain political authority. A regime can be overthrown, but its successor will immediately face the problem of assumption; what attitude should it take toward the debts it has inherited from its predecessor? A new regime will also inherit the preexisting matrix of economic difficulties, as well as the added costs imposed by the transition from one regime to another. Anyone who argues that present circumstances cannot go on indefinitely should be asked: Why not? Latin-American countries can and do have persisting double-digit inflations, and poor countries cope with their fiscal problems.[20]

In macro-economic terms, the compulsion to face unpleasant choices is most likely to come from abroad. Every major European nation is now more dependent on the international economy than the international economy depends on it. For example, while Sweden imports 30 percent of its national product, it accounts for only 2 percent of world trade and 6.6 percent of trade in Europe. In such circumstances, world conditions outside the control of national governments influence greatly a large portion of domestic prices. An overloaded government finds that a relatively high rate of domestic inflation will promptly lead to the devaluation of the purchasing power of its currency in international markets; for example, the British pound and the Italian lire have declined to less than half their former value relative to the German Deutsche Mark since 1970. In an attempt to cover the gap between domestic commitments and costs of international trade, a government may borrow from abroad. But, as the McCracken Report notes, "Access to international financing is at times so easy as to tempt governments to postpone needed adjustments, but can then abruptly become difficult as shifts occur in market sentiment regarding individual countries' credit-worthiness."[21] A balance-of-payments crisis thus can force an overloaded government to make hard choices about its political economy.

The International Monetary Fund provides the institutional mechanism for funding the adjustments a government must make to reduce the load on its economy. When a country goes to the IMF (Britain and Italy were the two major Western nations forced to do so in 1976–77), it finds that there is no international political community (i.e., a system within which financial burdens are shared, with the more prosperous subsidizing the less prosperous, as if there were common citizenship). The behavior, as distinct from the title, of the European Economic Community provides ample evidence of national interest taking precedence in international politics. British and Italian politicians have learned the hard way that other nations will not make substantial and unrequited economic sacrifice for the sake of others. Their efforts to lobby German, Japanese, and American governments to stimulate world trade have been rejected by the latter three countries on the grounds that it would only import inflation. In the tart words of a German economist, "If a country suffers from unemployment and inflation, it cannot be helped by other countries."[22]

A country that comes to the IMF for a loan by definition has immediate and serious fiscal problems. The loan is valued not only for the money it provides, but also as a "Good Housekeeping Seal of Approval" of its fiscal policies, useful in sustaining world confidence in its currency, and in financing additional loans from abroad. The IMF is not interested in managing the economy of a country that has mismanaged its own affairs. The chief countries putting up the money to finance loans wish only to be assured that the borrowing nation is taking actions to remove the causes of its immediate difficulties. The negotiations for an IMF loan effectively become a mechanism that forces an overloaded government to act to reduce its overload.

A behavioral mechanism within a society that forces government to act can arise from the steady fall of the real purchasing power of take-home pay of large numbers of citizens. (This can occur concurrently with conditions leading up to an international balance-of-payments crisis.) In a period of widespread and well-publicized economic recession like the 1970s, most citizens do not expect their living standards to continue to rise. However, there are strong psychological and institutional grounds sustaining what Sir John Hicks has called "real wage resistance."[23] When the total aggregate amount of money available for wages is falling, individual citizens ask: "Why should this cut fall on me?" Their union leaders and employers may not be confronted with demands for more real income but only for enough to match a rising cost of living. Ironically, the demand for 15 to 30 percent increases from an individual point of view can be a conservative act, that is, simply an attempt to preserve existing levels of real take-home pay.

At this point, political bankruptcy can occur, for the overloading of resources encourages civic indifference. As government increasingly appears ineffectual and also threatens conservative self-interest (i.e., the maintenance of take-home pay) individuals may be expected to adopt a *"Sauve Qui Peut"* attitude. Instead of street demonstrations or television confrontations, indifference can be registered through inaction and avoidance (e.g., companies ignoring planning directives from governments or union leaders ignoring requests for wage restraints). Ordinary citizens can redefine their economic affairs to create a new "private" sector, which government does not know about or tax. In place of a black market in selling goods, a black market in labor can grow up. Untaxed wages are worth twice as much as wages attracting direct taxes at a marginal rate of 50 percent, and half again as much as wages taxed at 33 percent. In Italy, black work amounts to as much as one-sixth or more of the total effort in the economy, and the American GNP may be underestimated by at least 10 percent because of the "subterranean economy." Even in Sweden, surveys of public opinion show that a majority do not regard tax evasion as a serious offense; many justify it on grounds that it is a reasonable reaction to the country's high rates of income tax.[24] Even something as legal as the growth of do-it-yourself activities is symptomatic of the *demonetization* of labor, as individuals find that unpaid work is worth more money than services that must be paid for from pay subject to tax.

Unless inertia forces that push public policy costs up faster than the national product are stopped or reversed, then three major Western nations—Britain, Italy, and Sweden—could well face the choice between containing the growth of public policy or endorsing the long-term reduction of take-home pay.[25] Take-home pay has already fallen in each of these countries for at least two years since 1974. In Britain, for example, it fell by 12.3 percent in the 26 months from December 1974 to February 1977.[26] These three countries have reached a crossroads, traveling by very different routes. In Italy, a rapidly growing economy has been outpaced by the costs of public policy ballooning even more rapidly, due to old-style patronage motives and new welfare programs. In Britain, the squeeze arises because the economy has grown even more slowly than the slow-growing costs of public policy. In Sweden, a reasonable rate of economic growth has gradually failed to keep up with public policies that have grown substantially and steadily from an already high share of the national product in 1950.

The other major Western nations analyzed in detail—America, Germany, and France—are far from immune to the prospect of being forced to choose between reducing public policies or take-home pay. In America the costs of public policy have grown more slowly than in any country except Great Britain, and the economy has grown faster than Britain. But if the trends of the 1970s continue, rising costs of public policy could put the squeeze on take-home pay by 1984. Germany is more vulnerable than America, for it has financed a high rate of growth in public policy costs by a similarly fast-growing economy. But if the trends of the 1970s, rather than the quarter-century since 1951, continue, then the squeeze on take-home pay could threaten by 1980. France has combined greater fiscal caution with a high rate of economic growth. Until two years ago, it appeared capable of sustaining a growth in take-home pay indefinitely, but in 1977 its economy too had fiscal difficulties that, if continued, could threaten a squeeze within the next five years.

In an overloaded political economy, a government can make two effective choices: it can emphasize cuts in take-home pay or in public policy. International organizations such as the IMF tend to be indifferent to which is cut, as long as consumption is scaled down to match the national product. But those within the country care greatly about what happens to them.

From an economist's perspective, money is money, whether it is in the hands of government or individuals. But politically, money is power, and the question is how much influence individual citizens, as well as collective institutions of government, have on how it is allocated. Proponents of collectivist political views assume that public expenditure is desirable, because it is determined by government. An individual is responsible only for himself and his family, but public institutions are considered to be responsible for the collective interests of all members of society. From this perspective, the growth of government control of the national product and the decline in self-oriented or "selfish" individual control is good in itself.

While the growth of government has undermined nineteenth-century liberal and individualistic economic doctrines in Western nations today, the collectivist doctrine of government depends on the nineteenth-century liberal faith in the direction of government by popular elections. But today it is as much a myth that government policies are controlled directly by elections as it is that large business corporations are controlled by their shareholders. Oligarchical pyramids of power remain pyramids of power, whatever flag flies from the top. To increase individual dependence on government for goods and services in kind, as well as for cash-transfer benefits, would be to centralize in the hands of organizational hierarchies or oligarchies far more power than is the case in the mixed economy, where a rising take-home pay has increased individual choice as well as collective choice. Whatever personal value judgment one makes about this phenomenon, it would mark a great change from government as we have known it in the Western world in the past quarter-century. And whatever the intellectual or ideological arguments advanced on behalf of such a course, it is worth noting that no political party successful in gaining office advocates a systematic reduction of take-home pay to enhance collectively determined public policies.[27]

To reduce loads on government by stopping the inertia growth of public policy requires rethinking the meaning of affluence. In an overloaded Western society, politicians may no longer feel affluent, but their society remains affluent. An overloaded political economy is not poor but imbalanced, a condition that could befall a relatively wealthy nation such as Sweden or Germany, as well as Britain or Italy. To reduce inertial commitments for spending on public policy does not require cutting past spending, but only limiting *future* growth, a principle that is easy to state though hard to implement.[28] What government needs to do is to delay or deny expectations of future spending (e.g., capital spending on new hospitals, schools, roads) to balance irrevocable future commitments (e.g., incremental salary increases for public employees) against some savings (e.g., not hiring replacements as public employees resign or retire), and to ration any increase in spending commitments from new public policies according to achieved rather than happily forecast levels of economic growth. In short, a government can continue to increase public spending, barring the catastrophe of a long-term decline in the absolute level of the national product; but when it is heavily overloaded, it must hold back increases for a few years, until take-home pay has managed to start rising again, so that an increase in public policy and take-home pay can go together once again as in the decades of treble affluence.

Remedying the defects of an overloaded economy does not require the abolition of programs or public agencies, something that governments are notoriously bad at doing.[29] But it does mean that there is a need to put the brakes on the growth of some major spending programs accounting for most of the costs of public policy:

1. Social policy accounts for half or more of governmental spending in nearly every major Western nation. Health, education, and pensions are the chief programs spending money under this heading. None of these could be abolished, because of popular political reaction. But citizens cannot claim—whether legally or as a moral badge of citizenship—a right to the maintenance of *improved* standards under each heading. Every major Western nation already makes some charges for education at higher levels, and for health services as well. In addition, state pensions are subject to payments from future beneficiaries, and in Continental countries pensions reflect the "ability to pay" as they are in part earnings-related.

2. A government could additionally or alternatively slow down its rate of capital expenditure on economic infrastructure, such as roads and housing. It could also limit subsidies to private and publicly owned firms and industries.

3. There is today little money that Western nations could hope to save in defense cuts, for defense costs have been falling in relative importance, and wages and updating of equipment consume a high fraction of defense bills.

4. Similarly, the rapidly rising cost of servicing government debt—because of higher interest rates as well as more debt—can be reduced only after a government resolves its problems of overload.

To contain the cost of public policy does not require government to desist from enacting new policies and programs but only to take care about their funding implications. Among the variety of policies that could be enacted without loading up government are (1) policies that increase net revenue (e.g., more effective tax collection); (2) money-saving policies of decriminalization and deregulation (e.g., legalizing soft drugs and reducing paperwork); (3) ad hoc expenditures on nonrecurring activities (a Bicentennial, hosting the Olympic games, or a Royal Jubilee, however expensive, by definition are not annually recurring expenses); (4) public works with low maintenance costs (e.g., statues in public parks rather than opera houses or university buildings); or (5) activities where user charges are levied (e.g., building swimming pools rather than public libraries). Clearly, fiscal criteria cannot be the only bases of choice, but neither can they be ignored.

The resistance of politicians to containing public spending is usually grounded on a simple proposition: the voters will not stand for it. But public opinion surveys reject the assumption that citizens expect government inevitably to spend more and more on public policy. A survey of *Aspirations and Affluence* in America, Britain, Germany, and the Netherlands, taken at the height of the decade of treble affluence in 1968, found substantial differences in economic expectations within as well as between these countries. Only 12 percent of Germans and no more than 31 percent of Americans expected their living standards to rise continuously in the future as in the past. Citizens are divided in their views. The national distribution of opinion is on aggregate tipped toward optimism, but not by much. In Germany the optimists expecting continued growth outnumbered the pessimists by 11 percent, in Britain by 17 percent, and in America by 35 percent. In each country, the don't knows and the uncertains held the balance.[30]

When economic conditions change, popular expectations change with them. At the height of the boom in the United States in 1964, 65 percent expected prosperity to continue in the year ahead, whereas at the beginning of 1975, 70 percent expected economic conditions to worsen. Both times the majority was right. At the beginning of 1977 a Gallup international survey found that from 62 to 85 percent of Britons, Frenchmen, and Italians expected the next year to be a time of economic difficulty, and unemployment to rise. In America and Germany, pessimists also outnumbered optimists.[31] If politicians gave citizens what they expected, then they could be delivering them bad news rather than good news.

To contain the growth of public policy sufficiently to prevent or reduce overloading of government is, in technical terms, a Pareto optimal solution. No one need be made worse off in terms of real take-home pay, nor would anyone need to be deprived of public policy benefits already provided, and some might be benefited by increased take-home pay. It is arguable whether the measures required should be described as cuts, for they are no more and no less than means of delaying the speed with which public policies grow. The prudent fiscal course is to expand spending in keeping with real rates of growth, and not to spend future growth (which may or may not arrive as expected) for the sake of present policies.

The alternative courses that government might follow are less than Pareto optimal. To cut the take-home pay of the great bulk of members of society in the name of collectivism would almost certainly jeopardize legitimate authority, as those whose earnings were undermined became indifferent or refused to comply with the directives of a government promoting such a policy. Alternatively, to cut real take-home pay by a policy of controlling wages so that they rise more slowly than prices (including the costs of public policy) would be to risk political authority by encouraging citizens to become indifferent to a government incapable of conserving their existing take-home pay. A third route into political bankruptcy is unintentional. Politicians could maintain the illusion that they can continue to deliver the benefits of public policy without risking any political costs, while the political economy for which they are responsible becomes increasingly overloaded.

The growth of government then presents a real challenge to governors. It is a challenge of using political authority to control an economy without threatening the existence of that authority. It is also the challenge of teaching citizens certain ageless truths about the impossibility of a free lunch. Finally, it is a challenge of dealing creatively with social and economic problems in the face of an awkwardly heavy weight of taxation.

Notes

1. See Richard Rose and B. Guy Peters, *Can Government Go Bankrupt?* (New York: Basic Books, 1978), a comparative analysis of America, Britain, France, Germany, Italy, and Sweden.
2. See Assar Lindbeck, *Endogenous Politicians and the Theory of Economic Policy* (Stockholm: Institute for International Economic Studies, Seminar Paper NO. 35, 1973) and "Stabilization Policy in Open Economics with Endogenous Politicians," *American Economic Review* 68, NO. 2 (May 1976): 1–19.
3. In other words, our model is grounded on the legal obligation of government to provide policies, a "ghost within the machine," rather than on putative social-psychological expectations of citizens for an ever rising material provision of benefits.
4. For an outstanding review of theories of the increase of public expenditure, see Daniel Tarschys, "The Growth of Public Expenditure: Nine Modes of Explanation," *Scandinavian Political Studies* 10 (1975): 9–31. On uncontrollable expenditures, see, e.g., *The Budget of the United States*, 1977 (Washington, D.C.: U.S. Government Printing Office, 1976), p. 34, and Barry M. Bleichman, Edward D. Gramlich, and Robert W. Hartman, *Setting National Priorities: The 1976 Budget* (Washington, D.C.: Brookings Institution, 1975), pp. 193 ff.
5. For a seminal discussion of this topic, see W. J. Baumol, "Macroeconomics of Unbalanced Growth: The Anatomy of the Urban Crisis," *American Economic Review* 57 (1967): 415–26.
6. See H. M. Treasury, *Public Expenditure White Papers: Handbook on Methodology* (London: HMSO, 1972), p. 25; R. M. Spann, "Rates of Productivity Change and the Growth of State and Local Government Expenditures," in T. E. Borcherding, ed., *Budgets and Bureaucrats: The Sources of Government Growth* (Durham, N.C.: Duke University Press, 1977), pp. 100–129.
7. See J. M. Buchanan and R. E. Wagner, *Democracy in Deficit: The Political Legacy of Lord Keynes* (New York: Academic Press, 1977).
8. The Treasury calculated that a 2.4 percent annual increase in Gross Domestic Product in the five-year period 1974–79 would increase privately financed personal consumption in aggregate by £110 million: at 3.4 percent £430 million, and at 3.8 percent £560 million. In the preceding five years, the British economy had grown by an average rate of 2.4 percent. See *Public Expenditure to 1979-80* (London: HMSO, 1976, Cmnd. 6393), table 1.1.
9. See Daniel Bell, "The Public Household," *The Public Interest*, Fall 1974.

10. The shift in past allocation patterns shown in table 3.1 might be described as a shift in preference of individuals from goods bought with take-home pay (e.g., color television sets and cars) to goods and services financed through government (e.g., higher pensions, better education, and recreation facilities). To note that relative preferences can change through time is also to accept that in future, e.g., in conditions outlined later in this paper, there could be a shift in the opposite direction, favoring take-home pay.

11. Cf. the old and invalidated forecast of Colin T. Clark, "Public Finance and Changes in the Value of Money," *Economic Journal* 55 (1945): 371–89, and the latter-day jeremiads of Milton Friedman, "The Line We Dare Not Cross: The Fragility of Freedom at Sixty Percent," *Encounter* 47 (November 1976).

12. See "Alternative is 'Savage Action and 3 million jobless,'" *The Times* (London), September 30, 1976.

13. Note that in his request to Congress of February 4, 1977, for authority to reorganize executive branch departments, President Carter explicitly asked to remove the Reorganization Act of 1949's requirement that the President state how much money would be saved by reorganization. Instead, the President wished to use words to describe "improvements in management, efficiency and delivery of federal services." See the verbatim text in *Congressional Quarterly Weekly Report*, February 12, 1977, p. 274.

14. See D. E. Butler and A. King, *The British General Election of 1966* (London: Macmillan, 1966), p. 5.

15. The potential growth rates of GDP 1975–80, hypothesized by OECD in "A Growth Scenario to 1980," OECD *Economics Outlook No. 19, Special Supplement* (Paris, July 1976), table 54, imply, consciously or otherwise, that public policy costs will continue to rise at a faster rate still. Cf. Rose and Peters, *Can Government Go Bankrupt?*, table 3.2.

16. See the McCracken Report, *Towards Full Employment and Price Stability* (Paris: OECD, 1977), p. 317.

17. For a very perceptive discussion of this problem, se John H. Goldthorpe, "Social Inequality and Social Integration in Modern Britain," in Richard Rose, ed., *Studies in British Politics* (3rd ed.; London: Macmillan, 1976), pp. 84–104.

18. For the failings of a command economy that does impose wage and price controls, see, e.g., Alec Nove, *The Soviet Economy* (3rd ed.; London: Allen & Unwin, 1969).

19. See, e.g., Craufurd D. Goodwin, ed., *Exhortation and Controls: The Search for a Wage-Price Policy, 1945–71* (Washington, D.C.: Brookings Institution, 1975); Samuel Brittan and Peter Lilley, *The Delusions of Incomes Policy* (London: Maurice Temple Smith, 1977); and for the breakdown of Swedish wages policy in 1976, see Birgitta Nedelman and Kurt G. Meier, "Theories of Contemporary Corporatism: Static or Dynamic," *Comparative Political Studies* 10, NO. 1 (1977): 39–60.

20. See Felipe Pazos, *Chronic Inflation in Latin America* (New York: Praeger, 1972).

21. McCracken Report, *Towards Full Employment*, p. 32.

22. See the statement of Professor Herbert Giersch to the McCracken Report, p. 248. More generally, note the emptiness of the declaration of the Economic Summit in London, May 1977, and President Carter's readiness to reaffirm national interest doctrines in an important pre-summit interview with Europeans, *The Times*, May 3, 1977.

23. See Sir John Hicks, *The Crisis in Keynesian Economics* (Oxford: Basil Blackwell, 1975).

24. See, e.g., Paolo Farnetti, "Some General Aspects of Governmental Overload in the Present Italian Political and Social Situation, 1964–76" (Berlin, ECPR Workshop on Governmental Overload, March 1977); and Joachim Vogel, "Taxation and Public Opinion in Sweden: An Interpretation of Recent Survey Data," *National Tax Journal* 27, NO. 4 (1974): 499–513.

25. For a full discussion of the future implications of present trends, see Rose and Peters, *Can Government Go Bankrupt?*, chap. 7. In these forecasts, the fundamental question is not what technique is used, but whether one assumes the immediate future will resemble patterns of the 1970s, or those of the 1950s and '60s.
26. See the Treasury figures in House of Commons, *Weekly Hansard*, May 4, 1977, Written Answers: col. 185.
27. Collective choice inevitably becomes significant in proposals to equalize income as a means to that end. But treble affluence is equally important, for only with treble affluence would it be possible to alter incomes so that no one would be worse off in absolute terms, as below-average incomes were raised toward the mean.
28. On the general tendency of spending to growth with age of programs, see Harold Wilensky, *The Welfare State and Equality* (Berkeley: University of California Press, 1975).For the failure of a "success," the British PESC (Public Expenditure Survey Committee), compare Aaron Wildavsky, *Budgeting: A Comparative Theory of Budgetary Processes* (Boston: Little, Brown, 1975), chap. 19, and Maurice Wright, "Public Expenditure in Britain: The Crisis of Control," *Public Administration* 55 (Summer 1977): 143–70.
29. See Herbert A. Kaufman, *Are Government Organizations Immortal?* (Washington, D.C.: Brookings Institution, 1976).
30. See George Katona, Burkhard Strumpel, and Ernest Zahn, *Aspirations and Affluence: Comparative Studies in the United States and Europe* (New York: McGraw-Hill, 1971), pp. 44 ff.
31. See the *Gallup Opinion Index* (Princeton: Report NO. 138, January 1977), pp. 2–3. For a more detailed discussion of popular attitudes toward the political economy, see Richard Rose, "Ordinary People in Extraordinary Economic Circumstances" (Glasgow: University of Strathclyde Studies in Public Policy NO. 11, 1977).

EDWARD K. HAMILTON

4.On Nonconstitutional Management of a Constitutional Problem

I

The past forty years of evolution in American governance are an impressive testament to the influence of pragmatism on our social and political philosophy. Without any fundamental amendment of the Constitution, and with only two genuinely sweeping redirections of judicial interpretation, we have totally transformed the scope of purpose, the scale, and the order of complexity of the public sector, as well as the difficulty in holding government accountable. This masterwork of incrementalism confirms our post–Civil War talent for effecting major adaptation without doctrinal confrontations serious enough to threaten the fabric of the republic. It also owes much to the capacity of the Framers to sense how much they could not foresee, and their consequent care that all except the few most sacred propositions and structures could be changed without altering organic law.

However, the more durable part of the deep malaise now evident in popular attitudes toward government probably represents the price of sustained incrementalism. Such change depends on a delicate balance between fact and myth. The greater the innovation, the more necessary that it be linked to a reaffirmation of traditional principles. The three great watersheds of change in this period have been crises of strikingly different kinds: the Great Depression, World War II, and the mid-1960's crisis of economic morality when we discovered that years of unprecedented general prosperity did not eliminate poverty or guarantee a decent level of public services. Each crisis produced a massive expansion in the role of government generally acknowledged to be legitimate. Each produced a corresponding enlargement in government operations and costs. But none resulted in major challenge to the average citizen's conception of the nature of the federal system and the relation of the multiplying numbers of governmental units within it.

Evidence now abounds that (1) the facts of federalism have diverged so far from the classic myth that the rhetoric of political persuasion is largely irrelevant to the real world; (2) unless ways are found to achieve consensus on revisions in the myth—without necessarily revising the Constitution—attempts to deal with our deepest social pathologies are likely to be ineffective and brutally expensive; and (3) even if this revision is achieved, there is substantial basis for doubt that the political and economic incentives created by the current division of labor and authority among jurisdictions can be blended into a satisfactory set of instruments for supplying the protections and services now generally demanded from government.

If this case can be made, a student of the Constitution might remind us, the straightforward remedy would seem obvious. The document contains an orderly procedure for amendment, or even for total revision. But few would maintain that the present strength of the American political consensus is sufficiently impressive to warrant confidence that a wholesale revision would yield more improvements than new defects. The problem is more subtle. It is to formulate, explain, debate, and solidify a new set of federalist principles to underlie a nonconstitutional revision of the nature of our union that has already partially occurred. Out of the ruins of the classical theory of separate levels of government, separately financed, the nation needs to develop either a broadly based rationale for the current jungle of inextricably intertwined units, or an effective constituency for reform. In this area, as in many others, our national response to the question "A New America?" is subject to conscious influence only if we are better able to come to terms with the current state of the nation.

This essay attempts a modest exploration of the main directions of past change in the federal system, the critical characteristics of the current situation, the reasons that pressures on the federation may be somewhat different in the future than in the past, and the indicators that may most reliably suggest which direction we are taking. It closes with a brief discussion of major problems and options that seem likely to present themselves in the years immediately ahead.

II

The vast literature of judicial speculation on the intent of the Framers probably says nothing more accurate than that these people would be uniformly aghast at the living patterns that characterize twentieth-century America. The Framers did not construct a governmental framework for a predominantly urban nation. Quite the contrary, their writings suggest consensus on the distaste for urban civilization expressed some decades later by Tocqueville.

> In towns it is impossible to prevent men assembling, getting excited together, and forming sudden passionate resolves. Towns are like great meeting houses with all the inhabitants as members. In them the people wield immense influence over their magistrates and often carry their desires into execution without intermediaries.... I regard the size of some American cities and especially the nature of their inhabitants as a real danger threatening the future of democratic republics of the New World, and I should not hesitate to predict that it is through them that they will perish, unless their government succeeds in creating an armed force which, while remaining subject to the wishes of the national majority, is independent of the peoples of the towns and capable of suppressing their excesses.

The Framers, an extraordinarily gifted assembly, did not indulge their anti-urban sympathies to the extent of the national police force implied by Tocqueville's position. But they did take pains to vest all subfederal sovereignty in units of sufficient size and diversity to assure that the passions and other evil humors they perceived as inevitable products of city life would be filtered through the more measured and balanced judgmental processes they associated with rural culture before any governmental decision could be taken. Thus, they gave no constitutional stature to even the largest local governments; they prescribed no procedures for state cooperation in governance of contiguous urban settlements that crossed state boundaries; nor did they place any limits on the discretion of states in making their internal allocations of governmental labor and authority. Because the states were much more substantial entities than the union at the time, it is not surprising as a matter of practical politics that a Constitution achieved through their consent contains very few checks on their internal affairs. Still, it is important to understand that the leaders of the day viewed it as undesirable that urban concentrations develop which either would dominate state governments by the sheer size of their populations, or which would evolve a sense of local political identity separate from that of the state that might be translated into purely urban decisional mechanisms for governance of more than the most localized of public functions.

The structural expression of this point of view was, in the image developed by Morton Grodzins, "layer cake Federalism." The Constitution contemplated clear separation between state and federal governments, with each provided with the sources of public revenue necessary for support of the functions assigned to it. This emphasis upon separate powers over separate purses was elegantly phrased by Alexander Hamilton in his discussion of the division of taxing authorities in the *Federalist* (NO. 31): "A government ought to contain in etself every power requisite to the full accomplishment of the objects committed to its care, and to the complete execution of the trusts for which it is responsible, free from every other control but a regard to the public good and to the sense of the people." Thus, the notion of major transfers of resources between the federal government and the states does not arise in the Constitution.

For the first 140 years of our history, a few important exceptions such as the land grants for state colleges to the contrary notwithstanding, the prevailing attitude was that expressed by President Franklin Pierce in 1854 when he vetoed a bill that would have provided federal land grants to the states to support facilities for the insane: "[Should Congress] make provision for such objects, the fountain of charity will be dried up at home, and the several states, instead of bestowing their own means on the social wants of their people, may themselves, through the strong temptation, which appeals to states as to individuals, become humble supplicants for the bounty of the Federal Government, reversing their true relation to this Union." One would hardly need to change a word to render this pronouncement suitable to express the first reaction of President Ford and a majority of the Congress to the New York City fiscal crisis of 1975. Yet the subsequent reversal of

Ford's position and provision of direct federal aid to New York City signaled the very advanced state achieved by the transition, continuing in Grodzins' imagery, from "layer cake Federalism" to "marble cake Federalism."

This transition had begun to take shape in the late nineteenth century at the base of the "cake" in the relation between state and local governments. By and large, state constitutions had placed more restrictive controls on executive authority than the national Constitution had placed on the President. And, although state legislatures were clearly sovereign, local police powers, responsibility for minimal aid to the poor, and regulation of land use within incorporated areas (if any) were generally in the hands of local government, following the British tradition. State governments primarily concerned themselves with facilitating and regulating commerce, supervising the development of new land and the incorporation of new localities, administering justice, governing unincorporated areas, and providing for some public institutions (e.g., universities and mental hospitals) that clearly would not be provided by the ordinary workings of the market, by private industry, or by local governments. But the urbanizing effects of the industrial revolution and the surge of poor immigrants from Europe made this simple division of labor unworkable in the fastest-growing states. From the political standpoint, the center of attention and relevance for most state politicians moved with the voters — into the cities. The shift of focus had major effects on all practitioners, from the governor in need of urban votes to the rural member of an unreapportioned (and therefore rural-dominated) state legislature striving to keep the cities in their place. From an economic perspective, the costs of providing even the most minimal care to the urban poor were more and more obviously beyond the revenues produced by the taxes that the states had authorized cities to levy, as the philosophical proposition that minimal care should in fact be provided was growing in strength, albeit over strong resistance. Meanwhile, the great scandals of the big-city corruption had severely undermined public confidence in the municipality as an efficient administrator.

Thus, both political and economic logic in the centers of subfederal sovereignty argued for a sharp increase in the state role in local affairs. The great weight of the traditional concept of federalism showed clearly in the effort to achieve this concept without obscuring the basically separate nature of state and local governments. Thus, as the welfare function became a state concern, its administration and financing were often shifted from cities to counties, the latter being designed, after the British shire, to serve as administrative outposts of the states. The local revenue base to meet the enlarged costs of traditional local services (e.g., police, fire) in the swelling cities was generally provided through grudging transfer of most property-tax authority from the states to localities, to be replaced in the state exchequers by sales and eventually by income taxes. Cities, for their part, launched major programs of annexation, and in a few cases of merger with surrounding counties, in an attempt to assure that the rapid increases in revenue-generating capacity created by the settlement of their outskirts would be available to support growing public-service costs in the urban cores. By 1934, therefore, 24 states had designated their counties as primary units for welfare administration, and 11 of the 20 counties of more than 500,000 population (including New York, Philadelphia, Baltimore, San Francisco, and Denver, among others) had completed some form of consolidation of city and county governments. In general, it could still be persuasively argued at that time that the functions of the three levels of government were distinguishable, that their revenue sources were largely independent, and that there was reasonable identity between the point of decision on spending and the point of publicly visible responsibility for persuading the people to support the revenue measures required to support that spending.

However, the Great Depression placed what eventually proved to be intolerable stress on the "layer cake" concept. The crash caught the nation in the early stages of transition from laissez-faire national economic governance to a somewhat more activist philosophy. The response was correspondingly ambiguous. On the one hand, it was evident that decisive action could not come from the states unless they were vested with very substantial new financial authorities, including the power to run a large cumulative deficit. (Because state finances are regulated by state constitutions, formal action to force this would probably have required an overriding amendment of the national Constitution.) In any event there was little patience for the delays, complexities, and presumed inefficiencies involved in attempting to address so pressing a national problem while maintaining strict financial separation among governments. On the other hand, the suddenness and depth of the collapse seemed to underscore the temporariness of the situation. It was tempting, both as an intellectual matter and as a matter of political salesmanship, to view the depression as a short-term aberration that could and should be dealt with by brief suspensions of traditional federalist rules that could be lifted when normalcy had been restored. This perception made it possible to avoid the substantial problems evident in the two straightforward approaches suggested by adherence to the "layer cake" theorem: that the federal government turn over to the states the revenue-generating capacity necessary for them to support massive new income subsidies and pump-priming efforts, or that the national regime—the states and the Supreme Court willing—mount these operations as directly administered functions.

To be sure, the federal program did in fact administer some aspects of the recovery program. But the largest and most fateful share was provided through a hybrid, and avowedly temporary, approach to federal organization that could be justified both as a reaffirmation of state sovereignty and as a legitimate use of the constitutional power of the Congress to raise federal revenues and to supervise their use. The essence of the new arrangement was to abandon Alexander Hamilton's dictum and turn a growing portion of the federal government into what might be termed a bank for the states, granting and (later) lending matching money as the clients generated their contributions and proved their qualifications to receive federal subsidies according to federally set criteria which permitted very wide variations in policy and practice among the states. Overriding the objections of groups that urged a uniform national income maintenance policy, such as the

1935 President's Commission on Income Security, this banking concept was locked formally in place in the landmark Social Security Act passed in that year. By the end of the decade, the banker relation was the channel for more federal funds than had been contained in the entire federal budget only a few years before.

The parallel history within states was much more diversified, with the populous and industrialized states behaving more nearly according to the federal model. The development of state subsidies for local operations had begun some time before. However, in the decade beginning in 1932, the states doubled the share of local spending that they subsidized for education and highway purposes, and they multiplied their share of local welfare financing sixfold. The interpenetration of state and local budgets became pronounced in many of the larger states, but on the whole state resources were still carefully restricted to "areas of state interest," which did not include the traditional municipal service staples. There were several dozen municipal bankruptcies, and a number of very near misses—notably in New York City—which were largely dealt with through state and private measures advertised as temporary emergency steps.

The aftermath of World War II demonstrated that even though the national economy had mushroomed during the hostilities, the end of the depression did not bring the end of the social problems to which the banking-type federal functions were addressed. Indeed, as the pace of urbanization quickened, the suburbs burgeoned, and the postwar readjustment effects—including the baby boom—emerged, the political pressure to extend federal-state matching, particularly in transportation and housing, became irresistible. It also became evident that the intervening decade of decentralized policy making had resulted in so diverse a collection of state social-welfare policies and benefits, most of which were federally subsidized, that uniform national standards would be extremely difficult and expensive to impose.

More important, however, there was little sense of need for such standardization. Diversity was widely perceived as an asset, representing the capacity of the American system to permit subnational communities to apply their own values and reach presumably more sensitive judgments about local standards of decency than could be dictated from Washington. This view also helped to explain the relative equanimity with which the country watched the major metropolitan areas splintered into a myriad of overlapping jurisdictions (e.g., nearly 1,200 in the Chicago area, more than 1,100 in and around New York) too complex for even the most determined citizen to hold in his mind the division of responsibility among them. But the politics of local administration were also influential. The psychology of flight from inner-city problems was the very heart of the suburban mentality. It dovetailed neatly with the perception of professional politicians that sole and visible responsibility for local administration promised no benefits to a budding career, but could easily destroy one if some snafu demonstrated that the officeholder could not "even" pick up the garbage or deploy policemen. This perception had long fostered the growth of the city manager system, wrich ironically had been initiated in part by the strong mayors. Now this consensus on the negative value of visible local administrative authority provided solid support not only for the proliferation of jurisdictions but also for the plethora of plural decisional bodies—boards, committees, commissions, and the like—which provided a certain protection in the anonymity of individual members when trouble developed.

Some of the same factors underlay the simultaneous acceleration in the trend toward "privatization" of public-sector functions, which added another dimension of complexity to the organizational scene. With the exception of the Department of Defense, the federal agencies formed after the war were designed less as direct operators than as contract supervisors, overseeing huge collections of private enterprises engaged to perform stated tasks. The preference for corporate-style organization also included new and expanded public-benefit corporations and free-standing public authorities at all three levels of government, along with a flood of special districts at the regional and local levels. In most cases, these districts overlapped preexisting local jurisdictions, and were governed by complicated mixtures of state-, local-, and district-selected officials.

Within the states, the great engine of state absorption of previously local financial burdens was the growth of elementary and secondary education, which produced unworkable public-school economics for many localities. In most areas, however, this did not in itself breach the state-local separation because school districts and local government were separate jurisdictions. Expansions of state support in such areas as highway programs and public health efforts, however, did begin to signal a basic change in the nature of state support. Meanwhile, the capacity of states to raise revenue became more and more superior to localities as state after state enacted an income tax. The absence of any metropolitan level of revenue raising made the state the residual financier as the stresses of urbanization and intrametropolitan migration made the local tax base in older core cities unequal to the costs of maintaining services.

By the mid-1950s the syndrome of inner-city shrinkage and decay had begun to take clear shape, irreversibly tangling the aging urban cores with their respective states in a financial embrace as indispensable as it was unpleasant. Although metropolitan areas continued to expand rapidly, most of the core cities began a steady shrinking process that masked very brisk two-way traffic in which most of the leavers did not depart the area, but simply took their higher incomes to the suburbs. The combination of shrinking numbers, shrinking average incomes, and growing average per capita demand for public services added up to an impossible mismatch between revenue-generating capacity and the costs of vital services. Slowly at first, and then with growing momentum, the larger states expanded their banker roles toward localities. In the 1954–74 period they expanded their share of financial support for local budgets by more than half; by the end of the period such states as New York were allocating more than 80 percent of state revenues to aid to localities. The banking function had become much the most financially significant state activity in most of the states that contained large cities, while in such states as South Dakota it remained relatively minor.

However, at no point in any state did this evolution proceed according to any long-term plan. States typically did not admit of the possibility of any increase in local subsidies in advance of a point of absolute and generally acknowledged desperation. This was as true before the Supreme Court forced reapportionment of state legislatures, beginning in 1962, as it was afterward, for the Court's decision moved the balance of power within most state bodies from rural areas to the suburbs, which were not noticeably more inclined to recognize state responsibility for city finances. As Gelfand has demonstrated, the ruling event in all principal state movements was perceived emergency and the correlative perception that no alternative existed. Rarely was the theory of state interest precisely enough defined so that a clear rationale for growth in the state share of local financial burdens could be discussed. Never was it widely admitted that the fiscal mismatch of the core cities was an inevitable consequence of the combination of poverty concentration and jurisdictional separation from access to the affluent sections of the metropolis.

Despite repeated experience to the contrary, state budgets continued to be planned and projected on the basis of current state-local burden-sharing arrangements, and city charters continued to contemplate that pressures for local expenditure increases could be met by local actions, without regular recourse to the state. When both premises proved faulty year after year, the event was typically treated as an unexpected and irregular happenstance, which qualified for attention only if dire and immediate consequences would flow from inaction. When addressed, it was dealt with in a subsidy pattern that strove mightily to preserve the principle that the state had only limited and specialized interests in a few local service areas. The separation was also carefully maintained with respect to borrowing authorities, to the extent that states and their client localities often had quite different ratings applied to their bonds regardless of the degree to which their respective financial viabilities were linked.

But the resulting flow of services was far from adequate in the eyes of many. The superlative behavior of the macro economic indices in the 1962–66 period served only to accentuate the plight of the poor, particularly those in the inner cities. It was clear that neither the traditional state and local resource base nor the crisis ad-hocery of emergency adjustment would make a dramatic improvement in their fortunes without imposing a tax burden on both industrialized states and core cities that would drive out the revenue base that remained to them. This realization combined with the unique political circumstances of 1963–64 to generate enactment of more than two hundred new domestic federal programs—many of them sweeping—within the years 1965–68. The same opinion trends contributed to a major change in public attitudes that had the result of drastically reducing the number of people who, although qualified for benefits and services, had previously chosen not to apply for them. Direct federal payments to states and localities rose from less than $3 billion in 1954 to about $60 billion in 1976, or from just over 11 percent of state and local revenues to nearly 30 percent. Moreover, the nature of federally subsidized programs became substantially more open-ended and even less connected to direct federal administration. Reacting in part to the administrative complexity inherent in the traditional categorical grant-in-aid form of federal-state banking relations (which Douglas Yates has fetchingly dubbed "ordeal by paper"), such newer benefits as Medicare, Medicaid, and food stamps were given the character of economic rights attached to individuals, theoretically to be provided without budgeted limit on demonstration that the individual met the qualifications established for the grant.

As these new federal commitments unfolded, all levels of government were adjusting to a surge in labor costs, the dominant component in all their budgets. The upward revaluation of public goods and services represented by the Great Society contained an element of recognition that public instrumentalities could not be expected to compete with the private sector for first-class talent when government salaries, particularly for middle- and upper-level managers, were not remotely comparable. In the federal case, this realization led to enactment of the Federal Pay Reform Act of 1963, which established the principle that the salaries of federal workers should be adjusted annually to maintain "comparability" with private-sector workers carrying similar responsibilities. In states and localities — whose employees averaged about 30 percent lower annual earnings than federal employees — upward movement was much more uneven and closely tied to other factors, notably the growth of collective bargaining; but the direction was the same, particularly in large states and urban governments. Brookings research has documented the fact that, as state and local employment tripled between 1955 and 1973 (rising from about 7.5 percent to 12 percent of the national work force), average earnings progressed from about 92 percent of the average for all private industries to about 104 percent of that average. This still compared unfavorably with the 143 percent average achieved by federal workers, but it represented substantial change from the 88 percent recorded for subfederal workers in 1945. In historical terms, the adjustment largely restored the relative earning position that state and local employees had occupied in 1929 (when they were at 107 percent of the industrial average), but did not yet approach their position in 1939, when they received more than 116 percent of the industrial average.

Overall, the effect was an upward ratcheting of government salaries (along with those paid in universities, foundations, and most other elements of the nonprofit industry) at a rate about 20 percent higher than the growth in private-sector earnings. Thus, urban areas, especially core cities, were faced with the triple pressure of rising (and largely nonignorable) per capita demand for traditional services, an explosion in mandatory and optional nontraditional services partially financed by other tax bases, and a powerful upward surge in the unit cost of the labor necessary to perform both varieties of service. If there had remained any question about the infeasibility of return to arm's-length relations between banker governments and their clients, the grotesque contrast between these pressures and the condition and prospects for the inner-city tax base should have removed all doubt.

The final abandonment of Alexander Hamilton's principle was signaled by the enactment of General Revenue Sharing in 1972, but the event seems not to have really registered upon the consciousness of most citizens until the New York City crisis of 1975. The enactment of revenue sharing was a historic but relatively untraumatic occurrence (at least as compared with the surmounting of previous major philosophical barriers to federal subsidy) that essentially reflected the plight of the states in the wake of the first recession since the budgets of many of them had become heavily dependent upon a revenue source—the income tax—that was susceptible to a very severe damage from sudden stagnation in the general economy. Unaccustomed to predicting or dealing with volatile revenue behavior, unequipped with reserves or other techniques for absorbing the shock of revenue shortfalls, without controllable, non-labor-related expenditures (other than aid to localities) that could be reduced easily and quickly, and deprived of the capacity to finance deficits in any way other than by cutting expenditures or raising taxes, the states almost uniformly found themselves in greater financial embarrassment at a time when political wisdom argued against imposing further taxes on a frightened electorate in the grip of the first economic downturn in almost a decade. In most states and cities taxes did in fact get raised, but the associated clamor for national action was sufficiently loud to persuade a Republican President, and later a quite conservative Chairman of the House Ways and Means Committee, to sponsor legislation granting all states and cities an unappropriated lien on a portion of federal income tax proceeds.

This action should have thrown into sharp relief the scissorslike effect on the federal structure of the 1960's commitment to governmental activism. Pressure on first city and then state tax bases in densely populated areas had steadily expanded the geographic breadth of revenue sources, while growing interest in more and more tailored public services had striven to bring the point of expenditure decision down closer to the local and even sublocal bodies that individual citizens might reasonably aspire to influence. The theoretical contribution of Nixon's "New Federalism," albeit modest, was largely to bless this divorce of revenue and expenditure decision bases as a natural and even traditional construction of the Constitution. The same concept had earlier been embodied in state relations with localities, as evidenced by the rise in general state support to local budgets from $600 million in 1954 to nearly $5 billion twenty years later. Again, however, the increase was concentrated in a few of the populous states and was apparently arrested during the sweeping retrenchment in state spending (from 4.6 percent annual increase to 0.6 percent) that occurred after the tax-raising shock of 1971.

However, two other elements were necessary to provide sufficient drama to intrude the breakdown of traditional federalism onto the crowded agendas of opinion makers. First, it was necessary that an important and identifiable jurisdiction be poised on the brink of a financial collapse that would severely damage its parent state and perhaps the financial integrity of the nation at large. Second, the nature of the peril had to be defined in terms of a manageable number of actors within a finite time frame, rather than the Tolstoyan exercise in historical process that had characterized management of annual fiscal emergencies during the previous fifteen years. The New York City crisis provided these elements in ample measure, and thereby awakened many opinion leaders to the reality of "marble cake" federalism. The sheer scale of New York City and its singular dependence upon short-term borrowing (a practice originally developed to compensate for late arrival of federal and state subsidies) crystallized in the minds of reluctant and unbelieving officials and citizens alike the financial stakes at risk for the entire structure of public and private finance. In time, it also demonstrated that the risk of total abandonment of troubled urban cores was no more tolerable than had been the threatened failure of one of the nation's largest employers a few years before. Yet, once again, the response stopped short of formal recognition that the problem was based on long-term structural difficulties which were likely to generate many variations on the same theme in the years ahead. Clearly terrified by their brush with the maelstrom of inner-city finance, President and Congress—in the face of unanimous contrary urgings by all manner of local officials—declared the New York City crisis a regrettable but temporary condition resulting from the failure of a single city to "live within its means." The fact that no older inner city had met this standard for about three decades (if the standard implies providing local services only to the degree that they can be supported from the local tax base), was conveniently ignored. Subsequent events in Detroit, Cincinnati, and other cities suggested that this attitude simply pushed forward the day of reckoning and increased the probability that it would be dealt with in the traditional crisis atmosphere rather than on the basis of any concerted federal or state planning.

The New York City scenario also represented a continuation of unwillingness at the federal level to address the question of the net impact of federal policy on jurisdictional form at the state and local levels. The "layer cake" view had exerted a strong disincentive against direct or overt approaches to this problem. In theory, it was simply none of Washington's business how states and localities arrayed themselves. This principle still carried substantial political power. Nevertheless, it had been at least obliquely attacked in the Economic Opportunity Act of 1965, when the concept of community-wide action (usually meaning a base of action larger or smaller than the central city) had been put forward in a modest way, much to the distaste of most city officials. The rapid demise of this effort had been followed by a series of partially conflicting incentives and disincentives to metropolitanization that were independently administered by a variety of federal agencies, usually without the consent or cooperation of the affected states. These efforts also seemed to have little effect, with a few possible exceptions in such areas as health-facility planning and environmental pollution control. Following a mildly successful attempt to get the federal government's own house in order by systematizing the geographic regions used to administer its major agencies, another attempt was made to incorporate all relevant jurisdictions into the decision process (including, particularly, the state governors) through a review process (the so-called A-95 sequence) that was said to be a required component of many federal decision procedures.

Meanwhile, states and cities had moved in a modest way to create loose collectivities of governments in some regional and metropolitan areas. In general, these took the form of Councils of Governments (COG) that were typically without substantial decision authority, but that contained some minimal capacity to provide common staffing and a regional discussion forum for governments that wanted to make use of such facilities. Largely independent of the process of COG formation, a brisk traffic developed in the transfer of functions from local jurisdictions with narrower tax bases to ones (e.g., counties) of broader or more specialized revenue-generating power; a 1976 survey showed that about one-third of approximately 3,300 responding municipalities reported the transfer of one or more functions or components of functions during the previous ten years. The potential of the federal government to induce state and jurisdictional change was amply demonstrated by the rush to create and partially finance metropolitan transit organizations when Washington finally capitulated and began appropriating tiny sums for subsidization of first capital and then operating expenses of such enterprises. Nevertheless, in 1977 it was still fair to say that the basic right of federal authorities to engage in state and local jurisdictional architecture is by no means established, the jurisdiction-influencing policies followed by different federal agencies are very different, and no durable tendency toward metropolitanization of major functions, or of the generation of revenues to support these functions, has yet appeared in most states.

As reasonably solid data on demographic and income trends for the period after 1970 have begun to be available, it appears that major changes in the 1955–70 pattern have taken place and may suggest a future quite different from the past. These trends and their implications will be discussed in section IV.

III

The net legacy of these fits and starts is a federal "system" that bears little relation to the pre-1935 model or, more importantly, to the model that most Americans carry around in their heads. For purposes of domestic governance it is the most gigantic mechanism ever devised to transfer resources from the point of generation of income to thousands of categories of individuals and institutions eligible for public subsidy. The minority of this flow that is focused upon the poor has principally involved transfer from the outer rings of our metropolitan complexes to the inner cores, a feat of extraordinary difficulty where the supramunicipal jurisdiction is controlled by residents of the outer rings, and where those rings may not even be contained within the same state. Paradoxically, the very bulk of these huge transfer mechanisms obscures their visibility to most citizens. So many are the linkages, so fragmented the financing and authority, and so byzantine the decision channels that many citizens seem to be driven back to the "layer cake" perception in simple defense of sanity. The more thoughtful have long since abandoned hope for simplicity, an inevitable casualty of industrialization. There is, however, a yearning, as yet unfulfilled, for some set of consistent principles that can at the same time order the meshing of governmental fiefs and provide a rationale for their future evolution that promises to bear some reasonable relation to real prospects rather than to empty exercises in nostalgia.

As will be discussed in the next section, there is reason to believe that factors emerging during the most recent years make these future prospects quite different from past experience, and that these developments will make rationalization of the "system" even more difficult. Before proceeding, however, the analysis already presented supports the following heretical truths about the present federal framework.

1. The dominant domestic functions now performed by the "banker governments" (the federal and state levels), other than making formula payments to individuals, are to generate revenue and transfer it to narrower jurisdictions which either cannot or will not be self-sufficient.

2. This role is not temporary; neither does it show any signs of declining in significance. Federal aid now accounts for about 30 percent of state spending, and federal and state aid to localities supports more than 40 percent of big-city spending, including education. With the enactment and renewal of revenue sharing, this involvement extends to every aspect of subfederal governance. Allocative principles based on restricted areas of federal or state interest are at least sick unto dying.

3. In the older and most populous states and cities, no policy change that involves any substantial increase in state or local spending can in practice be effected without intergovernmental consultation and financial cooperation. Once commenced, this cooperation becomes a very hardy feature of the budgetary landscapes of all parties concerned. This rule of involvement increasingly applies to such delicate matters as collective bargaining policies, state and local burden sharing, and the setting of state and local tax rates.

4. The rapidly expanding states (Texas, Arizona, Florida) and cities (Houston, San Diego, Phoenix) have more policy flexibility but thus far less politicocultural inclination to use it.

5. The extended initiation and control linkages in so large and diverse a "system," together with the long lead times implied by the necessity to coordinate so many unsynchronized units, has greatly reduced the influence of elected officials upon real-world outcomes, and severely diluted the capacity for deliberate and predictable influence by any individual or faction. This problem has been compounded in recent years by a marked tendency toward shorter average tenure in elective and appointive office at all levels.

6. Many of the largest states and cities are so interdependent financially that questions of major default will expose them as a single financial entity in which one component's credit worthiness stands or falls with the other's. There are also strong links between all public jurisdictions in

terms of the marketability of their securities, as was demonstrated when municipal interest costs rose across the nation by an estimated $3 billion (or half the annual yield of revenue sharing) in the wake of the 1975 New York City crisis.

7. The diversity of state policies and attitudes is profound, and, in practice, susceptible to change only by positive (that is, financial) incentives applied from the federal level. Sanctions on the states for noncompliance have been largely ineffectual. And even full federalization of functions has not necessarily been effective in reducing state spending, standardizing benefit levels, or eliminating administrative complexity, as was demonstrated by the 1974 federalization of programs to aid the aged, disabled, and blind.

8. Whatever discipline has been alleged to flow from the perceived lack of financial recourse by urban governments to umbrella jurisdictions in the event of fiscal distress has been severely diluted everywhere and may have largely disappeared in the poorest cities. Conversely, there seems to be a fairly strong disciplinary potential in the attitude of the private money market, although ways have not yet been found to standardize risk assessment for most public entities.

9. The commingling of governmental levels seems to have severely attenuated the link between the intent of voters and the postelection sequence of events, particularly at the local level. The "ambassadorial" function of local elected and appointed executives (to the state and the national capitals) is often as invisible to the electorate as it is critical to meaningful action. In general, candidates' programmatic platforms continue to ignore the necessity of intergovernmental cooperation to effect any major change, so that voters have little sense of how many cooks are required to produce edible broth.

Put in simplest terms, having been unwilling to recognize the existence, legitimacy, and permanence of bank-type relations among governments, we have been unable to learn how to control them or manage them efficiently. We do not know how the banker governments should go about deriving program criteria and performance measures for local authorities that tread the thin line between helpful direction and inefficient meddling. We do not know how best to maximize the quantity and quality of governmental product when the point of finance is split and often two or even three levels removed from the point of final output. We do not know what disciplinary forces can resist impulses to excessive spending when the spender bears no responsibility for raising the revenue being allocated. And we do not know an effective means for providing policy-making and administrative traction to short-lived, politically chosen officials, and thereby to the voters who selected them. This is not to say that there is no useful research or experience on each of these questions. But the body of knowledge and hypothesis is pathetically small in comparison with the importance of the problem, and its utility is further limited by our basic unwillingness to accept the fact that the classical concept has been abandoned.

IV

The post-1970 statistics tracking national demographic trends point up some important differences in many of the factors that shaped developments during the previous fifteen years. Most critical, of course, is the dramatic reduction in the birthrate, which reduction shows some signs of durability. If so, prospects are that the age profile of the country will shift markedly upward, increasing the category of citizens who are most generously provided with public subsidies. The shift in concentration of population is also important; the 1970 census was the first in which more than 50 percent of the population was located within fifty miles of the East and West coasts, and the remarkable acceleration in the growth of the "sun belt" metropoles in the first five years of this decade indicates that entirely new migratory patterns are well under way.

As a result, as George Peterson has shown, not only do the inner cities of the Northeast and Midwest continue to shrink in population and, even more important, in employment opportunities, but some of their surrounding metropolitan areas (as of 1976, those around Cincinnati, Cleveland, Detroit, New York, and Pittsburgh) are shrinking as well. Similar but less pronounced phenomena seem to be occurring in a number of older western urban complexes, notably San Francisco, Oakland, Los Angeles, and Denver. These developments include some complete turnabouts, such as the net out-migration of blacks from central cities that occurred during 1970–74. But the figures also contain many reaffirmations of earlier trends, such as the fact that the average family moving into inner cities during this period had an annual income of about $1,200 lower than that of the average family moving out.

Demographic movements are complemented by changes in fiscal policies in the populous states, and by growing tension with and political estrangement from their needier client cities. It seems clear that 1972 was a watershed year for spending patterns at both subfederal levels, as the average annual spending increase of the previous decade was slashed by nearly 90 percent. Ironically, this occurred at the same time as the collection of revenue generated by the painful tax increases of the preceding year. This revenue, expanded by inflation and by the recession tendency to underestimate the tax yield that will be realized from a given rate applied during a recovery phase, was swelling their coffers to the extent of a $10 billion overall surplus in the state and local sectors. More significant, however, was the general signal from state capitols that the window dispensing subsidy increases to localities was shut and was unlikely to be opened to the late-1960's level for some time, if ever. The steady increases in state-aid formulas that had been a major escape valve for urban fiscal pressures during the 1960s became increasingly rare in the more industrialized states. Shaken by the realization that a recession, over which they could exercise no substantial control, could create volatile revenue behavior in the face of inflexible expenditure commitments, states took a number of other steps to shore up their fiscal shock absorbers, including more conservative projection of revenues and the regular budgeting of surpluses and reserve funds. These actions, together with the effect of federal revenue sharing, were evident in the much lower order of distress that the states suffered during the subsequent recession of 1974–75.

One particularly general device employed by states in their efforts to lessen fiscal risk was more aggressive use of the "transformers" by which they convert open-ended, entitlement-type federal subsidization of individuals into finite commitments which can be budgeted by subfederal governments that must provide substantial matching funds but have no means of financing major deficits if claims exceed resources. The usual technique was a flat ceiling on the portion of the statutory standard of need (e.g., for Aid to Families with Dependent Children) that would actually be paid to eligible recipients during a given year. In extremis, this could be converted into an immediate "ratable reduction" in the course of the current year. Rarely if ever was the need standard itself reduced, a difficult political task in the context of stagflation that was inflicting greatest hardship on the poor. But the level of actual payment fell below 60 percent of the standard in some states, and in only 20 states was the need standard fully met through the period. This practice was critical to the success of the states in holding the largest and yeastiest elements in their budgets (other than education) in check.

On the other hand, inner cities, plagued by the mismatch between tax base and service demand, were rather more ravaged by the second recession of the decade. Although they too benefited from revenue sharing, this source represented less than 2 percent of big-city budgets and was not sufficient to avoid major damage. Despite partially successful efforts to halt the growth in employee salaries and benefits, the disappearance of the option of increased state aid forced most of the declining urban cores to impose substantial degradations in services. Some were dramatic, as in the case of New York's dismissal of more than 40,000 employees, or Detroit's short-lived suspension of 20 percent of its police force. Most were less eye-catching, such as the major northeastern city that suspended all street maintenance for at least three years. Taken as a whole, however, the core-city picture was one of steady, sometimes largely invisible disinvestment that raised the the specter of decline into what I have elsewhere termed general service default — the inability to provide a level of service consistent with the minimal requirements of prevailing community standards of decency. It was becoming evident that this form of decay could be at least as effective in discouraging job creation and maintenance as would be the higher tax rates necessary to allay it.

But both states and cities were reeling in the face of taxpayer reaction to fifteen years of state and local tax increases which had doubled the share of the national income devoted to these governments. Property owners were in particularly general revolt, and relief of their burdens was complicated by decisions in some major states (notably California and New Jersey) that basing the quality of education on the differential capacities of school districts to generate property-tax revenues violated the equal protection clauses of state constitutions. Barring enactment of one of the as yet unaccepted equalization schemes that take into account the unusual service demand placed on core cities, the prospect was that their relative paucity of schoolchildren would react in state aid formulas with their wealth of high-priced buildings to produce a greater local financial burden simply to maintain the same level of educational quality. There were also some signs of efforts to extend the "*Serrano* principle" (named for the plaintiff in the California school case) to other urban services, an extension well within the bounds of rational extrapolation if the basic principle were accepted. If such a movement were to develop, it would require the discard and replacement of the allocative principle now most widely in use for supporting and distributing local services.

The property-tax struggle was one component of a general trend toward divergence of the circumstances of older, declining core cities from those of most states and less afflicted municipalities. Indeed analysis of upward pressures on overall state and local spending in the 1960s led some scholars to pronounce them largely transitory and unlikely to recur, so that the aggregate state and local sector could look forward to taking in about 1 percent more revenue than needed to finance services of present scope and quality each year through 1986. The basis of this optimism lay in four key assumptions: (1) upward pressure on state and local expenditures will ease considerably because of the halt in growth of demand for services (particularly education) as population growth slows; (2) state and local capital needs will either be much more heavily subsidized by federal grants, or will simply be ignored; (3) no new problems will be addressed or services developed unless their costs can be entirely met by reductions in existing services; and (4) public-sector salaries will move back from the accelerated growth rate they have exhibited during the past fifteen years to a rate that is the same as the average in the private sector.

The controversiality of these assumptions is obvious, but it seems clear that they are most dubious when applied to the distressed inner cities. Thus emerges the prospect of an inverse relation between the degree of urban distress and the probability that the shrinking inner cities will be able to mobilize political support from sister jurisdictions on the basis of shared experience and interests. The bleak financial prospects of the distressed states and cities imply that others will be enjoying relative affluence and cannot be expected to be pleased to join in what will necessarily be ever more visible transfers (viz. the present New York City loan program) to less fortunate places. If it is deemed important that minimal living and service standards in core cities be maintained, the dangers are two: that the necessary resource transfers will not occur because of the absence of political support, or that the condition of any transfer to the needy will be nearly equivalent transfer to the nonneedy.

Thus, recent experience suggests that both the political and the economic strains on the federal structure will be more pronounced in years ahead than they have been in years past. Our past muddling-through has been heavily dependent upon rapid average rates of economic growth, relatively cheap energy, ample capacity for capital formation, and the capacity of the states to offset, however disparately and inadequately, the chronic fiscal mismatch in the core cities. None of these factors appears as favorable now as in earlier years. Differences among states are likely to increase, in terms of both attractiveness as places of investment and living quality acceptable to the middle class. The result could be a reverse of the past pattern in which the federal government has been willing to "carry" a high percentage of the costs of southern state governments as the price of much larger dollar (but smaller percentage) contributions to much more elaborate governments in the North. But it is not clear that the politics will work in reverse, particularly if the "sun belt" cities and states use their remaining advantages (e.g., transfer of functions to large counties, easy processes for municipal annexation) to avoid the worst of the aging problems that characterize cities in the Northeast quadrant. At the least, such changes would exert stronger and more divisive pressures upon our jury-rigged federal linkages. The question posed is whether a federation formed to protect diversity among states can deal with increasing concentration of its have-nots in a small minority of state and local jurisdictions of steadily weakening political influence.

V

The key exogenous influence upon the evolution of federalism will clearly be the perceived economic and cultural utility of geographic proximity. So far, despite extravagant expectations of change from such technological innovations as cable television, this utility seems at a high and stable level—the level that has concentrated 75 percent of the population in 2 percent of the land area. As long as more than 80 percent of bank accounts, 75 percent of federal income tax collections, and 80 percent of the value added to manufactured goods are located in urban areas, the present stresses, or worse ones, will endure. Rapid urbanization has clearly mellowed into a fairly constant aggregate balance between urban and rural populations, but there is no current suggestion of a massive movement away from preferences for densely settled areas.

Given continued stability in this balance, the most revealing benchmark is likely to be the relation between the point of financial responsibility and the point of control. Revenue sharing, as we have seen, represents an almost complete separation of the two. About 25 percent of all other federal payments to states and localities are now provided in the form of "block grants," which at least theoretically allow more local discretion in their use, although sometimes on the condition of providing information (e.g., inventories of existing city housing stocks) that requires establishment of wholly new facilities and practices in state and local jurisdictions. Should this separation continue to gain momentum, the principal effect is likely to be steady enhancement of the role of the states, which can largely regulate effects upon cities irrespective of direct federal aid to them or of mandatory "pass throughs" of federal funds initially granted to the states. This control can be exerted through manipulation of state subsidies. If such measures become a serious problem, counteracting them may eventually require a difficult choice between what amounts to federal controls on state allocations of state resources, and the designation of the most distressed cities (or of core areas within them) as direct federal wards by some agreement with the relevant states.

In the near term, however, the main determinants of trends are likely to be (1) whether federalization of welfare finance is determined to entail federal administration and solely federal determination of benefit levels and eligibility standards; (2) how any program of national health insurance that may be enacted is financed and administered; (3) whether a general program of federal aid to inner cities (and/or guarantees for their securities) is developed, and what role is given to the states in its administration; (4) whether collective-bargaining rules governing state and local employees are established at the federal level as well as at the state level; and (5) whether the federal government develops a coherent policy with respect to its influence upon local jurisdictional forms.

Within the states, the critical question is whether—and for how long—state governments can increase subsidies to inner cities without (1) paying the price of equivalent subsidies to localities that do not need them, and (2) eschewing direct control of client government administration. The divorce between financial responsibility and control grows easier in direct proportion to the remoteness of the financier. Modern state governments still enjoy some degree of detachment from city administration, but this distance is clearly decreasing. As in the aftermath of the New York City crisis, it seems probable that it will be the inclination of the state, and of any private investors involved, to establish a semipermanent institutional bridge to major cities so as to maintain direct supervision of their most expensive clients. Over time this could produce a quite serious negative reaction from an inner-city population of steadily decreasing influence in the decision councils of the state. At some point this friction, in the absence of such preemptive federal action as that mentioned above, could lead some states to consider massive shifts of local power to larger jurisdictions, perhaps to counties. Ironically, this may be the only practical route to metropolitanization.

These indicators etch the outline of the options likely to be placed before us as the overburdened structures of traditional federalism groan under the strain of dealing with a population that refuses to deploy itself tidily within the governmental vessels provided for it. History suggests that the least promising option is also the most probable. Our instinct in such matters has been to treat the strain as a temporary imbalance, and our instinct is likely to be to go on doing so. But the weaknesses that seem to be developing in the adjustment mechanisms which have made that policy marginally viable suggest that the price of ignoring the gap between constitutional theory and operating practice is rising and will rise faster in future. Rightly reluctant to risk wholesale amendment of the Constitution to close the gap, our challenge is to effect a new consensus and appropriate modus operandi within the permissive framework afforded by the current form. This will require leadership and foresight of the same order as that exhibited by the Framers in setting forth the original structure, and possibly a higher tolerance for frustration, in that the results are unlikely to have the decisive and tangible characteristics of a single document. Whether these qualities of leadership are forthcoming will bear heavily on the nature of any "New America."

MARTIN SHEFTER

5. New York City's Fiscal Crisis: The Politics of Inflation and Retrenchment

The current New York City fiscal crisis is above all a political crisis. Its origins lie in a set of political changes the city experienced in the 1960s, which led municipal expenditures and indebtedness to grow at an explosive rate. And the eruption of the crisis has produced a further transformation in the structure of the city's politics.

This is not to deny that changes in the city's demographic and economic base over the past three decades have contributed to the problems the municipal government faces. The migration of more than a million poor blacks and Puerto Ricans to New York since World War II has placed pressures on the municipal budget at the same time that the movement of business firms and middle-class whites to the suburbs has reduced the city's capacity to finance new expenditures. But these developments, which are commonly cited to explain the city's difficulties, cannot in themselves account for the crisis; unemployed men and fatherless children do not, after all, have the authority to appropriate public monies or float municipal bonds. To account for the rapid growth of the municipal budget and debt, one must explain why public officials responded as they did to these changes in the city's demographic and economic base — an explanation to be found in the transformation of New York City politics in the 1960s.

During that decade, the regime that had formerly governed New York City collapsed, and a new coalition of political forces attempted to seize control. This initiated a pattern of political activity that has characteristically led to rising public expenditures and indebtedness, financial collapse, and ultimately budgetary retrenchment and a reorganization of politics, shifting the balance of power to the owners of the public debt. This pattern of political and fiscal change is not unique to New York City in the 1960s and 1970s; it has appeared both in other places and in earlier periods of the city's history.

Two Routes to Retrenchment

The political conditions that lead city governments to increase municipal expenditures at a rapid rate and accumulate large deficits are similar to those which encourage national governments to pursue highly inflationary fiscal and monetary policies. Such policies are likely to be adopted in the following combination of circumstances: (1) a social group that has recently gained political power begins to assert claims on the government for greater public benefits or a larger slice of the national income; (2) the government responds to these claims either because it is allied with the group in question or because it cannot withstand its opposition; and (3) the government is too weak politically to finance these new claims by reducing the flow of benefits to other groups, or by raising taxes. To cover the difference between expenditures and revenues, both municipal and national governments can borrow money. In addition, national governments can print money — in large quantities, if necessary — to finance their deficits, and hence deficit financing on the national level can generate rampant price inflation.

These political conditions have prevailed, as the historian Charles Maier has noted, during the major episodes of national inflation in this century. The hyperinflations in Central Europe in 1919–22, for example, followed the creation of democratic regimes in Germany and Austria, which for the first time granted representation in the government to working-class parties. These regimes, however, were threatened by antidemocratic forces on the Right and dared not alienate the nation's industrialists. The only economic policies compatible with the maintenance of a tacit coalition between labor and industry were highly inflationary: the industrialists would not tolerate any new taxes on corporate or personal incomes, and the government thus increasingly financed its operations by resorting to the printing presses.

Similarly, in Latin America, periods of severe inflation characteristically occur after the rise of regimes that speak for the urban or rural lower classes, but — because of their political weakness, administrative incapacity, or corruption — cannot collect taxes from the middle and upper classes, or prevent the wealthy from sending their money abroad, or foster economic development. The Peronist regime in Argentina, for example, sponsored the organization and political incorporation of labor, but failed to industrialize the nation and generate the wealth necessary to pay for the benefits provided its supporters. Consequently, claims to the national income that the government granted exceeded the national income, and inflation followed.

The European nations now experiencing the highest levels of inflation — Portugal and Italy — are characterized by politics most closely approximating the pattern outlined above. The Italian case is too complex to describe here, but the Portuguese situation is quite straightforward. Following the revolution of 1974, which granted the Portuguese political rights they had been unable to exercise freely for fifty years, a succession of weak governments (six in two years) either encouraged, or found it impossible to resist, the demands of the army for an immediate withdrawal from Portugal's colonies, of agricultural laborers for land, of workers and civil servants for wage increases, and of unions for greater control over factories and offices. The result was a rise in the nation's wage bill, a decline of labor and military discipline, the influx of more than half a million refugees from Angola who had to be housed and fed by the government, a rise in government deficits, and consequently an inflation rate in 1975 of 46 percent.

The conditions fostering very high levels of inflation are inherently unstable. Double- or triple-digit inflation can lead to a credit or liquidity crisis, to balance-of-payments difficulties, and ultimately to a recession. When this occurs, industrialists become less willing to accept inflationary policies. Middle-class *rentiers*, who generally are the most seriously injured by inflation, and who find it difficult under normal circumstances to assert themselves politically against better-organized groups, can erupt into an angry political force when inflation threatens to wipe out the fruits of a lifetime of thrift. And the banks, which are in a position to extend the necessary loans for stabilizing the nation's currency and refinancing its international debt, gain enormous political leverage by their ability to attach conditions to their aid. If all these interests coalesce, they can overturn the government that fostered inflation, and install a government that will implement a program of retrenchment.

Retrenchment involves eliminating nonessential public expenditures. What this commonly means in practice is that groups that have only recently gained a measure of power will be deprived of whatever benefits they won by being incorporated into the political system. For the purposes of retrenchment, these groups must either be driven off the political stage or compelled to accept a more modest role.

Historically, the first of these alternatives is probably the more common: retrenchment often occurs at the expense of democracy. In 1922, for example, the Austrian government received a stabilization loan from the League of Nations by agreeing in the Geneva Protocols to abrogate parliamentary authority over all financial matters for a period of two years. And the agreements that brought stability to Weimar Germany involved the overthrow of the last coalition government in which a working-class party had representation. In Latin America, typically only military governments can carry out retrenchment policies that international lending agencies insist on. Argentina — and Chile — provide stark examples of what the implementation of a retrenchment program can entail.

The alternative route to retrenchment involves a system of discipline imposed upon the new political group not by an alliance of domestic conservatives and foreign bankers, but rather by the leadership of the group in question. And this can lead to harsh measures. The halt to the leftward drift of Portugal's revolution and the rise to power of the moderate Socialist government of Mario Soares came only after many offices of the Portuguese Communist party were firebombed, leftist groups in the military were smashed, the army was purged by a stern disciplinarian, General Ramilho Eanes, and the Socialists allied themselves with the two most conservative parties behind his presidential candidacy. And the success of Italy's current retrenchment program ironically depends upon the ability of a Leninist party — the Italian Communist party — to impose its new line (the "historic compromise") on restive party militants and compel the unions affiliated with the Communist labor federation to limit their wage demands.

Boss Tweed and Tammany Hall

New York City's budget rises and falls in response to a political logic similar to the one outlined above. Periods of increased public expenditures and indebtedness follow upon the rise to power of new but loosely organized political coalitions, and periods of retrenchment are associated with the expulsion of these new forces from the political arena, or their subjugation to tighter political discipline.

In New York City, these new political forces have generally been coalitions of elements of the city's business community and members of ethnic groups that had previously been politically weak. Such political coalitions have traditionally been pieced together by machine politicians, who placed new ethnic groups on the public payroll to win their votes and at the same time sponsored the public projects favored by their allies in the business community. This method of purchasing political support can be costly. On three occasions in the city's history—in 1871, 1933, and 1975—it has led to a fiscal crisis that enabled the banks owning the city's debt to insist that municipal expenditures be drastically reduced as part of a bailout plan. The politicians in office when the city amassed its debt are then discredited by their responsibility for the city's difficulties, and weakened by the retrenchment program; this in turn permits the political agents of the bankers to call themselves reformers and win the next election. This experience chastens the defeated political forces and enables a more sober leadership to emerge among them. It also gives the new leaders an incentive to organize their followers more tightly, and upon returning to power they can be less generous in dealing with their rank-and-file supporters and more accommodating in dealing with their erstwhile opponents.

The rise and fall of the Tweed Ring illustrates this process clearly. Boss Tweed was allied with businessmen who operated chiefly in local markets—building contractors, real-estate men, street-railway promoters, savings bank owners, and manufacturers, who benefited from Tweed's ambitious program of opening up new streets and transit lines in the northern sections of the city. Uptown development had previously proceeded slowly; city officials had been more responsive to the elite merchants and bankers operating in national and international markets—interests that were oriented to the downtown district and the port and that regarded as utterly profligate uptown development on the scale proposed by Tweed.

Tweed also sponsored the political incorporation of the immigrant Irish. In the three weeks prior to the election of 1868, the judges allied with the Tweed Ring naturalized several thousand new citizens, and expanded the number of registered voters in the city by more than 30 percent. The attachment of these new voters to the Tammany organization was reinforced through placing many on the public payroll, and through a public-welfare program that bore some marked similarities to the poverty programs of the 1960s. (The poverty programs funneled public monies into community groups and Baptist churches in black neighborhoods; Boss Tweed's public-welfare programs channeled public funds into charitable institutions and Catholic churches in Irish neighborhoods.)

The cost of bringing local businesses and immigrants into the political system was high. The budget of the Streets Department, for example, quadrupled in Tweed's first years as Deputy Commissioner. It was especially high because the Ring was structurally weak. Tweed was unable to command the obedience of other politicians; instead, he was compelled to purchase with cash bribes the support of state legislators, county supervisors, and even his immediate associates. To finance its operations, the Ring levied a surcharge on all city contracts. And because the Ring was weak, Tweed hesitated to raise taxes sufficiently to meet the city's current expenses, let alone to cover the costs of the capital improvements he sponsored. Just as Mayors Lindsay and Beame were to do a century later, Tweed funded short-term revenue notes into long-term bonds. In the last four years of Ring rule in New York, the city's outstanding indebtedness tripled.

The Ring was brought down by the city's creditors, who were driven to act by two events that destroyed their tolerance for a regime based upon the two groups from which Tweed drew his support. The first was the Orange Riot of July 1871, sparked by a parade of Irish Protestants celebrating the Catholic defeat at the Battle of the Boyne. Catholic spectators threw stones at the troops protecting the marchers, and the troops responded with a volley of gunfire that killed thirty-seven spectators. The press blamed the city government for provoking the disturbance, and respectable elements in New York concluded from the incident that a municipal government dependent on the political support of the Irish could not preserve public order. The second event that led the city's financial elite to move against the Ring was the suspension of trading in New York City bonds on the Berlin Stock Exchange and the refusal of bankers in London, Paris, and Frankfurt to extend any more loans to the city, after a series of exposés in the press revealed the extent of municipal corruption and the size of the city's debt. The collapse of the city's credit threatened the solvency of all the New York banks owning municipal securities. To protect itself, the city's financial community felt it imperative that the Ring be overthrown. This was accomplished, in the words of a contemporary pamphlet, through an "insurrection of the capitalists": A group of the city's most prominent businessmen, the Committee of 70, organized a tax strike, and a thousand property owners refused to pay their municipal taxes until the city's accounts were audited. In addition, the city's bankers refused to lend the municipal government the money needed to meet the city payroll and cover debt-service payments until a reformer, Andrew Haswell Green, was appointed Deputy Comptroller with absolute authority over the city's finances. The *coup de grâce* was given the Tweed Ring when the Committee of 70 entered a slate of candidates in the 1871 municipal elections and won control of the city government.

The collapse of the Tweed Ring enabled "Honest John" Kelly, in alliance with a group of wealthy, nationally oriented Democrats, to seize control of Tammany Hall. Kelly inferred from the Tweed episode that Tammany could not survive if all elements of the business community united against it, and that to avoid such opposition it must shed its reputation for corruption and profligacy. He accomplished this by purging Tammany of its more disreputable elements and by centralizing and strengthening the party organization. (It has been said that Kelly "found Tammany a horde and left it an army.") Kelly then used this organization to elect a succession of respectable merchants to the mayoralty, discipline lower-level Tammany officials engaged in the grosser forms of corruption, and make himself Comptroller, in which position he pursued an extremely tight-fisted policy of retrenchment.

By creating the modern Tammany machine, Kelly and his successors, Richard Croker and Charles Murphy, established a mechanism for incorporating immigrants into the city's political system in a way that was tolerable to, if not entirely to the liking of, the city's propertied elite. This involved extruding from the political system competing contenders for control over the city's immigrant masses. Kelley's victory represented the triumph of a respectable lower-middle-class leadership group among the Irish (Kelly himself was married to a niece of Cardinal McCloskey), and the maintenance of this group's control entailed the defeat of both the lower-class gangs that had formerly played an important role within Tammany and the trade-union and socialist movements that at various times (most notably the 1880s and the 1910s) had attempted to assume political leadership of the working classes.

The preservation of Tammany's hegemony, however, required that the machine's subordinate functionaries be tightly disciplined and that new ethnic groups be given a share of the spoils. When the hold of the machine's central leadership weakened, as it increasingly did after Murphy's death in 1925, Tammany officials were free to enrich themselves without limit, and to freeze out newcomers. The bacchanalia of corruption during the administration of Jimmy Walker, and the inability of Tammany's fragmented leadership to face up to, or impose upon their subordinates, the stringencies that the Great Depression required, set the stage for the New York fiscal crisis of 1933, and the triumph in the municipal election that year of a coalition of reformers, businessmen, Italians, and Jews under the leadership of Fiorello LaGuardia.

From Accommodation to Community Participation

The last political leaders in New York to successfully pursue Kelly's strategy were Carmine DeSapio, Alex Rose, and Robert Wagner. These leaders won a secure position for Italians and Jews in New York politics by helping to expel from the political system those elements of their ethnic constituency who were least acceptable to other groups in the city. DeSapio consolidated his hold over the Democratic party by purging Tammany of its gangster element, which was primarily Italian, but included Jewish district leaders such as Sidney Moses and Harry Brickman. Rose established the influence of the Liberal party by destroying the Communist-dominated American Labor party, which was heavily Jewish, although its most prominent ally was the Italian-American Congressman Vito Marcantonio. Both DeSapio and Rose created tightly centralized party organizations, and when they united behind the same candidates, municipal elections involved as little competition as they had during the heyday of machine rule in the 1920s. In the mayoral race of 1957, Robert Wagner, who had the support of both organizations, won 72 percent of the vote and defeated his Republican opponent by almost one million votes.

The politicians who governed the city during the 1950s defused opposition by accommodating its major organized interests. The downtown business community was satisfied because control over the development programs that were of prime interest to them was placed in the hands of Robert Moses and/or various public authorities responsible only to their bondholders. Municipal civil servants and the prestigious civic associations were granted substantial influence over the city's major service-delivery agencies. And in making revenue and expenditure decisions, elected officials paid special heed to the views of the city's tax-conscious lower-middle-class homeowners. Consequently, during Mayor Wagner's first two terms, the city government did little that aroused controversy, and its expense budget increased at an average annual rate of only 6.6 percent between 1953 and 1960.

This political calm was shattered in the late 1950s and early 1960s by the emergence of three new political groups in New York—the Democratic reform movement, the school-integration movement, and the movement to unionize city employees. The effort of politicians to gain power in the city by allying with these movements destroyed the regime constructed by DeSapio, Rose, and Wagner and initiated the present era of budgetary inflation.

The first of these to gather force was the reform movement in the Democratic party. In the face of its threat, Mayor Wagner undertook to salvage his career in 1961 by turning on his political mentor, DeSapio, and seeking renomination with the support of the reformers and the municipal civil service. The steps Wagner took to win their backing—especially his sponsorship of a new city charter —weakened the regular party organizations, loosened some of the restraints upon budgetary inflation in New York, and made him more dependent politically on groups demanding services. Consequently, municipal expenditures increased during Wagner's third term at an average annual rate of 8.9 percent. Significantly, in 1961 the city's expense budget fell into deficit for the first time since the depression, and it continued to do so during each year of Wagner's third term.

In 1965, the reformers and liberals abandoned their former allies in the municipal labor movement, and supported the mayoral candidacy of John Lindsay. The political forces backing Lindsay sought to drive the civil-service unions from power and seize control of the municipal bureaucracy themselves. Lindsay centered his 1965 campaign around an attack upon the "power brokers" (i.e., the civil-service union leaders); he undertook to reorganize the municipal bureaucracy into ten superagencies, which would be responsive to his leadership; and he regularly contracted with outside institutions (such as the RAND Corporation, the Ford Foundation, and various universities) to perform tasks formerly conducted by municipal civil servants. To gain political support, the Lindsay administration allied itself with the third new political movement of the 1960s, the black civil rights movement. Blacks were useful allies because they could be used to legitimize the administration's efforts to seize control of the bureaucracy, which was criticized for its failure to adopt "innovative" programs that were "responsive" to the needs of the black community. And the alliance Lindsay cultivated with blacks provided the administration with shock troops to attack the bureaucracy from below, a function served by the mechanisms of community participation established by the administration.

New York City's budget during the early Lindsay years reflected this political strategy and the political constituency of the administration. The three major municipal programs in which expenditures rose the most rapidly during the 1966–71 period were higher education (251 percent), welfare (225 percent), and hospitals (123 percent). The clientele of two of these programs (welfare and public hospitals) is predominantly black, and the explosion in expenditures for the third (public education) occurred after the emactment of an open-admissions program that tripled black enrollments at the City University. Moreover, the staff providing services in each of these programs (whose salaries account for much of the increase in expenditures) is composed of large number of highly educated and well-paid professionals. To be sure, federal and state assistance under Aid to Families with Dependent Children and Medicaid helped the city pay for some of these new expenditures. But even as far as the city's own funds (so-called tax-levy expenditures) were concerned, welfare and higher education were by far the fastest growing budgetary categories during the first five years of the Lindsay administration.

The Lindsay administration was not in a position to finance the benefits it provided to its constituency by reducing, or even holding the line on, expenditures for other municipal programs, because Lindsay's victory in the mayoral election of 1965 did not destroy the influence of the unions that represented the employees of the more traditional municipal agencies. After Lindsay's election, the city-employee unions might no longer have had an ally in the mayor's office, but they retained their capacity to strike, to lobby before the state legislature, and to support or oppose candidates in future municipal elections. By the end of his first term, the mayor discovered how vulnerable he was to each of these maneuvers. He initially attempted to break the power of the unions by refusing to enter into the give-and-take of labor negotiations, by inviting strikes, and by then seeking to mobilize public opinion (and, in one instance, the national guard) against the unions. These efforts repeatedly failed, and Lindsay eventually learned that he could not govern the city without the cooperation of the unions. In addition to the wage increases they obtained by striking, the unions were able to secure very lucrative retirement benefits from the state legislature during the Lindsay years, because as the regular party organizations in New York grew weaker, many state assemblymen and senators from the city found the civil-service unions to be their most effective source of campaign assistance.

Finally, Lindsay himself was desperately in need of such assistance in his campaign for reelection in 1969. To win union support and pay off his campaign debt, he gave the unions everything they demanded during the 1969–70 round of contract negotiations. In these ways, the civil-service unions were able to secure substantial salary and benefit increases for city employees during his tenure, thereby compelling the mayor to increase expenditures for the agencies employing their members. During the 1966–71 period, the budgets of the traditional municipal departments—Police, Fire, Sani.ation, the Board of Education—did not double or triple, as expenditures did for welfare, hospitals, and higher education, but they nonetheless did increase on the average by 66 percent.

Setting the Stage for Financial Ruin

The Lindsay administration did not find it politically possible to obtain either enough additional state aid or enough additional taxing authority to finance all these expenditure increases. Although state aid payments to the city did rise substantially during the Lindsay years, there were limits to the willingness of upstate and suburban legislators to tax their constituents for the benefit of New York City. And the state legislature, when it considered New York City financial legislation, followed a set of informal procedures that enabled political forces unfriendly to Lindsay to block some of his proposals for tax increases and that favored the passage of legislation authorizing the city to borrow money to close its annual budget gap.

The Republican and Democratic leaders in the Assembly and Senate would round up votes necessary to pass New York City financial legislation only if every single assemblyman and senator from the city voted in favor of the bills in question. In practice, this informal requirement for unanimous consent meant that these bills had to meet with the approval of each of the major interests enjoying access to the city's legislative delegation, the legislative leaders, and the governor. One such group was the lower-middle-income homeowners, who were unable to defeat Lindsay in mayoral elections, but did send Republican assemblymen and senators to Albany to defend their interests. These legislators found it politically difficult to vote for tax increases, and to avoid losing their votes, the mayor and governor found it necessary to substitute bond and note issues. The city's major banks, whose views were represented in such deliberations by the governor, were quite happy to endorse deficit spending, because bond and note issues provided them with healthy commissions and good investment opportunities. Moreover, so long as the office boom of the 1960s continued—assisted by capital projects the city and state constructed with borrowed funds—it appeared that rising municipal tax receipts would enable the city to cover its debt-service payments.

The Lindsay administration was ultimately compelled to abandon its efforts to break the power of the public-employee unions, to seize control of the municipal bureaucracy, and to use the authority of the city government for new purposes. These efforts suffered a number of serious setbacks at the end of the mayor's first term and the beginning of his second. Lindsay's efforts to decentralize the city school system precipitated a bitter controversy and a teachers' strike—the Ocean Hill strike of 1968—and the settlement of the controversy was something of a defeat for the most militant advocates of community control. The upper-middle-class liberals and blacks who comprised the core of the Lindsay coalition were unable on their own to provide him with the votes he needed to win reelection in 1969, and Lindsay was consequently compelled to come to terms with the civil-service unions. And the administration's plans to place a large, low-income housing project in the middle-class neighborhood of Forest Hills in 1971 generated intense local opposition and had to be drastically scaled down.

The defeat of Forest Hills chastened Lindsay, and the growth rate of the city's budget slowed considerably. From 1966 through 1971, operating expenditures had increased at an average annual rate of 16.5 percent. In 1972, the growth rate of the city's budget declined to 8.6 percent; in 1973 it was 9.3 percent. Moreover, much of this budgetary growth resulted from rising prices, and the deceleration of the city's budget after the Lindsay administration had received its political chastening is thus particularly dramatic when measured in constant dollars: annual expenditure increases in constant dollars averaged 11.5 percent from 1966 through 1971; they averaged 3.7 percent in the next two years. Abe Beame's election as mayor in 1973 simply confirmed that a new political and fiscal plateau had been reached. Mayor Beame's budgets, again measured in constant dollars, grew at an average annual rate of only 2.8 percent.

This new political and fiscal plateau did not involve a return to the *status quo ante* of 1965. The new players in the political game, who had been ushered onto the field by John Lindsay, were not expelled—apart from a few unruly ones who had attempted to drive out some of the older players. And the claims of these new players to a share of the gate were recognized. Consequently, as Mayor Lindsay left office and Mayor Beame came in, the city's budget was more than three times as large as it had been at the close of the Wagner administration.

In the mid-1970s, however, it was far more difficult than it had been in the late 1960s for New York City to honor the claims on its budget granted during the Lindsay administration. Inflation drove up the cost of providing a fixed bundle of municipal services, and the failure of the city's economy to recover from the recession of the early 1970s made it increasingly difficult for New York to cover these rising costs. Moreover, by the mid-1970s there was an explosion in the costs of the retirement benefits that the municipal government and the state legislature had granted to city employees during the previous decade. In 1965, the city's retirement costs had been $364 million; by 1974, they had risen to $1.121 billion, and in 1976 they were $1.480 billion. In 1965, the city's annual debt-service payments had been $470 million; by 1974, they had risen to $1.269 billion, and in two more years they reached $2.304 billion. In order to close the gap between current expenditures and current revenues, and refinance the short-term debt as it fell due, the city resorted ever more heavily to borrowing. By 1975, the city's cumulative short-term debt had risen to $5.3 billion. The budget Mayor Beame initially presented to the state legislature for fiscal year 1976 anticipated a further deficit of $460 million, and had the city been able to borrow all that it wanted in 1975, its short-term debt might have amounted to as much as 33 percent of the entire outstanding short-term municipal debt in the United States! The city's request for huge grants and additional taxing authority from the state legislature, and its enormous demands upon the municipal-securities market for additional loans, set the stage for the New York fiscal crisis of 1975.

The Rise of the Banks

The fiscal crisis of 1975 was precipitated by a combination of events resembling the taxpayers' strike and bondholders' coup that had brought down Tweed a century earlier. The Republican state senators from New York City banded together in May 1975 and agreed to present a common front against the pressure from their party leaders and colleagues to vote for legislation granting additional taxing authority to the city. The refusal of these spokesmen for the city's taxpayers to consent to any new taxes increased the city's demand for credit and thereby weakened the market for New York City securities. Later that month, the major New York banks refused to underwrite or purchase any more New York City notes and bonds and thereby drove the city to the verge of bankruptcy.

There is little reason to believe that the Republican legislators and the New York bankers foresaw the enormous consequences their actions would have, or that in precipitating the crisis they were motivated by anything beyond the desire to protect the short-run economic interests of the groups they represented and their own short-run political and institutional interests. As for the Republican state legislators, they were heavily dependent on the support of small-property owners, who were being squeezed by the combination of inflation, recession, high levels of taxation, and rent control in New York, and were increasingly voting on the Conservative party line. Moreover, in 1975 the governor's office was occupied by a Democrat for the first time in sixteen years and hence Republican legislators no longer had a compelling reason to support a tax package hammered out in negotiations between the governor and mayor.

As for the major New York banks, there were a number of strictly economic reasons why they were becoming increasingly reluctant to purchase the city's securities. Other more lucrative investment opportunities (foreign loans, leasing, consumer financing) had recently been developed by the banks or had been made available to them by amendments to the Bank Holding Company Act, and the failure of the Real Estate Investment Trusts had created liquidity problems for many of them. But, most importantly, as the city's short-term debt began to skyrocket, it was becoming increasingly clear to outsiders as well as insiders that the city was engaged in a great ponzi game: It was financing current expenditures by borrowing, and paying off old debt by issuing new debt. So long as dealing in New York municipal securities had been a high-profit, low-risk venture for the city's banks, they had been quite happy to participate without asking too many embarrassing questions of city officials. But when eleven major New York banks realized in the spring of 1975 that the outside world would shortly be able to figure out what the municipal government had been doing, they unloaded $2.7 billion in New York City securities that they owned. With the banks flooding the market with old New York bonds at the same time the city was seeking to sell additional hundreds of millions in new municipal notes and bonds, the market in the city's securities collapsed.

This collapse confronted the banks with immediate and grave dangers. Unless the city could borrow additional money, it could not redeem its old notes and bonds as they fell due, and if the city defaulted on these obligations, the value of New York securities remaining in the banks' portfolios would plummet. If this occurred, not only would the banks suffer a direct loss, they also could be sued by the clients whose money they had invested in New York notes and bonds. Thus the major New York banks sought desperately to keep the city from defaulting: they pleaded with out-of-town banks to purchase New York securities; when that failed, they pleaded with the federal government to guarantee the city's bonds. Indeed the very desperation of the banks made it possible for the architects of the plan that bailed out New York to squeeze additional loans out of the banks to shore up the city's finances.

In addition to these short-run economic dangers, the fiscal crisis presented the banks with long-run political opportunities. It has enabled the banks (and, more generally, the city's corporate elite) to gain a dominant voice in municipal affairs. Some of this influence rests on the ability of the banks to extract concessions from the city government in return for lending it money. But the banks have actually lent the city less money than either the municipal-employee pension funds or the federal government. The major reason the banks have become so influential lies instead in the following combination of circumstances. First, the city must be able to regain access to the municipal credit market, unless some other means of managing its cash flow, financing capital projects, and discharging its outstanding debts becomes available. Second, the city has no chance whatever of regaining access unless its most prominent bankers and business leaders are prepared to assert that they are satisfied it is managing its affairs in a prudent and economical fashion. Third, public officials at the municipal, state, and national levels have accepted the banks' claim that if the business community's retrenchment program is adopted, the market *will* reopen to the city—in other words, that enactment of the retrenchment program is sufficient, as well as necessary, for the city to regain access to the market. This claim is, to say the least, highly conjectural.

In the name of making New York bonds marketable, nthe banks have managed to extract enormous concessions from the city. In the process, the local business elite has come to play a larger and larger role in governing the city, and the conduct of public policy in New York has increasingly come to reflect the priorities of the business community. The state initially created a Stabilization Reserve Corporation (SRC) to market a new series of bonds for the city, and it specifically set aside the proceeds of certain city taxes to cover the debt-service payments on these bonds. When these bonds failed to sell, a new state-appointed board, the Municipal Assistance Corporation (MAC), was created to replace SRC. In addition to being granted the authority to issue bonds and use municipal tax revenues for debt service on these securities, MAC was given the power to revamp New York City's accounting system. When the MAC bonds also failed to sell, the state, at the urging of the banks, passed a statute requiring the city to balance its budget within three years and limit its annual expenditure increases to not more than 2 percent during that period, and creating an Emergency Financial Control Board (EFCB) empowered to freeze the wages of city employees, approve all city contracts, and supervise city finances.

The EFCB is composed of two state officials (the governor and state comptroller), two city officials (the mayor and city comptroller), and three private citizens appointed by the governor. The governor resisted pressure to appoint a labor and a minority representative, and selected instead top executives of the New York Telephone Company, American Airlines, and Colt Industries. In addition, the mayor—at the urging of the business community—established the Mayor's Committee on Management Survey, chaired by the president of the Metropolitan Life Insurance Company, to reorganize the municipal bureaucracy along business lines. And in response to pressure from the banks, the mayor fired one of his oldest associates as First Deputy Mayor, and appointed prominent business executives to three of the most important financial and managerial positions in the city government: Deputy Mayor for City Finances, Budget Director, and Director of Operations. Just as the New York banks in 1871 were able to install their man, Andrew H. Green, as Deputy Comptroller, thereby gaining control of the city's finances, the leaders of the New York financial and business community over the last two years have been able to install their representatives in key positions, thereby gaining effective control over the city government today.

These spokesmen for the city's business community have argued, with considerable justification, that New York has little alternative but to close the gap between expenditures and revenues by reducing expenditures. Tax increases would encourage more employers and taxpayers to leave the city, thus exacerbating New York's economic and fiscal problems. Among the city's expenditures, however, two categories have been the particular targets of New York's fiscal overseers. The first are labor costs. In response to pressure from MAC and the EFCB, the city instituted a wage freeze and eliminated 56,000 employees from its payroll. This represents a 19 percent reduction in the city's labor force. The second are programs with predominantly black clienteles—youth services, addiction services, compensatory higher education—which have suffered disproportionately severe budget and personnel cutbacks. Moreover, personnel have been fired in disproportionate numbers from job categories—clerical, paraprofessional, and maintenance—heavily staffed by Blacks and Puerto Ricans. Consequently, between July 1974 and February 1976, the number of Hispanics employed by mayoral agencies declined by 51 percent, and the number of black males declined by 40 percent. What retrenchment has meant in practice is that the city has curtailed the benefits it provides to two of the groups—civil servants and blacks—that had gained a measure of political power in the 1960s.

The Fall of the Blacks and the Unions

Squeezing out the blacks has been a rather simple matter. Black leaders had mobilized their constituency in the 1960s by relying upon the resources provided by federal and local agencies, and by drawing upon the publicity and support of the press, national foundations, and universities. In the early 1970s, however, the Nixon administration turned sharply to the right, and federal expenditures for community organization were cut drastically. At about the same time, the Lindsay administration abandoned its mobilization strategy, and the various institutions in the not-for-profit sector committed wholeheartedly to social activism in the 1960s felt the pinch of a declining stock market and reduced federal social expenditures, and became far less aggressive politically. Finally, upper-middle-class youths, who had provided much of the manpower for community organization drives in the 1960s, turned to other causes in the following decade: environmentalism, consumerism, feminism, or simply careerism. The New York fiscal crisis represents the culmination of this trend: blacks have simply been abandoned by their erstwhile supporters. It appears that the upper-middle classes, who in the flush 1960s saw blacks as useful allies in the drive to extend their influence over municipal government, have concluded in the harsher climate of the 1970s that their political interests can better be served by entering into an alliance with the banks. The *New York Times*, for example, has uncritically accepted the most questionable assumption underlying the retrenchment program advocated by the city's business leadership—the notion that retrenchment will restore the city's access to the capital market—and it now attacks the civil service not in the name of responsiveness and innovation but rather in the name of economy and productivity.

It has been a far more troublesome problem to deprive the city employees of the gains they achieved in the late 1960s and early 1970s, because city employees are far better organized than blacks, and their power is less dependent on the steadfastness of their allies. Nonetheless, the civil-service unions have been compelled to accept a wage freeze, layoffs, longer hours, and heavier workloads. In addition, they have been induced to invest (or to commit themselves to invest) some $3.7 billion of their pension-fund assets in New York City and MAC bonds. Indeed, since the onset of the fiscal crisis, the tables have been entirely turned in municipal labor relations. No longer do the unions and the city bargain to determine which of the unions' demands the city will accede to; now the question has become which of the city's demands the unions will accede to. How has this been accomplished?

In an immediate sense, the tables were turned by the state's Financial Emergency Act, which granted the EFCB the power to review—and to reject—municipal labor contracts. But one must ask why the unions have agreed to play by these new rules, instead of striking to obtain higher wages. The most direct explanation for the unions' meekness is that strikes would almost certainly fail. New York's creditors and potential creditors regard the wage freeze as the acid test of whether public officials in New York are prepared to mend their ways. Were city and state officials to bow to the demands of a striking union, the city's present and future sources of credit would dry up. If the unions were to strike nonetheless—in an effort to compel the mayor and governor to choose between losing access to credit once the city's current cash balance was depleted, and an immediate and total disruption of municipal services—the mayor and governor would probably take the latter. The success of a strike ultimately depends on public tolerance—or more concretely, whether the public will countenance the use of the national guard to perform the functions of striking workers. Mayor Lindsay floated the idea of using the national guard during the 1968 sanitation strike, and quickly discovered that it was totally outside the realm of political possibility at that time. It is a measure of how dramatically New York politics have been transformed since the fiscal crisis that the municipal unions dare not tempt the mayor to make such a proposal today.

Another reason for the remarkable restraint of the unions during the crisis is that they have an enormous stake in the city's fiscal viability. Bankruptcy would cause the value of the New York City and MAC bonds owned by the union pension funds to plummet. More importantly still, bankruptcy would throw the city into the hands of a receiver with the unilateral authority to abrogate union contracts, slash wages, order wholesale firings, and reduce pension benefits. This would mean the end of collective bargaining and would threaten the very existence of the unions. To avoid these dangers, municipal union leaders have undertaken the task of selling the retrenchment program to their members, convincing them that they have no alternative but to bear with it. And by doing this, they have made it unnecessary for the bankers and business leaders to rely upon harsher measures to implement the program. In this respect, since the fiscal crisis the municipal labor leaders have played a role in New York politics similar to that played by John Kelly after the overthrow of Tweed: they have assumed the job of disciplining the municipal labor force, just as Kelly imposed a system of discipline upon the ward heelers in Tammany. In praising Victor Gotbaum for being "responsible" in urging his members to bear with the wage freeze, the editorial writers for the *New York Times* were saying in 1975 precisely what the editor of the *Commercial Advertiser* said a century earlier of Kelly, in somewhat more forthright terms: "Kelly has ruled the fierce Democracy in such a manner that life and property are comparatively safe.... It requires a great man to stand between the City Treasury and this most dangerous mass.... Dethrone Kelly and where is the man to succeed him?"

Sources of Instability

There are, then, some striking similarities between the financial and political developments in New York since the fiscal crisis of 1975, and those in the aftermath of Tweed's downfall a century ago. In each case, municipal expenditures exceeded municipal revenues, and the city was compelled to bring the two into line by reducing its expenditures. Retrenchment has involved a reduction in the flow of benefits to groups that had recently acquired political power, which in turn means that the members of these groups must endure a new and more stringent fiscal and political order. This process of financial and political contraction has been accomplished, in part at least, with the cooperation of leaders from the very groups that are being compelled to lower their sights and accept the harsher discipline of the new order.

The parallel is not perfect, however. The most obvious difference is that blacks and Puerto Ricans have thus far been less successful in defending their economic and political gains than the Irish were under John Kelly, or for that matter, than the civil-service unions have been during the present crisis. Another difference is that the regime currently governing the city is less tightly organized, centralized, and broadly based than the Tammany of Kelly, Croker, and Murphy. Consequently, no single organization today is capable of subjecting both the electorate and public officials to its discipline. And for these reasons, the modus vivendi that has emerged among the major actors in New York politics in the present crisis is not entirely stable.

The structural weakness of the present New York regime, and the substantial exclusion of blacks from it, could lead to the collapse of the entire set of accommodations sustaining the retrenchment program so far. One potential threat to the success of the current retrenchment program arises from the weakness and lack of discipline of some of the city's public-employee unions. If the leaders of a union are to risk negotiating a contract that reduces their members' benefits, they must be politically secure; if they are to get their members to approve such a contract, the union must be organizationally strong. Victor Gotbaum and the union organization he leads (the State, County, and Municipal Employees) may well be strong enough to impose discipline on its rank and file, but some of his colleagues in the municipal labor movement are not so well situated. The leadership of the Patrolmen's Benevolent Association (PBA), in particular, is very insecure, and the union itself is highly factionalized and quite weak. It is not surprising, therefore, that two successive PBA presidents, Ken McFeely and Douglas Weaving, refused to agree to the wage freeze and were reluctant to negotiate a contract that—in the city's judgment, at least—stayed within the EFCB's guidelines. When Weaving finally did hammer out an agreement with the city's negotiators, it was rejected by the union's delegate assembly, and bands of policemen, encouraged by Weaving's political opponents within the union, staged a series of protests and demonstrations. Unable to mediate successfully between his members and the EFCB, Weaving resigned, as McFeely had done before him. The refusal or inability of any one union to accept wage restraints, of course, makes it more difficult for the other unions to do so.

The very fact that New York City employees are represented by a number of independent unions is another potential source of instability: each union can attempt to exploit its peculiar advantages, and pass the burdens of moderation on to the other unions. On a number of occasions the United Federation of Teachers (UFT) has sought to do exactly this. The UFT is probably the most politically powerful of the city-employee unions, because it can both draw upon its own resources and count on other groups to rally to the cause of education. Thus the UFT relied on its strength in the state legislature to secure passage of the Stavisky-Goodman bill in the spring of 1976, which directed the mayor to restore $150 million of the funds he had cut from the Board of Education's budget. And the UFT has been the only civil-service union to stage a strike during the first two years of the financial crisis. The contract settlement that ended the brief teachers' strike in September 1975 provided salary increases for senior teachers, which the Board of Education financed by reducing the length of the school day and by failing to rehire any of the teachers laid off earlier. In all probability, when the UFT and the board agreed to this contract, they anticipated that they would be able, with the support of aroused parents' groups, to pressure the mayor into giving the schools enough money to rehire teachers and restore the full school day.

The Stavisky-Goodman bill and the 1975 UFT contract indicate other tensions that can undermine the retrenchment progam—those between the handful of officials in New York directly responsible for the city's finances and the hundreds of officials in legislative and administrative positions without such a responsibility. The overriding concern of the mayor and comptroller of New York City, and the governor and comptroller of New York State, is what might be termed the "cash-flow imperative." The city simply must have cash on hand to pay its bills when they fall due—especially to meet its payroll and debt-service obligations—if the government of the city is not to grind to a halt. The cash-flow imperative is the central preoccupation of these four officials, because they bear the ultimate responsibility for the day-to-day administration of the city's affairs, and for obtaining the loans the city needs to continue operating. This is a less immediate concern to city and state legislators, and to administrative officials who are only responsible for spending money but not raising it. And because politicians in New York today (in contrast to the situation during the heyday of Tammany rule) are independent political operators who are not subject to the discipline of a common party organization, the mayor and governor have found it difficult to compel other officials to pay heed to the imperatives imposed upon the city by the capital market.

The inability of the mayor and the governor to control other politicians provides groups demanding services with the opportunity to get their way by mobilizing other public officials against them. The Stavisky-Goodman bill, for example, was strenuously opposed in the name of fiscal responsibility by Mayor Beame and Governor Carey—both of whom, it should be noted, are moderately liberal Democrats. Nonetheless, the UFT and its allies were able to secure overwhelming majorities in the State Assembly and Senate to pass the bill—even though the governor had vetoed it, the legislature had not overridden a gubernatorial veto in more than one hundred years, and one house of the legislature was controlled by moderately conservative Republicans. The UFT was also able to pressure the EFCB into approving its labor contract, although questions had been raised by the EFCB staff about whether the contract was consistent with the wage freeze, by getting the two U.S. senators from New York to urge ratification in public testimony before the board. Likewise, the Board of Higher Education and the Health and Hospitals Corporation, which as quasi-independent agencies have somewhat more leeway to maneuver politically than regular city departments, have attempted to resist budget cuts by getting various elected officials to support their cause. In this way, they hope to isolate and pressure the mayor and governor.

The Electoral Threat

The final difference between the regime governing New York today and the regime Kelly and his successors constructed involves perhaps the most serious threat to the retrenchment program. The Tammany machine in the days of Kelly, Croker, and Murphy rested on a very broad and tightly controlled electoral base. The structure of electoral politics in New York today is quite different. A substantial proportion of the city's electorate—particularly its potential black and Puerto Rican electorate—does not vote. And many of the groups that do vote, but have acquiesced in the retrenchment process so far, are capable of acting independently in the electoral arena to protect themselves from the full rigors of retrenchment. The potential thus exists for elections to disrupt the retrenchment process. If black leaders were to mobilize a broader electoral base now than in the past—and they now have a stronger incentive to do so—public officials would not find it so easy to slash expenditures on programs with a black clientele. And if various groups that have acquiesced thus far to retrenchment were to adopt a new stance and enter into a new set of electoral alliances, public officials might find it politically impossible to heed the imperatives imposed upon the city by the capital market.

In short, the structure of electoral politics in New York today is such that political campaigns can generate serious strains within the retrenchment coalition, and can result in the election of public officials committed to opposing aspects of the retrenchment program. Just how real this possibility is can be seen by examining the potential electoral resources commanded by blacks, homeowners, liberals, and city employees, and by considering the various ways candidates might construct coalitions among these groups in their effort to win municipal elections.

Blacks and Puerto Ricans participate in elections in far smaller proportions than other major groups in the city. (During the first round of the 1973 Democratic mayoral primary election, for example, a total of 3,828 votes was cast in the predominantly black 54th Assembly District in Brooklyn, while 23,080 votes were cast in the predominantly Jewish 45th Assembly District a few miles to the south.) This is a consequence, at least in part, of the peculiar role blacks and Puerto Ricans played in the city's politics in the 1960s—one that contrasts sharply with the role the Irish played in New York politics a century before. While the political leaders of the Irish were rewarded in direct proportion to the number of votes they commanded, for the most part black leaders in the 1960s were not rewarded on this basis, because their support was valued less for the number of votes they could swing in municipal elections than for the legitimacy they were able to confer upon public officials or public programs in the eyes of federal grant-givers, national opinion leaders, and the most ardent supporters of these officials and programs. To the extent that black leaders were able to obtain administrative appointments, influence over policy making, access to the mass media, federal or foundation grants for their organizations, or election to public office in predominantly black constituencies, all without a large mass following, they had no compelling incentive to undertake the effort involved in mobilizing such a following.

The legitimacy that black leaders can confer on the officials or programs they support has been a far less valuable political commodity in the mid-1970s than it was in the late 1960s, and blacks have consequently suffered heavily from retrenchment. The immediate reason why blacks have borne the brunt of the recent wave of firings, of course, is that the city removes workers from the municipal payroll in reverse order of seniority. Black leaders have predictably denounced this practice as "racist" and "anti-black." The city has adhered to it nonetheless, because any alternative would be denounced with equal vehemence by the civil-service unions, and the mayor is less willing to arouse their ire than that of the black leadership. If it were the case, however, that blacks and Puerto Ricans cast as large a proportion of the vote in the Democratic primary as their proportion of the city's population (roughly one-third), rather than voting at less than half that rate, it is likely that the mayor would have taken greater pains to protect blacks from the full force of the "last-hired, first-fired" rule. He might, for example, have cut more deeply into job categories occupied predominantly by whites, rather than by blacks.

Such political lessons are not likely to be lost on black politicians. To the extent that black leaders in the future will be rewarded only in proportion to the help they are able to give their friends at the polls, or the harm they are able to inflict on their enemies, they will have a stronger incentive than they had in the 1960s to mobilize the enormous pool of black nonvoters. At the same time, retrenchment will provide black politicians with the inducement to adopt a new leadership style, and it may well spark leadership struggles within the black community. The skills involved in organizing large blocs of voters and forging coalitions in the electoral arena are not the same as the ones rewarded and hence encouraged by the city's political system in the 1960s. In this way, the current fiscal crisis may well foster leadership changes within the black community akin to those among the Irish a century ago, which favored the respectable and taciturn John Kelly over both the fiery Irish nationalist O'Donovan Roosa and the disreputable gambler

John Morrissey. Such leadership is by no means alien to blacks: it is the style of the black labor leader (e.g., Bayard Rustin or Lillian Roberts) rather than the black preacher. There are some indications that such a transformation may in fact be taking place today. In announcing his candidacy for the 1977 Democratic mayoral nomination, for example, Percy Sutton ignored racial issues and focused his remarks solely on the problem of crime, an issue around which he clearly hopes to mobilize a biracial electoral majority. Over the long run, then, the fiscal crisis may do for blacks what the overthrow of Tweed did for the Irish: it may facilitate their incorporation into the political system under a chastened and more sober political leadership.

Whatever its long-run consequences, however, in the short run the incorporation of the enormous reserve of black nonvoters into the electoral arena can only upset the current retrenchment program. The success of this program is contingent upon the political feasibility of firing a large fraction of the city's minority-group employees, and cutting heavily into the budgets of municipal agencies providing services to blacks and Puerto Ricans. No black leader could hold on to his following while tolerating a retrenchment program whose burdens fall so disproportionately on his constituency. (Although his general strategy entails avoiding racially divisive issues as much as possible, even Percy Sutton rose to the defense of John L. S. Holloman, the black director of the New York City Health and Hospitals Corporation, whose removal from office was engineered by the EFCB and Mayor Beame because he resisted cutting the budget of the public hospital system, most of whose patients and a majority of whose nonprofessional personnel are black and Puerto Rican.) The entry of thousands of blacks into the electorate would give black politicians the bargaining power to back up their demand that the burdens of retrenchment be redistributed. Any such changes would of course be resisted by the groups that would be disadvantaged, and elected officials might well find it impossible, within the constraints imposed upon the city by the municipal-bond market, to arrange a new set of fiscal and political accommodations acceptable to the city's unions, taxpayers, business interests, liberals, and blacks.

Who Should Bear the Burden?

The civil-service unions are also in a position to use their electoral influence to improve their bargaining power in the retrenchment process. The unions can deploy manpower and money in political campaigns, and public employees and their spouses constitute a substantial voting bloc, especially influential in primary elections. A natural strategy for a candidate would be to court the support of the unions and middle-class Jews (the group whose turnout rate is the highest in the city's electorate) by casting himself as the defender of the city's traditional public programs, especially its public schools and colleges, and its subsidized middle-income housing program and rent-control program. The two chief sponsors of the Stavisky-Goodman bill, one of whom had his eye on the presidency of the city council and the other on the mayoralty, were clearly laying the groundwork for such a campaign appeal when they introduced their bill in the state legislature.

Elections and political campaigns can also lead to changes in the relative influence of the two groups most strongly committed to budgetary cutbacks—the city's downtown business elite and its homeowning population—and might thereby disrupt the retrenchment coalition. Since the eruption of the fiscal crisis, bankers and corporate executives have wielded enormous power in their role as mediators between the city and the capital market. They are able to exercise far less leverage in electoral politics, however, because apart from the Republican organization in Manhattan, they have no organizational presence. On the other hand, representatives of the city's homeowners have played little direct role in governing the city since the onset of the fiscal crisis (no spokesman for this group sits on the EFCB or MAC), but they are an important force in the city's electoral politics. Tax-conscious homeowners are a major bloc in the electorate, and their representatives play a considerable role in municipal elections through the regular Democratic and Republican organizations in Brooklyn, Queens, and the Bronx, and through the Conservative party.

The question of who speaks for retrenchment in the governmental and electoral arenas is significant because the politicians who represent the city's homeowners are likely to cultivate alliances that differ considerably from the ones the bankers have struck. It would be natural for a candidate seeking the votes of the homeowners (who are chiefly lower-middle-class Catholics) to advocate that the municipal bureaucracies that employ and serve them (the Police and Fire Departments) be spared drastic budget cuts, and that reductions be made instead in programs (especially welfare) that have a black clientele and employ middle- or upper-middle-class personnel. Nothing could be more calculated to alienate the reformers and liberals, who have been happy to join a retrenchment coalition led by men of their own class or a higher social class (like Felix Rohatyn), and would find it hard enough anyway to overcome cultural and ethnic antipathies sufficiently to collaborate with politicians speaking for lower-middle-class Irish and Italians.

Finally, reformers and liberals may come to play a different role in the city's politics during and after an election campaign than they have since the eruption of the fiscal crisis. Since 1975, reformers and liberals have followed the political leadership of the banks. In electoral politics, however, they have the ability to act independently, and they command a number of important resources—organizational skills, money, talent, energy, and a committed mass following. During an election campaign, these resources could be deployed in one (or both) of two ways. One alternative, which might be called the West Side option, would be for liberals to recultivate an alliance with blacks, oppose budgetary cutbacks, attack the banks, and—apart from calling for increased federal aid—ignore the issue of how the city is to pay its bills. The second, the East Side option, would be for liberals to maintain their current alliance with the banks, insist that the city has no choice but to cut its budget, attack the politicians and union leaders (the power brokers?) responsible for getting the city into its present mess, and—apart from opposing appeals to racism—ignore the blacks.

Campaigns can thus open the question of who should bear the burden of retrenchment, and elections can compel public officials to commit themselves to protect various municipal programs from budgetary cutbacks. When this source of strain is considered along with the other tensions besetting the retrenchment coalition, it is little wonder that New York City's creditors and potential creditors are reluctant to trust their fate to democratic politics.

The Logic of Political Contraction

There are, as I noted above, two fundamental routes to retrenchment. One, the path of political organization and internally imposed discipline, preserves at least the forms of democracy. The other, the path of political contraction and externally imposed discipline, does not. Any particular entrenchment program may of course involve elements of both self-discipline and political contraction. Although New York City recovered from the fiscal crisis of 1871 by pursuing for the most part the path of self-discipline, there were aspects of the post-Tweed regime that could scarcely be considered democratic. For example, the reform charter under which the city operated from 1873 through 1897 included provisions for "minority representation" guaranteeing the anti-Tammany forces at least one-third of the seats on the Board of Aldermen. And Tammany relied, at least in part, on its control of the police to deal with opponents who challenged its hegemony over the working classes: The police commonly intervened against unions in labor disputes, and dealt rather harshly with anarchists, socialists, and communists.

These qualifications aside, New York City recovered from its 1871 fiscal crisis without abandoning the forms of democracy because John Kelly and his successors discovered a way, in a city where the ownership of property was not widespread, to reconcile mass political participation with the security of private property. They accomplished this by constructing a political machine that exchanged patronage for votes, and had both a broad base and a centralized structure and was therefore able to subject voters, public officials, and public employees to its discipline.

No such political organization exists in New York today. This is why the process of retrenchment in New York is currently beset by so many tensions, and why political campaigns and elections could so easily upset the retrenchment program. And it is for this reason that legal and institutional reforms that would sharply limit the scope of local democracy are being seriously considered in New York today.

New York City's creditors are well aware of the dangers threatening the retrenchment process. This explains the character of the proposals that the banks have advanced, and that public officials themselves have supported, in an effort to make the city's bonds marketable. For example, at the insistence of the banks, the statute creating the Municipal Assistance Corporation diverted the revenues of the stock-transfer tax and sales tax from the city's general fund, and earmarked them for debt-service payments on MAC bonds. And in February 1977 Mayor Beame proposed that revenues from the city's property tax be set aside in a fund under the State Comptroller for the purpose of meeting debt-service payments on New York City bonds and notes. Together, these reforms would deprive locally elected officials in New York City of the authority to determine how the monies raised by the city's most productive taxes are to be spent. (An analogous reform on the federal level would be a constitutional amendment depriving Congress of its authority over the $150 billion raised by the federal income tax, declaring that this money must be spent for national defense, and placing it in a fund controlled by the Joint Chiefs of Staff.)

In a similar vein, Governor Carey proposed that a "health czar" be jointly appointed by the mayor and governor to exercise all the authority of the city and state governments over hospitals and health care in New York City. This would permit both the mayor and governor to disclaim responsibility for the health czar's actions and would thus give him enough freedom from popular pressures to accomplish what officials subject to such pressures find impossible to do—order the closing of hospitals.

Finally, in March 1977, the banks proposed that a state-appointed Budget Review Board be established as a long-term successor to the EFCB. The Review Board would have the power to review the city's budget before it was adopted, to reject it if—in the board's judgment—it was not legitimately balanced, and to approve or disapprove all subsequent budgetary changes and all city borrowing. If city officials refused to obey the orders of the Review Board, it would have the authority to assume total control over the city's finances, and even to prefer criminal charges against municipal officials. The banks also proposed that restrictions be placed upon the city's ability to issue short-term debt, that a fund be created to cover revenue shortfalls and expenditure overruns, and that city officials be required to observe various reporting requirements and internal budgetary controls.

As these proposals indicate, a process of political contraction is well under way in New York. And the logic behind that process seems to be inexorable. If New York City is to manage its cash flow, finance capital projects, and pay off its accumulated deficit, it must enjoy access to credit. It will obtain such access only if its creditors are convinced that the city is able to repay the money it borrows. The city can pay its debts only if its current expenditures do not (as they presently do) exceed its revenues. Since the city's ability to increase its revenues through additional taxation is reaching the point of diminishing returns, it has no alternative but to reduce its expenditures. If elected officials find it politically impossible to reduce municipal expenditures, then the city can obtain the loans it requires only if outsiders are empowered to do the job for them, or if their authority to do otherwise is restricted by law.

In the absence of a political leadership with the power that John Kelly had to impose restraints upon public officials, New York City's creditors have searched for other means to ensure that their loans will be repaid. And in an effort to provide such guarantees, the city has been driven down the second route to retrenchment—that of political contraction. To be sure, New York City is not the Weimar Republic or Argentina. David Rockefeller is not in a position to organize bands of black-shirted thugs to beat up municipal union leaders and break up meetings of West Side reformers, nor is Felix Rohatyn likely to propose that welfare recipients be disqualified from voting in municipal elections. The process of political contraction, however, can proceed not only by direct assaults on the rights of newly powerful groups but also by removing authority from the hands of elected officials amenable to the influence of these groups and transferring it to officials insulated from popular pressures. Moreover, statutes can be enacted and standards placed in the covenants of twenty-year municipal bonds that limit the freedom of elected officials within the domain where they do retain some authority. And, as Boss Tweed learned, the criminal law can be used to keep profligate politicians in line. Just such reforms have been enacted or are being proposed in New York in an effort to make the city's bonds marketable. Whatever may be the long-run consequences of the city's fiscal crisis, as a result of these reforms, the citizens of New York may be left over the next decade with very little control over how they are governed.

David T. Stanley

6. Cities in Trouble

The Troubled Scene

What Is "Trouble"?

A discussion of which cities are in trouble, why, and what can be done to help them should begin with a definition of "trouble." For the purposes of this paper, trouble is *a city government fiscal situation so unfavorable as to impair borrowing ability, require reduction of municipal services, pose a threat to public health and safety, and thus diminish the quality and satisfaction of urban life.*

City trouble can be divided into two main types: (1) *fiscal crisis*, in which the city has neither cash nor credit to meet near-term expenses such as payroll and supplies; and (2) *long-term decline*, in which the city's economy, social conditions, and general enjoyment of life are slowly deteriorating. Neither type means that a city is "dying" or "uninhabitable"—cities cannot and will not be destroyed. Funds will be found somehow to meet crises. The declines may continue but the cities will live on among growing crime, filth, flammability, and despair. Nor does trouble necessarily mean *bankruptcy*, which requires formal, voluntary action by local government to request a federal court to supervise a debt-restructuring plan.

Trouble (as described in this paper) is *not* the annual struggle to balance the budget without raising taxes or cutting services. This occurs even in affluent localities with superior credit ratings like Fairfax County, Virginia, or Montgomery County, Maryland. Such governments feel distress, but the difficulty is of a completely different order.

The Spread of City Trouble

City trouble has a widespread impact. The city government tries to solve its budget-balancing problems by raising taxes, imposing fees, reducing its work force, and cutting down on purchases and construction. These measures are bad for the local economy. Businesses may move away or cancel plans to expand. This hurts not only the city but the suburbs, where many employees live and where some suppliers of central-city businesses operate.

As a city's finances become shaky, its bonds and notes may be hard to sell, will decline in price, and will cost the city more in interest. The effects can reach to other cities, as in 1975, when New York's problems caused a general lack of

95

confidence in municipal securities which drove up interest rates. Under such circumstances, banks with large holdings of city obligations are put under strain.

Other levels of government are also affected. The state governments concerned may have to extend special credits, make extra grants, and correct and supervise the cities' financial practices. The financial stability of states containing large, troubled central cities is impaired: nearly half their budgets is spent on these cities.[1] The federal government's provisions for general revenue sharing, block grants, and categorical grants are put under particular pressure. The question of special federal aid to New York City occupied much of the time and attention of both the Congress and the President in 1975.

The problems of troubled cities are, therefore, national problems—for federal and state governments, for private businesses, and for citizens. They are also, as this paper will show, problems that are intractable, grim, and discouraging. Solutions are much easier to conceive than to put into effect, considering the political balances in our federal system.

Which Cities Are in Trouble

To answer this first question, one must consider briefly the second, "Why are they in trouble?" Causes and indicators of difficulty are naturally intertwined.

Fiscal Crisis: Reality or Threat?

To start with, no cities are *bankrupt*—that is, petitioning for formal proceedings in federal bankruptcy court under either the old Chapter IX of the Bankruptcy Act or its new 1976 amendment.[2]

Two cities, New York and Yonkers, have been *insolvent*—unable to pay debts as they mature. They also faced immediate, critical difficulty in getting cash to pay expenses. Both cities were rescued by action of the New York State legislature, which advanced money and put them under financial control boards, virtual receiverships. A third city, Buffalo, found it impossible to sell a bond issue until the price was raised and new arrangements were made for organizing an underwriting syndicate.

The next questions are What cities are likely to follow New York and Yonkers into insolvency and cash crises? And how soon? These pressing questions simply cannot be answered because the variables are so numerous, the data so inadequate for comparisons, and the motivations—both of city officials and of financiers—so complex.

There are, of course, fiscal danger signs. These are early warning indicators, not trip wires or triggers, and warnings can be evident for years without leading to fiscal crises. Also, any set of figures raises methodological questions and can be questioned with reference to local financing conditions and accounting and budgeting practices. Despite these caveats, analysts can identify patterns of fiscal danger.

TABLE 6.1 PERCENTAGE OF 1973–74 SHORT-TERM BORROWING
COMPARED TO REVENUE

Toledo	34	Louisville	19
New York	28	Cleveland	15
Buffalo	27	Detroit	15
Chicago	26	San Antonio	14
Boston	21	San Francisco	14

Philip Dearborn, of the District of Columbia Municipal Research Bureau, presented several indicators—and the cities to which they point—last year. The two most significant to this discussion are: (1) deficiency of revenues compared to expenditures in 1971 and 1974 (New York, Boston, St. Louis, and Buffalo);[3] and (2) deficit cash position in 1971 and 1974 (New York, Chicago,[4] Philadelphia, Detroit, and St. Louis).[5] If a city frequently or consistently permits expenditures to exceed revenues, it will deplete its cash balance and eventually strain its credit-worthiness. Yet one cannot predict when the financial community will shut off credit. It happened to New York only when investors and banks were unwilling to buy short-term notes to finance operating expenses.[6]

Dearborn also reports other indicators: the amount of short-term debt outstanding at the end of a fiscal year (only in New York, Chicago, and Buffalo)[7] and increases in bonded debt, which he finds neither unduly large nor rising at an excessive rate.[8] Terry Clark, of the University of Chicago, has combined several indicators of "fiscal strain"—long-term debt, short-term debt, expenditures, and tax effort—for fifty-one cities. The top six cities included in his preliminary research are New York, Boston, San Francisco, Newark, Buffalo, and Atlanta.[9]

Already some names are being repeated. John Craig and Michael Koleda, of the Center for Health Policy Studies, National Planning Association, have prepared a listing—in which these names recur—of cities whose short-term borrowings in 1973–74 amounted to more than 10 percent of their revenues (see table 6.1).[10] This measure should not be used alone, however. Municipal short-term borrowing may be constructive and perfectly safe.

A final indicator of potential fiscal crisis is the financial rating of general obligation bonds. The rating should be of paramount importance because the financial community's loss of confidence in a city's ability to repay may be the immediate cause of fiscal crisis. Nevertheless, the quality of the analysis behind the ratings

...can best be described as undistinguished. Even in the spring of 1975, Moody reaffirmed its "A" rating of New York City bonds. Earlier, during the Lindsay years, both Moody and Standard and Poor had upgraded New York City's bond rating to an "A" position, although it subsequently became clear that at just this time the city began to accelerate its accumulation of hidden budget deficits.[11]

Moody's A rating indicates "upper medium grade obligations. Factors giving security to principal and interest are considered adequate, but elements may be present which suggest a susceptibility to impairment sometime in the future."[12] Since there is basis for concern at or below this rating level, the list of cities whose general obligation bond ratings are below Aa should be considered (see table 6.2).[13]

TABLE 6.2. CITIES RANKED BY OBLIGATION BOND RATINGS

New York	Caa	St. Louis	A
Newark	Baa	Boston	A
Detroit	Baa	Baltimore	A-1
Philadelphia	Baa	New Orleans	A-1
Buffalo	Ba	Jacksonville	A-1
Cleveland	A	Pittsburgh	A-1

Such ratings are more confirmations than predictors of fiscal trouble. The market will usually point to problem cities by showing increasing yields for their issues and the best-informed insiders will supply some analytical background.

One final listing, from an anonymous Washington source with a key responsibility for analyzing state and local obligations, gives the cities in greatest fiscal danger as Philadelphia (budget gimmickry, large unfunded pension obligations) and Boston (limited tax base, big pay increases), followed by Buffalo (small tax base, relatively large short-term borrowing) and (somewhat "safer") Detroit and Newark.

All these judgments are merely approximations of fiscal danger. No one can say with certainty what city, if any, may be next because there are so many variables to consider for each case. The fact that a few names reappear is significant; it is even more so if the same names also show long-term economic decline.

Long-Term Decline

Many of the same cities, often those with similar background characteristics, are in the second kind of trouble—long-term socioeconomic decline. Such a decline cuts revenue growth, drives up expenses, and is intertwined with fiscal distress.

Richard Nathan and Charles Adams of the Brookings Institution have prepared a "hardship index" to compare cities on six different economic and social measures: (1) unemployment, percentage of civilian labor force unemployed; (2) dependency, persons under 18 or over 64 as a percentage of total population; (3) education, percentage of persons 25 years old or more with less than twelfth grade education; (4) income level, per capita income; (5) crowded housing, percentage of occupied housing units with more than one person per room; and (6) poverty, percentage of families below 125 percent of low-income level. Each city is compared first with its own suburbs and then with other cities (see table 6.3).[14]

Another list of troubled cities, based on adverse demographic and economic characteristics, was presented to Congress by Thomas Muller of the Urban Insti-

TABLE 6.3. CENTRAL-CITY HARDSHIP INDEX

Compared with Balance of SMSA		Compared With Other Central Cities	
Newark*	422	Newark*	85.5
Cleveland*	331	St. Louis*	75.5
Hartford	317	New Orleans*	72.6
Baltimore*	256	Gary	70.0
Chicago*	245	Miami*	62.5
Atlanta*	236	Birmingham	61.8
St. Louis*	231	Youngstown	60.3
Rochester	215	Baltimore*	60.0
Gary	213	Cleveland*	59.6
Dayton	211	Detroit*	58.6
New York*	211	Buffalo*	57.2
Detroit*	210	Jersey City	56.6
Richmond	209	Hartford	56.2
Philadelphia*	205	Louisville*	55.9
Boston*	198	Cincinnati*	53.5
Milwaukee*	195	Providence	52.7
Buffalo*	189	Springfield (Mass.)	52.0
San Jose*	181	Tampa	50.9
Youngstown	180	Sacramento	50.4
Columbus*	173	Grand Rapids	50.3
Miami*	172	Atlanta*	50.1
New Orleans*	168	Philadelphia*	50.0
Louisville*	165	Chicago*	49.3
Akron	152	Pittsburgh*	47.1
Kansas City*	152	Dayton	46.9
Springfield (Mass.)	152	Rochester	46.3
Fort Worth	149	Richmond	46.2
Cincinnati*	148	Boston*	45.8
Pittsburgh*	146	New York*	45.3
Denver*	143	Akron	43.4

*Cities among the 40 most populous.

tute. Muller's characteristics, in simplified form, are "municipal danger signals" (outmigration, loss of private jobs, high local tax burden, rising proportion of low-income households, and low increases in per capita income) and other factors that usually correlate with the "danger" list (inability to annex or otherwise share in regional tax base, high per capita debt service costs, high unemployment, and large concentration of employment in manufacturing). According to Muller, large cities with declining populations and most of the above characteristics include Buffalo, Boston, Cleveland, Detroit, New York, Philadelphia, and St. Louis. Cities with declining populations and several of the characteristics, but whose fiscal outlook

TABLE 6.4. CITIES WITH DECLINING OR NO-GROWTH
TAXABLE PROPERTY BASE, 1970–75

New York	Cleveland	Buffalo
Chicago	San Francisco	Cincinnati
Detroit	St. Louis	Toledo
Baltimore	Pittsburgh	Newark

is more favorable than that of the above seven, are Cincinnati, Chicago, Baltimore, Pittsburgh, New Orleans, San Francisco, Milwaukee, and Seattle. "A number of smaller cities, such as Newark, are also in the danger category."[15] If some single-indicator economic rankings are asaembled, familiar names again appear (see tables 6.4[16] and 6.5[17]).

It has not been possible in this paper to penetrate deeply into the complex world of social indicators to see if the cities in fiscal and economic trouble are suffering other kinds of quality-of-life trouble. A 1972 Urban Institute study does explore such factors, but the results are too limited to be helpful here.[18]

TABLE 6.5. CITIES WITH HIGH PERCENTAGE OF POPULATION
RECEIVING WELFARE PAYMENTS

Boston	16.9	New York	12.4
Baltimore	16.3	New Orleans	11.4
Philadelphia	16.2	Detroit	11.2
St. Louis	15.8	Chicago	11.1
Newark	14.4		

I have extracted and examined data on two social indicators as related to population—suicides in 1973 and reported major crimes in 1974—and have concluded that the rankings of cities according to these indicators bear no relationship to the rankings already reported on fiscal and economic matters.

After a research exercise on fiscal, economic, and demographic considerations, Craig and Koleda, of the National Planning Association, categorize the forty largest cities (see table 6.6).[19] Another listing is *Newsweek*'s "ten cities to watch," which "may encounter difficulty servicing their debts in the months ahead": Boston, Buffalo, Cleveland, Detroit, Hoboken, Jersey City, Newark, Philadelphia, Wilmington, and Yonkers.[20]

My own list of most troubled cities is based on a combination of subjective judgments on fiscal outlook, condition of economic base, securities rating, leadership and farsightedness displayed by local political leaders, and the degree of state government supportiveness and is reinforced by the frequency with which these cities appear on the lists already quoted.

TABLE 6.6. THE STATE OF THE CITIES, 1975–85

Declining and Vulnerable Cities	Declining but Basically Healthy Cities	Growing Cities
New York	Los Angeles	Houston
Chicago	Washington, D.C.	Dallas
Philadelphia	Indianapolis	San Diego
Detroit	Milwaukee	San Antonio
Baltimore	San Francisco	Memphis
Cleveland	Boston	Phoenix
St. Louis	New Orleans	Columbus
Pittsburgh	Seattle	Atlanta
Buffalo	Jacksonville	Fort Worth
Cincinnati	Denver	San Jose
Newark	Kansas City	Oklahoma City
	Minneapolis	Nashville
	Toledo	
	Portland	
	Oakland	
	Louisville	
	Long Beach	

New York: unable to borrow, economy depressed, state fisc weakening

Buffalo: relatively high short-term debt load, sunken tax base, unemployment

Detroit: inadequate long-range revenue prospects in a high-cost area despite some industrial recovery, low level of state aid

Newark: significant physical deterioration, low level of services, angry adversary groups in citizenry

St. Louis: slow recovery in economic base, payroll likely to increase

Boston: high in tax burden yet facing expensive payroll costs and unfunded pension liabilities

Cleveland: low in tax effort, past errors in financial management

Philadelphia: budget barely balanced, large pension obligations, effort to force mayor out of office

No one can predict which cities will experience a cash or credit crisis. A city could be thrown into such a crisis by a natural disaster, major management mistakes or scandals, or civil commotion. However, a city nearing a crisis may be saved by local civic leadership, state legislation and supervision, federal aid, help from neighboring communities, and supportive tolerance by the local financial community.

Why Are They in Trouble?

The reasons for a city's fiscal trouble are very grave, interlocked, and—for the most part—long-term. Their impact varies from city to city, and they are given differing emphasis by researchers and public officials; but, in general, cities are in difficulty because of

> Static or declining populations and economic bases
> Rising costs of public services (primarily personnel), due in part to inflation
> Lagging growth in revenues, due in part to the mid-seventies recession
> Expedient, indifferent fiscal management, due to the natural political psychology of local governments

Declining Population and Economy

One can say of the most troubled cities that their economies are going nowhere and their people (the more productive) are going elsewhere. Central cities, in general, lost four times the population between 1970 and 1975 as between 1960 and 1970. Seventy-three percent of cities over 200,000 in population declined in size in the early 1970s, and "cities such as Buffalo, Cleveland, Pittsburgh, and St. Louis lost more than one-fifth of their total net population in the thirteen years 1960–73."[21] The movement is to nearby suburbs and other regions. The growth of suburban subdivisions, shopping centers, and business buildings is evident daily. Meanwhile, the metropolitan areas that are growing substantially are concentrated in the South and Southwest. The people who are moving away from the cities tend to be richer, better educated, and younger than both those they leave behind and those they join. Hence, this movement "weakens economically and socially the areas being abandoned and strengthens the receiving areas."[22]

Meanwhile, the number of jobs in troubled cities either declines or fails to grow as fast as employment generally in the nation. Muller, of the Urban Institute, computes a reduction in private employment between 1970 and 1973 of 3.6 percent in Cleveland, 6.3 percent in Philadelphia, and 7.2 percent in New York.[23] Considering total employment, Syracuse University economists show declines from 1965 to 1972 in New York, Philadelphia, and St. Louis at a time when

TABLE 6.7. PERCENTAGE OF JOB LOSSES, 1960–70

Detroit	18.8	Milwaukee	10.2
Buffalo	15.8	Baltimore	4.6
St. Louis	14.2	Philadelphia	4.1
Cleveland	12.9	Boston	4.0
Newark	12.5	Cincinnati	3.8
Chicago	12.1	New York	1.9

employment nationally *grew* 20 percent, inferring that "the private economy in cities will not offer a rate of growth sufficient to sustain continued rapid city government budgetary expansion."[24]

Reviewing the period from 1960 to 1970, Seymour Sacks estimates job losses in twelve cities (see table 6.7). Twenty-two other large cities had employment *gains* ranging from 0.5 percent to over 100 percent.[25] The New York City scene is particularly bleak:

> From a peak of 3.8 million jobs in 1969 employment in New York City declined by more than 11 percent to 3.4 million by the end of 1975, the lowest total employment in the City since 1950.... While employment in the nation as a whole was growing by 8.3 percent, the job losses in New York City resulted [from] both employment reductions by firms remaining in the City and reductions in the number of firms. This decline was across all sectors of activity.... If employment in New York City had grown at the national rate it would have 1.03 million more jobs than it now has, nearly 25 percent more.[26]

And New York, as noted earlier, is only one of twelve major cities with a declining or static tax base.

The troubled central cities are deteriorating amid suburbs that seal them in and prevent them from sharing in the economic growth of the area. Growing cities, by contrast, have been able to annex adjacent areas.[27]

Rising Costs

Declining cities are high-cost cities. The fact that population, business, and jobs are reduced does not mean that municipal services, and the staffs and facilities to provide them, are reduced correspondingly. On the contrary, declining cities have more employees per citizen and higher pay per employee than growing cities (see table 6.8).[28]

TABLE 6.8. COMMON CITY FUNCTIONS IN 1973[29]

	7 Large Growing Cities	14 Large Declining Cities	New York
Expenditures per capita	$152	$264	$ 396
Employees per 1000 residents	8.7	13.0	13.0
Average monthly wage	$812	$958	$1,115

Costs within the troubled cities have risen sharply in recent years, as have costs in all large cities and indeed in state and local governments generally. Spending per capita grew 163 percent from 1962 to 1972 in all state and local governments and 198 percent in twenty-eight big cities. (Of the twenty-eight, seven were growing, fourteen were declining, six were formerly growing and are now declining, and one, New York, was treated separately.)[30] The main components of the cost increases were:

1. More employees: an 11 percent increase in per capita employment from 1967 to 1972 in the largest declining cities and a 13 percent increase in the largest growing cities.[31] Cities generally had employment increases in these years, followed by a sharper rise in 1972–73 and a slowdown in 1974.[32] Employment went up mainly because of increasing demand for services to city residents, stimulated in part by the availability of federal and state grants and normal bureaucratic accretion ("Parkinson's Law"). Instead of reducing the demand, the 1974–75 recession stimulated it, at the same time impairing the cities' ability to pay for the added workers.

2. Higher pay in the state and local government sector (up 69 percent, 1965 –73, compared with 56 percent in private industry).[33] According to another study, pay for common municipal services increased from 12 to 20 percent between 1970 and 1973 alone.[34] These increases were partly the consequence of a general rise in pay levels nationally and partly a result of the advances in public-sector unionism, which enabled employees to bargain effectively for "their share" of public resources, even to the point of higher pay than the private sector offered for comparable work.

3. Increases in fringe-benefit costs, which add about 30 percent to every payroll.[35] In several cities these increases ranged from 18 to 31 percent between 1970 and 1973.[36] Retirement contributions alone went up 9 percent a year from 1967 to 1972 and over 10 percent a year in 1973 and 1974. These fringe costs are also a reflection of unions' effectiveness. As pay became competitive, the unions turned to benefits as a means of getting more. Pensions are a particular cause of fiscal concern because enormous cost increases are built in for future years when unfunded or partly funded obligations come due as employees retire.[37]

According to the Maxwell School economists, about 27 percent of city cost increases in 1967–72 was attributable to inflation. Another 17 percent was due to "real compensation growth"—what employees received in excess of cost of living increases. The remaining 55-plus percent resulted from "input quantity"—more employees, materials, and supplies. The inflationary factor was 25 percent in 1972–74, resulting in a loss of over $2 billion in municipal purchasing power.[38]

This study has concentrated on pre-1974 data because of its greater availability. In 1974 and 1975 the troubled cities were also having great difficulty keeping costs down because of genuine service needs, continuing inflation, and political and bureaucratic pressures.[39] Among thirty of the largest cities, operating fund expenditures in 1973 or 1974 increased an average of 6.8 percent over the previous year. Some cities showed decreases; most had increases (see table 6.9).[40]

TABLE 6.9. AVERAGE ANNUAL OPERATING EXPENDITURES
(PERCENTAGE OF CHANGE, 1973–74)

St. Louis	17.7	Philadelphia	3.1
Boston	15.4	San Francisco	2.3
Chicago	12.4	Detroit	1.6
New York	10.1	Cleveland	1.5
Cincinnati	8.7	Baltimore	0.1
Columbus	8.4	Pittsburgh	− 7.1
Milwaukee	6.8	Buffalo	− 8.0

Lagging Revenue Growth

Revenues are not keeping up with rising costs. Tax revenues would have increased only 15 percent (compared with the 25 percent increase in expenditures) if cities had taxed at 1972 levels the 1972–74 inflationary increase in their tax bases.[41] Cities face a losing battle, with expenses responding more to inflation than do revenues.

Nevertheless, the declining cities have tried harder. Among cities studied by the Urban Institute for the 1967–72 period, "growing cities managed to cut their effective property tax rates by more than 25 percent...while the declining cities were obliged to raise their rates by nearly 25 percent."[42] Between 1967 and 1973, large declining cities increased per capita revenues by 113 percent (compared with growing cities' 95 percent) despite slower increases in per capita income and wealth.[43]

In the District of Columbia government's annual study of tax burdens in the nation's thirty largest cities, the top eight in estimated burden of major taxes for a family of four with a $10,000 income were Boston, Milwaukee, New York, Buffalo, Chicago, Philadelphia, Los Angeles, and Baltimore; for a family with a $15,000 income the list is the same, with the ranking of the last four changed.[44] All but Los Angeles are troubled and declining.

In 1975 my study of five troubled cities found a 12 percent increase in the real estate tax in New York City, which was already insolvent and hard pressed to make up major deficits; the other four (Buffalo, Cleveland, Detroit, and St. Louis) were experiencing level or slightly rising revenues. Officials were convinced that the outer limits of taxpayer tolerance had been reached, psychologically and politically. Resistance to further increases has been a nationwide phenomenon even in more affluent jurisdictions. "The 90% rejection rate in the November 1975 bond elections set an all-time record."[45] At the same time, the fiscal squeeze in cities was aggravated by the 1974–75 recession, which cut growth in sales and earnings taxes, dampened potential growth in the property tax base, increased tax delinquencies, and raised the work load of city services as inner-city unemployment rose.

The recession made revenue-raising efforts especially counterproductive in the declining cities. A rise in the property tax rate or the imposition of some new tax might not be the only reason for a company's leaving the city or deciding not to move in, but it would be an important consideration. Even for firms remaining in the city, the higher taxes would soak up funds that might otherwise be used for more economically stimulating purposes.

Lack of support from local revenues caused cities to turn to state and federal aid. For six declining cities studied by the Urban Institute, almost two-thirds of all additional revenue in 1965–73 came from other levels of government or was borrowed.[46] But state and federal aid began to fall off in 1974 and 1975. Federal budgetary policies and the declining fiscal health of the states show little grounds for optimism about grant receipts in the future.[47]

Federal grants to cities brought fiscal hardships as well as relief. As the deputy mayor of New York City complained to his congressmen,

> Federal matching and maintenance requirements were designed to assure expansion of total outlays for specific programs. When applied to the city at this time, the requirements often have a counterproductive effect. In many cases the lack of necessary local matching funds means that federal funds and the projects that they support must be forsaken. In other instances, the city is often forced to make painful cuts in other worthy locally supported programs to satisfy matching and maintenance of effort requirements for federally aided programs. In these cases, the allocation of our dwindling fiscal resources is seriously skewed by federal policies contrary to local needs.[48]

The income problems of declining cities have been neatly and emphatically summarized by Peterson:

> From the revenue side, the fiscal crises of 1975 were the product of an unhappy coincidence of timing. The abrupt slowdown in the growth of intergovernmental aid during 1974–75 forced the older cities back upon their own resources at just the moment these resources gave out because of the recession. The necessity of suddenly financing their own expenditure growth (including the wage increases demanded by workers originally hired under federal programs but for whom no more federal assistance was forthcoming) would have strained the cities' fiscal capacity under the best of circumstances. As it was, the simultaneous failure of local and intergovernmental revenue sources precipitated genuine fiscal distress. The newer, growing cities have been spared the worst of this budgetary pressure. Their local revenue sources stood up better during the national recession; they had never embroiled themselves in federal financing to the extent that the old central cities had and thus suffered less from the slowdown in federal aid; and the changeover from programmatic assistance to revenue sharing actually improved their situation.[49]

Financial Mismanagement

This final reason is of a lower order of importance except in New York City, where palpably unsound budgeting and accounting practices and massive short-term borrowing were important factors in the city's crisis.[50] If the city had had prudent, statesmanlike financial management over the last decade or two, it still would have been in trouble—not so deep or so soon, but clearly in trouble. The economic decline and the effects of inflation and recession were inexorable.

Other cities are not yet in genuine fiscal crisis, although they are candidates. They are still able to meet their obligations. Although they cannot properly be accused of financial mismanagement, two types of shortcomings need to be mentioned. First, it is most difficult to determine a city's vulnerability to fiscal trouble from its published budget, balance sheet, and income and expense statements without being familiar with local policies and idiosyncrasies in accounting. Comparison of operating revenues and expenditures is difficult if there is no capital budget, if there are gray areas between the operating budget and the capital budget, or if there are several different operating funds. Federal grants, for example, may or may not be included in the general operating budget. Interfund transfers may confuse the income-expense balance in various funds. The availability of cash or investments to meet an unexpected stringency may not be clear.

A city's accounting practices may meet the standards of the Municipal Finance Officers Association and may present a clear picture to insiders, but may not adequately reveal potential difficulties to federal agencies, potential investors, or public policy groups. Individual cities, state fiscal agencies, and local governmental public interest groups should review and update the "warning signs" publicized by the Advisory Commission on Intergovernmental Relations,[51] then recommend accounting practices to make the warnings more explicit.

Second, city officials tend to take a short-term view, surviving each fiscal year by improvisations or expedients that may detract from the city's long-run fiscal integrity. Some such actions smack of gimmickry: (1) Cleveland sold the city sewers in 1974 to a new independent authority and used most of the proceeds for general operating expenses that year; (2) St. Louis in 1975 pushed five quarters of federal revenue sharing money into four quarters of local budgeting; (3) St. Louis also avoided paying for a twenty-seventh payroll period in the fiscal year 1975–76 by including the final payday in the following fiscal year.

Other cities have scraped through fiscal years by getting special state grants, which have no assurance of being repeated. They have eliminated (or cut down) employee pay raises, even though increases will have to be given in future years when the fiscal situation is likely to be even worse. It is easy for remote observers to criticize apparent shortsightedness and to urge that local revenues be raised, debt trimmed down, and marginal services cut out; yet the local political pressures operate in the opposite direction. Expedient manipulations to squeeze through another fiscal year may be more an inevitable cost of our political system than clear cases of executive failure.

DAVID T. STANLEY

What Can Be Done to Help Them?

Before proceeding to remedies, a summary of the trouble may be helpful. Fiscal crisis, as defined, is not clearly imminent for any of the troubled cities (except New York, whose crisis of course continues). Their efforts to stay out of crisis, mainly by cutting costs so that debts can be repaid, contribute to the long-term decline. Some relief can be expected as recovery from the recession continues and as inflation is reduced. However, such recovery and such reduction will be felt less by the troubled cities than by those whose economies are in better long-term health and whose costs are lower. The total prospect for the troubled cities is grim. What can be done, both by their own governments and by the state and federal governments? Answers can be considered, first, for action in the event of fiscal crisis and, second, for efforts to deal with long-term decline and to keep the cities out of fiscal crisis.

Cities in Fiscal Crisis

If fiscal crisis is clearly imminent—cash not available to meet bond or note payments, payrolls, and suppliers' bills—emergency action on all levels is required. New York City's experience is instructive in considering remedies. Solutions will be easier in other cities because the dollar measure of their problems is so much smaller and because their credit history is better.

ACTION BY THE CITY. If the problem is little more than one of cash flow, city officials may be able to sell short-term notes to the financial community. In the more likely event that investors' local patriotism is no longer equal to such an appeal, they may still agree to a negotiated moratorium on payments on some of the city's securities. This is *de facto* default, and major creditors are not likely to agree unless they can see an upturn in the city's finances in a few months. To turn to higher levels of government for help, city officials must be in the position of having made extraordinary efforts to increase revenues and to cut expenses. They likely will be at the statutory tax limit, unable to impose new taxes without state approval. They will have "frozen" new major purchases, construction, filling of job vacancies, and increases in pay and benefits. Yet if it *is* a crisis, none of these steps will be enough, and help from other levels of government will be needed.

ACTION BY THE STATE. Fiscal crisis for any city, no matter how much it has done to solve its own problems, makes emergency state action obligatory and imperative. The governor, comptroller, and legislature will need to consider these options in consultation with officials of the troubled city and with private financiers:

1. Making an emergency cash grant to keep city services functioning while more enduring remedies are developed. Such a grant may require the sale of special short-term securities.
2. Authorizing new city revenue measures, such as a commuter earnings tax, a "piggyback" addition to the state sales tax, or a new or increased city

tax on business franchises or transactions. Such measures are politically nauseous. They probably have been considered earlier and rejected but may be enactable under crisis conditions.

3. Revising the state's formulas for distributing to local governments either general-purpose revenue or special-purpose funds (such as education, transportation, or housing). Any such changes would benefit troubled cities at the expense of suburban or rural governments, which can be counted on to object and to demonstrate their own genuine needs for state help.

4. Authorizing a special bond issue for relief of the city's immediate debt load, thus backing up the city with the state's credit. Such a bond issue would have to specify the source of repayment—in the case of New York, from a portion of city sales tax proceeds. Such a step will be hard to sell and expensive in states whose own finances, already under strain, are used in large measure for support of cities, as noted earlier.

5. Stiffening state control over, and participation in, city financial decisions. New York City's Emergency Financial Control Board, which is chaired by the governor and which has a majority of his appointees, must approve the level of the city's budget and the more important spending commitments. Lesser measures could be considered by other states for other cities, such as revision of the budget procedures and accounting system, more detailed auditing, and new limitations on the city's obligational authority. A New York-like takeover is more likely, however, because state political leaders will need to provide assurance of controls in return for these extraordinary assistance measures.

ACTION BY THE FEDERAL GOVERNMENT. In this respect, as in others, generalizations from the New York City experience are hazardous. No other city is the second largest government in the nation, the national capital of finance, commerce, and the arts; and no other city's fiscal collapse is so threatening to the credit of other cities, to the solvency of its state government, or to the economic life of a wide area. Despite heroic and well-planned emergency efforts by the New York State government, only mhe federal government could really save the situation. For other cities in genuine fiscal crisis, the following federal actions may be considered:

1. Loans to provide operating cash at times of low cash flow. This was the solution specifically adopted for New York City. If the same remedy is made available to other cities in fiscal crisis, it would be only sensible to enact more generalized legislation that would define the situation in which a city would become eligible for such loans, e.g., inability to enter credit markets, operating budget unbalanced, possibilities of state aid exhausted; set time and money limits on such aid; and

provide, as in the case of New York, for federal monitoring of the city's fiscal performance.

2. Federal guarantees of state loans to provide rescue operating funds for cities in fiscal crisis. This remedy would emphasize and reinforce the state's responsibility for action but would put a fiscal safety net under the state's funds. As in the case of the direct loans, provision would be made for eligibility criteria, limitations, and performance monitoring.

3. A one-time cash grant, either directly to a city or through a state government, to put the city on its feet fiscally. This is the "bailout" idea, though that term was more loosely used during congressional consideration of aid to New York City. This action would be hard to justify and to enact. Its sponsors would have difficulty answering such questions as How do you know the city will stay on its feet? Why not make preventive grants to all hardpressed cities to forestall fiscal crises? Are you rewarding the fiscal incompetents?

FILING IN BANKRUPTCY COURT. This option is set apart because it is a local-federal option. Under the newly amended Chapter IX of the Bankruptcy Act, a local government may voluntarily file a petition in federal bankruptcy court to have the city's debt reorganized under a plan approved by the bankruptcy law judge.[52] Like bankruptcy filings by individuals and businesses, this remedy is a last-resort kind of action. It was an option that at first seemed attractive to President Ford and others for New York City. A bankruptcy proceeding would stop any pending legal actions against the city by bondholders, suppliers, or other creditors. The city would be enabled to work out a plan for paying off its debts in reduced amounts, or over an extended period of time, or both. It would be able, presumably with court support, to modify unreasonably burdensome pension obligations, other fringe benefits, and pay and work-rule provisions of union contracts. Without a formal bankruptcy proceeding, city officials could never reduce city obligations and expenditures to levels consistent with its means because the political and bureaucratic obstacles are overpowering.

Considerations on the negative side are at least as strong. The matter does not get into bankruptcy court unless the city voluntarily files a petition—an act subjecting the mayor and council members to virtually unbearable political stigma. Chapter IX has been used in recent decades only for a handful of municipalities and special-purpose districts, not by large cities. Under the amended law, a flood of litigation by creditors may be expected. To make the matter even more complex, the city would need to borrow to keep going during the bankruptcy case, and the obligations thus incurred would themselves be subject to court challenge. Worse yet, bankruptcy law judges are unversed in the complexities of municipal and intergovernmental finance and in the underlying political relationships. Finally, it is arguable whether going through a bankruptcy proceeding will make a city more welcome in the financial community than it would be if other means of relief were employed. All in all, city fiscal remedies seem better negotiated in state and federal legislative environments than in bankruptcy courts.

Cities in Long-Term Decline

Remedies to keep a city out of fiscal crisis and to reverse, or at least to stop or retard, its long-term decline should be as urgently sought as those to get a city out of crisis. Unfortunately, they are not. Governments tend not to change their ways unless disaster impends, especially when those changes may cost much money at a time of anti-government feeling. Yet if deterioration of cities is unchecked, more widespread crises are probable.

Longer-term remedies for cities in trouble may be considered under two different assumptions: first, that no significant changes are made in the structure and functions of the governments concerned; and second, that such changes may be made.

Assuming that governmental boundaries—both geographical and organizational—remain as is, there is much that can be done.

ACTION BY THE CITY. First, attention must be given to what the city government itself can do. We must put an administrative step before substantive actions; otherwise those actions will go unnoticed.

1. *Putting more clarity and order into the city's fiscal processes and statements.*[53] Higher levels of government, investment bankers, and local taxpayers need to know where the city stands each fiscal year and how the prospects look for the future. This means, in the typical city, revision of the fund structure, the accounting system, the budget formulation process, and the ways of controlling expenditures. Such changes are complicated and difficult to make in a time of trouble but are necessary before further decline occurs.

2. *Making sure that potential economic revitalization measures are fully mobilized and vigorously directed.* The question must be raised whether the potential of the city and its surrounding area for employing city residents in commerce and industry has been fully exploited.

3. *Cutting expenditures, or at least stopping their growth.*[54] This is regarded by some critics as the only solution. It certainly is a prerequisite for gaining the cooperation of state and federal officials and of the financial community. Troubled cities generally have been cutting down, judging from my own trips to five of them within the past year. The process typically begins with a freeze on filling jobs (except perhaps in the most urgently needed services) and a slowdown of construction and major purchases. Next, unfilled jobs are usually abolished, saving the pay and benefits allocated for those positions. It is hard to evaluate claimed savings from this source without knowing whether the jobs would in fact have been filled, and if so, when. Some cities (New York and Buffalo are examples) have cut down on "provisional" non-civil service employees, thus eliminating some of the less experienced and less qualified workers. This is a wise move but is hardly a significant source of savings.

This topic leads to a much-touted but at present overvalued area, *productivity programs*. The application of systems analysis, job engineering, operations research, and other sophisticated techniques could result in major savings in local governments. The field of productivity management in government is growing, and there are some positive findings in the literature.[55] So far the scope is narrow, limited mainly to trash removal programs (high capacity mechanized equipment, engineered routes) and fire departments (development of "slippery water," programmed deployment of fire fighting forces). Further progress is desirable but will be slow and difficult. Local government services have so many employees that significant savings require elimination of a large number of them. In many services people cannot be replaced by equipment; even when this is feasible, there would be high procurement and transitional costs and opposition or foot-dragging by employee unions.

Closely related is the idea of turning some services, presently monopolized by city governments, over to the private sector—by contracting out, by issuing vouchers to citizens with which to obtain service, or by having citizens do more themselves.[56] Here again there are bureaucratic and community obstacles. It is a political fact of life that local governments exist not only to provide services but also to provide jobs. Nevertheless, productivity and privatization programs, however difficult to put into effect, do offer potential savings. Such innovative efforts must be encouraged, but they are not soon likely to be an important fiscal factor.

Meanwhile, city officials can and do hold down increases in employees' pay and benefits, either by fiat or by increased toughness at the bargaining table. The unions have agreed in order to minimize layoffs. So it is that, at a time when the cost of living was rising about 8 percent annually, there were no pay raises in 1975 in New York and St. Louis, only a 3.5 percent "bonus" in Buffalo, and a ten-cent-an-hour increase (later raised to twenty-five cents) in Cleveland. To a significant extent, then, the employees were paying for the cities' deficits. One can argue that there are too many employees and that they have been well paid, but this will not convince the police officer who has four dependents and a mortgage; he will be back at the bargaining table next year, and his city treasurer may be even less able to help him then than this year.

The next step—one that is already being taken—is employee layoffs, which result in reduced protection and services. In various cities there are fewer (and older) men on each fire engine; fire companies are traveling farther to fires; police special squads and strike forces have been deactivated; drug abuse patients have been put on waiting lists; preventive maintenance has been abandoned in hospitals; library and museum hours have been reduced; and park maintenance has been cut back. Such reductions are scattered and not yet deep, but there are more to come.

Layoffs in some cities (New York, Detroit, and Cleveland) have had reduced impact because hundreds of laid-off employees have been reemployed at federal expense under the Comprehensive Employment and Training Act (CETA).

This has been a welcome solution, but it has drawbacks; it makes the layoff process much more complex if there is a succession of reductions; it uses funds intended to upgrade difficult-to-employ citizens; and it may be cut back by the federal government.

To summarize: it is desirable and necessary to make efficiency-productivity reductions, but the average troubled city would do astonishingly well to save 10 or 15 percent of its operating budget in this way. Beyond that point, expenditure reductions may be politically necessary under the circumstances, but they are not helpful in the long run. They hamper economic recovery, make the cities less safe and attractive, cause hardship for employees, and do nothing for the main underlying problem, the need to strengthen the urban economic base.

Finally, troubled cities must do all they can to *increase revenue from local sources.*[57] We have already noted, however, that most of them are so high in tax effort that increased taxes are economically counterproductive. Cities that are still below statutory or constitutional taxing limits and whose tax effort is lower than others in similar circumstances should consider increases. In Cleveland and Cincinnati, for example, a family of four with a $15,000 income has an estimated tax burden of 7.3 percent, compared with 19.3 percent for Boston, 13.2 percent for New York, and 12.5 percent for Buffalo.[58] Whether the local voters will permit a tax increase is another question.

Central cities are attracted to taxing earnings of suburbanites who work downtown. Such citizens, it is argued, should share in paying to remedy the problems on which they turn their backs daily at quitting time. The counterargument is that commuters already pay city taxes both directly and indirectly as they occupy rented offices, eat lunch, and shop. Besides, the legislative body concerned, as Detroit and Washington, D.C., have discovered, may not let the commuter tax be imposed.

ACTION BY THE STATE. States may be doing everything within their fiscal power to reverse or slow down the long-term slide of the troubled cities, yet, as noted earlier, that fiscal power may be weakening partly *because* of the troubled cities. Three principal kinds of action need to be emphasized.

1. *Leading major efforts at economic revitalization.* The state is helped when any business comes to a city or does not leave it. The influence of the governor's office and the power of the legislature to provide incentives can aid local promotional efforts. Troubled cities still have persuasive selling points (labor supply, transportation, communications, educational support), and the state can help make the most of them.

2. *Overhauling the whole state-local revenue and local aid structures.* The troubled cities are unlikely to climb out of their morass by themselves. They need the more versatile and elastic taxing power of the state. More specifically, states need to enact progressive income tax

laws or make less progressive taxes more progressive. The proceeds should be used in large part for aid to local governments, with priorities favoring those whose economic situation has deteriorated, primarily the troubled cities. New Jersey and Connecticut, with their troubled cities Newark and Hartford, have demonstrated over the decades how difficult it is to take this kind of remedial action. Even without such a revenue change, state governments should reexamine their distribution patterns to determine if they adequately reflect such priorities. The more a troubled city decays, the greater the danger of fiscal crisis and thus of a greater burden on the state.

3. *Imposing stronger surveillance of local government fiscal operations.* State standards, reporting requirements, and supervision and audit mechanisms should be reviewed in the light of New York's experience to prevent other cities from slipping into fiscal crisis. Requirements should be rechecked concerning cash and investment position, remedies for potential deficits, adequacy of accounting reports, realism of budget formulation procedures, and strength of expenditure control systems. This may seem very obvious, but how closely were state governments watching while their cities declined fiscally?

ACTION BY THE FEDERAL GOVERNMENT. Much that cannot be accomplished by the city itself or by its state government remains for the attention of the federal government, with its superior taxing capacity and its established distribution structure of general revenue sharing, block grants, and categorical grants.

1. *Reconsidering the pattern of distribution for federal dollars.* A recent analysis by the *National Journal* shows some striking differences

TABLE 6.10. COMPARISON OF PER CAPITA FEDERAL SPENDING
AND PER CAPITA FEDERAL TAXES PLUS DEFICIT

Region	Federal Spending Per Person	Federal Taxes Per Person (including federal deficit)	Difference (spending less taxes)
New England	$1,470	$1,533	$ – 63
Mid-Atlantic	1,325	1,594	– 269
Great Lakes	1,064	1,518	– 454
Great Plains	1,287	1,374	– 87
South Atlantic	1,454	1,303	151
South Central	1,327	1,137	190
Mountain	1,615	1,238	377
Pacific	1,745	1,497	248

among regions when per capita federal spending is compared with per capita federal taxes plus shares of the federal deficit (see table 6.10).[59]

The troubled cities are in the "minus" regions, paying out more to the government than they receive. A reversal of this situation is needed in policies for federal construction, purchasing, placing of contracts, and awards of discretionary grants.

Revision of general revenue sharing is another option. At this writing, it appears that Congress will reenact revenue sharing for more than five years at approximately present amounts and without significant change of statutory conditions. The present distribution formula "displays a moderate favoritism toward the older central [i.e., troubled] cities."[60] Nevertheless, such cities would be helped further by removal of the "145 percent ceiling" provision, which limits the amount of per capita assistance.[61] The Ford administration recommended raising the ceiling to 175 percent over a period of years, but Congress has not agreed.

2. *Providing countercyclical aid.* The troubled cities, handicapped by abnormally high unemployment and destined for slow recovery, will benefit from a federal law recently passed over the President's veto. It provides for public works grants to state and local governments, with preference to those governments with high unemployment rates, and for emergency grants to stimulate economic recovery if the national unemployment rate exceeds 6 percent; the higher the rate goes, the more money is authorized.[62] The law requires evaluation by the Comptroller General of its impact on state and local government operations and by the Congressional Budget Office and the Advisory Commission on Intergovernmental Relations of its economic effects.

A form of countercyclical aid has been supplied through federal manpower (CETA) funds, which, as noted earlier, have become a form of subsidy of regular operations in some troubled cities. At present, the Department of Labor is stiffening its resistance to such use of the money; Congress has expressed its disapproval of using federally financed public service employees to replace laid-off regular employees;[63] and the President has proposed terminating the entire program.[64]

3. *Assuming full financing of welfare.* This change, urged for years by the Advisory Commission on Intergovernmental Relations, would be of little interest to most troubled cities but a major boost to New York. Welfare is a city problem only where (*a*) the state requires substantial local government contributions, and (*b*) county and city governments are joined. Federal assumption of the costs has debatable aspects,[65] but would relieve New York City of much of its current operating deficit.

4. *Taking more aggressive leadership in economic revitalization of the troubled cities.* Some federal measures to retard or reverse economic

slippage—the need to continue CETA grants and to revise the general distribution pattern of federal dollars—have already been mentioned. A necessary related step is the extension and increase of the community development block grants (urban renewal, rehabilitation loans, open space, neighborhood facilities, water and sewer facilities, and land acquisition). Congress is now considering the extension of the law beyond its initial three years, including some formula changes to benefit central cities in particular. It would be desirable, from the troubled cities' viewpoint, to raise the funding level above its present approximate $3.1 billion, but pressure to hold down federal spending on domestic programs may well prevent this. This program is the logical instrument for remedying central city decay. A new Congress might choose to start a special drive to assist cities whose long-term decline is most alarming, but this seems unlikely. The troubled-city problem is serious, but not immediately threatening enough to energize the necessary legislative action. Any additions to congressional spending on urban programs are likely to help suburbs as well as central cities.[66] To make the prospect even worse, the leading candidates for President in 1976 did not find aid to troubled cities to be an attractive political issue.[67]

If the trouble is severe enough to justify altering existing arrangements, relieving the cities of functions or restructuring local government are additional options.

FUNCTIONAL SHIFTS. Some city services can be moved to state or county jurisdiction, made independent (as a separately supported district or authority), or yielded to the private sector. Such shifts are common: a 1975 survey by the International City Management Association of over 3,000 municipalities found that 31 percent of all cities studied and 79 percent of cities over 500,000 had transferred at least one function in the previous ten years.[68]

The most likely functions for the troubled cities to transfer, both because they are heavy drains on the treasury and because they are more easily separated than other functions, are:

1. *Institutions of higher education*, as in New York City. They can be absorbed by the state system, put under a newly chartered nonprofit organization, or abandoned, letting their competitors take over their functions.

2. *Hospitals and clinics*, as in New York, Detroit, and St. Louis. They can be closed, merged with community voluntary hospitals, or shifted to county jurisdiction.

3. *Public Schools*, in cities where they are an integral part of the city fiscal process, as in New York and Buffalo. They could be shifted to independent school districts.

Although this summary oversimplifies complex political and emotional matters, the extremity of the remedies needed is evident. Functional shifts will call for active state involvement, prolonged negotiations, and solution of a host of fiscal and legal puzzles. Any such shifts, particularly in the fields of education and health care, should be preceded by expert utilization studies to avoid wasteful overlapping: not every university in or near a city needs to have a criminal justice school or a graduate school of business or a nursing school, for example; nor does every hospital need a complete array of the more expensive services.

STRUCTURAL CHANGE. This is a matter interrelated with functional shifts but separated here to clarify the difference. Troubled cities may ease both their revenue and expenditure problems by a fundamental change in local government structure.[69] Councils of governments (COGs), which provide a measure of collaboration and a few common services, are a step in this direction, but will normally hesitate to trespass on the organizational turf of municipalities. More meaningful coordination and real fiscal advantage may be found in a thorough review leading to decisions about which services will be rendered at the county level and which at the town level (as in the Rochester, New York, area).[70]

There is even more advantage in actual city-country consolidation, as in Nashville, Jacksonville, and Indianapolis.

> In those areas which are in the traditional pattern of central city decline with modest suburban growth, increasing the regional responsibility for financing and delivery of services would greatly advantage core city residents, but such assistance, if the past is a sufficient guide, will be bitterly opposed by suburban residents. Such a change, however, might contribute to the continuing economic viability of [the] entire metropolitan area. If Indianapolis and Jacksonville, for example, had not regionalized their governments, their central cities would today be experiencing severe financial problems.[71]

If the decline is spreading to the troubled cities' suburbs, this remedy clearly has more dubious prospects.

Another successful model of metropolitan organization since 1967 is the Twin Cities Metropolitan Council in the seven-county region of Minneapolis-St. Paul, Minnesota, a "council of 30 gubernatorially appointed members,...a regional agency of substantial authority which controls the activities of special districts and can shape and control the physical development and growth of the region. A companion piece of state legislation provided for a regional tax sharing plan which on a formula basis allows all local governments in the region to benefit from non-residential growth in the region despite its location within a single jurisdiction."[72] The high potential of such a plan results from its supremacy in certain respects over the existing local governments, a fact which would probably make it hard to enact in some areas.

DAVID T. STANLEY

What Can Be Done?

It is hard to do *anything* about the troubled cities. The basic cause of their difficulties, their withering economic bases, is also their most intractable problem. Corrective action is also blocked by natural inertia, the tendency to feel that it is "the other guy's problem," and a reluctance to disturb long-established balances of power. The situation calls for the emergence of strong, sure-handed, cooperative leadership at all levels of government. Such leadership, where it can be found, will create the necessary sense of urgency and provide the innovative drive to put the right package of remedies into effect. Mayors Lugar and Flaherty have in different ways demonstrated this point. The remedies will vary from city to city, but there will be basically two main kinds:

The first is the *disaster package*, for genuine fiscal crisis, which will propose

State and local action to supply operating cash
Extraordinary local efforts, with state authority as needed, to increase revenues and cut expenses
Emergency state grants, based if necessary on new security issues
State control of major city fiscal operations
Federal loans or loan guarantees if needed for cash requirements
Filing in bankruptcy court—only if other attemped solutions fail

The second is the *stronger bootstraps package*, for the problems of long-term decline, which advocates

Improvement of fiscal processes and records
Economic revitalization steps
Expenditure cutting for improved productivity and retention of highest-priority services
Fullest realization of local revenue potential
Restructuring state taxation and fund distribution to localities
Close state surveillance of all city fiscal operations
Revised federal spending and granting patterns, giving more of an edge to declining areas and localities
Revision of local government functions and structures to achieve fiscal and economic viability

Enough of the first package must and will be used to keep basic city services functioning, though possibly at a low level; we cannot be so sure about the second. With effective leadership at federal, state, and local levels, our troubled cities can be greatly improved; without it they will continue to deteriorate.

Notes

1. Roy M. Bahl, Bernard Jump, and David Puryear, "The Outlook for State and Local Government Fiscal Performance" (testimony prepared for the Joint Economic Committee, U.S. Congress, Washington, D.C., January 22, 1976), p. 4.

2. Public Law 94-260, April 8, 1976.

3. Philip M. Dearborn, "Statement on Fiscal Health of Major Cities" (presented to the Subcommittee on Intergovernmental Relations and Human Resources of the Committee on Government Operations, U.S. House of Representatives, Washington, D.C., July 15, 1975), p. 3 and table 1. (The 1971 figures are drawn from Dearborn's report, *City Financial Emergencies: The Intergovernmental Dimension,* Report A-42 of the Advisory Commission on Intergovernmental Relations [Washington, D.C.: Government Printing Office, 1973]. He uses the 32 most populous cities, subtracting San Jose and Washington.)

4. "...Chicago collects property taxes in the year following the one for which they are levied, with the result that the city always shows a fund deficit on a cash basis" (Dearborn, "Fiscal Health of Cities," p. 3).

5. Ibid., p. 3 and table 2.

6. George E. Peterson, "Finance," in William Gorham and Nathan Glazer, eds., *The Urban Predicament* (Washington, D.C.: Urban Institute, 1976), pp. 64–66.

7. See note 5 above.

8. Dearborn, "Fiscal Health of Cities," p. 3.

9. Terry Nichols Clark et al., "How Many New Yorks? The New York Fiscal Crisis in Comparative Perspective" (report no. 72 of Comparative Study of Community Decision-Making, University of Chicago, April 1976), p. A-5.

10. John Craig and Michael Koleda, "The Future of the Municipal Hospital in Major American Cities," (Washington, D.C.: National Planning Association, April 1976), table 7. Mimeo. Their universe was the forty most populous cities.

11. Peterson, "Finance," pp. 66–67.

12. *Pitfalls in Issuing Municipal Bonds* (New York: Moody's Investors Service, 1974), p. 13.

13. *Moody's Municipal and Government Manual* (New York: Moody's Investors Service, 1976, as updated by periodic releases). Dearborn's list of cities (see note 4) was used, plus the next eight most populous cities.

14. Richard P. Nathan and Charles Adams, "Understanding Central City Hardship," *Political Science Quarterly* 91 (Spring 1976): 51, 55. The authors cover 55 of the 66 largest SMSAS.

15. Thomas Muller, "Statement on the Fiscal Outlook for State and Local Governments" (presented to the Subcommittee for Urban Affairs of the Joint Economic Committee, U.S. Congress, Washington, D.C., January 22, 1976), p. 11.

16. Craig and Koleda, "Municipal Hospital," table 6.

17. U.S. Congressional Budget Office, "New York City's Fiscal Problem: Its Origins, Potential Repercussions, and Some Alternative Policy Responses," mimeographed (Washington, D.C., October 10, 1975), p. 16. These are early 1975 data from urban areas with the highest proportion of population receiving AFDC assistance; the recipients of general assistance were then added.

18. Michael J. Flax, *A Study in Comparative Urban Indicators: Conditions in Eighteen Large Metropolitan Areas* (Washington, D.C.: Urban Institute, 1972). Since 1972 the Institute's philosophy on this subject has changed. See "Social and Urban Indicators," *Search* 4 (May-August 1974), pp. 1–2; and Flax et al., "Social Indicators and Society: Some Key Dimensions," in *The Social Economy of Cities,* vol. 9 of *Urban Affairs Annual Reviews* (Beverly Hills: Sage Publications, 1975).

19. Craig and Koleda, "Municipal Hospital," table 8.
20. *Newsweek,* November 10, 1975, p. 25.
21. Peterson, "Finance," p. 44.
22. Alan K. Campbell, "The Future of Metropolitanism" (speech given to the Fifth Colorado Urban Conference, Denver, April 2, 1976), pp. 2–3. See also *New York Times* series on movement to the sun belt, February 8–13, 1976; and Thomas Muller, *Growing and Declining Urban Areas: A Fiscal Comparison* (Washington, D.C.: Urban Institute, 1975), p. 6.
23. Muller, *Urban Areas,* pp. 16–18.
24. Bahl, Jump, and Puryear, "State and Local Government," pp. 9–10. (Employment data are collected not for cities but for SMSAs and counties. The authors caution: "The only appropriate comparison that can be made is of employment in central cities which are coterminous with counties.... This comparison also forces exclusion of government and proprietorship employment.")
25. Seymour Sacks, "The City as a Center of Employment," quoted in Roy M. Bahl, Alan K. Campbell, David Greytak, Bernard Jump, and David Puryear, "The Impact of Economic Base Erosion, Inflation, and Employee Compensation Costs on Local Governments" (Occasional Paper No. 23, Metropolitan Studies Program, Maxwell School of Citizenship and Public Affairs, Syracuse University, September 1975), p. 4 (hereafter cited as OP 23).
26. Roy M. Bahl and Alan K. Campbell, "The Economic and Fiscal Outlook for New York City" (paper presented to the Mediation Panel for the Negotiations between the Metropolitan Transportation Authority and the Transit Workers Union, New York, March 24, 1976), pp. 2–3.
27. Peterson, "Finance," pp. 72–73; Muller, *Urban Areas,* pp. 76–78.
28. Muller, *Urban Areas,* pp. 33–51; Peterson, "Finance," pp. 40–51.
29. Peterson, "Finance," p. 48.
30. Ibid., pp. 41, 48.
31. Muller, *Urban Areas,* p. 39.
32. Bahl, Jump, and Puryear, "State and Local Government," p. 18.
33. Ibid., p. 21.
34. OP 23, p. 16.
35. Bahl, Jump, and Puryear, "State and Local Government," p. 23.
36. OP 23, p. 16.
37. Bahl, Jump, and Puryear, "State and Local Government," p. 26. Also see "Financial Disclosure Practices of the American Cities: A Public Report" (New York and Ann Arbor: Coopers & Lybrand and the University of Michigan, 1976).
38. Bahl, Jump, and Puryear, "State and Local Government," pp. 12–16.
39. David T. Stanley, "Running Short, Cutting Down: Five Cities in Fiscal Distress" (Washington, D.C.: Brookings Institution). Mimeo.
40. Dearborn, "Fiscal Health of Cities," table 3.
41. Bahl, Jump, and Puryear, "State and Local Government," p. 14.
42. Peterson, "Finance," p. 57.
43. Muller, *Urban Areas,* pp. 67–68.
44. "Tax Burdens in Washington, D.C. Compared with Those in the Nation's Thirty Largest Cities, 1974" (Washington, D.C.: District of Columbia Department of Finance and Revenue, 1974), table A. Mimeo.
45. Irwin T. David, "Evaluating Municipal Revenue Sources," *Governmental Finance* 5 (February 1976): 14.
46. Peterson, "Finance," pp. 59–60.
47. See "State Fiscal Survey: Fiscal Years 1974, 1975, and 1976 (estimated)" (Washington, D.C.: National Governors' Conference, December 1975), esp. pp. 1–4. Mimeo.

48. Letter from John E. Zucotti, First Deputy Mayor, City of New York, to Representatives Edward Koch and Benjamin Rosenthal, March 8, 1976.

49. Peterson, "Finance," p. 62.

50. New York City's financial errors have been so widely publicized and analyzed that they will not be rehashed here. For optional reading, see particularly Wyndham Robertson, "Going Broke the New York Way," *Fortune*, August 1975; and Steven R. Weisman, "How New York Became a Fiscal Junkie," *New York Times Magazine*, August 17, 1975.

51. Dearborn, *City Financial Emergencies*, p. 4.

52. Public Law 94-260, April 8, 1976.

53. See several articles on improvement of governmental accounting in *Governmental Finance* 5 (May 1976).

54. This subsection and the one that follows draw on findings from my visits in 1975 to New York, Detroit, St. Louis, Buffalo, and Cleveland; they are developed in my recently completed study, "Running Short, Cutting Down."

55. See productivity publications of the Urban Institute, the Labor Management Relations Service, the International City Management Association, the National Commission on Productivity and Work Quality, and the New York City Office of Management and Budget.

56. See statement of William G. Colman, "Partial Privatization of the Public Sector," in *Fiscal Relations in the American Federal System* (Hearings of the Subcommittee on Intergovernmental Relations and Human Resources of the Government Operations Committee, U.S. House of Representatives [Washington, D.C.: Government Printing Office, 1975], pp. 453–58; and Allen E. Pritchard, "Private Delivery of Public Services," in *Urban Options I* (Columbus: Academy for Contemporary Problems, 1976).

57. For a convenient and knowledgeable review of this subject, see David, "Municipal Revenue Sources."

58. "Tax Burdens," table A.

59. Joel Havemann, Rochelle L. Stanfield, and Neal R. Peirce, "Special Report: Where the Funds Flow," *National Journal* 8 (June 26, 1976): 881.

60. Peterson, "Finance," p. 87.

61. "...no county can receive per capita assistance that exceeds 145 percent of the per capita average for the state as a whole, and no locality can receive an amount that exceeds 145 percent of the per capita average of the county in which it is located" (ibid., pp. 88–89). See also Richard P. Nathan et al., *Monitoring Revenue Sharing* (Washington, D.C.: Brookings Institution, 1975), pp. 158–60, 169.

62. Public Law 94-369, July 22, 1976. Also see analysis in Emil Sunley, "The State and Local Sector," in Charles L. Schultze, ed., *Setting National Priorities* (Washington, D.C.: Brookings Institution, 1976), pp. 400–404, and Peterson, "Finance," pp. 91–92.

63. Public Law 94-369, Sec. 201(5).

64. Peterson, "Finance," pp. 88, 90–91.

65. Ibid., pp. 93–96.

66. Demetrios Caraley, "Congressional Politics and Urban Aid," *Political Science Quarterly* 91 (Spring 1976): 42–43.

67. Joel Havemann, "It's Not That Candidates Don't Care about the Cities—Nobody's Asking," *National Journal* 8 (April 17, 1976): 514–18.

68. "Municipal Transfers of Functional Responsibilities," *Urban Data Service Report* 7 (Washington, D.C.: International City Management Association, September 1975).

69. For an up-to-date, useful review of this subject, see Charles R. Warren and Alan K. Campbell, "A Revival of Interest in Metropolitan Governance," *New York Affairs*

3 (Spring 1976): 3–14. This issue contains other useful articles on metropolitan government as well.

70. "Two-Tiered Government in Monroe County, New York: A Report of the Greater Rochester Intergovernmental Panel," Rochester, New York, June 30, 1975.
71. Warren and Campbell, "Metropolitan Governance," pp. 16–17.
72. Ibid., pp. 6–7.

Richard L. Lucier

7. Gauging the Strength and Meaning of the 1978 Tax Revolt

Proposition 13 was appraised as the "most important U.S. political-economic event of 1978, perhaps even the 1970s" by MIT economist Paul Samuelson.[1] Indeed, even its California setting added interest to this intriguing tax measure: "other states are watching closely, because California has long been at the leading edge of innovation and social change in the United States."[2] Did the June 6 vote in California signal the beginning of a national revolt against taxes and government?

Chase Econometrics concluded that "the main driving force behind Proposition 13 was not local conditions in California, but rather the arrival of the long-awaited taxpayer revolt, and is truly nation-wide rather than localized in the southwestern fringe of the nation."[3]

Chase also concluded that a Proposition 13-type amendment would have passed with a large, "lopsided majority" if it had appeared on the ballot in most other large industrialized states where, similar to California, property taxes were above national average proportions of state personal income.[4] However, such conclusions may not be warranted. The tax and spending limitation measures voted on in November 1978 — as well as the proposition voted on in California on June 6, 1978 — can be analyzed to discover whether a tax revolt occurred or is occurring; whether the conditions conducive to passage in California are likely to exist elsewhere; and what conclusions regarding state and local government taxing and spending can be drawn from the 1978 voting results.

Popular rhetoric about the tax revolt has obscured the impact of Proposition 13 and the 15 tax and spending measures voted on in November 1978. A major source of confusion over the measures and their effects is the different uses and meanings given to the term "tax revolt." Two uses of the term are evident. The first concerns a vote on a tax-reduction measure that will result in a reduction in government services; I will refer to this meaning as "tax reduction–service reduction." The second use concerns a vote on tax limits, which will result in either reduced reliance on a particular tax source, or the imposition of spending limits, which may result in a slowdown of a government's spending increases. I will refer to these measures as "tax-spending restraints." Both meanings constitute a protest vote by taxpayers, but the effects differ substantially. They differ in their impact on the ability of governments to provide services.

Tax-reduction measures will lead to reductions in government services. Tax-spending-restraint measures will cause no or only minimal reductions in government services. Of course, stringent restraints may so limit the use of a tax source or spending increases that service reductions might result. Thus, the distinction between the two uses of the term "tax revolt" is a matter of degree and immediacy of impact. Tax reduction–service reduction measures are expected to cause immediate reductions in government service provisions while tax-spending restraints may have government service-reduction consequences, but reductions are not anticipated nor immediate.

The themes and conclusions of this paper include these perceptions:

1. A tax revolt—in the sense of an antigovernment, antitax expression of frustration by voters with little concern for the impact on government services (the tax reduction–service reduction meaning)—did not occur in California and was evident in only one state, Idaho, in 1978.
2. Proposition 13 was a unique phenomenon that, due to the particular set of circumstances in California, made it possible for voter-taxpayers to reduce their property taxes without significantly reducing their receipt of state and local government services.
3. The limitations on state government spending approved in four states in November owe their origin to measures adopted earlier in other states —not California—and are intended for quite different purposes. They are tax-spending restraints.
4. Voters in 1978 sought to accomplish either, or both, of two objectives: first, to limit increases in property tax burdens, and, second, to limit the rate of increases in state government spending.

National Climate: State-Local Fiscal Systems and Public Attitudes

State-local fiscal systems have grown at a faster rate than the private sector of the economy since World War II.[5] This growth is conducive to taxpayers' desires to reduce or limit further increases in the state-local public sector relative to the private sector. However, the state-local sector has been growing at a lower rate, relative to the private sector, since 1975.[6]

Public opinion surveys provide a reading of public attitudes toward particular taxes and levels of government. Results of a May 1978 national survey indicated that the local property tax was viewed as "the worst tax—that is, the least fair" by 32 percent of the respondents.[7] The federal income tax was considered the least fair by 30 percent, 18 percent named the state sales tax, and 11 percent cited the state income tax. Significantly, the local property tax was viewed as the least fair by 44 percent of those surveyed in the West. Contributing to this attitude was the larger increase in housing prices in the West than in other regions of the United States.[8]

Public attitudes toward levels of government, reflected in polls taken in June 1978, showed that 39 percent of those surveyed nationally felt they got their "money's worth from the tax dollars" they paid to local government compared to 30 percent who named state government and 21 percent who named the federal government.[9] In a June 1978 survey question, "Which level of government do you think wastes the biggest part of its budget?" 62 percent named the federal government, 12 percent named state government, and 5 percent selected local government.[10]

The coupling of public attitudes toward taxes and levels of government highlights the ambivalence of the voter-taxpayer toward local government. Local governments, including school districts, are considered as providing the most value received for tax dollars paid of the three tax levels of government. Yet, the property tax—the major source of local government revenues (some 60 percent nationally)—is viewed as being the least fair tax. It is likely—and consistent with the November 7 voting results and the approval of Proposition 13 in California— that a restructuring of the property tax might redress the incongruity of opinion regarding local government and its method of financing its local activities.

California—The Setting and Vote on Proposition 13

Several factors contributed to the two-to-one majority approval given California's constitutional amendment:

1. California is one of twenty-three states in which statewide propositions can be placed on ballots by citizen petition.
2. The above-national-average housing value increases in the West were often larger in California. The California legislation analyst reported that housing value increases in some metropolitan areas were 2.5 percent per month.
3. California's property tax assessment system is one of the best administered in the country. The assessment system was the first to be computerized nationally; housing sales at higher market values were updated and recorded efficiently.[11]
4. The state average property tax rate per $100 of assessed valuation had been reduced by 4.6 percent in 1977–78 compared with the 1976–77 level. But that reduction did not offset the 14.4 percent increase in assessed valuation over the same period, and property tax payments increased by an average of nearly 10 percent statewide.[12] Many taxing jurisdictions were on a three-year assessment cycle so that an

average home would be reassessed at 30 to 40 percent more than its previously assessed value.

5. Local property assessors, who had urged lower property tax rates but did not have rate-setting powers, sent notices of increased assessments for 1978 to property owners ahead of the July 1 deadline. Assessment increases and property tax bills were received by property owners before the June 6 election.

6. The state had a large, growing, and consistently underestimated budget surplus, and legislators could not agree on its disbursement. The "NO on 13" coalition had made dire predictions regarding the impact of the proposition on local governments—using estimates of the size of the surplus (and the potential amount of state aid to local governments) given them by the state. A few days before the election, state budget officials announced that the surplus was some $2 billion more than the coalition had been reporting.[13]

Increases in property values, assessments, and property tax payments—combined with a $5 billion state budget surplus—were the major factors that accounted for the approval of Proposition 13 in California. The vote in California was not necessarily a manifestation of a new conservatism, an antigovernment or antipoor (with racist overtones) backlash, or a vote of no-confidence in public schools and local government. Some voters may have voted for Proposition 13 for one of several of the motives mentioned above; but, given public attitudes toward local government spending, the property tax, and the large state budget surplus, voters were presented with an opportunity that proved irresistible—substantial property tax relief and minimal reductions in local government services.

Proposition 13 was expected to reduce local government revenue by an average of more than 23 percent for California's cities, counties, school districts, and special districts. Property tax receipts were reduced by an average of nearly 57 percent for these units of local government.[14] State aid, totaling more than $4 billion, reduced revenue losses to an estimated 9.7 percent of 1978–79 revenues—subject to a number of conditions and requirements likely to reduce local decision-making authority and autonomy.[15] Local government revenue losses may be even smaller than the 9.7 percent figure. William Oakland has estimated the local government revenue shortfall at only 2.5 percent. Employment data and other local government budget information are consistent with Oakland's estimate of minor revenue losses.[16]

A *Los Angeles Times*–CBS News statewide survey of voters as they left the polling places revealed that California voters realized that state aid was available and could be tapped for the assistance of local governments. A large majority, 71 percent, of those voting for Proposition 13 said that drastic property tax cuts could be achieved without significant reductions in government services.[17] Thus, the tax revolt in California corresponds to tax-spending restraint rather than to tax reduction–service reduction.

Proposition 13-Type Measures on November 7 Ballots

Proposition 13-type measures did not sweep the country. They appeared on ballots in only three states—Idaho, Nevada, and Oregon. The western setting of these measures was related to housing value and property tax increases in that region of the U.S. The conclusion that the appearance of these measures on ballots in three states—and their approval in Idaho and Nevada—is supportive of the occurrence nationally of a tax reduction–service reduction interpretation is misleading.

As table 7.1 shows, the initiatives voted on in Idaho, Nevada, and Oregon (Measure 6) were tax reduction–service reduction measures. Voters in Idaho approved a measure that has the legal status of a legislative act—the constitution cannot be amended by referendum. As a legislative act, the measure must conform to the Idaho constitution. Conformity will be difficult; the measure conflicts with the constitution in some thirty-five instances.[18] The legislature and the courts must work out the myriad of inconsistencies before the measure takes effect on October 1, 1979 (even the effective date is disputed!). When, and if, the conflicts are resolved, the measure is expected to reduce local government property tax revenue by more than 30 percent. The state does not have a large budget surplus, and the two-thirds approval required to raise state and local taxes makes local government service cuts very likely.

The overwhelming approval of the Proposition 13-type constitutional amendment in Nevada occurred in a tax climate similar to California. Property values in the urban areas of Nevada had soared recently, and the state budget surplus was expected to total nearly 17 percent of FY 1978 state expenditures (compared to a surplus of about 20 percent in California). Thus, property tax cuts could be made and state aid could be increased to offset local government revenue losses. With substantial state aid, the measure could be categorized as tax-spending restraint rather than as tax reduction–service reduction. However, the Nevada constitution can be amended only if the measure is resubmitted and approved a second time by the voters. Reconsideration of the amendment will occur in 1980. The state legislature has an opportunity to enact tax relief before 1980, and such action might obviate reconsideration of the amendment. The Nevada vote, then, can be seen as a protest vote carrying instructions to the legislature. No immediate effects on local government revenues and services follow from the Nevada vote. Nevada voters took advantage of the opportunity to register their displeasure with property taxes *without* having to face the service reduction consequences.

Both Idaho and Nevada had state limitations on local government property tax rates. However, property tax rate limits do not keep property tax payments (or burdens) from increasing when property values and assessments rise. The Nevada legislature, therefore, may have to consider whether to follow the example of 13 states and enact limits on property tax payments to avoid reapproval of the Proposition 13 copy by voters in 1980.

TABLE 7.1. TAX AND SPENDING LIMITS VOTED ON IN JUNE AND NOVEMBER 1978

	Legal Nature	Object of Limit	Level of Govt.	Growth	Override	Mandates	Vote	Comments
Prop. 13-Type Limits								
California	Constitutional Amendment	Property Tax	Local	2% annual increase in assessed values from 1975–76 base	Constitutional Amendment	Not specified, state assumed $1 billion of county health, welfare and food stamp costs in state aid package	Approved, 2 to 1	Property tax rates were reduced to a maximum of 1% of market value; no new taxes on real property may be approved by ⅔ of each legislative house, new local taxes must be approved by ⅔ of "qualified electors."
Idaho	Statutory Enactment	Property Tax	Local	2% annual increase in assessed values from 1978 base	Statutory Enactment	Not specified	Approved, 58% to 42%	Same as California. Conflicts with state constitution in more than 30 particulars.
Nevada	Constitutional Amendment	Property Tax	Local	2% annual increase in assessed values from 1975–76 base	Constitutional Amendment	Not specified	Approved, 78% to 22%	Same as California. Amendment must be approved by voters in 1980 before it takes effect.
Oregon (Measure 6)	Constitutional Amendment	Property Tax	Local	2% annual increase in assessed values from 1975–76 base	Constitutional Amendment	Not specified	Defeated, 48% to 52%	Same as California with exception of 1½% maximum property tax rate.
Spending Limits								
Arizona	Constitutional Amendment	Spending	State	7% of personal income in Arizona	⅔ vote of each legislative house	Local governments must reduce property taxes commensurately with state assumption of local program costs	Approved, 78% to 22%	Current fiscal year spending is 6.5% of Arizona personal income and has never exceeded 7%.
Colorado	Constitutional Amendment	Spending	State and Local	Per capita spending tied to U.S. CPI	⅔ vote of each legislative house following governor's declaration of an emergency	Prior legislation had required the state to reimburse local governments for new or increased state-mandated services	Defeated, 41% to 59%	7% statutory limit on state spending approved in 1977, and local government property tax financed spending limited to 7% increase over prior year's level. State income tax revenues indexed to CPI in April 1978.

Hawaii	Constitutional Amendment	Spending	State	Spending tied to growth in state product	2/3 vote of each legislative house or declaration of emergency by governor	Not specified	Approved, 2 to 1	State sales and income tax revenues earmarked for education and welfare programs.
Michigan (Headlee)	Constitutional Amendment	Spending / Property Tax	State / Local	State spending tied to personal income, local property tax payments tied to U.S. CPI (Florida "full disclosure" plan)	Emergency declared by governor and 2/3 vote of each legislative house	State required to reimburse local governments for state mandated programs	Approved, 52% to 48%	Amendment would not require reductions in state spending nor state aid to local subdivisions.
Nebraska	Constitutional Amendment	Spending	Local	5% annual increase over previous year; larger increases if population increase more than 5%	3/5 vote of the unicameral or majority vote by local political subdivision	Not specified	Defeated, 45% to 55%	State laws had placed a 7% limit on local government property tax financed spending in June 1978.
Oregon (Measure 11)	Constitutional Amendment	Spending	State and Local	State and local government spending tied to growth in personal income in Oregon	2/3 vote of each legislative house	Not specified	Defeated, 45% to 55%	State budget surplus, 10.5% of FY 1978 state expenditures, to be used for property tax relief for homeowners and renters
Texas	Constitutional Amendment	Spending	State	Spending tied to growth in state product	Majority vote of each legislative house to spend beyond limit; 2/3 vote to increase taxes	Not specified	Approved, 84% to 16%	Florida "full disclosure" plan adopted to limit property tax payment increases. Intangible personal property tax repealed, and homestead exemption increased as part of the amendment. Large state budget surplus of $4 billion.
Tax Limits							
Alabama	Constitutional Amendment	Property Tax	Local	20% jurisdiction-wide following state-wide reassessment	Constitutional Amendment	Not applicable	Approved, 55% to 45%	Assessment basis changed.
Massachusetts	Constitutional Amendment	Property Tax	Local	Not applicable	Not specified	Not applicable	Approved, 2 to 1	Cities and towns permitted to classify and tax residential property at lower rates than commercial property.
Michigan (Tisch)	Constitutional Amendment	Property Tax	Local	Assessment ratio cut from 50% to 25% and annual assessment increases limited to 2½%	Constitutional Amendment	Not specified	Defeated, 37% to 63%	State income tax rate limited to maximum of 5.6% compared to present 4.6% rate, school districts allowed to impose a 1% rate local income tax.
Missouri	Constitutional Amendment	Property Tax	Local	Not applicable	Constitutional Amendment	Not applicable	Approved, 2 to 1	Authority to rollback property tax levies transferred from local governments to the General Assembly.

Oregon voters had protection from property tax burden increases. Counties, municipalities, and school districts in Oregon operate under a state-imposed property tax payment limit. Property tax payments were not as high and were not increasing as fast in Oregon as in California due to the 6 percent constitutional limit on growth of the property tax base. Under Oregon's property tax system, property tax payment increases of more than 6 percent could occur only with voter approval. The California property tax system, as mentioned, allowed payment increases without voter approval whenever housing values and assessed values increased. Thus, in Oregon the approval of Measure 6 would have reduced local government spending or led to increased state control if the moderately large state budget surplus had been used to replace local property tax revenues. Taxpayers had effective protection from property tax increases, and with that protection they did not have sufficient incentives to reduce property taxes and either local spending or local control.

Limitations on Government Spending

Many observers have lumped spending limits voted on in seven states in November with Proposition 13. This view is erroneous. The November spending-limit measures are more similar to measures adopted in New Jersey, Colorado, and Tennessee—not to Proposition 13. The limits on spending adopted in those three states apply primarily at the state level and limit increases in state expenditures. They are tax-spending restraints. Proposition 13 had its primary impact at the local level by cutting and limiting the property tax as a revenue source. Several factors—including the receipt of the state-aid package—caused Proposition 13 to be a tax-spending restraint rather than a tax-reduction–service reduction measure.

Limitations on state government spending are a recent phenomenon. The first was enacted in New Jersey in 1976. It limited increases in state government spending to the same growth rate as per capita state income.[19] The Colorado legislature, in 1977, limited state spending increases to no more than 7 percent over the previous year's level.[20] Like New Jersey, the Colorado law coupled the limit on state spending increases with local property tax relief. In March 1978, Tennessee became the first state to place a constitutional limit on state expenditures. The amendment tied state expenditure increases to the growth rate of the state's economy.

Brief experience with spending limits in these three states has been positive; state officials support their continuation. The limits have been sufficiently flexible (with the possible exception of Colorado) to allow the states to maintain services, yet the public has gained protection from state-spending increases that outpace ability to pay and the growth of the state's private sector. The Colorado limit is potentially severe since inflation has exceeded the 7 percent ceiling.[21]

Voters approved constitutional amendments to limit increases in state spending in four states in November (see table 7.1). Voters in Michigan (Headlee amendment) tied state spending to increases in state personal income growth.[22] State government expenditure increases were tied to growth in the state economy in Hawaii and Texas. The ceilings placed on spending increases in both states are above current levels of expenditure and will not necessitate reductions in state government budgets.

Constitutional spending limits were defeated in Colorado, Nebraska, and Oregon (Measure 11). The spending limits defeated in these three states shared two major similarities which may account for their defeat. First, they applied to local government spending (to both state and local government spending in Colorado and Oregon and to only local government spending in Nebraska). Second, limits on property tax payments or levies had been enacted previously.

Colorado's counties, municipalities, school districts, and special districts were constrained by law to a maximum increase in property tax payments of 7 percent over the previous year's level. Had the constitutional amendment been approved, local government spending would have been limited for the first time — the 7 percent, statutory limit on property tax-financed local spending increases would have been supplanted by the constitutional spending limit. Voter-taxpayers had protection from tax payments of more than 7 percent in property tax payments and, with that protection, apparently did not wish to limit local government spending further.

The constitutional amendment defeated by Nebraska voters would have limited local government spending increases in FY 1979–80 to no more than 5 percent over FY 1978–79 levels unless political subdivisions experienced population growth in excess of 5 percent. The vote against the amendment should be understood in the context of two tax bills passed in a special session of the Nebraska unicameral legislature on June 8, 1978. Legislative Bill 1 placed a ceiling of 7 percent annually on increases in proportions of local government budgets financed by property taxes. The ceiling could be exceeded by majority vote in a political subdivision. Legislative Bill 2 gave political subdivisions the authority to prohibit increases in property-tax-financed budget growth by a majority vote in a petition-initiated election. Both statutes provided controls over property taxes by (1) limiting increases in property tax payments; and (2) allowing local governments, at their option, to freeze property-tax-financed spending at existing levels. The November 7 vote suggested that the control over property tax payments afforded by legislative action in June made controls on local government spending unnecessary or undesirable.

Measure 11 in Oregon was placed on the ballot by the legislature as an alternative to Measure 6 which was a copy of Proposition 13. Like the constitutional amendments defeated in Colorado and Nebraska, Measure 11 would have placed local government spending under a constitutional limitation. Cities, counties, and many school districts were operating under a constitutional limitation on annual increases in property tax payments (see the discussion of Measure 6 above). The existing limit had kept property taxes from increasing as fast in Oregon as in California. Also, property tax payments beyond the 6 percent limit could be approved to finance local government services. Thus, property tax payments were controlled and they had not increased as readily as in other states — notably California.

Voters in Oregon could, and did, increase their property tax burdens to buy more local services. In 1977–78, 47 percent of statewide property tax revenues were the result of voter-approved increases beyond the 6 percent limit.[23] The constitutional control over local government spending proposed in Measure 11, which could be exceeded by a two-thirds majority vote of each legislative house in Oregon, would have been in addition to the constitutional limitation on property tax payments. This latter limitation could be exceeded by a majority vote locally. Thus voter control over property tax payments with local ability to override the limit appeared to be sufficient; voters did not impede local government spending further.

To recapitulate, limits on state government spending increases approved in November by voters in Arizona, Hawaii, Michigan (Headlee admendment), and Texas are comparable to the constitutional limits adopted in Tennessee in March 1978. They are tax-spending restraints and do not necessitate reductions in state-provided services. The constitutional spending limits defeated in Colorado, Nebraska, and Oregon (Measure 11) would have applied to local spending. The Colorado and Nebraska measures were on the boundary between tax reduction–service reduction and tax-spending-restraint measures since inflation can be expected to exceed the 7 and 5 percent (respectively) increases in spending. Measure 11 in Oregon was a tax-spending-restraint measure since spending could have increased at the same rate as personal income. The three measures were defeated in states that had enacted property tax payment controls previously. These results suggest that property tax payments — not local government spending — were the concern of voters. This explanation is consistent with the public opinion survey results discussed earlier. However, the heavy reliance on property tax revenues to finance local government spending means, of course, that alternative revenue sources must be found if local spending is to increase.

Property Tax Limits

State limitations on local government power to raise property tax revenue are found in most states. In 1977, state constitutional and statutory restrictions on local property tax rates and payments were in force in 45 states and the District of Columbia. The most recently adopted state limits have been payments or levy limits, and the Florida "full disclosure" plan. Under the latter, a lower property tax is applied to inflation-induced assessed value increases to raise the same total property tax revenue as was raised in the previous year (or a specified percentage increase in revenue over the previous year). In order to realize higher property tax revenues, elected officials must hold public hearings and go on record as proposing higher property tax payments and increased local expenditures. The Florida plan is designed to hold local elected officials publicly accountable for additional spending financed by increases in property tax payments. Without this procedure, property tax payments would increase due to existing rates applied to inflated property values—without voter approval.

Property-tax-related constitutional amendments were on November 7 ballots in Alabama, Massachusetts, Michigan, and Missouri. The amendments were adopted in three of the four states. The Alabama, Massachusetts, and Missouri amendments provided homeowner property tax relief by changing the administration, base, or assessment procedures used with local property taxes.

The Tisch amendment in Michigan was defeated. It would have cut local property tax revenues in half. Partial replacement revenues could have come from an increase in the state income tax and increased state aid to local governments from that revenue source. The amendment also would have allowed public school districts to impose a local income or payroll tax of up to 1 percent. The amendment would have cut the major source of local government revenue—the property tax—by 50 percent without providing full substitute revenues. Local government spending would have been reduced. This consideration did not seem to be outweighed by the desire for property tax relief. Had a tax revolt occurred in Michigan, one would have expected the Tisch tax reduction–service reduction amendment rather than the Headlee tax-spending-restraint amendment to win voter approval.

Conclusions

Care should be taken in analyzing and drawing conclusions from Proposition 13 and the other tax and spending measures voted on in November 1978 elections. The California vote has been interpreted in a variety of ways and it has been and will be invoked to support tax and spending limits and cuts at all levels of government. Are policies such as these consistent with recent election results? What were voters saying in California and in 12 other states?

First, regarding Proposition 13, California voters responded to rising property tax payments and a large state budget surplus by voting for cuts of more than 50 percent in their property tax payments. Voters knew that local government property tax revenue losses would be lessened by increased state aid; the question was not whether the state surplus would be used to assist local governments but what the amount of aid and allocation among governments would be. California voters expected property tax cuts without significant reductions in local services, and their expectations were fulfilled. The California measure was less a tax reduction–service reduction than a tax-spending restraint. A large source of local revenues shifted from the local property tax to state taxes. Property tax reductions were not at the expense of local services, but they were at the cost of decreased local control.

RICHARD L. LUCIER

Second, measures virtually identical to Proposition 13 were approved in two states in November. The Nevada measure was approved in a tax climate similar to California's, but the measure will not amend the state constitution unless approved again in 1980. Nevada voters took the opportunity to vote against rising property taxes without having to suffer the service reduction consequences. The Idaho vote may constitute the only evidence of an antigovernment tax revolt in that it represented a tax reduction–service reduction in the terminology herein developed. Local government service cuts are likely since a state budget surplus is not available to provide substitute local revenues.

Third, the November election results suggest that voters wanted to control —i.e., restrain—the growth of state government spending. Increases in state spending were tied to growth in the state's economy or personal income. The constitutional amendments approved in Arizona, Hawaii, Michigan, and Texas will keep each state's public sector from growing faster than state output and income. These four measures are patterned most closely after the constitutional amendment passed in Tennessee in March 1978.

Fourth, voters did not want limits placed on local government spending. They feared the potential local-service reductions. Constitutional amendments to limit local spending were defeated in Colorado, Nebraska, and Oregon.

Fifth, voters did not want property tax payments controlled. The Headlee amendment in Michigan and the constitutional amendment in Texas limited increases in property tax payments and placed controls on state expenditure increases. Voters in Alabama, Massachusetts, and Missouri approved constitutional amendments intended to slow the growth in local and residential property taxes. Further, the defeat of constitutional amendments in Colorado, Nebraska, and Oregon suggest that with the protection afforded by property tax payment limits, voters did not wish to constrain local government spending further.

Sixth, voters did not want property tax cuts at the expense of local government programs and services. Tax reduction–spending reduction measures were defeated. The Tisch amendment in Michigan and Measure 6 in Oregon would have accomplished both objectives, and voters rejected them. Proposition 13 reduced property taxes without reducing local services because of the state budget surplus. A similar solution is possible in Nevada. The Idaho measure is the only example of a state's voters choosing local service reductions and property tax cuts.

The Congressional Budget Office concluded: "It is probable that state and local officials will respond to the signal sent by California taxpayers, even if not required to do so by their own voters."[24] Federal officials are responding to the signal also. Elected officials have and will continue to point to Proposition 13 and, to a lesser degree, to the November 1978 election results, as signaling a public desire for less government and lower taxes. Many people undoubtedly feel that way. However, the conclusion some observers have drawn—of the public pointing a shotgun at government, pulling the trigger, and being unconcerned with the effects on government services—is inaccurate. The public is more discerning in its attitudes and judgment regarding government and taxes. As national opinion surveys point out, the public discriminates among levels of government and particular taxes, and the 1978 voting results are consistent with those attitude surveys— remarkably so when one considers the differing fiscal environments in which the tax and spending measures were considered. Simply put, the tax and spending measures voted on in California on June 6, 1978 and in twelve other states on November 7, 1978 do not add up to a national revolt against state and local government and taxes. Public policy founded on such an understanding of the mood of the public is misplaced and is a misinterpretation of the signals sent by voters.

Notes

1. As quoted in David R. Francis, "Odd Effects of California's Proposition 13 Crop Up," *Christian Science Monitor* 26 (June 1978).
2. "California: Will It Choke Off Its Boom?," *Business Week*, July 17, 1978, p. 55.
3. Chase Econometric Associates, Inc., "Will the Taxpayer Revolt Sweep the Country?" *Macroeconomic Forecasts, 1978*, June 1978, p. 7.
4. Ibid.
5. For example, state-local direct general expenditures, including those financed by federal aid, have increased from about 9 percent of U.S. personal income in 1948 to over 20 percent in 1977; state-local government employees per 10,000 population have increased from 240 in 1948 to 485 in 1977. See John Shannon, "After Proposition 13— Questions for Commission Consideration" (memorandum to Wayne F. Anderson, Advisory Commission on Intergovernmental Relations [ACIR], August 25, 1978).
6. State-local general expenditures from own funds has declined from 11.6 percent of gross national product (GNP) in 1975 to an estimated 10.6 percent in 1978; state-local taxes as a percentage of GNP have declined from 9.7 percent in 1975 to an estimated 9.5 percent in 1978. Similarly, state-local payrolls have been reduced from 9.1 percent of state personal income in 1975 to 8.9 percent in 1977. See ibid.
7. ACIR, *Changing Public Attitudes on Governments and Taxes* (Washington, D.C.: U.S. Government Printing Office, 1978), p. 2. The local property tax and the federal income tax have been at the top of this poll, and have alternated rank, since 1973.
8. The National Association of Realtors reported that the average price of a single family home increased by more than 50 percent from $47,000 to $70,600, between February 1976 and February 1978 in the West. Increases, from a lower base price, were 20 percent in the Northeast, 27 percent in the North Central Region, and 18 percent in the South over the same two-year period.
9. Ibid., p. 5. A majority felt that they did not get their money's worth from federal, state, or local government. By a narrow margin, 45 to 44 percent, school districts were considered to give their money's worth. A Gallup poll, also taken just after Proposition 13 was voted on, found local government rated first as giving "the most value for your tax dollars." Earlier surveys, from 1972 to as recently as May 1978, showed the federal government, then local, then state government as giving the most for your money. It was not clear to ACIR, nor to other observers, whether the different wording and sequence of questions accounted for the apparent shift in attitude. See the ACIR discussion on pp. 4 and 5.

10. Ibid., p. 5.

11. "Taxes Were Fair, If High," *State Government News,* July 1978, p. 4.

12. Jerome Evans, "Proposition 13: The Morning After," *State Government*, Spring 1978, p. 75.

13. "How Do You Spell Relief: The Impacts of the Taxpayers Revolt," *The National Voter* (Washington: League of Women Voters of the U.S., Fall 1978), p. 3.

14. California State Legislature, *Summary of the Conference Report on SB 154, Relative to Implementation of Proposition 13 and State Assistance to Local Governments* (Sacramento: June 23, 1978), p. 1.

15. Conditions for the receipt of state aid are discussed and analyzed by many observers. See, for example, Evans, pp. 75–80. National City, California, found the strings attached to state aid too burdensome and in violation of the principle of home rule. It became the first municipality to refuse state aid. See Kile Morgan (Mayor), "A City Pays the Price of Prop 13 – Without State Aid," *Christian Science Monitor* 26 (July 1978): 23.

16. William H. Oakland, "Proposition XIII – Genesis and Consequences," *San Francisco Federal Reserve Bulletin*, forthcoming. (See pp. 16–19 particularly.) Also, see Wallace Turner, "Little Impact Seen in Tax Slash," *New York Times*, February 11, 1979.

17. William Schneider, "Proposition 13's Biggest Booster Was Inflation – Not Anger Against All Government," *Los Angeles Times*, June 11, 1978. At the time voters marked their ballots in California, the amount of state aid and the probable local government revenue losses were not known by the voters. However, the expectation that state surplus funds would be used to assist local governments and prevent service reductions equal to property tax revenue reductions was on voters's minds and was a factor in their decision on Proposition 13.

18. Letter from Lawrence Seale, Administrator, Division of Budget, Policy Planning and Coordination, State of Idaho, Boise, dated August 25, 1978 to Gerald Miller, Director, Office of Management and Budget, State of Michigan.

19. City and county government spending was limited to a maximum increase of 5 percent over the previous year's appropriations as part of a package which instituted a state income tax. The proceeds of the income tax were earmarked, by constitutional amendment, to local property tax relief.

20. Property-tax-financed spending by local governments was limited to a 7 percent annual increase.

21. In 1978 the Colorado legislature passed a law indexing state income tax payments to prevent income tax revenues from growing faster than the incomes of Colorado taxpayers. State budget surpluses, which had been accumulating, were to be retained by the state in a contingency fund and additional surplus funds were to be distributed as property tax relief.

22. The Headlee amendment will roll back local property tax rates if assessments increase at a faster rate than the U.S. consumer price index (C.P.I.). The amendment in Michigan also required the state to reimburse local governments for costs imposed upon them by the state. Michigan law had limited municipal and county property tax rates previously but property tax payments or levies (i.e., assessed values multiplied by property tax millage rates) had not been controlled.

23. Robert W. Smith and Lynn Frank, *Oregon's Proposed 1½% Limitation on Property Taxes* (Salem: Oregon Budget Management Division, Executive Department, August 1978), p. 3.

24. U.S. Congress, Congressional Budget Office, *Proposition 13: Its Impact on the Nation's Economy, Federal Revenues and Federal Expenditures* (Washington, D.C.: U.S. Government Printing Office, July 1978), p. 29.

Decision Making

PART THREE

Decision Making

PAUL R. SCHULMAN*

8. Nonincremental Policy Making: Notes Toward an Alternative Paradigm

Two major paradigms have come to dominate the scholarly analysis of public policy and quite possibly, the policy-making process itself. One is the decision model of incrementalism; the other a "divisibility" model of piecemeal public programs with negotiated and specialized payoffs.

Incrementalism, described by Charles E. Lindblom, is a decision model that asserts the propensity of organizations to move in small steps.[1] Because of (1) disagreement on primary values and policy objectives, and (2) the difficulty of gathering and processing information on which to evaluate a wide range of potential policy options, policy makers typically arrive at their decisions by assessing only "limited comparisons to those policies that differ in relatively small degree from policies presently in effect."[2] The strategy of incrementalism is one of continual policy readjustments in pursuit of marginally redefined policy goals. Long-term plans are abandoned in favor of short-term political implementation.

The divisibility paradigm is not unrelated to incrementalism. It asserts, basically, that any large policy undertaking is simply the aggregation of many politically self-contained subprograms and activities. Policy is the distribution of discrete goods in portions—in line with prevailing configurations of power or publicized need.[3] This divisibility assumption, of course, lies behind the concept of "pluralism" invariably applied to the analysis of industrialized democracies.[4] It is implicit in the emerging "public choice" school of policy analysis.[5]

The divisibility paradigm supports the perception of the public interest as simply the sum total of countless individual interests.[6] As Anthony Downs has aptly described the paradigm in practice: "Each decision-maker or actor makes whatever choices seem to him to be the most appropriate at that moment, in light of his own interests and his own view of the public welfare."[7]

*The author wishes to thank Francis E. Rourke and Matthew A. Crenson of the Johns Hopkins University, as well as T. Alexander Smith, David M. Welborn, and T. McN. Simpson of the University of Tennessee for their advice and criticisms regarding this study. In addition, officials of the National Aeronautics and Space Administration and the National Science Foundation, giving generously of their time, immeasurably advanced the work. Finally, a great deal of support and encouragement were provided by Francis E. Rourke, to whom this essay is gratefully dedicated.

These two paradigms, as mentioned, enjoy a currency both in policy analysis and policy practice. Few critiques of these outlooks have appeared, and those criticisms which are offered suffer from inflated normative judgments and anemic descriptive insights.[8]

Yet the breadth of application accorded incremental and divisibility outlooks has not been without its costs. In particular, these paradigms have deprived policy analysis and public administration of attention to a class of policy enterprises which fit into neither framework. This chapter is about that class of policies. These are enterprises distinguished by their demand for *comprehensive* rather than incremental decisions; synoptic rather than piecemeal outlooks and vision. These policies are characterized by an *indivisibility* in the political commitment and resources they require for success.

This class of nonincremental, indivisible policies is perhaps small but is nonetheless significant. It consists of large-scale government undertakings commanding major shares of the public budget. Frequently these undertakings involve the application of new technologies to major political or social problems. Nonincremental policies must be cast within large-scale and risk-taking frameworks if they are even to approximate acceptable levels of goal-seeking performance. Again, as we shall see, these are characteristics for which conventional analytical models are inadequate.

In order to explore adequately the implications of nonincremental, indivisible policy, one case has been selected from this class for explication. Its analysis, supplemented by references to additional policy examples, will illustrate three primary characteristics of major significance—characteristics which elude the present coverage of policy-making models. The policy is U.S. manned space exploration—a large and revealing undertaking.

The Nonincremental Policy Start-Up

The first characteristic associated with this special class of policies to which we have been referring is important. *Nonincremental, indivisible policy pursuits are beset by organizational thresholds, or "critical mass" points closely associated with their initiation and subsequent development.* These policies must rely for their success on factors that come into play only at high levels of political and resource commitment. Manned space exploration elaborately illustrates this point.

On May 25, 1961, President John F. Kennedy, in a special message to Congress, proclaimed the goal of landing a man on the moon and returning him safely to earth. This was to be accomplished before the end of the decade—an undertaking explicitly designed as a major national commitment. In communicating his intentions to the Congress the President indicated that space-related budget allocations were to be enlarged, and that the pace of spacecraft and booster development was to be accelerated. In the ensuing five fiscal years National Aeronautics and Space Administration appropriations rose from $1.8 billion to $5.2 billion, and the total number of employees associated with space exploration programs (both within and outside of NASA) climbed from less than 60,000 to 420,000 at its peak.[9]

Yet the Kennedy announcement came a full four years after the birth of the "space race"—the launching of the Soviet satellite *Sputnik I*. What had happened to the nation's space enterprise during this four-year interim? The answer is highly significant. It illustrates the "start-up" dilemmas of the nonincremental policy enterprise.

Public Policy vs. Public Pressure

The history of manned space exploration in this interim period between the Sputnik launch and the Kennedy commitment is one of opinion intensity in the midst of organizational insufficiency. The Sputnik launch (and its even more spectacular sequel—the canine-carrying *Sputnik II*) had aroused in the United States both alarm at the technological and projected military capabilities of the Soviet Union, and exasperation at the slow pace of U.S. missile and rocket development. Although survey data during the immediate post-Sputnik period are sketchy, available studies suggest both a high degree of worldwide awareness of space events and a subsequent belief that space achievement was in some way linked to national prestige and international power.[10]

Gabriel Almond, in an early survey of opinion in Great Britain, France, Italy, West Germany, and the United States, discovered an "extraordinarily high" public recognition of initial satellite launch achievements. "Almost every respondent in the countries surveyed was aware of the launching of the first satellite and of the fact that Russia had launched it. Subsequent awareness of the first American success was also high."[11] This awareness was reinforced by the perceived linkage of space achievement to national strength. As Almond concluded, "One of the most stable popular beliefs of the postwar era—the belief in the scientific and technical superiority of the United States—has been rudely shaken, and its place taken by anxious estimating that fluctuates with each report of a significant step forward in satellite launchings."[12]

In the United States itself, opinion intensity was high following the Sputnik launches—even though public attitudes were not particularly coherent. "The opinions held by many Americans regarding this first step into space were sometimes inconsistent, occasionally rich in non sequiturs, and frequently illogical."[13] Nevertheless, public demand for a policy response to the Sputnik achievement was strong. A Survey Research Center poll conducted shortly after Sputnik reported that "77 per cent thought that the Russian satellite should make 'a difference in what we are doing about the defense of this country', with...47 per cent going for a crash program on weapons development."[14]

Set apart from this intensive public arousal was the inchoate and disordered organizational and administrative framework associated with the development of U.S. space exploration capabilities. The major components in this matrix were: the National Advisory Committee for Aeronautics (NACA), a small research and consultative agency for the aeronautics industry and other divisions of the Federal government; the three military branches, each conducting piecemeal research and development operations in line with its own particularistic notions of what space exploration was all about; and, of course, the U.S. aircraft industry, only marginally involved in space flight research (apart from weapons development projects) and confronted with a traditional reliance on "in-house" rocket development on the part of such government organizations as the Army Ballistic Missile Agency.[15]

This period in the development of the space program — in which high levels of public arousal confront underdeveloped organizational forms — is extremely interesting, for it illustrates an important relationship between public policy and public pressure. Public pressure generally oscillates freely within a political system — frequently enlarging rapidly, then declining suddenly.[16] Such oscillations can occur anywhere along a continuum of intensity primarily as a function of complex determinants of attitude and attention.

Yet public policy is not similarly free to move along a continuum insofar as its scale is concerned. Again much has been said in policy analysis about the incremental nature of program advances. Yet *relative to public pressure*, public policy is beset by a dependence upon organizational features which cause it to enlarge or contract in discontinuous "jumps" — as jurisdictional, manpower, or budgetary plateaus are reached.

In fact, given the highly disparate ways in which policy and pressure enlarge, *it is unlikely for them ever to be appropriately matched.* Pressure expands as a continuous function (although as mentioned earlier it is subject to wide and rapid fluctuations along its intensity continuum). Policy undertakings, on the other hand, enlarge as a step function; they are beset by discontinuities that reflect thresholds associated with their expansion. Enabling legislation, for example, is frequently required for the initiation of a policy pursuit. Once established, a policy does not expand far from the dimensions of its genesis without soon confronting jurisdictional, manpower, and appropriations boundaries. Then it must *leap* over these boundaries — it must secure an enlargement of its legislative authorization, upgrade its manpower supplies, and justify an increased level of appropriated funds.

Significantly, this process does not come to define a smooth gradient. It generally occurs in spurts. Nonincremental policies in particular must expand greatly *if they are to expand at all.* Only then can they overcome the inertia, external resistance, or internal start-up problems which act as barriers to policy expansion. It is perhaps a telling illustration of this all-too-ignored discontinuity of policy enlargement, that a general analysis of public programs by the Tax Foundation concluded: "The general pattern characterizing the growth of...new [federal] programs is this: sharp increases in the first two years as the programs get into fuller operation, relatively modest increases in the third and fourth years, followed by a steep jump of the sort depicting major expansion or legislative extensions of the program."[17]

Let us review again the policy-pressure relationships mentioned above. As pressure builds for government action within a specific issue setting it is likely to confront a partial vacuum in ongoing public policy. The beginnings of the ecology "movement" amply illustrate this phase—where increased public concern over problems of environmental quality quickly overbalanced the minimal regulatory standards of the federal government. This initial stage is one of *underscaling* in public policy. Such an underscaling also characterized the organizational insufficiencies of the space program in the period on which we have so far been concentrating.

Eventually, of course, public policies are generated in response to escalating public pressure. But, again, the discontinuous nature of policy expansion makes it difficult to match appropriately government performance with fluctuations in public "demand." Frequently, the appearance of government activity itself can contribute to the dissipation of public arousal. Secure in the symbolic reassurance that "something is being done," the public shifts its fleeting attentions to other issues of greater currency and fashion.[18] This decay in public concern can lead ultimately to a condition in which policy performance actually exceeds public demand, which might well be termed an *overscaling* dimension to public policy. At this extreme of the policy-pressure relationship, bureaucratic programs can persist long after generalized support for such pursuits has subsided. In regulatory policy making this is typically the stage at which the "capture" of the agency by a specialized constituency can occur. Because public arousal has waned, the regulatory agency must turn for its support to the one social component whose attention and watchfulness remain unwavering—the very interest which the agency seeks to regulate. Should policies in general fail to locate steadfast constituencies during this period of overscaling, the result must invariably be that saddest of administrative spectacles—the politically orphaned agency, an object (in Norton Long's words) "of contempt to its enemies and despair to its friends."[19] The overscaling dimension too has become an important part of the manned space exploration story.

In essence the expansion-support "game" is one at which the nonincremental, indivisible policy enterprise is considerably disadvantaged. This is so because of the extreme start-up lags to which it is subject. Nonincremental policy is beset by substantial discontinuities in both enlargement and payoff. Continuing the description of manned space exploration will illustrate this point more fully.

We left space exploration in the interim period between the first Soviet Sputniks and the Kennedy moon-landing commitment. This was an era of a "lagging, directionless space program,"[20] or, as one critic expressed it, a "space maze and missile mess in Washington."[21] In February of 1958 the Advanced Research

Projects Agency (ARPA) was established in the Department of Defense to coordinate and oversee diverse military missile and space satellite programs. This was an initial effort to upgrade U.S. space exploration in light of conspicuous Soviet successes, yet it proved to be hopelessly underscaled in relation to distinctive organizational thresholds and inertia which had to be overcome. These thresholds are a critical feature of the nonincremental policy enterprise.

The Dilemma of "Thinking Small"

The first problem is a psychological one. Perhaps no barrier is more essential for nonincremental policy to breach and overcome permanently than the penchant for thinking small. Overcoming this trait is a major necessity in developing the imagination and receptivity closely associated with organizational innovation.[22] In addition, thinking small is also a detriment to the planning and jurisdictional extensions upon which nonincremental policy depends.

Before the lunar landing commitment, underestimates on the rate of technological advance and the engineering "do-ability" associated with manned space programming were commonplace. No less a figure than Hugh Dryden, NACA Director and a future Deputy Administrator of NASA, asserted a scant four years before Sputnik: "I am reasonably sure that travel to the moon will not occur in my lifetime...."[23] Such myopia was certainly understandable, yet adequate space planning required both foresight and an obstinate faith in the future approaching that which drives the classic "revolution of rising expectations." It was not until this radical departure in perspective could find a congenial institutional environment that efficient preparation for manned missions could begin.

Thinking small also served as a barrier to the jurisdictional expansion upon which space exploration depended. NACA, the central research agency in the administrative network concerned with space exploration, actively resisted the Eisenhower administration's efforts to upgrade its policy-making jurisdiction. "By February 1958, as the Eisenhower administration began wrestling with the complexities of formulating a national program for space exploration, NACA had taken the official position that, with regard to space, it neither wanted nor expected more than its historic niche in government-financed science and engineering. While NACA should become a substantially bigger instrument for research, it should remain essentially a producer of data for use by others."[24]

This reluctance to accept an enlarged organizational assignment (and, indeed, to participate in a timely institutional growth) led ultimately to the demise of NACA later that same year. In its place the National Aeronautics and Space Act of 1958 established a national space advisory council (The National Aeronautics and Space Council) and NASA (which absorbed most of NACA's personnel). NASA was created to attain another major threshold associated with a nonincremental policy such as space exploration. This was the requirement for administrative consolidation.

Consolidation Requirements

Even though the Space Act provided for a distinctive civilian/military apportionment of space exploration activity between NASA and DOD, NASA immediately on its formation began to press for the acquisition of key research groups and programs located within the military services. In less than three months NASA had acquired Project Vanguard from the Navy (as well as the 150 staff members and $25 million in appropriations connected with it), lunar probe and earth satellite projects from the Air Force, and the Jet Propulsion Laboratory (complete with Caltech staff and $100 million in appropriations) from the Army.[25] It even attempted to take over the Army Ballistic Missile Agency amid shrieks of outrage from that agency. Although delayed by Army opposition, NASA's ambitious consolidation plans were not to be denied. In March of 1960 NASA formally acquired the ABMA and most of its "von Braun team" of key researchers.

These acquisitions reflect the importance to the nonincremental, indivisible policy enterprise of consolidating control over those suboperations upon which it closely depends. In industrial settings consolidation of this type is referred to as vertical integration — an effort to amalgamate raw materials and component production processes within the same managerial framework as that governing the creation of a final marketable product for which these subprocesses are important. (Of course, at the same time NASA was accomplishing a type of horizontal integration — eliminating the potential sources of space exploration programming competition.)

The nonincremental policy requires an extensive consolidation because of the close interdependency of its component parts. Uncertainty or performance failures in any one suboperation can threaten the success of them all. Many research and development projects require parallel breakthroughs on a variety of problem fronts. The development of a rocket guidance system, for example, demanded simultaneous advances in both computer miniaturization and thruster engine design.

For manned space exploration, consolidation was an essential organizational threshold to surpass, given the extremely diverse and ramified operations upon which any manned-mission plans would depend. "Whether it was given special responsibilities or not, NASA had to concern itself with the nation's overall space program *if it was to optimize its own.*"[26]

Administrative consolidation also allowed NASA to recruit, both from industry and from other government agencies, highly qualified technical personnel to work on its programs. In part, consolidation triggers the rising expectations essential to mobilize the manpower required for nonincremental policy making. As one NASA official observed: "We believe that we are attracting quality people...because we have salaries which are competitive, plus a new, attractive and exciting program, and an *expanding mission* which creates the possibilities of greater opportunities."[27]

Closely related to the administrative consolidation requirements are the following specific start-up thresholds which space exploration policy making had to overcome.

The Indivisibility Dimensions of Research

A great deal of organizational management theory centers around the importance and inevitability of specialization, both for bureaucratic supervision and for institutional problem solving. Yet this attention to specialization has resulted in the partial neglect of those operations for which specialization is not entirely appropriate. One of these, oddly enough, is the major research project — the very setting in which specialized knowledge would seem most important. But a large-scale research problem is frequently interdisciplinary — cutting across lines of specialization and imparting an indivisibility to organizational tasks. For problems such as these "research teams are only divisible down to a minimum effective scale."[28] Conversely, research teams must first attain this scale if they are to mount an effective attack upon a critical problem.

Major research progress in space flight technology was delayed until interdisciplinary groups could be assembled on a scale which would multiply their problem-solving effectiveness. Below this threshold a host of conflicting theories and experimental results remained largely unreconciled while still other "good ideas" went begging for attention.

In discussing indivisibilities associated with space research it is also important to note the extent to which much of this research was "equipment-intensive." The study of acceleration tolerances, for example, required the construction of large centrifuges in order to simulate the stresses of space flight. Research into designs and materials which would safeguard spacecraft reentry into the earth's atmosphere depended upon sophisticated hypersonic wind tunnels and was delayed pending the construction of such devices. Advanced manned-mission planning in general was predicated upon prior unmanned missions of research and experimentation. It was considered essential "to strengthen NASA's program for the unmanned exploration of the moon, using hard-landing Ranger spacecraft and soft-landing Surveyor spacecraft. The unmanned exploration of the moon was considered an absolutely essential step prior to manned landing."[29]

This equipment-intensive characteristic of much space exploration research heightened the thresholds associated with its start-up. The design and construction of specialized instrumentation and simulation devices was expensive, and the scarcity of such equipment served to confine research activity to a few isolated groups with access to these devices. These expense and isolation problems which typified space research are not at all unlike the features associated with large-scale scientific research in general.[30] These were responsible for important lags in research progress prior to the policy acceleration that organized and funded research groups at critical levels of problem-solving effectiveness.

Land Acquisition and Facilities Construction

Another feature of manned space exploration to which start-up thresholds were attached was land acquisition and facilities construction. Enormous quantities of land and elaborate spacecraft tracking, construction and testing facilities were required before any manned-mission planning could realistically begin.

The Atlantic Missile Range alone required more than 100,000 acres of land. While some of this land had been acquired earlier by the Air Force, far larger tracts were needed by NASA in order to construct an adequate launch facility at acceptable margins of safety. Their acquisition clearly reflects the threshold problems attendant upon the nonincremental policy enterprise. As it developed, the buying of land was a process not readily susceptible to gradualism. It required both executive branch clearance and specific congressional authorization — actions which in turn were predicated upon elaborate programming justifications. Significantly, it was not easy to attain these requisites on a small scale because of a peculiarity in the approval process. *Program plans had to be large if they were also to be persuasive.* Larger scale plans communicated a sense of urgency and purpose. In a very real sense, the scale of the acquisition request was a major factor in upgrading the probabilities of its own fulfillment.

A further problem in the land acquisition process was the need for land holdings to be concentrated at the early stages of agency planning. This was important because the very act of land acquisition (and of the publicized prospect of its subsequent development) raised the price (and in some cases altered the zoning) of surrounding land in highly unfavorable directions. This made it far more difficult to acquire additional land later.

It was for precisely this reason that NASA Administrator James Webb, in requesting congressional authorization for land acquisition within the Atlantic Missile Range area, argued vigorously for permission "to take all the land we can visualize that would be required. Once we get this, I do not think it will be possible to get any more land there. It will be too expensive."[31]

Qualitative Correlates of Scale

A final class of start-up thresholds consists of those space exploration requisites which were only qualitatively realized under the impact of scale. Reliability in space hardware, for instance, a critical dimension to any manned-mission planning, was closely dependent upon a large number of trial tests and subsequent "debugging" after prolonged use. As one NASA official described the problem: "We never quite know, when we launch a satellite, what is going to be the limiting point because we have not been in business long enough to establish these numbers. What you need to do is the thing you have always needed to do to develop long operational life; that is, to start to develop, to debug, and to build life through use."[32]

Another qualitatively derived function of scale is the external support upon which any nonincremental policy depends for success. Frequently, as mentioned, such support stems from the rising expectations which policy objectives are able to generate. In any case, major public approval and the prospect of its continuance is required to render the initial start-up costs worthwhile. An enormously expensive operation such as space research "cannot be turned on and off like a faucet. It must be planned in advance, given adequate leadtime, and funded in such a way that there is assurance that it can move along systematically."[33]

As James Webb has contended:

A common denominator of large-scale endeavors is the necessity of a continuing "critical mass" of support. There must be enough support and continuity of support to retain and keep directly engaged on the critical problems the highly talented people required to do the job, as well as to keep viable the entire organizational structure.... Any uncertainty or shortfall in the support factor is apt to have far-reaching effects and force the endeavor into serious difficulties.[34]

In a very real sense, a nonincremental, indivisible policy pursuit must attain a "capture point" of public goal and resource commitment. Albert O. Hirschman has stressed the importance of this capture point in a study of major development projects in Third World nations. In observing these capital-intensive national enterprises Hirschman notes the extent to which potential project difficulties are frequently underestimated at their outset. He then asserts that if a development project is to overcome these misestimations "its operators must be 'caught' by the time the unsuspected difficulties appear—caught in the sense that having spent considerable money, time and energy and having committed their prestige, they will be strongly motivated to generate all of the problem-solving energy of which they are capable."[35]

Hirschman argues that many agricultural projects fail precisely because they are too short-term and small-scale to reach this capture point. When unanticipated problems arise, these projects are prematurely abandoned. In effect, they fail because of a reluctance "to throw good money after what looks like bad, but could be turned into good, if only the requisite rescue effort were forthcoming."[36]

To be sure, this policy entrapment effect is not without its hazards. The attainment of a capture point may well lead after all to the casting of good money, time and effort after that which really *is* bad. This, it will be recalled, was a major argument against much of the U.S. military escalation in Vietnam.

Yet entrapment is important to the nonincremental public policy enterprise. It can assure the continuity of support so essential to policies of this class. At the same time, entrapment safeguards the nonincremental policy from many of the unanticipated problems associated with its pursuit. In space exploration, the Kennedy commitment sustained mission goals through even the darkest hours of equipment failure, cost overruns, and ultimately, the tragic spacecraft fire that took the lives of three Apollo astronauts.

Start-Up Requirements and Initial Space Decisions

In assessing these nonincremental start-up requisites, it is small wonder that a major political commitment, in fact a presidential mandate, was necessary to energize manned space exploration policy. As space administrators readily conceded, "Science is, and cannot be, the driving force for space exploration."[37] It was indeed President Kennedy's national commitment that "galvanized the lagging, directionless space effort around a dramatic, not-too-distant goal."[38]

The full magnitude of the start-up operations to which reference has been made is well illustrated by budgetary data compiled for the early period of the space program. Figure 8.1 illustrates NASA expenditures from fiscal years 1961 through 1966, and highlights the research and development component of these expenditures. It is revealing to note two things in connection with these expenditures: the steeply rising rate of overall space spending, and the degree to which R&D-classified outlays approximate the total NASA funds spent. Seldom has a government agency increased its appropriations as rapidly as NASA. This strongly reflects the political support associated with the Kennedy moon-landing commitment. But the proportion of R&D expenditures is also significant. More than 80 percent of NASA's funds went into starting up the space exploration enterprise—filling the gaps in theory, technology, and equipment required for space exploration to advance. (It is interesting to note, by way of contrast, that in 1961, only 2.9 percent of the total U.S. GNP was spent on R&D. In that year the average industry expenditure was 4 percent of sales.[39])

Another illustration of the dimensions of the space exploration start-up is provided by employment data compiled during the 1960–66 period. Figure 8.2, depicting total employment on space exploration programs both within and out-

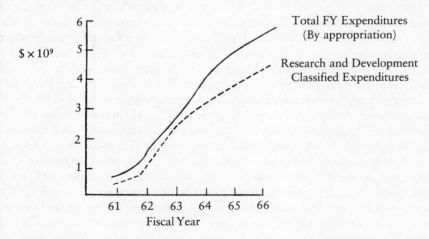

Figure 8.1. NASA Expenditures (FY 1961–66)

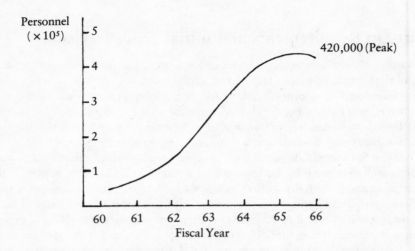

Figure 8.2. Total Employment on NASA Programs (1960–66)

side of NASA, emphasizes the personnel mobilization required to pursue exploration objectives. This manpower tool represents substantial private industrial expansion as well as extensive programs of training and recruitment. It is unlikely that such a work force could have been assembled without the prospect of a major *and continuing* space exploration commitment.

What we have seen so far of the start-up problems associated with manned space exploration illustrates the degree to which the model of incremental decisions fails conspicuously to account in this case for an observable reality. The start-up thresholds attached to nonincremental policy represent problems for which comprehensive (and even optimal) decisions are required. In reviewing the lunar landing program James Webb has argued: "We could not stop with doing 80 or 90 or 99 per cent of what we needed to do and come out reasonably well." Indeed, for a lunar landing "a partial success is likely to be a complete failure."[40]

Lindblom asserts, in his description of incrementalism, that "policy is not made once and for all; it is made and remade endlessly. Policy making is a process of successive approximations to some desired objectives in which *what is desired itself continues to change under reconsideration.*"[41] Yet contrast this with the extended planning and the continuity of support so essential to the nonincremental policy enterprise. The Kennedy commitment and the prospects for extended exploration missions were the major reasons that elaborate and expensive space start-up requirements were deemed worthwhile. Manpower training and recruitment closely depended upon the fixed future perceived for space programs. Shifts in policy objectives of the sort postulated by Lindblom would, under these circumstances, have jeopardized the future of the space program. They would have seriously undermined the continuity of support which space exploration policy, in this its start-up phase, so desperately required.

Finally, the incremental model of decision making greatly misrepresents the reality of administrative thresholds themselves. The appropriations, manpower, research, and facilities growth in the immediate aftermath of the Kennedy commitment was far more than marginally removed from the policy "state" by which it was preceded. Indeed marginal additions to a nonincremental, indivisible policy in the period of its start-up *will consistently fail to translate into incremental gains in policy performance.* Major, comprehensive commitments of personnel and resources are required before even limited pay-offs are derived. Thus it is extremely difficult to adjust input decisions to subsequent changes in output performance—a characteristic which renders nonincremental policy resistant to the process of marginal refinement postulated by Lindblom.

Instability in Nonincremental Policy

Apart from the problem of start-up thresholds, another major characteristic besets the nonincremental, indivisible policy pursuit: *nonincremental policy is in essence unstable—devoid of middle ground between self-generating states of growth and decay.* Again we turn to space exploration for the appropriate illustration.

During the mid-1960s manned space exploration rode the crest of what amounted to a dynamic and highly complex policy "movement"—a movement characterized by heightened technological and national aspiration, persistent political pressure for congressional appropriations, and seemingly open-ended prospects for organizational growth. It was perhaps during this period that a "match" was approached in that elusive balance between public policy and public pressure. Start-up thresholds had largely been overcome and space policy *outputs* (in the form of repeatedly successful manned missions) reached their maximum levels of public support.

Yet this match was to be short-lived. As Downs suggests in his analysis, "The Issue Attention Cycle," public support can quickly subside as a cycle of issue saliency runs its course.[42] This sudden ebb in public pressure can leave the nonincremental policy precariously overscaled relative to the political resources which exist for its support. It is precisely at this point that nonincremental policy may become exceedingly burdensome and vulnerable.

As both budgetary and employment data reveal, the sharply accelerating pace of space exploration in the early 1960s gave way toward the end of the decade to a major decline in policy support, even before the lunar landing objective was achieved. NASA appropriations declined from $5.2 billion in fiscal year 1965 to $2.8 billion in 1973. Even more dramatic evidence of space policy decline is provided by the statistics of total manpower employed on NASA programs. As figure 8.3 depicts, total personnel dropped from the fiscal year 1965 peak of 420,000 to a low of approximately 108,000 in 1972.

Associated with this appropriations and manpower slide has been increased public and congressional criticism of space exploration in general, a decline in

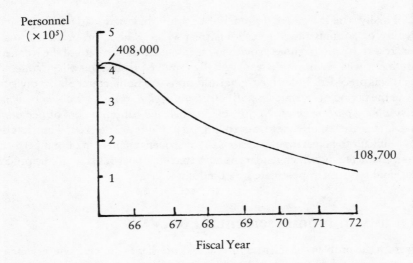

*Figure 8.3. Downturn in Total Employment
on NASA Programs (FY 1966–72)*

morale among remaining space program employees, and specific decays in organizational performance throughout the space policy bureaucracy itself.

As early as 1965, Gallup polls began to report significant erosion of both public interest and support where expensive, nonmilitary space exploration undertakings were concerned. A July 1965 Gallup poll, seeking to uncover opinion on the question "Which country—the United States or Russia—do you think is farther ahead in the field of space research?" elicited a 26 percent "Don't know" response. This would seem to indicate a sizable disinterest in the space exploration "race" among the American people. The same poll revealed a 36 percent preference among those contacted for decreased space exploration expenditures, as against 42 percent in favor of keeping those expenditures the same and 16 percent in support of their increase.[43]

Even more dramatic evidence of diminishing public space policy support is provided in a 1967 Gallup poll. Here, in response to the question "Do you think it is important or is it not important to try to send a man to the moon before Russia does?" a full 60 per cent of those interviewed assessed the landing race as "not important."[44]

By February 1969, in fact, 40 percent of Gallup poll respondents called for a reduction in space research expenditures as against 41 percent approving present levels of those expenditures. In addition, a July 1969 poll (on the threshold of the lunar landing) revealed that 53 percent of those interviewed opposed a Mars manned landing as a follow-on goal to the Apollo program. Only 39 percent favored such a goal.[45]

Closely related to this erosion in general support for space policy was an increase in specific criticism directed at NASA programs and their expenditure requirements. A number of congressional critics began to question the "pork barrel" distribution of NASA facilities. Public debates also began over the relative merits of manned versus unmanned flight. Such debates were particularly heated at times of NASA setbacks or Soviet achievements (such as the Lunakhod series) in purely instrumented space flight and experimentation.

National opinion leaders such as Senator Edward Kennedy and the Reverend Ralph Abernathy began to speak out against space exploration as a diversion of scarce national resources urgently needed elsewhere. In the aftermath of Vietnam war escalations, space exploration came to be viewed in some circles as an extension of military and defense policies and was opposed on that basis. Finally, "counterculture" values led to a condemnation of space exploration as an extravagant exercise in mindless technology.

This increased opposition to space exploration has led in recent years to serious declines in morale within the space policy bureaucracy. Employee layoffs coupled with the failure to establish follow-on goals have contributed to the perception that the future is "running out" on the space program. This perceived termination of manned missions lies at the root of an intensified scientist-engineer controversy within NASA. The prospects of limited flight opportunity have intensified feelings of discrimination on the part of scientist-astronauts who have lost out in competition with pilot-astronauts in past mission assignments and for whom few future space flight opportunities remain.[46]

Declines in Organizational Performance

The sense of decline that has developed within the space policy bureaucracy has had important consequences for the effectiveness of that organization in the attainment of its objectives. A number of specific performance problems have emerged that could become highly significant given the close ranges of control tolerance upon which successful space flights depend. One of these difficulties lies in the movement of highest quality personnel out of NASA into areas of greater perceived excitement and career opportunity. Despite indifferent, or distinctively unfavorable, job markets, much of NASA's most valuable managerial and scientific talent has left the agency for brighter prospects in universities, private industry or other government agencies. This exodus has left the space program without some of its most imaginative and capable personnel. As one former NASA official privately asserted: "Programs like Apollo attract people who like challenges. Once the major problems are solved they are no longer interested. Those left behind are really mediocre, and they establish a self-fulfilling mediocrity within the program."

One of the most consistent areas of concern throughout the history of the space program has been that of hardware reliability and quality control. Space flight equipment, of course, requires the greatest technical care and precision in its design and manufacture. The image of the "white room" with its sterilized, dirt-free environment has come to symbolize the "assembly line" of the space age. Yet behind the elaborate rules and assembly procedures, the monitoring and testing technology, is a recognition that no matter how detailed or sophisticated the safeguards "if the employee doesn't care whether or not he makes a mistake, he will probably err."[47]

Operating under this assumption NASA has carefully developed programs to add a motivational component to quality control. NASA astronauts have made repeated visits to divisional facilities and contractors to upgrade the morale of space employees by increasing their sense of importance and identity with respect to space exploration goals. The lunar landing commitment itself provided a major incentive for extra care in spacecraft assembly. Workers on Apollo hardware felt a special motivation to upgrade and sustain the quality of their job performance as a means of personal participation in an endeavor of historic proportions.

Yet, in recent times, along with the declines in public support and employee morale which have beset the space policy bureaucracy, an erosion has occurred in quality control capability. One NASA official conceded in a private interview that "the number of anomalies has risen alarmingly in each successive flight after [Apollo] 11." Another reports that with this erosion "worries about quality have become a fetish with higher management."

These statements are very important. *Apollo 11*, it will be remembered, was the first lunar landing mission. It marked the fulfillment of that commitment to which most of NASA's activities over the decade of the '60s had been dedicated. At the same time it represented the end of a period of clear direction for space exploration policy. One goal had lapsed, and no new ones had appeared to take its place.

This lack of direction probably contributed importantly to NASA's problems in quality control. Without the *esprit* which characterized the space challenges of the early 60s a lapse has developed in what might be termed the institutional "will to be careful." This may explain why hardware failures (or "gliches") have been occurring with increasing frequency in even tried and tested spacecraft systems.

Dissolution of the Space Policy Bureaucracy

In addition to performance shortfalls, related decays can now be observed in the structure of the space policy bureaucracy itself. An organizational fragmentation and contraction has hit the space program and appears to be moving it in the direction of the inchoate administrative arrangements which characterized the immediate post-Sputnik period. Appropriations and manpower cutbacks are, again, highly influential here but so too is the failure to establish follow-on goals for a nonincremental policy.

University laboratories represent one structural decay already well established. Cutbacks in NASA's training grants and the elimination of its Sustaining University Program have pushed a number of university labs out of their involvement with space programs. Those laboratories which remain attached to the program find the general decline in NASA's experimentation interest a deeply foreboding sign of the future. As one observer notes: "The dilemma of the laboratories is that they require lead times of 18 months to two years to develop instrumentation for satellite experiments and to train graduate students to handle the data. With nothing in the offing they can count on in the 1970's, they are having a difficult time maintaining a trained laboratory staff and keeping students on tap."[48]

Besides university laboratories, a number of small aerospace contractors have either dissolved under the impact of space appropriations cutbacks or are in serious trouble to the extent of their dependence upon contract revenues. Other former contractors have detached themselves from space exploration assignments in favor of more promising long-term prospects elsewhere. Even major contractors have not escaped internal upheavals during the recent period of fiscal and manpower retrenchment. Shrinkage of the aerospace industry has raised among some the "immediate concern...that the...manufacturing and testing establishment developed to build Apollo will fall apart."[49]

These space exploration declines—in public support, appropriations, personnel, morale, organizational structure and performance—all illustrate the fundamental instability inherent in the nonincremental policy enterprise. Nonincremental policy is not likely to realize a point of equilibrium or "steady-state" between support-mobilizing expansion and downward spirals of disillusionment and decline. There is perhaps nothing which space exploration demonstrates more convincingly than this very point.

Recognizing these exceptionally thin margins between policy expansion and decay, space policy makers have exhibited an impressive resourcefulness in attempting to maintain growth in their programs. Both Soviet and American space administrators, for example, have repeatedly praised the achievements of the other side in an effort to generate competitive spirit for increased efforts at home.[50] In recent times, as the enthusiasm for international competition has waned, NASA officials have stressed the possibilities of international *cooperation* in space as an incentive to the Nixon and Ford administrations to upgrade space funding.

As one astute observer describes it: "The reasoning goes like this: If NASA could establish an opportunity for improved Soviet-American relations through cooperation in space, this would presumably create the need for a series of post-Apollo missions of historic proportions. Considering the current politics of detente with the big powers, it would be hard for the White House or Congress to say no to funds for such an effort."[51]

The recent Soviet-American joint orbital flight, first announced during former President Nixon's Moscow summit, would appear to testify to at least the partial success of this new approach.

Attempts at a Policy Steady-State

To describe the instability associated with manned space exploration as a nonincremental policy, is not to deny that efforts have been made to find a point at which space programs could be stabilized. The Apollo Applications and Skylab projects have both been attempts to locate that intermediate ground where the continuity of space exploration missions could be assured.

Skylab, in particular, was conceived as a balanced, well-paced series of orbital experimentation missions — a "holding program which keeps the technology alive, but barely so, until the nation recovers its interest in new frontiers and decides to become venturesome again."[52] But at its outset Skylab suffered in competition with the Army's Manned Orbiting Laboratory (MOL) program. Those Skylab missions which were undertaken were troubled by a public indifference as well as by manufacturing flaws in the Skylab itself.

Another stabilization effort, the Apollo Applications Program (AAP) failed dramatically to elicit the enthusiasm necessary to counterbalance the costs involved in its undertaking. In a study of post-Apollo planning in NASA, Emmette Redford and Orion White reported that "the AAP program remained throughout its development in a highly fluid state, without objectives ever being firmly decided upon."[53] They concluded:

> The AAP, after being squeezed into acceptable dimensions by NASA's top leadership, the Bureau of the Budget, and the Congressional budget process, would have been given adequate support if it had not run into competition with other demands on national resources. What mainly brought it down...was apparently the budgetary stringency produced by the Vietnam war, the Great Society program, the riots in the cities and the fear of continued inflation.[54]

In this conclusion, however, Redford and White ignore the essential nonincremental and indivisible nature of space exploration policy. It is equally plausible that what really destroyed the Apollo Applications Program was its very *formulation* as an incremental and balanced policy alternative. Once "squeezed into acceptable dimensions," it lost the persuasive content that would have justified its proposed expenditures.

This is precisely the problem of nonincremental policy. Without major mobilizing commitments (such as landing a man on the moon and returning him safely) these policies simply cannot generate and sustain the support required for their collective payoffs.

A deepseated paradox is at work here. In order to fit comfortably into an incremental, piecemeal framework the AAP was cast in a form which was basically not large enough to be persuasive. Then, without being able to generate its own collective political commitment, the AAP was suddenly too large for available amounts of public support.

Escalation and the Space Shuttle

These dilemmas faced by space policy managers in sustaining their programs have certainly not gone unheeded by top leadership in either the aerospace industry or the White House itself. NASA has, of course, targeted many of its public pleas for support directly toward presidential ears. Intensive industry and congressional pressure has also been brought to bear for the upgrading of space exploration policy goals.

In response to these pressures President Nixon appointed in 1969 a special Space Task Group, consisting of then Vice-President Spiro Agnew, Science Advisor Lee A. Dubridge, Air Force Secretary Robert C. Seamans and NASA Administrator Thomas O. Paine, to assess follow-on goals for space exploration. The group urged the adoption of a Mars manned landing goal, but at a "moderate pace"—no specific date and no overriding national priority were to be attached to the endeavor.[55] Yet the President was not yet willing to make any political commitment of this order, and efforts to find a middle ground on which space exploration policy (and expenditures) could unobtrusively rest continued.

As organizational decay continued, however, even a highly cautious Richard Nixon could not escape the dilemma of the nonincremental policy enterprise. On January 5, 1972, the President authorized NASA to undertake development of a partially reusable space "shuttle"—designed for near-space transit and estimated to cost approximately $5.5 billion within a six-year time period.

The space shuttle commitment represents an expensive goal with which to upgrade once again the manned space exploration program. The shuttle is predicated upon the notion that extensive investment is required in the immediate future in order to reduce the cost of space flight far in the future. The shuttle is a political commitment (by a reluctant President) to rescue the space policy bureaucracy from the decay spiral in which it had been caught. Thus it is with nonincremental policy—it is not readily balanced in any organizational steady-state.

At its height, space exploration constituted a policy "movement" fueled by high aspirations, public pressures, and seemingly open-ended prospects for organizational growth. Significantly, the instability described herein is a major characteristic of social movements in general. They must mobilize increasing numbers of persons to their support or they risk disintegration and decay. At the other extreme, the very success of a social movement can jeopardize its continuance insofar as success leads to institutionalization and its crystallization in bureaucratic form. Hannah Arendt has noted in this connection "the perpetual motion mania of totalitarian movements which can remain in power only so long as they keep moving and set everything around them in motion."[56] She contends that totalitarian movements "if they do not pursue global rule as their ultimate goal...are only too likely to lose whatever power they have already seized."[57]

The correspondence between social movements and nonincremental policy is striking and politically significant. Both require an extensive mobilization of public resources and support for their start-up. Both must then maintain this mobilization above a critical level or they will rapidly disintegrate. Both, in effect, require the presence of expansive goals as the primary means of protecting themselves from erosions in support.

The escalation of goals is a major requirement and a major dilemma of nonincremental policy. As Albert Hirschman has noted: "The promise of some sort of utopia is most characteristic of larger-scale undertakings such as the launching of social reforms or external aggression because they are likely to require heavy initial sacrifices."[58] Utopian promises (and sharply rising expectations) in themselves frequently contribute to explosive social instability. They are hardly likely to lead to public policies that are readily susceptible to balance or long-term steady-states.

Public Policy and Indivisibility

A final, summary trait of nonincremental policy now presents itself. *Nonincremental policies are beset by an indivisibility which defies disaggregation into piecemeal decisions or additive partial advancements.* This means simply that for nonincremental policies a "self-containment" demand must be observed. Policy requirements as well as outputs must be provided at high levels or they cannot be provided at all.

Space exploration required elaborate and expensive start-up investments before it really got underway. Because of the delayed payoff of the policy, a major political commitment was essential in order that these initial start-up costs would be judged worthwhile. *No short-term, piecemeal or incremental commitment* could have mobilized the support and generated the expectations that space exploration required to surpass its start-up thresholds.

Perhaps this "threshold effect" lies at the heart of nonincremental policy. Thresholds themselves are highly important to the understanding of a great many social processes. As Kenneth Boulding has observed:

> [Social] depreciation and appreciation are not continuous functions of use or load, but exhibit threshold or overload phenomena, which is what causes crises... Continuous functions, which are fine for celestial mechanics, are characteristic of social mechanics only over small ranges of variation, and most social problems arise because of discontinuous functions—the road that suddenly jams up as one more car appears on it, the river that refuses to clean itself under a single addition of sewage, the international system that breaks down into war, or the city that erupts into riot when some small straw is laid onto some existing back.[59]

Thresholds make it exceedingly difficult for a series of small incremental steps to add up in cumulative fashion to one big comprehensive step. *They detach piecemeal decisions or resource commitments from corresponding or proportionate policy payoffs.* This is a critical oversight in incrementalism and the divisible goods model of policy making, and an area to which a great deal of corrective attention should be directed.

In examining this last trait of nonincremental policy it is appropriate to offer additional examples of public enterprises which might fit into this class. Consider urban renewal undertakings, for instance. In urban areas it is becoming increasingly apparent that the rejuvenation of the inner city is an operation to which thresholds or critical masses are attached. Slums represent resource and structural "sinks" — downward cycles of dilapidation and capital depreciation. The influx of limited recovery-inducing elements into the slum environment — in the form of public housing projects, piecemeal slum clearance efforts and private capital investment — is rarely sufficient to overcome the "sink" effect which characterizes the slum. The decay rate of public housing, as well as shrinking inner-city investment returns testify to the failure of small-scale, incremental policy interventions to effect slum rejuvenation.[60]

Perhaps only massive efforts, commitments or expenditures will result in a cycle of rejuvenation which would overcome the sink effect and establish itself as self-sustaining. Major capital inflows will begin to justify private inner-city investment. This investment will in turn enlarge the urban job market, providing resources and incentives for the repair and rebuilding of slum housing. The subsequent appreciation of this housing will add to the supply of inner-city capital, and so on.[61]

If this were so, an urban redevelopment policy, unless cast on a scale approaching its critical resource thresholds, has little chance of realizing — *or even approximately realizing* — its ends. The potential challenge here to a strategy of incrementalism is unmistakable. A series of small decisions or steps, below a policy threshold, will not advance the policy even incrementally in the direction of its goals. Yet at a critical point of personnel or resource commitment, a "takeoff" can occur in policy output — yielding vastly multiplied gains in goal-seeking performance.

The need to breach thresholds and to maintain an organizational transcendence of these limiting factors, places severe constraints on the "divisibility" of the nonincremental policy enterprise. It is likely that urban transportation policies frequently fall victim to their own indivisibility requirements. Rapid transit systems in particular possess underlying scale demands — they must attain a requisite coverage or they simply cannot cope with traffic densities in sufficient degree to justify their costs. Additionally, these systems require firm commitments to detailed plans, and an early construction start-up before labor and materials costs rise prohibitively, and before land acquisition and rezoning resistance coalesces.

Given these requirements, it is easy to understand why, despite feasibility studies, campaign promises, and the establishment of urban transportation planning agencies, urban transport policy remains underdeveloped. Rapid transit systems, because of their indivisibility characteristics, acquire a rigidity which will not permit them to surmount successfully the compromise, delay, and reduction processes of urban political bargaining. These are essentially processes of *disag-*

gregation, and they push transportation ventures below those critical thresholds on which they rely for success.

Indivisibility of the same type can also afflict large-scale planning efforts in general. Plans, after all, create their own support requirements and must generate political commitments and public aspiration in order to fulfill them. Disaggregation can undermine the base of support required for adequate plan implementation. It can seriously disrupt the internal "logic" upon which the plan must rely for its persuasiveness. In this connection Gerhard Colm has argued that "it is very important to recognize that a one-year plan cannot be obtained merely by dividing, say, a five-year plan into five equal parts."[62]

Indivisibility, of course, leads to a major vulnerability in the nonincremental policy enterprise. To a large extent its success depends on the degree to which it can be shielded from the ever-present forces of political disaggregation. Yet this very shielding requirement contains enormous political implications.

Nonincremental Policy and Its Political Consequences

It often happens that nonincremental managers, painfully aware of the vulnerabilities to which their programs are subject, will go to great lengths to establish congenial political environments. Frequently, a nonincremental policy will be "oversold" to the public in order to gain the support and resources deemed essential in the overcoming of thresholds. Once oversold, it becomes difficult to modify the basic objectives of the policy without threatening the political foundations upon which its support has been based. For manned space exploration the Kennedy lunar landing commitment became the major sustaining but at the same time the major constraining factor with which space policy makers had to deal.

Yet this overselling effect is not confined to space exploration alone. Theodore Lowi has noted an identical tendency in large-scale foreign policy undertakings as well. The war in Vietnam, Lowi argues, was rigidified by the very way in which it was sold to the public:

> No policy has escaped injury to itself and to national interests and international stability in the years since American statesmen have felt the need to oversell policies *in order to avoid coming up with a partial decision.* The war in Vietnam has been just another instance of the point. The fighting in the South was not of our making. The crisis was. The escalation was. The involvement in Vietnam was sold by American image-makers as a case of unambiguous aggression and therefore of the need for military victory. Perhaps it was both of these things, but to sell it on the front pages that way in order to ensure support at home left world diplomats, including our own, *with almost no options.*[63]

If Lowi's point is true, it hints strongly at major rigidities implicit in nonincremental foreign policies. The perceived need to accommodate thresholds (i.e., to avoid "partial decisions") can lock foreign policy makers into unyielding, "all-or-nothing" commitments.

This rigidity has major consequences for all policies of a nonincremental nature. It renders them resistant to the compromise and adjustment processes of political bargaining—frequently the major means by which public accountability is imposed. At the same time, their rigidity places nonincremental policies at a disadvantage in responding to shifting political coalitions—a demand essential to the maintenance of public support.

Compounding these difficulties is the instability of nonincremental policy itself. As mentioned earlier, policies in this class are unable to balance themselves within resource or aspirational steady-states. Because of this, a twofold political problem presents itself. In what way besides overselling are policy makers to ensure the requisite support for their undertakings? Without overselling, thresholds can render nonincremental policy so vulnerable to political "adjustments" that it exceeds existing capacities for bureaucratic support. Policy managers, in this case, are likely to experience a continuing frustration in starting up their programs and in mobilizing sufficient resources to offer an adequate chance of goal attainment.

The second half of the political dilemma is that of *disengaging* from rigid, nonincremental policy endeavors which have entered into a self-escalating spiral of growth. Disengagement is difficult to accomplish because of heightened aspirations and bureaucratic forces which support such spirals. (It is also likely if accomplished to lead to serious organizational perturbations as a concomitant retrenchment cycle sets in.) The war in Vietnam would appear to illustrate this disengagement dilemma to a frightening degree.

The Inapplicability of Trial Programs

Another policy implication attached to nonincremental, indivisible undertakings is their challenge to the ever-popular limited-scope trial program. These programs are frequently employed in policy settings because, in the event of failure, not too much in the way of prestige or organizational resources has been risked in them. If they succeed, they provide a blueprint for adjustments in design and an enlargement of application. These advantages have led many policy makers to urge that we "expand the area of governmental and public affairs activity in which new ideas can be tried out as limited-scale programs."[64]

If nothing else, this analysis of nonincremental policy suggests that trial programs can have severe limitations. It suggests that small-scale policy efforts may not necessarily replicate larger ones. Trial programs cannot hope to duplicate those critical commitment and resource thresholds upon which nonincremental, indivisible policy pursuits must rely.

As a result, limited-scale programs are likely to be seriously misleading indicators of nonincremental policy performance. Such programs may indicate a potential for success which is really mythical where larger forces must come into play. Perhaps more importantly, they may project failure where success is possible, given resource commitments on the requisite scale.

All of these policy implications hint strongly at the need for new analytical attention to nonincremental policy, and particularly the need to identify, prior to policy commitment, *which public undertakings are likely to have thresholds attached.* This identification might allow for more enlightened political decisions and the subsequent design of more congenial organizational environments should commitments to nonincremental policies be undertaken. In the meantime, however, no such analytical imagination appears likely until alternatives to the incremental and divisibility paradigms which dominate policy analysis are presented.

Nonincremental Policy: The Conceptual Challenge

To review briefly, this essay has described a class of policy undertakings which elude much of the analytical weaponry of political science. Nonincremental policies require large start-up investments unfulfillable by incremental or piecemeal commitments. They are policies which are nonequilibrating with respect to growth — that is, they are devoid of middle ground between expansion and decay. Lindblom, in his description of incrementalism, stressed the importance of marginal and continuous decisional refinements to the policy process. Yet the policies of which we have been speaking are precisely those for which this strategy is inappropriate. They cannot attain the equilibrium *which would allow these adjustive actions to be successful.*

It is important to recognize the extent to which incremental and equilibrating outlooks dominate political science. Policy analysis repeatedly stresses the degree to which marginal balances are struck between bureaucrat and client, between policy goals and public pressure, and between bureaucratic decisions of the present and organizational routines of the past.

In addition, many of the emerging trends in the analysis of public policy lead in the direction of further elevating decentralized, divisible processes as the "stuff" of policy making. The "public choice" school of policy analysis applies economic models to its assessment of policy activity. In effect, this approach assumes the existence of a decision "market" in which the disaggregated forces of competition, bargaining, and exchange are the determining factors in policy output. Related to this analytical outlook is a developing political persuasion which endorses the increased decentralization of public decision making.

Perhaps the best argument for this public policy "approach" has been presented by Alan Altshuler. Altshuler asserts that it is now necessary "to think more systematically about the virtues of disaggregation versus integration, pluralism versus coordination, and the free market versus regulation in social life."[65] Altshuler calls for a "debureaucratization" in public policy—wherein bureaucratic decisions are supplanted by popular decisions (as in citizen participation and community control) and by market decisions (in which a market adjustment of individual preferences, such as in voucher plans, replaces centralized efforts at planning or control).

There is obviously a great deal to be said in behalf of the public choice and decentralization movements in public policy. Yet there is a real danger, again, that such outlooks will command a disproportionate amount of both analytical attention *and* political support—at the expense of important nonincremental and indivisible policy objectives to which thresholds are attached. This is a problem of theoretical and practical dimensions.

In political theory at present, decision-making models, as well as most models of the political system itself, describe deviance-minimizing, self-stabilizing, and equilibrating operations exclusively. Yet as we have seen, nonincremental policy frequently entails a high-level, unstable process of deviance *amplification* —a performance "takeoff" based upon systems of mutual causation.[66] Entirely new models must be fashioned to account for deviance-amplifying processes before we can hope to analyze enterprises like manned space exploration adequately.

Meanwhile, a deep disillusionment has come to surround the public's assessment of nonincremental political commitments to large-scale policy. In this era of skepticism little support exists for ambitious and expensive undertakings in the public sector. Peculiarly, however, interest in large-scale *goals* remains; and herein lies a major dilemma. Solutions are still urgently sought to problems of poverty, unemployment, and urban decay. Demands continue for major improvements in transportation, housing, energy supply, and environmental quality. Yet the decentralization movement may force us to rely for their resolution upon small-scale, disaggregated policy efforts.

It may well be that many of these efforts will be successful. But the danger exists that in a number of problem areas, incremental policy attempts will fail repeatedly as each falls below some critical effectiveness threshold. Perhaps only nonincremental modes of policy making will prove adequate in satisfying many of our implicit societal aspirations. The decentralization movement threatens to undercut seriously the political support upon which such nonincremental enterprises would have to depend.

The point of this essay is not to attack the public choice or decentralization movements in public administration, nor even to challenge the unity of the incremental model of policy making. The purpose of this essay is to argue for *additional* analytical frameworks to account for the phenomena which lie outside present theoretical coverage. New departures in policy analysis are called for if we are to understand many large-scale public undertakings and their problems. Such understanding is important—both to the development of political science and to the success of public policy.

Notes

1. See Charles E. Lindblom, "The 'Science' of Muddling Through," *Public Administration Review* 19 (Spring 1959): 79–88; Lindblom and David Braybrooke, *A Strategy of Decision* (New York: Free Press, 1963); and Lindblom, *The Intelligence of Democracy: Decision-Making Through Mutual Adjustment* (New York: Free Press, 1965).
2. Lindblom, "The 'Science' of Muddling Through," p. 84.
3. For a description of "divisible" policy making, see Robert A. Dahl and Charles E. Lindblom, *Politics, Economics, and Welfare* (New York: Harper & Brothers, 1953); E. E. Schattschneider, *The Semi-Sovereign People* (New York: Holt, Rinehart and Winston, 1960); and Robert A. Dahl, *Pluralist Democracy in the United States* (Chicago: Rand McNally, 1967). A more critical appraisal of the same phenomenon can be found in Theodore J. Lowi, *The End of Liberalism: Ideology, Policy and the Crisis of Public Authority* (New York: Norton, 1969).
4. For the classic statement regarding pluralism, see, of course, David B. Truman, *The Governmental Process* (New York: Knopf, 1951).
5. The public choice or economic market models of the policy process are presented in such works as James M. Buchanan and Gordon Tullock, *The Calculus of Consent* (Ann Arbor: University of Michigan Press, 1962); Warren F. Ilchman and Norman T. Uphoff, *The Political Economy of Change* (Berkeley: University of California Press, 1969); Robert L. Curry and L. L. Wade, *A Theory of Political Exchange* (Englewood Cliffs, N.J.: Prentice-Hall, 1968); and William C. Mitchell, *Public Choice in America* (Chicago: Markham, 1971).
6. An excellent description of this "realist" approach to the public interest can be found in Glendon A. Schubert, *The Public Interest* (Glencoe, Ill.: Free Press, 1961), chap. 4.
7. Anthony Downs, *Urban Problems and Prospects* (Chicago: Markham, 1970), p. 37.
8. See, for example, Yehezkel Dror, "Muddling Through—'Science' or Inertia?" *Public Administration Review* 24 (September 1964): 153–57; Dror, *Public Policymaking Reexamined* (San Francisco: Chandler, 1968); and Amitai Etzioni, "Mixed Scanning: A 'Third' Approach to Decision-Making," *Public Administration Review* 27 (December 1967): 385–92.
9. "Statistical Report," *National Aeronautics and Space Administration*, Programs and Special Documents Division (Washington, D.C.: U.S. Government Printing Office, 1971). For a review of the process of commitment, see John M. Logsdon, *The Decision to Go to the Moon* (Cambridge: MIT Press, 1970).
10. See Gabriel A. Almond, "Public Opinion and the Development of Space Technology," in *Outer Space in World Politics*, ed. Joseph M. Goldstein (New York: Praeger, 1963), pp. 71–96; Donald N. Michael, "The Beginning of the Space Age and American Public Opinion," *Public Opinion Quarterly* 24 (Winter 1960): 573–82; and Albert J. Lott and Bernice E. Lott, "Ethnocentrism and Space Superiority Judgments Following Cosmonaut and Astronaut Flights," *Public Opinion Quarterly* 27 (Winter 1963): 604–11.
11. Almond, "Public Opinion and the Development of Space Technology," pp. 73–74.
12. Ibid., p. 77.
13. Michael, "The Beginning of the Space Age," p. 581.
14. Ibid., p. 579.
15. See, for an account of this period, Richard S. Lewis, *Appointment on the Moon* (New York: Viking, 1968).
16. For an interesting discussion of public opinion "stages" and their determinants, see Anthony Downs, "The Issue Attention Cycle and the Political Economy of Improving Our Environment," Royer Lectures, University of California, Berkeley, April 13–14, 1970.
17. *Growth Trends of New Federal Programs: 1955–1968* (Washington, D.C.: Tax Foundation, 1967), pp. 19–20.

18. In this context, see Murray Edelman, *The Symbolic Uses of Politics* (Urbana, Ill.: University of Illinois Press, 1964).

19. Norton E. Long, "Power and Administration," *Public Administration Review* 9 (Autumn 1949): 257.

20. Richard S. Lewis, "The Kennedy Effect," *Bulletin of the Atomic Scientists* 24 (March 1968): 2.

21. Donald W. Cox, *The Space Race* (New York: Chilton, 1962), p. 69.

22. See, for example, Chris Argyris, *Organization and Innovation* (Homewood, Ill.: Irwin, 1965), for a discussion of how innovative output can vary as a function of organizational culture.

23. Hugh L. Dryden, as quoted in Lloyd S. Swenson, Jr., James M. Grimwood and Charles C. Alexander, *This New Ocean: A History of Project Mercury* (Washington, D.C.: U.S. Government Printing Office, 1966), p. 56.

24. Swenson, Grimwood, and Alexander, *This New Ocean*, p. 77.

25. Robert Rosholt, *An Administrative History of NASA: 1958–63* (Washington, D.C.: U.S. Government Printing Office, 1966), pp. 45–48.

26. Rosholt, p. 106 (italics supplied).

27. Abe Silverstein, Director, Space Flight Programs, NASA, in *Hearings Before the Senate Committee on Aeronautical and Space Sciences*, June 7–12, 1961 (Washington, D.C.: U.S. Government Printing Office, 1961), p. 177 (italics added).

28. Harry Townsend, *Scale, Innovation, Merger and Monopoly* (London: Pergamon, 1968), p. 25.

29. Rosholt, *Administrative History of NASA*, p. 194.

30. For a discussion of the organizational features related to the conduct of large-scale scientific research, see Derek J. deSolla Price, *Little Science, Big Science* (New York: Columbia University Press, 1963); and Alvin M. Weinberg, "The Impact of Large-Scale Science upon the United States," *Science* 134 (July 21, 1961): 161–64.

31. James E. Webb, Testimony in (FY 1963 Authorization) *Hearings Before The Committee on Aeronautical and Space Sciences, U.S. Senate, 87th Congress, Second Session* (Washington, D.C.: U.S. Government Printing Office, 1962), p. 35.

32. Silverstein, *Hearings Before the Senate Committee on Aeronautical and Space Sciences*, p. 83.

33. Rosholt, *Administrative History of NASA*, p. 88.

34. James E. Webb, *Space-Age Management: The Large Scale Approach* (New York: McGraw-Hill, 1969), pp. 62–63.

35. Albert O. Hirschman, *Development Projects Observed* (Washington, D.C.: Brookings Institution, 1967), p. 18.

36. Ibid., p. 20.

37. Dr. Eberhard Rechtin, Director, Jet Propulsion Laboratory, California Institute of Technology, in *Hearings Before the Senate Committee on Aeronautical and Space Sciences, 88th Congress, First Session* (Washington, D.C.: U.S. Government Printing Office, 1963), p. 138.

38. Lewis, "Kennedy Effect," p. 2.

39. Daniel Hamburg, *R&D: Essays on the Economics of Research and Development* (New York: Random House, 1966), pp. 13 and 41.

40. Webb, *Space-Age Management*, p. 149.

41. Lindblom, "The 'Science' of Muddling Through," p. 86 (italics added).

42. Downs, "The Issue Attention Cycle," pp. 12–15.

43. Gallup Opinion Index, NO. 3 (August 1965): 16.

44. Gallup Opinion Index, NO. 22 (April 1967): 19.

45. Gallup Opinion Index, NO. 45 (March 1969): 17, and NO. 50 (August 1969): 20.

46. See "NASA: Trouble in Paradise," *Newsweek* 74 (September 22, 1969): 73–74; and Marti Mueller "Trouble at NASA: Space Scientists Resign," *Science* 165 (August 22, 1969): 776–79.

47. James F. Halpin, *Zero Defects: A New Dimension in Quality Control* (New York: McGraw-Hill, 1966), p. 3.

48. Richard S. Lewis, "Goal and No Goal: A New Policy in Space," *Bulletin of the Atomic Scientists* 23 (May 1967): 19. See also in this connection W. Henry Lambright and Lauren L. Henry, "Using Universities: The NASA Experience," *Public Policy* 20 (Winter 1972): 61–82.

49. Richard Lewis, "Our Terra-Lunar Transit System: Where Will It Take Us?" *Bulletin of the Atomic Scientists* 25 (March 1969): 22.

50. For a discussion of this point, see Francis E. Rourke, *Bureaucracy and Foreign Policy* (Baltimore: Johns Hopkins Press, 1972), pp. 47–48.

51. John Noble Wilford, "Cooperation in Space," *New York Times*, December 6, 1971.

52. Lewis, "The End of Apollo," *Bulletin of the Atomic Scientists* 24 (September 1968): 5.

53. Emmette S. Redford and Orion F. White, *What Manned Space Program After Reaching the Moon? Government Attempts to Decide: 1962–1968* (Syracuse: Inter-University Case Program, 1971), p. 140.

54. Ibid., p. 223.

55. See "The Post-Apollo Space Program: Directions for the Future," *Space Task Group Report to the President* (Washington, D.C.: U.S. Government Printing Office, 1969).

56. Hannah Arendt, *The Origins of Totalitarianism* (New York: Harcourt, Brace and World, 1966), p. 306.

57. Ibid., p. 392.

58. Hirschman, *Development Projects Observed*, p. 31.

59. Kenneth Boulding, "Discussion," in "The Political Economy of Environmental Quality," *American Economic Review* 61 (May 1971): 167.

60. For a discussion of the urban decay spiral, see William J. Baumol, "Macroeconomics and Unbalanced Growth: The Anatomy of Urban Crisis," *American Economic Review* 57 (June 1967): 415–26. Also, Harry W. Richardson, *Urban Economics* (London: Penguin, 1971), pp. 133–45.

61. For an analysis of these potential "accelerator effects" in urban renewal, see Wilbur R. Thompson, *A Preface to Urban Economics* (Baltimore: Johns Hopkins Press, 1965), pp. 299–302.

62. Gerhard Colm, *Integration of National Planning and Budgeting* (Washington, D.C.: National Planning Association, 1965), p. 24.

63. Lowi, *The End of Liberalism*, p. 179 (italics added).

64. Adam Yarmolinsky, "Ideas Into Programs," in *The Presidential Advisory System*, ed. Thomas E. Cronin and Sanford D. Greenberg (New York: Harper & Row, 1969), p. 99. For a further discussion of experimental policy making, see Alice M. Rivlin, *Systematic Thinking for Social Action* (Washington, D.C.: Brookings Institution, 1971), pp. 108–119.

65. Alan Altshuler, "New Institutions to Serve the Individual," in *Environment and Policy: The Next Fifty Years*, ed. William R. Ewald (Bloomington: Indiana University Press, 1968), p. 425.

66. For an excellent discussion of the deviance-amplification process, see Margoroh Maruyama, "The Second Cybernetics: Deviance-Amplifying Mutual Causal Processes," in *Modern Systems, Research for the Behavioral Scientist*, ed. Walter Buckley (Chicago: Aldine, 1968), pp. 304–13.

IRENE RUBIN

9. Universities in Stress: Decision Making Under Conditions of Reduced Resources

The purpose of this article is to present some suggestions on the relationship between reduction in resource levels and changes in patterns of organizational decision making. Results will be presented from a study of five state universities experiencing financial stress.[1] These results will be compared with models of decision making discussed in the literature.

To date, there have been few studies on how decision making changes under conditions of lowered resource levels. The most important contributions have been those of Cyert and March and March and Cohen.[2] The variables they used or implied and the hypotheses they developed have been combined and compared to the data collected in the current study. The ways in which the current work supports or refutes their hypotheses are discussed. A supplementary model is suggested, which describes aspects of decision making not included in the earlier work.

The work of Cyert and March emphasized changes in allocation procedures as resource levels drop. The authors argued that allocation criteria become more explicit, and resources tend to be spent more on solving organizational problems and less on providing prestige for the subunits. They illustrated these themes by describing decision making about the purchase of a new piece of equipment under conditions of high, medium, and low resource levels. A self-corrective mechanism that prevents the reduction in resource levels from becoming too severe was also postulated.

March and Cohen offered a more abstract model of improved decision making. They hypothesized a two-stage model in which decision making is initially thrown into confusion but gradually improves as a result of reduced resources. March and Cohen emphasized the proportion of decisions resolved rather than ignored or postponed, shifts from one solution to another, the number of times a decision is made, the quality of the information base of an organization, and the frequency with which stored information is used in decision making.

When the work of Cyert and March and March and Cohen is combined, the resulting model predicts initial chaos followed by improved decision making.

Improved decision making is measured by six variables: (1) completeness of relevant information, (2) quality of information used, (3) definitiveness of decisions (the number of times a decision needs to be made), (4) the existence of explicitly formulated criteria for decision making, (5) the degree to which decisions are made with a view to maximizing goals, and (6) the timeliness of decisions.

In adapting and combining the theoretical formulations of March and his co-authors, some liberties have been taken with their decision-making variables. The changes have been made for two reasons: some of the variables used in their analyses are implicit rather than explicit, and some of the variables they describe are not measurable.

The Study

The research is based on a case-study analysis of five state universities undergoing financial stress. The initial plan of the study called for three universities varying in their degree of research emphasis. A fourth university was added because it was a second campus of one university already in the study. The ability of administrators to shift funds and cuts from one campus to another made this addition necessary. Data from a pilot study were included in the current analysis when the information collected was nonconfidential and comparable to that collected afterward.

The universities in the study had experienced growth during the late 1960s and early 1970s, followed by a reduction in the level of budget support from 1972 through the present. In the earlier period, the rate of increase of budgets was faster than inflation, while in the later period it was slower than inflation. These figures are shown in table 9.1.

The data were derived from a combination of interviews, documentary materials, and participant observations. Budgeting and allocation procedures were discussed with administrators in open-ended structured interviews. Budget council sessions were observed at one university, and minutes of budget council meetings were read at a second university. Self-studies describing allocation procedures were utilized. The information capacity of the university was explored

TABLE 9.1. ANNUAL CHANGE IN APPROPRIATED FUNDS,
IN PERCENTAGES, ROUNDED*

	1968	1969	1970	1971		1972	1973	1974
Research U.	7	7	10	11	:	−4	5	5
Urban U.	29	22	28	12	:	2	6	3
Rural U.	29	19	21	18	:	−3	1	1
Crossroads U.	19	18	29	15	:	1	2	5
Inflation**	6	6	6	6	:	5	5	10

*Complete budget data were available for only four of the universities.

**Source of the inflation index is June O'Neill, *Resource Use in Higher Education* (New York: McGraw-Hill, 1971). It has been updated by Charles Anderson of the ACE. The base year was 1963–64.

both at the Office of Institutional Studies, and with deans and department chairpersons. Budget and enrollment data were used extensively.

Comparative data for the period of growth were obtained in several ways. Former administrators were asked what decision making had been like in the early period. Current administrators were asked whether there was any logical or necessary difference in decision making during growth and retrenchment. They were asked about changes in criteria for allocation and for tenure awards. Budget staff were asked about technical changes in procedures for budgeting and allocation. Administrators were also asked about changes in the amounts of information they requested from subordinates, and about changes in the amounts of information requested from them by their superiors. The answers of superiors were checked against the versions of subordinates and, to the extent possible, interview results were compared with results from analysis of quantitative data representing the outcomes of decision processes.

While it would have been desirable to have more quantitative measures for both periods, this was often impossible. First, although the information capacity of the universities was improving, records seldom went back more than a few years. Second, individual personnel transactions were not public. Consequently, the estimates of administrators were often the best sources of information available.

In all, there were 50 formal interviews, 25 with higher-level administrators, and 25 with department heads. The same five departments were used in each university. The average interview lasted about one hour and was conducted in one session. In addition to respondents for formal interviews, there were a number of interviews with general informants who were chosen for their knowledge about campus affairs. Both informants and respondents were promised anonymity.

Changes in Decision Making

In this section the observed changes in decision making are described. The aptness of the two-step model in predicting the results is discussed, and a supplementary formulation is offered.

The greatest success of the Cyert and March model was in its description of the changing allocation patterns from the period of abundance to the period of restricted resources. They argued that the allocation decisions that used to be based on the self-interest of the subunits came to be based more on the solution of organizational-level problems. This change was observed repeatedly during the field work. This change was accompanied by increasing explicitness of decision-making criteria, and an expanded and improved information base. These changes generally occurred in a two-stage sequence, of chaos followed by improved decision making, as predicted by the model.

The process of allocation to the departments illustrates the change from an incremental and almost casual system of allocation during expansion to a more systematic and comparative approach during retrenchment.

During the period of abundance, any department head could get the resources needed if a good case could be made for them. In the extreme case, an informant described admnistrators asking a roomful of chairpersons, "Who wants a new position?" and allocating the positions to those who raised their hands. Informants indicated that there was more money in those years than the universities could absorb with new programs. Money lapsed back to the state unspent at the end of the year, and authorized faculty positions went unfilled. There was no need to compare the requests of the subunits with each other.

When this period of abundance came to an abrupt halt, the administrative response was to gather up loose resources to hold against contingency. The only criterion used was that such money be unobligated; there was no comparison of need between units.

Gradually, the impact of this policy began to be felt. The quality of the institution and its ability to adapt to changing enrollment patterns was weakened. Administrators reportedly began to move toward a less haphazard form of allocation. While loose funds were still gathered up, they were returned to the departments on the basis of priority orderings. Resources such as freed time for research, sabbatical leaves, and secretarial help were allocated on the basis of newly devised criteria laid out by administrators.

For example, one dean listed the criteria he used to determine whether a department head should be allowed to replace a faculty member who was leaving. He included the ratio of instructional faculty to students, compared with norms of departments in other comparable universities; the extent that the replacement would add to the quality of the department; and the priority of the position in comparison to others they would like to create. Such comparisons had not been made previous to the stress period because the positions had remained in the department, to be filled at the department's discretion.

The criteria established to compare existing with proposed programs, to evaluate faculty for sabbatical leaves, and to award freed time for research were also newly created when resources became limited. During abundance, faculty who applied for sabbaticals (and were eligible) could get them automatically. Freed time for research was assumed rather than allocated. But as the total amount of such resources dropped, criteria were devised for allocating them. While these criteria continued to include departmental interests, such as ensuring a minimum number of sabbaticals per department, they also included comparisons between individuals on the basis of merit and between departments on the basis of need. The criteria used reflected goals to be achieved by the university as a whole.

In addition to devising schema for the allocation of scarce resources, administrators also felt the need to reallocate resources from shrinking to growing departments. Such reallocation served several organizational goals: first, it enabled the university to remain adaptive to enrollment trends; and second, it prevented some departments from becoming increasingly expensive as expense was calculated in the state cost study. Since allocation to the university as a whole was based on the cost study, it was important to prevent such an increase in costs.

Did the administrators succeed in reallocating resources during retrenchment, or did the departments manage to maintain their budget levels regardless of falling enrollments? To answer this question, the proportion of budget earned was compared with the proportion of credit hours generated for all liberal arts and sciences departments in each university. The results were summed across departments and expressed as Gini coefficients. The analysis was done for two points in time: just before the financial stress began and after three years of stress. Since enrollment patterns were changing, unless there was substantial reallocation based on enrollment, the degree of mismatch between budget and enrollment would increase. This would increase the Gini coefficients. On the other hand, if there was substantial reallocation on the basis of enrollment, the match between budget and enrollment could be improved. This would lower the Gini coefficients. The results are shown in table 9.2.

It is apparent that none of the universities failed to reallocate on the basis of enrollment. Departments were not successful in maintaining budget levels despite falling enrollment; administrators did manage to allocate with a view to solving organizational problems during retrenchment.

In addition to the changes in allocation processes just described, there was also an expansion of the universities' information base. This was caused in part by the increased requests for information from outside agencies, including the federal government and the state control board. But the expansion of information capacity also stemmed from internal needs to cope with retrenchment, such as better projections of enrollment by department, better recordkeeping of expenditures and fund balances, and more data on credit-hour production by departments. Administrators indicated that they needed more information during retrenchment for two reasons: they could not afford to make mistakes and they needed to justify their retrenchment decisions.

As administrators upgraded and expanded the information base, they created an initial phase of chaos. More information was requested from the subunits than could be effectively used. Surveys were launched without adequate preparation, so that the entire effort was wasted. Information was requested from the departments over and over again, in slightly different form. This initial period of chaos seemed to be passing at the time of the study.

TABLE 9.2. CHANGE IN THE DEGREE OF MATCH BETWEEN ENROLLMENT AND BUDGET, EXPRESSED AS GINI COEFFICIENTS (BETTER MATCH = SMALLER COEFFICIENT)

	1970–71	1973–74
Research U.	.278	.272
Urban U.	.177	.163
Rural U.	.184	.144
Crossroads U.	.234	.137
Teaching U.	.197	.189

The two-step model of initial chaos followed by gradual improvement was thus partially sustained by the data. But the model did not anticipate the continued uncertainty that made chaos a semipermanent feature of decision making. Nor did the model foresee some of the conscious obfuscation that occurred as a strategy of response to financial stress. The authors made the assumption that once the slack was gone and decision making had improved, resources would not continue to decline. This assumption required modification for the state universities in the study.

In the universities studied, the most important source of chaotic decision making was uncertainty introduced by retrenchment. This source of poor decision making was constant throughout the retrenchment period. It resulted in making decisions over and over with different assumptions, and it made long-term planning impossible.

There were two different sources of the uncertainty: one was the budget cuts themselves; the second was the bureaucratic context of the universities in the study. The budget cuts increased the scope of uncertainty because the entire budget, rather than just new programs, was subject to scrutiny. The response of administrators to threatened cuts increased uncertainty. They frequently adopted risky strategies to minimize the impact of the cuts. These included tactics such as budgeting lapsing funds in advance and underestimating the rate of inflation. Since these estimates are based on averages from previous years, they can easily be wrong for any given year. A fragile structure was built up in which the university could create its own deficits by misestimation. (New York City's three-year plan is an extreme example of this practice.)

For the universities studied, this uncertainty was aggravated by the structural context of higher education. Cuts could come at any of five times during the year. Preliminary approval of the budget request had to be given first by the trustees and lower boards, and then by the state board. The budget then went to the governor and the bureau of the budget. Then it went to the legislature. Finally, it went back to the governor, who could veto the appropriation. It was not unusual for the budget to be in doubt until after the fiscal year had already begun. In fact, sometimes the school year began in September without a firm budget.

The resulting uncertainty was exaggerated by the state board, which adopted a policy of changing allocation procedures to the universities every year in order to keep the university administrators off balance.[3] They had changed allocation schema four times in four years. The presidents were barely able to figure out why they had been cut the last time when a new allocation schema was implemented.

The best way to illustrate the effect of this uncertainty on decision making is through the example of one administrator's reactions to cuts announced late in the year. The following excerpts from an interview illustrate the extent of uncertainty, its sources, and its gradual resolution.

The informant began, "We found out about the governor's cuts about four or five days before he made it public. It was to be 6 percent off the base, but we did not know what the base was, and we started off thinking it would be 4 percent and not 6."

He went on to list the assumptions they made in dealing with this degree of uncertainty. They went through the categories of revenues guessing at which would be cut and which would not. They then made the decision as to what to try to protect.

Next, he drew up the alternatives. They could cut the size of faculty and personnel raises, they could cut the size of the margin built into the budget for price increases, or they could find money in the income fund. The income fund is money that the university raises rather than tax money appropriated by the legislature. A major component of the income fund is from tuition. He noted that they could try to increase tuition to increase the income fund. An alternative was to try to have the legislature appropriate for their use money in the income fund balance. That balance is usually created by underestimating tuition revenue.

Many of these alternatives were themselves laden with uncertainty. If they cut the margin for the price increases, they could get caught short later in the year. The option of increasing income funds by raising tuition required board, legislative, and gubernatorial approval. Even if the increase was approved, there was always the danger their appropriations from tax revenue would be reduced proportionally to the increase in tuition revenue.

After determining the options the administrator then developed an optimistic, a neutral, and a pessimistic strategy. Under each assumption, tradeoffs were made explicit and preferable courses of action were determined.

After all this was done, the governor announced that he would take 6 percent off each line, which invalidated all the previous work. Another set of alternatives was worked out, and then the legislature refused to act, leaving a further residual of uncertainty.

The administrator lamented, "In the meantime, we are waiting. Our budget for next year was done, and now we have to revise it. We have to decide whether to go back to the deans and department heads, or do it mechanically, giving them a percentage equal to the cuts. We'll go back to the deans. A 4.5 percent increase cannot be handled the same way as a 9.5 increase. Expense and equipment will be handled automatically—it takes too long to do it the other way."

This pattern of events, lacking relevant information, formulating alternatives under varying assumptions, making decisions between alternatives only to have the rules change and be forced to start again, was repeated at other universities. There was frantic telephoning, instant meetings, and general confusion about the emerging picture. Finally, there was the necessity of redoing internal allocations and redoing the budget request for the following year.

There are two important points to be drawn from the example cited at length here. One is that explicit criteria were devised to guide the decision making, even though these criteria sometimes had to be changed when the amounts of money involved changed. The second feature of this decision-making process was the necessity to make the same decisions over and over again.

The adaptations made by administrators coping with cuts and with uncertainty increased the uncertainty for their subordinates. For example, administrators engaged in the practice of authorizing faculty positions early in the year, but not allowing contracts to be signed until the budget was firmer. This was one way of making sure there were some resources to cut (unfilled but authorized positions) if cuts became necessary late in the year. This practice created uncertainty for department heads. They engaged in recruitment without knowing if they would have the position when they had the candidate.

Another response of administrators was to wait until the budget (and enrollment) was certain before giving permission to hire temporary faculty. This often meant until just before the beginning of the fall term. Department heads complained they could not plan. They did not know how many faculty they would have and which courses they would offer right up until registration. They could announce the course without an instructor's name, and hope they got someone to teach it, or they could wait and announce the course at registration. The students were equally irritated if they signed up for a course that did not meet or if they did not know about a course until too late. The late circulation of information regarding a course often reduced enrollment, which counteracted the benefits of hiring temporary faculty to cover popular courses.

To state the consequences of uncertainty in more general terms, administrators were reluctant to make commitments, and to expend funds once they were committed.[4] As a result, decisions were made too late to be of use. Secondly, uncertainty forced decisions to be remade at all levels of the organization.

A second source of deterioration in decision making was distortion of some kinds of information. For example, some administrators were very uncomfortable about the possibility of not being able to meet obligations because the margin of safety had become so narrow. In reaction to that discomfort, individuals began to make conservative estimates of resources and exaggerate expenditures. Frequently, only one or two other administrators knew of the decision to obscure the figures. Sometimes the error would be compounded by several administrators, each building in a margin of safety. In one university errors of over one million dollars were discovered to have accumulated from such procedures. As a result of these techniques, internal estimates of accounts lost some of their reliability. There was no motivation to do this when there were sufficient resources.

Information was also distorted in the attempt to protect certain kinds of expenditures by obscuring them.[5] One example of this obfuscation was the hiding of administrative costs. The control boards were convinced that there was much administrative fat in university budgets, and they set about to cut it out. As a consequence, there were changes in the way administrative costs were reported. Faculty and administrative positions were often lumped together in the category "academic." Some academic positions were redefined as nonacademic, such as computer applications positions. Sometimes positions were cut at the campus level, where they were obvious, and slipped in in an undifferentiated manner in the college offices. This was particularly true of counseling. Some costs of administration were included in the cost of instruction. Thus the line for an expenditure disappeared, while the expense and the function did not.

Other kinds of information also became less reliable in an attempt to protect those costs from being cut. It became increasingly difficult to estimate how much money was being spent on research, which was a second target of the cost conscious state board. Research assistants came to be defined as teaching assistants, without apparent change of function. The line item for sabbaticals was eliminated from the budget. The cost of sabbaticals had to be absorbed in the departmental budgets.

To this point, two sources of distorted information have been identified: the first was the withholding of information about fund balances in order to put in a margin of financial safety; the second was the attempt to hide expenses which had been identified by the board as likely to be cut. A third source of distorted information was the attempt to make subunits and programs look less expensive. For example, within the limits posed by enrollment records, departments rearranged some of the faculty time reports (with the apparent connivance of administrators). Since faculty time reports were used in the cost study on which allocations to the universities depended, such distortion was an entirely reasonable response.

A fourth source of distorted information was the intensified scramble for resources internal to the university. Since all positions that fell vacant in the departments were collected up at the dean's level for reallocation, departments began to hide vacancies. The number of faculty actually holding permanent positions became increasingly difficult to ascertain. Just as the department heads hid vacancies to prevent the dean from taking the lines, deans hid lapsing resources so that campus-level officials would not claim the funds. Thus figures on the amount of lapsing funds and the number of faculty positions became increasingly unreliable.

To summarize, the two-step model did not anticipate either the continued effects of uncertainty, or the systematic distortion of information which accompanied the retrenchment period.

A third problem with the two-step model is that it assumed termination of retrenchment at a favorable juncture for the organization. Since there is no well-defined point at which the organization is performing efficiently, budget-cutters may go right past the hypothetical point of maximum efficiency to impair organizational functioning and adaptability. If the amount of resources available for rewards and the likelihood of receiving rewards becomes too low, then individuals will stop trying to maximize goals. If this occurs, there will be a reduced likelihood of setting in motion self-corrective mechanisms to reduce the financial stress. The ability of the organization to innovate may also be seriously impaired.

In order to deal with the possibility that retrenchment might not be terminated at a favorable point, a supplementary schema was devised linking the probability of maximizing with the level of resources. The assumption has been made that individuals maximize when there is both a need to do so and a hope of succeeding if the effort is made. Utilizing this assumption, the following schema emerges: (1) during periods of abundance, there is no need to maximize; (2) when resources fall a little, there is both a need to maximize, and enough resources to reward maximizing behavior; (3) when resource levels fall even further, the need is increased but the likelihood of success is reduced so low the effort to maximize will not be made.

The evidence observed to support this model indicates the actual process did not occur in the order postulated. Rather, when the financial stress began, decision making changed from "no need" to "no hope." Administrators responded by trying to encourage maximizing, and to the extent that resources were available, succeeded in bringing about some improvement.

For example, during the period of expansion, tenure decisions had been lenient, in the research universities as well as in the teaching universities. Departments that wished to improve quality did not need to free up slots by not granting tenure. They could hire from the outside.

When financial stress began, several changes occurred. First, the level of new hiring slowed down (see table 9.3). The proportion of faculty who were tenured began to rise, even though it was still reasonably low on most campuses because of the recent hiring. The control boards, anticipating enrollment drops, feared that the increase in percent tenured would prevent the universities from reducing size when the time came. They put pressure on the university administrators to control tenure more strictly.[6]

TABLE 9.3. NEW HIRING, RURAL UNIVERSITY

Year	Total No. New Contracts	No. of New Permanent Contracts
1969–70	219	138
1970–71	250	111
1971–72	154	48
1972–73	158	34
1973–74	168	41

Because they could no longer change by growth, the departments had an interest in freeing up slots by nonrecommendation for tenure. But if they did so, they might not be given a replacement slot. Heads were forced by the low probability of success to continue to recommend mediocre faculty since the likely alternative was no faculty member at all.

This departmental strategy forced the decision between candidates on to higher-level faculty and administrative committees.[7] All administrators dealing with personnel affairs agreed that this had occurred. They reported that they were seeking ways of forcing the decision back on the departments. One solution they used in limited measure was to guarantee a department it would be able to replace if it made the difficult choice of nonrecommendation. This guarantee was given only to departments that had college support for improving the department. Where this agreement existed, the department heads willingly made the decisions between candidates. For the other departments, however, the chance of reward was too slight to motivate maximizing behavior. The deans could not guarantee replacement positions in the face of constant fears of budget cuts.

Satisficing decisions due to the uncertainty of reward for maximizing were observed a number of other times in the study. For example, at one university, the departments refused to go along with a modified zero-base allocation schema in which each department gave up 5 percent of its budget with the hope of gaining all or more than all the 5 percent back through new proposals. The likelihood of improving the departments' budgetary position was seen as so low that no effort was made to win the pool of funds.

When department heads were asked the best strategies for increasing their budget during the retrenchment period, they replied that they had strategies to protect the level of the budget, but not to increase it. They felt that if they tried to increase their budgets, they could end up worse off than they already were. Finally, some reported that they had stopped competing for funds for innovation. The competition was so keen that the likelihood of success was too small to motivate the effort involved in writing up proposals.

Stated in general terms, when resources were reduced, the motivation to maximize goals was increased while the likelihood of gaining rewards was decreased. When the chance of reward was reduced too far, administrators were not willing to risk trying to maximize goals.

Summary and Conclusions

For the universities in the study, retrenchment was accompanied by increased uncertainty. The separate effects of retrenchment and uncertainty, and their combined effect on decision making, are outlined as follows:

1. Reduced resources brought about changes in allocation procedures, including increasing the explicitness of decision-making criteria and increasing the utilization of resources to solve organizational level problems. These changes also contributed to the expansion of the information base and the increased use of this information in decision making. The budget reductions also contributed to the distortion of many kinds of information used in allocation.
2. Increased uncertainty had the effect of causing many decisions to be made again and again, and also caused many decisions to be less timely.
3. The combined effect of reduced resources and uncertainty was to reduce rewards so far that many decision makers did not try to maximize goals. The possibility of reversing the financial decline was thereby reduced.

As a result of financial stress and accompanying uncertainty, some aspects of decision making improved while others deteriorated. A two-step model of initial confusion followed by gradual improvement was found to be inadequate to describe many of the changes in the universities studied. The results of five case studies are too narrow a base on which to generalize, but they do suggest the limits of generalizability of earlier formulations, and they also suggest some avenues for future research.

Notes

1. The larger study deals with such issues as the effect of retrenchment on flexibility, differentiation, centralization, and the level of professionalism in the organization. It includes discussions of the tenure situation and changing evaluation practices. Readers interested in these issues are referred to my Ph.D. dissertation, "Financial Retrenchment and Organizational Change: Universities Under Stress" (University of Chicago, 1976). For a general orientation to universities' financial problems and budgeting practices, see Frederick Balderston, *Managing Today's University* (San Francisco: Jossey-Bass, 1974).
2. Richard Cyert and James March, *A Behavioral Theory of the Firm* (Englewood Cliffs, N.J.: Prentice-Hall, 1963); and James March and Michael Cohen, *Leadership and Ambiguity* (New York: McGraw-Hill, 1974).
3. This strategy was acknowledged to me by a member of the state board.
4. The relationship between uncertainty and reluctance to commit resources is discussed in James D. Thompson, *Organizations in Action* (New York: McGraw-Hill, 1967), p. 150.
5. Aaron Wildavsky, *The Politics of the Budgetary Process* (Boston: Little, Brown, 1974), p. 104.
6. At Research University, one administrator described the tightening of tenure in terms of a drop from 252 faculty receiving tenure to 150 receiving tenure "without a commensurate drop in the size of the cohort."
7. The changing location of the tenure decision, as well as the changing location of many allocation decisions, were part of a general tendency toward centralization. For more on this topic, see Irene Rubin, "Centralization and Retrenchment in the University" (paper presented at the annual meeting of the Midwest Sociological Society, 1976).

David W. Singleton, Bruce A. Smith,
and James R. Cleaveland

10. Zero-Based Budgeting in Wilmington, Delaware

In recent years, governments at every level have shown growing interest in adopting progressive management techniques. These techniques are in stark contrast to such factors as tradition and political considerations, which have historically played a central role in governmental management. The rapid growth in governmental expenditures in recent years, and the fiscal crises confronting many governmental units, have contributed significantly to the growing interest in adopting these modern approaches to management.

As in the private sector, the fundamental area of management in the public sector is the planning-budgeting-accountability process. Consequently, it is in this area that a large share of public sector management concern and improvement has taken place. Executive budgeting, performance budgeting, and the program planning and budgeting system (PPBS) all represent innovations—and advances—in this field.

One of the major drawbacks in most budgeting systems is their primary focus on the increases from year to year in various accounting categories, with little systematic regard for programmatic priorities and results. A relatively new approach to planning and budgeting—zero-base budgeting—aims to overcome this drawback by subjecting all proposed activities and expenditures to the type of intensive scrutiny normally reserved for proposed new programs. Zero-base budgeting, or ZBB, originated in the private sector and has been little used in the public sector. This article presents a case history of its implementation in the municipal government of Wilmington, Delaware.

With a resident population of 80,000, and a daily commuter influx from the suburbs of another 60,000, Wilmington is far and away Delaware's largest city, and its commercial hub. The city also houses half of the state's welfare recipients, a quarter of the senior citizens, a quarter of the persons with incomes below the poverty line, and nearly a third of the crime—although it represents only 15 percent of the state's population. Since 1960, the city's resident population has declined 17 percent.

For fiscal 1976, Wilmington's general operating budget was $34.8 million, of which $9.1 million was an operating subsidy to the local school district. In addition, the city operates separate funds for its water, sewer, and Marine Terminal operations, totaling $11.3 million in fiscal 1976, and administers another $10.2 million annually in federal, state and private grant funds. The city's capital budget for fiscal 1976 amounted to $12.5 million.

Wilmington's governmental structure, under home-rule charter, is characterized as "strong mayor-council" form. The present Mayor, Thomas C. Maloney, has held office since 1973. During that time, Maloney has established a national reputation for fiscal restraint, limiting the growth in the city's operating budget to only 18.9 percent for all four of his budgets combined—compared to 16 percent annually under his predecessor. A mainstay of Maloney's approach has been improved management of resources, and dramatic productivity improvements in a variety of city services.

In their continuing review of the planning-budgeting-accountability process in Wilmington, Mayor Maloney and his staff had identified a variety of disadvantages with the existing process—a fairly typical, although heavily detailed, line-item approach. Among the more significant difficulties were:

Insufficient information. The existing budget process provided little useful information about the nature and level of services provided, the reason for providing the service, the beneficiaries of the service, or the resources needed to provide a specific level of service.

Existing level assumed. In general, the budgeting process took as given the level of funding from the current year, and focused almost entirely on the increase sought for the coming year. Expenditures included in previous budgets usually required no significant justification.

No trade-offs. Although the city did not have sufficient resources to fund all services at the requested—or even current—level, there was no meaningful process available to make choices and trade-offs among the city's different services on anything even approaching a cost/benefit basis.

Impact of change unclear. There was no mechanism to predict the impact of significant changes in the funding of particular services, and no systematic way to identify the absolute minimum level of service (if any) which the city must provide. Similarly, there was no way to project the likely benefits of significant funding increases in a particular service.

Although these problems are relatively common to all levels of government, they were exacerbated in Wilmington's case by the severe and continuing fiscal problems which beset Wilmington and so many of America's older cities:

Little or no growth in existing revenue sources, coupled with a high level of inflation and excessive unemployment.

Locked-in union wage settlements in the 5–7.5 percent range.

Relatively "fixed" expenses, such as pensions, debt service, insurance, and the public school subsidy, consuming roughly half the available revenues.

Continuing demands for new programs (or continuation of programs formerly federally funded), particularly social services.

Strong aversion to any tax increases, which tend to accelerate the erosion of the city's tax base.

As a result of these concerns, members of Mayor Maloney's staff were attracted by the concept when they learned of the successful use of ZBB in the private sector.[1] After further research, discussions with a consulting firm having considerable ZBB experience, and consultation with city officials in Garland, Texas, one of the few jurisdictions which had utilized ZBB, a decision was made in the late autumn of 1975 to promptly implement ZBB in Wilmington.

In most organizations, the one type of budget request certain to receive intensive screening and analysis is the one that proposes to establish a new service. It is likely to be reviewed as to desirability and need for the service, beneficiaries of the service, reasonableness of proposed costs, potential future implications, and availability of funds—often in terms of relative priority of all proposed new services. Zero-base budgeting aims to apply this same type of process, in a more sophisticated manner, to all proposed expenditures.

Essentially, ZBB seeks to accomplish this through a process which divides all proposed activities (and expenditures) into cohesive units of manageable size, subjects them to detailed scrutiny, and ultimately establishes a rank-order of those units which, given unlimited resources, would be funded. A selected level of expenditure is then matched against the final rank ordering, and if funds are not sufficient to cover the entire listing, lowest priority items are left unfunded until the cumulative total of the funded priority list exactly matches the level of funding that is available. The final priority list, balanced with available funds, then becomes the budget.

ZBB is a sophisticated management tool which provides a systematic method of reviewing and evaluating all operations of the organization, current or proposed; allows for budget reductions and expansions in a planned, rational manner; and encourages the reallocation of resources from low to high priority programs. Because of the nature of the process involved, ZBB also tends to have some important fringe benefits, such as involving more managers in the budgeting process, providing more information and options to decision makers, and establishing a systematic basis for management by objectives and priorities.

The foundation of ZBB is a four-step analytic process. Conceptually, the steps are:

1. *Establish budget units.* A budget unit is a grouping of existing or proposed activities which might be identified as a "program." It might consist of only one distinct activity, as in the case of trash collection in Wilmington's budget, or it may consist of a group of closely related activities, as in the case of Wilmington's recreation program. In nearly every case in Wilmington, the budget units were smaller than a department, consisting of the previously established divisions within most departments. As a result, the budget units did not create a new and unfamiliar organizational structure, and each budget unit had a readily identifiable manager.

2. *Divide budget units into service levels.* Since the variety, quantity, and quality of service to be provided is usually a more realistic question than whether or not a given budget unit will be funded at all, each budget unit is divided into several alternative levels of service. In most cases in Wilmington, this began with a level at about half of current, and advanced in steps through a slightly reduced level, the current level, and a possible expanded level. Each level represents a forecast of the cost and service consequences of operating at that level. In Wilmington's budget, the 61 budget units were eventually divided into a total of 194 service levels, with from 1 to 7 levels per budget unit.

3. *Analyze service levels.* Given the relatively small size and programmatic cohesiveness of the budget units and the service levels, it is then possible to analyze each segment of the proposed budget in considerable detail. The need to provide a given level of a particular service may be explored. Potential alternative approaches to meet a particular need may be identified. The manpower and other costs proposed to provide a given level of service may be examined for reasonableness. A given level of marginal cost may be compared to a given marginal increase in the quality or quantity of service.

4. *Priority ranking of all service levels.* Following the analytic process, all of the potentially desirable service levels from all of the budget units, as revised and finalized, are rank-ordered into a single list. The basic concept is that a given service level is ranked higher than all of the service levels that would be foregone, if necessary, to make available the funds for that given service level. Meanwhile, a level of expenditure (typically the projection of revenue from existing sources) is selected. Since, generally, revenues are not sufficient to cover the entire list, the priority rankings determine which service levels will be funded and which will not.

In practice, the ZBB process is considerably more complex than this conceptual framework. Wilmington's experience with ZBB, in chronological order, is presented in the following sections.

Following Mayor Maloney's decision in the late autumn of 1975 to implement ZBB in Wilmington, a variety of planning and decision making became necessary. In recognition of the priority ascribed to the project by the mayor, two members of the mayor's staff were, from the outset, given essentially full-time responsibility for ZBB. Also, a consulting firm was retained to assist.

The first step was the development of a detailed timetable, from the starting point in mid-November 1975 to the charter-mandated City Council submission date, April 1, 1976. From the outset, it was recognized that the schedule was tight, with little allowance for slippage.

The major milestones of the schedule were:

Task	Completion
Determination of Agencies to be Included	December 5
Review and Approval of Budget Manual	December 12
Training Program	December 19
Preliminary Departmental ZBB Submissions	January 16
Final Departmental ZBB Submissions	January 30
Departmental Hearings	February 27
Preliminary Ranking and Revenue Estimate	March 5
Mayor's Approval of Final Ranking	March 19
Presentation of Budget to Council	April 1
Approval of Budget by Council	June 1

A fundamental decision was the comprehensiveness of the ZBB process. The possibility of including only some departments or only certain expenditures (such as personnel costs) was discussed. However, the ranking process which culminates ZBB was judged to be far more meaningful if all requests competing for the General Fund were ranked competitively.

While Wilmington's water, sewer, and Marine Terminal funds are maintained independently of the General Fund, it was decided to include all these funds in the ZBB process—although they would be ranked separately. This was done both to strengthen the overall resource allocation process, and also because any year-end surpluses in these funds are transferred to the General Fund, thus giving expenditures in these funds a direct impact on the General Fund.

Likewise, federal and state grant funds, which had never previously been included in the budgeting process (except for federal revenue sharing), were to be included. In each case, federal and state grant funds were to be identified as such, but shown as part of the relevant budget unit and service level. The inclusion of grant funds would provide significant additional information, not previously available to decision makers in a systematic manner. In many cases, these data would show major activities that had been little known to decision makers because they used no city funds. In some cases, the data identify critical areas with heavy dependence on grant funds, which might have to be assumed by city funds upon expiration of the grants.

The major exclusion frlm ZBB was to be the operating subsidy to the local school district. In view of the limited time available, the relative autonomy of the Board of Education, and the fact that the bulk of the schools' funding comes directly from state appropriations, it was considered infeasible to include the schools in the first implementation of ZBB.

The other significant exclusion from ZBB was to be so-called fixed expenses. Due to the lack of short-term control and discretion over these expenditures, items such as pensions, debt service, and insurance were omitted from the process.

Once the extent of the inclusion in ZBB had been determined, it was necessary to identify budget units. In the great majority of cases, budget units were selected to correspond with the established divisions within city departments. Thus, for example, Wilmington's Public Works department was divided into eleven budget units, corresponding to its eleven divisions, Planning and Development was assigned four budget units matching its established divisional structure, and the Auditing and Treasurer's departments were each assigned one budget unit, since there were no established divisions within those departments. In a few cases of very large divisions with highly varied functions, budget units were established to subdivide the established divisions. Thus, in the Department of Public Safety, the police and fire divisions were subdivided into, respectively, six and three budget units.

A critical step in the planning process was the development of forms. The unique needs of every jurisdiction make it improbable that any set of standardized forms can be used for ZBB. In Wilmington's case, consideration was given to such local factors as past budget practice, accounting system needs, availability of data, and other factors in developing ZBB forms. Where possible, the forms were designed to resemble the previously used budget forms. A total of seven forms were designed and utilized, although later experience suggests that the process can and should be somewhat simplified, with the number of forms reduced.

The final planning step was the preparation of a budget manual, containing ZBB instructions as well as traditional data, such as salary scales, hospitalization insurance premiums, and submission deadlines. Although it was recognized that the manual would have to be supplemented with training and technical assistance support, the manual did serve a useful purpose as the only written compendium of ZBB forms and instructions.

Recognizing the need for technical assistance, a team of nine budget analysts was assembled from the Mayor's Office, the Finance Department, the Department of Planning and Development and City Council's staff. All had past experience in fiscal analysis. After a period of intensive training, one of the budget analysts was to be assigned to each city department, to assist them in responding to the demands of ZBB.

With these steps completed, ZBB was ready for presentation to the city's departments for implementation.

The impending implementation of ZBB was formally announced to Wilmington's department heads by the mayor in late November 1975. Although — as with any radical departure from the past practice — there was some criticism and resistance, cooperation and support from the departments generally proved to be excellent.

Actually, the first involvement by most departments had been in early November, when the city's consultants met with department heads to gather their impressions of the former budget process, suggestions to improve the process, and sufficient information regarding departmental operations to identify budget units. This information was all used in developing Wilmington's ZBB format.

Following the formal announcement, department heads and budget unit managers (usually division managers) were split into two workshops, of about twenty-five participants each, for training. Each group received two half-day training sessions, at which budget manuals and forms were also distributed. The first session was an orientation to ZBB concepts and general procedures, while the second session was used to review specific instructions in the manual and to discuss samples of completed forms.

The first major process for departments—the preliminary analysis—focused largely on the definition of service levels. As the most radical and fundamental concept of ZBB, it is essential that service levels be soundly developed. Departments were given some guidance in defining service levels, but functioned largely on their own. For each service level of each budget unit, departments were asked to submit basic information.

Some departments felt that a reduced service level might be misconstrued as a recommendation to operate at that level, and resisted proposing reduced levels. As a result, all budget unit managers were instructed that service levels represented options, not recommendations, and the first level must not exceed 40–60 percent of the current expenditure level. Generally, a second level below current service was to be proposed, then the current level, and finally an improved level of service (when desirable), yielding a recommended minimum of four service levels. In fact, budget units ultimately submitted averaged three service levels each.

The structuring of service levels is cumulative. If a given service level is funded for a department, those that precede it will also be funded—although those that follow will not necessarily be funded. This assumption means that the costs for each level are costs to be added to prior levels in a department in order to produce the higher level of service.

Service levels vary either the quantity or the quality of a department's operations, or both. For example, in firefighting, the first service level might be either *quantity variation*—reduce by 50 percent the number of fire companies but maintain manning on each company as at present; *quality variation*—maintain the same number of fire companies as at present but reduce by 50 percent the manning on each; *both*—reduce both the number of companies and the manning on each by 25 percent.

Service levels were devised in all these manners in Wilmington. Sanitation, in Public Works, varied primarily the frequency, and thus the quality, of service:

Level 1: Once weekly pickup at curb
Level 2: Twice weekly pickup at curb
Level 3: Pickup from rear or side yard, plus special services and school pickups (current level)

The department apparently did not see sufficient marginal improvement to show possible service expansion to a fourth level (which could have been three times a week pickup).

Other departments defined service levels largely in terms of the quantity of services provided on a prioritized basis, holding quality relatively constant. For example, the police patrol division budget unit in Public Safety divided current and proposed services into six levels:

Level 1: Basic patrol and preliminary investigation of major crimes

Level 2: Preliminary investigation of all criminal complaints; response to priority noncriminal calls

Level 3: Follow-up on all criminal and noncriminal calls; operation of jail and selective parking enforcement

Level 4: Increased parking enforcement; full-service response to noncriminal calls

Level 5: Additional patrols, school crossing guards (current level)

Level 6: Expansion of patrol, parking enforcement, and school-crossing functions

Here, the department saw sufficient marginal improvement to show expansion to a sixth service level.

Whatever the approach, the objective was to show the department's assessment of what services should be provided if only a certain level of funding was available.

Once levels were defined, an estimated cost for each level was calculated. This did not prove to be difficult, since the bulk of the costs were personnel and fringe benefits, which could be readily correlated with the manner in which personnel were divided among the levels. The service levels and costs, along with certain additional data and a preliminary ranking by the department head were submitted by the departments in mid-January 1976. This provided the mayor's staff with an estimate of the total budget, and an opportunity to discuss possible revisions in the service-level structure and priority rankings with the departments. As a result of this process, several significant revisions were made.

In the latter part of January, departments completed the detailed final service-level descriptions. In addition to the information reported in the preliminary phase, more precise data and certain supplemental information were required for the final submission.

A unique feature of ZBB is the "program measures" reported for each service level. Up to seven measures could be selected for each budget unit, which would be repeated for each service level and reflect the increasing quality or quantity at each higher service level. Unfortunately, many departments had not accumulated such data, and were unable to provide the desirable level of documentation of program measures. However, this process has established a foundation for future years, and has led to efforts by several departments as well as the mayor's staff to begin the accumulation of more useful data.

The final service-level description was accompanied by a detailed line-item listing of all costs associated with that service level, including personnel, fringe benefits, materials, supplies, and equipment. These forms resulted in a considerable bulk of paperwork and a significant workload to the departments, although the work was more time-consuming than onerous.

In addition to the service-level and line-item listings, each department also submitted a departmental priority ranking of all budget units and all service levels within the department. A running cumulative total was included to show the amount required to fund the department to a particular priority level. Also, departments were asked to include a memorandum indicating the rationale for the order of prioritization selected.

The focus then shifted to the mayor's staff for the preparation of the city's consolidated budget.

The Mayor's Office review of departmental budget submissions began with a preliminary assessment of the city's financial position. Departmental general fund requests,[2] including requests for new or expanded services, amounted to $19.9 million, an increase of 15.6 percent over the existing budget. With a 1–2 percent revenue growth likely, requests would exceed revenues by roughly $2.6 million.

Wilmington's ZBB process presented a number of alternatives, which could be used singly or in combination to deal with the $2.6 million gap: (1) raise taxes to increase revenues; (2) reduce the cost of providing a specified level of service; or (3) not fund lowest-priority service levels.

The first alternative is generally least desirable. For policy reasons, it was ruled out in Wilmington at this time. The second alternative is generally most desirable, in that it tends to represent an increase in efficiency or productivity. In practice, this approach is most similar to traditional budgeting, with the prime emphasis on large or unusual expenditures, and expenditures showing significant increases from the current budget. Ultimately, Wilmington was successful in reducing the departmental budget requests by approximately $900,000, or 4.5 percent, through these line-item cuts.

Once revenues are established, and the cost of each service level has been reduced as much as possible, the third alternative—prioritizing—comes into play. This alternative represents the unique characteristic of ZBB. For Wilmington, this provided the mechanism for identifying $1.2 million in departmental requests that were of lowest priority, and would not be funded.

A major portion of the administration review process was consumed by departmental budget hearings. Each department was afforded a session of 3–6 hours duration, attended by both members of the mayor's staff and representatives of City Council Finance Committee. At the hearings, discussions focused on opportunities to reduce the cost of providing a specified level of service, as well as on the rationale for the structuring of the service levels and the prioritization of the department's service levels. Numerous minor changes in the costs of service levels were made at the hearings, generally with the consent of the department head. Changes in prioritization were not made at the hearings, although areas of disagreement with a department head's rankings were identified. Budget hearing discussions also covered program measures, beneficiaries of the service, involvement of grant funds, and marginal cost of increasing service levels.

The consensus of both departmental officials and members of the mayor's staff was that with the introduction of ZBB, the hearings provided a more comprehensive and penetrating view of a department's activities than hearings in previous years. Specifically, the basis for proposed expenditures was usually related much more directly and rationally to services provided than in the past. Also, more discussion of the value of specific services, and the need for specific services, was possible.

Separately from the hearings, members of the mayor's staff also reviewed the departmental submissions for completeness, clarity, arithmetic accuracy, and other largely technical considerations. This process, along with the hearings, resulted in minor adjustments to the total cost for most of the service levels.

Formal ranking of priorities is the crucial and distinctive step in ZBB. A variety of criteria may be used, both formally and informally. Some criteria are relatively general, probably applicable to any jurisdiction, while some are more related to local goals and objectives. Key criteria considered in Wilmington include

> Importance of the service level in terms of the perceived health, welfare, safety, and satisfaction of city residents
> Statutory, charter, and contractual commitments met by the service level
> Potential consequences of not providing the service level
> Federal and state funds received dependent on a particular expenditure of city funds
> Informal assessment of the quality of the service provided
> Cost effectiveness of the service level
> Preference, where feasible, to direct services to the public over administrative costs

The final analysis and ranking process began with the decision to lump together a group of services identified as essential, without further prioritization. Little benefit was seen in discussing whether the most fundamental service level of police, fire, or sanitation service is more important. Clearly, all these services will be provided, at least, at the first level of service. Thus, 34 of the 196 service levels were lumped together as a "basic" group, and ranked above all other services. Since most budget units had developed a first-service level of 40 to 60 percent of the existing funding level, the total cost of the "basic" group amounted to $10.0 million.

After isolating the "basic" group, $9.0 million in requested service levels remained, as against only $7.8 million in forecasted revenue. Efforts focused on analysis and ranking of the 162 service levels remaining.

Numerical ranking of 162 separate items is quite difficult—particularly when the 162 items are as varied as the service levels in Wilmington's budget. Consequently, the process began by dividing the remaining service levels into four groups: high priority, medium priority, low priority, and service levels not to be funded for policy reasons.[3]

The initial ranking of the remaining service levels showed that revenues were sufficient to cover the entire "high" and "medium" priority groups and part of the "low" priority group. Service levels undesirable for policy reasons were ranked below the "low" priority group, but were effectively eliminated from further consideration.

With the number of service levels to be ranked now reduced to groups of manageable size, all the service levels in each group were then numerically prioritized. For the "high" and "medium" groups, this was somewhat academic, since revenues were sufficient to fund all service levels in the group. However, it was judged important to establish these rankings as the first organized, comprehensive statement of the city's priorities.

For the "low" priority group the specific numerical ranking was of critical importance. Of the 56 service levels within the group, funds were sufficient for only about half. After rankings were assigned, a cumulative funding total was calculated to determine the point at which revenues were exhausted. An analysis of the rankings showed that many of the service levels below the cutoff point were new or expanded levels of service, although 21 levels of service currently being provided also fell below the cutoff. Two levels of new or expanded service ended up above the cut-off point.

The complete rankings, as proposed by the mayor's staff, were then presented to the mayor for his consideration. The mayor directed a number of minor changes, but generally expressed satisfaction with the priority order. However, the mayor was concerned that a number of existing service levels involving incumbent employees fell below the the cutoff, necessitating immediate layoffs and service cutbacks.

As an alternative, the mayor's staff developed a factor known as "special attrition." A factor had already been allowed for normal attrition, representing funds that would not be spent for salaries and fringe benefits during the period positions remain vacant between incumbents. Now, in order to avoid layoffs and abrupt service cutbacks, an additional factor was calculated representing anticipated savings from positions which would be left unfilled for the balance of the fiscal year when they become vacant. Although this may still entail modest service cutbacks, unless compensating productivity increases are achieved, they would occur on a scattered basis throughout the year. While the exact positions to be left vacant could not be identified, past turnover experience indicated that the savings budgeted for "special attrition" were reasonable and attainable.

Following the addition of "special attrition" and minor priority adjustments, the ranking was finalized. No layoffs would be required, although some existing services without incumbent personnel still fell below the cutoff. All told, the "basic" group and ranks 1–110 were shown as funded; ranks 111–162 were shown as not funded.

With the completion of prioritization the budget was then ready for final housekeeping details, printing and submission to City Council.

In a radical departure from most jurisdictions that have implemented ZBB, Mayor Maloney decided that the Council should receive the actual ZBB documentation. Other jurisdictions using ZBB have recast their budget in traditional format for legislative consideration and public distribution. Although this decision was sure to significantly increase the complexity of City Council's work, Mayor Maloney regarded Council's involvement in the ZBB process as critical.

City Council's exposure to ZBB had actually begun at the start of the City's involvement. The councilmen were thoroughly briefed before the decision was made to adopt the process, and had registered their support by adoption of a resolution. In addition, Council's Finance Committee Chairman and a staff member had attended all departmental hearings.

Council's consideration of the completed ZBB budget began with an orientation session, devoted to both the process and the output of ZBB. The ZBB budget represented such a total departure from past budgeting practice—in process as well as appearance—that a thorough orientation was essential.

As in past years, Council then proceeded to hold public budget hearings for each department. The hearings, which lasted from one to three hours each, repeated some of the discussion from the administration's budget hearings, but primarily served as a forum for the discussion of concerns of particular relevance to the councilmen. Several departments used the hearings to appeal either a ranking or a line-item cut made earlier by the administration. In a number of cases, members of the public or city employees raised questions about specific items in the budget. Members of the mayor's staff attended all meetings and were often asked to explain the rationale behind the priorization of a particular service level.

Prior to the hearings, Council agreed that no actual changes in the rankings would be discussed until all hearings were complete and all comments were heard. This avoided moving service levels up and down the ranking until all hearings were completed and the Council could put all the levels in perspective.

Initially many of the councilmen approached the budget much as they had approached past budgets. Most of the discussion concerned the incremental changes to line items. However, as the hearings proceeded, greater and greater attention focused on ZBB considerations. The rationale for a particular ranking, for example, was discussed more and more frequently. Much interest centered on the federal and state grant funds—information that the Council had never before had available in a systematic manner. There was also steadily increasing discussion of program measures and the marginal costs associated with a higher level of service.

One problem was the greatly expanded amount of paperwork. As part-time city officials, many councilmen had difficulty finding the time to digest the large volume of information on a department prior to the hearing. The line-item budget detail, a 1,000-page document, was simply too heavy and bulky to be readily taken home for review.

At the conclusion of the hearings, Council's staff checked with all councilmen to determine what changes in the administration's budget should be considered. After all had been polled, only five changes were proposed. Three proposed changes concerned service levels, with a total cost of $15,000, which had been ranked below the cutoff point but which Council wished to see funded. One change was a line-item cut of $6,000 within a funded service level, which the department head had argued for convincingly. The final proposed change of $8,000 was a service previously provided which the department involved had not included in their budget submission.

The latter proposal was most easily resolved by the administration's commitment to continue the service with personnel under a federally funded Summer Youth Program, thus not requiring any additional city funds.

Council met at some length to consider possible rerankings to accommodate the other desired additions to the budget. The process proved difficult. Every service level suggested for deletion, as a tradeoff, had its own supporters among the councilmen. Most of the service levels just above the cutoff point included incumbent personnel, whom the councilmen were not anxious to see laid off. A tax increase was seen as unpalatable.

Ultimately the small amount involved in the desired fiscal changes proved decisive. Council recommended to the mayor that the four service levels in question be reranked to include them in the budget and that all service levels then be reduced by 0.1 percent to provide the needed funds. Since extensive line-item cutting had already been undertaken, the mayor accepted the recommendation only with the understanding that the 0.1 percent savings would be achieved through attrition, by slightly increasing the time a position remained vacant between incumbents. Council agreed, and the appropriate rerankings were made. With these changes, the Council soon thereafter gave its approval to the entire budget.

Generally, City Council appears to have found ZBB preferable to the city's former process. A major reason appears to be that Council now gets more information, and more useful information, than they have ever had before. The ranked service-level format, although not legally binding on the mayor, provides Council with a strong moral commitment as to what services will be provided—whereas the old process had provided only a commitment as to what the line-item expenditures would be. Many councilmen have expressed a desire to continue the ZBB process in future years and possibly expand it to other areas, such as the operating subsidy to the school district and the city's capital budget.

It is important to establish the context in which zero-base budgeting was adopted in Wilmington. Essentially, it represented a logical step forward in a well-established process of fiscal restraint and improved management of resources. It followed earlier experimentation with other budgeting innovations, particularly program budgeting. It drew heavily on analytic and management staff resources that had been developed over an extended period. And it relied on the cooperation and support of the mayor, City Council, and city department heads. The process and the results could differ significantly in a different context. Insufficient time has passed to assess fully ZBB's impact on Wilmington. However, a number of conclusions may be drawn as to the benefits already derived, and the disadvantages.

On the positive side a key accomplishment has been the detailed identification of all the services provided by the city — regardless of funding source. Such information was never previously available in systematic form. Once identified, all programs and expenditures were reviewed to a level of detail usually reserved for proposed new programs.

Also beneficial is the establishment of a systematic prioritization of the city's services. This establishes a firm foundation for future years when the city's financial situation may require extremely difficult decisions, and helps assure that those decisions will be based on a well-developed set of priorities.

The ZBB process itself was beneficial in that it involved nearly all management personnel in the budgeting process, considerably more than in the past. Also, as a planning and budgeting process, ZBB involved these personnel in a far more comprehensive resource allocation process.

The ranking federal and state grant funds establishes a mechanism for identifying the importance of these funds to the city and anticipating the future demands to replace these funds with city funds when they expire. In effect, Wilmington has adopted a comprehensive planning and budgeting process for all its resources.

The statement of priorities and program measures by department heads serves as an excellent basis for a management by objectives program. In the past, the city's approach to management by objectives had been more general, making performance assessment more difficult. With the level of specific detail provided by ZBB, performance against objectives can be measured much more quantitatively.

ZBB has also involved City Council more meaningfully in the budget process. Specifically, it has given them a better picture of the issues involved and a direct involvement in the tradeoff process inherent to budgeting. Potentially ZBB could serve to very significantly increase the role of the legislative branch of government by providing more effective control of the planning and resource allocation process.

ZBB also has significant disadvantages. Foremost is the large increase in the time, effort, and paperwork required. Increased time devoted to the budget by city personnel, the need for consultants in the initial implementation, and increased printing costs probably resulted in a net increase of 100 percent in the cost of preparing the budget. The increased effort, and the high level of detail required, caused numerous complaints, especially from department heads. Particularly in the cases where a service is already rather well known to the city administration and City Council, such complaints are understandable.

The large size of the first service level in most budget units — 40 to 60 percent of current spending — may also have provided an opportunity to effectively shelter costs that might, if listed as separate service levels, be more seriously questioned. In a number of departments it appeared that overhead-type costs were unduly heavy in the initial service level, although if more time had been available, this could have been addressed by revisions in the proposed service levels.

Another limitation is the underlying assumption that the specified level of funding must be provided in order to obtain the specified level of service. Past experience suggests that improvements in efficiency and productivity may enable a specified level of service to be provided even with reduced funding levels. While the knowledge that reducing the cost of *each* proposed service level enables more service levels to be funded tends to encourage economy and stimulate productivity improvement, the stimulus may not be sufficiently strong to produce the desired results. Thus, it is desirable to undertake separate measures to promote efficiency and productivity in combination with the implementation of ZBB.

Wilmington's experience with ZBB has generally been positive and seems likely to lead to further use of ZBB in Wilmington. Combined with a variety of measures geared to improved organization effectiveness and economy, ZBB seems to be making a significant contribution. While ZBB would not necessarily prove beneficial in every jurisdiction, its implementation is certainly worthy of consideration.

Notes

1. Peter A. Pyhrr, "Zero Base Budgeting," *Harvard Business Review*, November–December 1970, pp. 111–21. *Zero Base Budgeting: A Practical Management Tool for Evaluating Expenses* (New York: Wiley, 1973).
2. Excluding fixed costs and the operating subsidy to the schools, which were not included in ZBB. These items were budgeted at $17.1 million.
3. For example, a proposed change in water billing procedure that would initially result in serious cash-flow problems.

REGINA E. HERZLINGER

11. Zero-Base Budgeting in the Federal Government: A Case Study

On February 14, 1977, President Carter asked each federal agency to develop its fiscal year 1979 budget using a zero-base budgeting system (ZBB), in accordance with instructions to be issued by the Office of Management and Budget (OMB). The substantial effort involved in fulfilling his request was to result in a "better" budget. Was this achieved? Were the benefits of the ZBB process worth the costs?

Many people were cynical of its prospects: "ZBB Is a Fraud" trumpeted a prominent *Wall Street Journal* headline.[1] Others were more sanguine about the process, some so euphoric as to contend that ZBB was the best thing since vitamin C, guaranteed to cure most organizational ailments.[2]

It is likely that ZBB, like most other managerial techniques, is neither a fraud nor a panacea. It is, rather, a process which can yield substantial benefits if properly implemented, but which can be neutral or even pernicious in its effect if sloppily or thoughtlessly executed. In order to better understand the technique of ZBB, its history in the Public Health Service (PHS) was carefully documented and evaluated through an extensive series of interviews. PHS was chosen because (1) it is representative of other large public organizations and (2) many observers felt that PHS had a fair measure of success in instituting the ZBB process.

This article describes the implementation of ZBB in the PHS, evaluates its efficacy, and generalizes these findings to the budgetary process in large public organizations similar to the PHS.

Background
The ZBB Process

In the incremental budgeting process traditionally used by government agencies, review is concentrated on proposed increases while the "base" (current level of spending) is given little scrutiny. In ZBB, the entire budget is reviewed, old programs as well as new, in three basic steps:

> Identification of "decision units"
> Formulation of "decision packages"
> Ranking and consolidation

A "decision unit" is usually an organizational entity that has an identifiable manager with the necessary authority to establish priorities and prepare budgets for all activities within the unit. The manager divides the unit's activities into a series of "decision packages," which are analyzed at various minimum, maintenance, and improvement funding levels. The costs and consequences of each package are documented, and the packages are then "ranked," either by the manager or group consensus (a task that is often the most sensitive part of ZBB). In large organizations, the decision packages are consolidated before being ranked in order to minimize the paper flow.

Starting from the top of the ranking, those packages that can be funded within the available total are included in the organization's formal budget request, unless the organization chooses to seek an increase in funding.

The Budgeting Process

Budgeting is one of the most ubiquitous topics in the literature of management as budgetary fads come and go with alarming regularity. The breadth of the literature on this subject is most likely due to the fact that the budgeting process is rarely successfully executed. Three aspects of budgeting are particularly controversial:

1. *The role of the budget.* Many organizations view the budget as that part of an integrated financial management cycle which bridges the planning and resource allocation functions to those of evaluation and control. Others view the budget as the method for delineating strategic plans and making critical resource allocation decisions. The difference between these two views is essentially one of timing. In the first, the budget is prepared *after* the plans and resource allocation decisions have been made; in the second, the budget is prepared *simultaneously* with fundamental planning and resource allocation decisions. ZBB fits neatly with both these views, either as an instrument of policy analysis and strategic choice or as a tool for assembling a budget that effectively communicates previously made plans and decisions.

2. *The scope or method of budgetary analysis* is another major area of controversy among the "incrementalists" who maintain that only additions to the base of the previous year's budget need to be analyzed, the "zero basers" who hold that the entire budget needs to be analyzed, and the "middle of the roaders" who think that any controversial program — whether old or new — ought to be subjected to an exhaustive zero-base analysis.

3. *The management of the budgetary process* is perhaps the most controversial area. Despite the fact that some procedures are generally followed by all well-managed organizations (i.e., the process is well delineated, governed by clear guidelines, and allotted an appropriate

amount of time and resources), there are substantial disagreements about the appropriate style for budgeting. Many organizations manage the process in a rigid, hierarchical manner, initiated and guided by the top layers of the organization. Some organizations prefer a more fluid, participatory style, spawned by the lower operational echelons. ZBB is premised on the notion that a participatory bottom-up style is central to the proper management of the budgetary process.

History of Zero-Base Budgeting

The concept of zero-base budgeting is a rather obvious one and has been traced as far back as 1924, when E. Hilton Young wrote:

> It must be a temptation to one drawing up an estimate to save himself the trouble by taking last year's estimate for granted, adding something to any item for which an increased expenditure is foreseen. Nothing could be easier, or more wasteful and extravagant. It is in that way obsolete expenditure is enabled to make its appearance year after year, long after reason for it has ceased to be.[3]

Its first formal use in the federal government occurred in 1962, when the U.S. Department of Agriculture experimented with ZBB. Aaron Wildavsky and Arthur Hammond reviewed the process and found it theoretically appealing but beyond the capacity of the agency to manage.[4] Despite its failure in the public sector, private firms, beginning in 1969 with Texas Instruments (TI), found the process of value. After Peter Phyrr of TI publicized his firm's positive experiences,[5] ZBB was used by an ever increasing number of corporations.

The manner in which it is used is somewhat surprising. A recent survey of fifty-four major corporate users found that ZBB was not widely regarded as a highly effective budgetary or resource allocation tool, but rather as a tool for learning more about the organization.[6] Similarly, George Minmier's evaluation of the ZBB process, as implemented in Governor Carter's administration of the State of Georgia, found that the process led to an improvement in the quality of management information and to greater involvement with budgeting, but that it had not changed the resource allocation or evaluation process in the state.[7]

Undaunted by these findings and by the widely publicized failures of previous attempts at budgetary reform in the federal government, such as the planning-programming-budgeting system, Carter made ZBB part of his platform and began its implementation shortly after his election.

The Public Health Service

In July 1944, Congress created the Public Health Service to serve as an umbrella organization for a number of medical research projects and health agencies being generously funded at the time. In the ensuing three decades, PHS became part of the newly created Department of HEW, and underwent numerous internal reorganizations (five from 1967 to 1972 alone). In 1977, when ZBB was instituted, PHS consisted of six operating agencies, among them the Health Services Administration (HSA), the Health Resources Administration (HRA), and the National Institutes of Health (NIH). Because of the complexity of their work and their powerful constituencies in Congress, many of these agencies, particularly NIH, were accustomed to operating with little, if any, interference from PHS.

One key official explained that the role of PHS was "not to make substantive decisions on where our agencies are going, but rather to create a mechanism so they can go where they want. We distribute blocks of funds to the agencies; they decide how to spend their funds." To help them carry out these duties, the Executive Office of PHS was well staffed and handsomely funded. However, the synergy originally envisioned among the different agencies constituting PHS never materialized, and the numerous reorganizations left their scars on PHS administrative personnel. The same official noted that "PHS was practically defunct in 1973."

After his election, President Carter had considerable difficulty filling the office of Assistant Secretary for Health. Quite a few people had refused the appointment. One appointee resigned after one month, "long enough to conclude that there is not much to [the job]."[8] At the time that work on ZBB began, PHS did not have a permanent presidential appointee at its helm.

Implementing ZBB in the Public Health Service

Introducing ZBB to the Executive Branch

When ZBB was instituted, the Executive Office decided that formal budget requests to Congress would retain the traditional format. Therefore, ZBB, once completed, had to be "crosswalked" to that format. Its advocates claimed that three major benefits of ZBB justified the double workload required:

1. ZBB leads to much better information about the extent and range of the organization's activities.
2. Because it requires a review of all activities (and not merely a review of new proposals), ZBB involves all managers in the budgetary process, forcing them to articulate their plans and motivating them to be creative about the process.
3. It clarifies organizational goals and therefore leads to greater cohesion and a shared sense of purpose across organizational levels.

As work on ZBB began, officials at PHS were optimistic that all three benefits would accrue to their member agencies. The agencies themselves, although wary of the incremental workload and cynical of the long-run future of ZBB, did anticipate a "clearer communication" among all levels of management. At OMB, the only person added to the staff to work on ZBB added the hope that "by going deeper within the agency, unneeded pet projects and functions that have outlived their usefulness will be eliminated."

The rest of the OMB staff was less enthusiastic. While they expected ZBB to help low- and middle-level managers articulate priorities and identify potential savings, they felt that time spent reviewing ZBB submissions distracted them from their proper mission. As one senior OMB official noted:

> OMB is not an investigative agency, nor a government-wide data bank, nor a postaudit function. Our examiners are spending much time right now helping the agencies structure their decision packages. They should be concentrating on larger problems....

Preparation for ZBB

In March 1977, a budget analyst in the Office of the Secretary (OS) of HEW convened a group of representatives from every HEW agency (each of the representatives had some training in ZBB) to produce the department's ZBB guidelines. After three weeks of work, OS issued a "FY '79 Budget Guidance" memorandum, with guidelines on budget funding levels, ranking procedures, and the formulation of decision units.

PHS began its ZBB preparations during the 1976 presidential campaign, when members of its central administrative staff were sent to ZBB training sessions. Near the end of March, PHS issued a document, referred to as the "Yellow Book," which specified decision units for each agency and gave instructions for assembling and ranking decision packages. The decision units were made identical to the existing budgeting activity structure to facilitate "crosswalking" and sufficiently large to minimize paper flow. NIH, for example, with a FY '78 budget request of $2.6 billion, was given eighteen decision units, eleven of them corresponding to its member institutes and the remaining seven to administrative and other support functions. One of those units, the National Heart, Lung, and Blood Institute, alone had a FY '78 budget of almost half a billion dollars. Although each agency could also identify other decision units for internal use, its decision packages were to be consolidated at the PHS-approved decision unit level. This requirement led to many of the problems later encountered with ZBB; the size of the decision units hindered subsequent analysis.

Managers of each of the decision units were to prepare at least three decision packages, reflecting "minimum," "maintenance," and "improvement" levels of operation. The first edition of the Yellow Book defined the maintenance funding level for each decision package as the President's FY '78 budget for that activity, the minimum funding level as 80 percent of the maintenance budget for that activity, and the improvement level as anything up to a 20 percent increase beyond the maintenance level, or $50 million, whichever was lower. These instructions were issued in a vacuum, however, since the Congress had not yet passed its version of the FY '78.

Many agencies were well into the budgetary process when a new set of definitions arrived. In the second edition of the Yellow Book (distributed on April 26), the definitions of minimum and maintenance budgets were revised to conform to HEW guidelines, issued on April 20, which provided that Carter's FY '78 budget be adjusted for certain built-in cost increases due to inflation. Each decision package was to consist of a cover sheet explaining the package, a "dollar data" form, and a "manpower data" form, the latter to be prepared with data gathered under each agency's Manpower Management Program.

Finally, the Yellow Book listed the six criteria that agency managers were to use for ranking decision packages: (1) health impact, (2) potential effectiveness, (3) sensitivity, (4) negative impact, (5) conformity with health strategy, and (6) appropriateness of the federal role. Almost all these criteria are justifiably used in making resource allocation decisions, but only one addressed the budgetary concern with effectiveness and efficiency.

OMB did not become formally involved until April 19, when it issued Bulletin 77-9, explaining ZBB terms and procedure. Its effect was nil, as described by a senior PHS official:

> It was not considered to be an action document. In fact, there were contradictions between that document and the budget guidance we had published up to that point. In those cases where there were contradictions, we told the agencies to follow the previous PHS guidance. Bulletin 77-9 played virtually no part in the PHS submission at that point, or in the submission to the Department later in the spring.

Ranking the Agency Submissions by PHS

On May 9, two weeks after the last guidelines were issued (after a massive effort), all six agencies submitted their budgets to the Executive Office of PHS. A few days before the individual agency submissions arrived, the Acting Assistant Secretary for Health sent to PHS a list (in order of importance) of five criteria to use in integrating the submissions: (1) containment of health care costs, (2) improved access to health care, (3) prevention of illness and disease, (4) knowledge development, and (5) all others. All these criteria were aimed at evaluating the fit between a particular activity and government policy. None questioned the success of the programs in meeting these policy goals.

The agencies criticized four aspects of these criteria:

1. The criteria were introduced *after* the agencies had completed their own rankings.
2. They differed from the six criteria previously articulated by PHS.

3. They were not appropriate to the nature of the work performed by the agency (for example, almost none of the bureaus had any impact on health cost containment).
4. The criteria were articulated by a temporary appointee.

Before applying these criteria, the budget staff of PHS consolidated the eight hundred packages they had received from the agencies. The staff director said:

> For NIH, the 354 decision packages in the original submission were consolidated into 110 for its eighteen decision units. For all the agencies, we validated each unit's maintenance-level packages by taking PHS criteria for the maintenance level and analyzing each line item. We dropped whatever didn't belong. Unfortunately, we couldn't do as thorough an analysis as we would have liked, in the time we had.

Each decision package was given a numerical rating according to its impact on the five priority areas. On the basis of those scores, the packages were grouped into minimum, maintenance, and improvement categories. The agencies' own rankings were ignored, except where very high or very low.

The PHS budget staff then met separately with the Division of Manpower Management, the Office of Policy Development and Planning, and the ten Regional Health Administrators to review the agency submissions. A number of reranking sessions followed, and after meeting with the Acting Assistant Secretary to review their progress, the staff sent a further reranking to the agencies. The agency directors were given twenty-four hours to appeal the rankings. After one final meeting when appeals were discussed, the budget staff issued a final ranking sheet to the agencies on May 25. No changes in rankings were allowed within PHS after that point.

Most of the changes that PHS had made in the agencies' original rankings appeared to be for political, not analytical, reasons. For example, HSA had given a low ranking to the PHS hospitals established in the eighteenth century to aid impoverished merchant seamen, feeling they were no longer necessary. However, the PHS staff felt it was politically unfeasible to suppress the hospitals and thus upgraded the ranking.

PHS analysis of the agency submissions (over $7 billion of decision packages) spanned the month of May, occupying over fifty people and a great deal of computer time and resources. In the end, the budget that emerged was not substantially different in size and emphasis from those of prior years.

ZBB in the Office oj the Secretary

When the PHS budget reached the Office of the Secretary of HEW on June 8, its numerous bulky volumes included each agency's now consolidated decision packages, a summary book with ranking sheets and tables relating to the FY '79 budget to previous budgets, a manpower analysis, and an overview letter explaining procedures and priorities. As was usual for review purposes, HEW divided the PHS agencies' budgets among four budget analysts in the Office of the Secretary. The four had already met with the Assistant Secretary for Planning and Evaluation to discuss health priorities.

The analysts had only two weeks for their review, far less than in past years. In order to assist them in managing this process, each of the decision packages was placed in one of three categories:

> *The Core:* those decision packages that would definitely be in the PHS budget
> *The Band:* decision packages to be studied with special attention
> *Improvement Budget:* decision packages of lowest priority

The placement of decision packages within the "core" area and the "band" area generally reflected presidential policy decisions rather than managerial concerns. In the course of their review, the analysts discovered the manpower statistics from PHS agencies were not reliable. Subsequently, they made some changes in dollar figures, disallowing some of the increases for inflation that PHS had instructed its agencies to include, and substantially changed the rankings within each of their three categories. However, they made virtually no changes *across* categories from their preliminary placement.

On June 30, approximately three weeks after his receipt of the PHS budget, HEW's Assistant Secretary for Management and Budget sent his recommendations to HEW's newly appointed Under Secretary, who with the Secretary and the rest of the OS staff spent the summer analyzing those programs in the "band" area of the budget of particular interest to the President.

Impact of Zero-Base Budgeting
Impact on the Budget

On September 15, the budget was sent to OMB. It was hardly affected by the ZBB effort. One official in the Office of the Secretary commented on the effects of the ZBB process from his vantage point:

> We've always tried to get PHS to give us their priorities but they never would. Now they have tried to give rankings. That's helpful to us. What bothers me about their standard decision package is that there is too much information to get on one sheet. The information is not as good as in previous years. And with very few exceptions, the agencies didn't really consider getting rid of programs. They just took 80 percent as minimum and proceeded from there without doing any serious analysis.

Impact of ZBB on the PHS Agencies

The response to ZBB from the PHS agencies varied. Some condemned it as a fruitless drain on resources, some were neutral, and a few felt ZBB to be helpful. Among the most hostile were the administrators of the National Institutes of Health and one of its members, the National Heart, Lung, and Blood Institute.

The National Institutes of Health (NIH) funds research projects, which may be conducted by outside contractors as well as NIH researchers. The projects are funded through a "peer review" process in which some three hundred committees, each with about thirty prominent scientists, recommend priorities and review most project applications.

NIH's egalitarian structure made the inevitably sensitive task of ranking even more difficult, and its administrators were chagrined by PHS's instructions. One commented:

> From those first meetings and instructions on ZBB, we understood that ranking would take place only at the improvement-budget level. Our administration knows our Institutes well; they have a good sense of their internal politics. They felt they could rank decision packages at the improvement levels. Then we got the Yellow Book and found we had to rank packages at the minimum and maintenance levels as well. They refused to rank below the improvement level.

The top NIH administrators presented their case to PHS:

> PHS said we didn't have any choice, but we refused. So we put together a list that appeared as a ranking, but was an alphabetical list. We told PHS that we weren't making choices at the minimum and maintenance levels.

Relations were aggravated by PHS's reluctance to allow the agencies to rerank their programs once PHS had made its decisions. As one senior NIH official said:

> We asked PHS, wherever you draw the line, we want to go back and do some more figuring. If the cutoff point is fifty decision packages, we'll want to look again and fund some at the top less and bring some in from the bottom. No one can make real priority decisions in a vacuum.

The National Heart, Lung, and Blood Institute (NHLBI), on the other hand, was potentially sympathetic to the ranking process. Its director, a medical researcher who also takes managerial responsibilities seriously, had already installed a system for setting priorities and linking those priorities to the budget. However, since the ZBB guidelines ignored the realities of biomedical research (necessarily long term and technical in nature), the director felt the whole process was "extremely threatening" to his program staff. He objected to the guidelines on the maintenance budget, explaining:

> For us, the commitment base is not the dollar level of the previous year. It is our long-term commitment to our research staff. Of the Institute's FY '78 budget of $450 million, $384 million is already committed. Good research takes a number of years to bring to fruition, and each program has a fixed life. The time to reassess it is when it becomes competitive again.

The NHLBI staff also objected to PHS's reranking of the Institute's decision packages.

> We have nothing against the ZBB process as such, but with the complexity of the research process, it is unrealistic to pass on the decision-making responsibility. You need real expertise to interpret and evaluate the state of knowledge and the opportunities in research fields.

In addition, the technical detail that could have helped others make informed decisions was all but eliminated when the Institute was forced to consolidate its 118 decision packages, painstakingly assembled, into just 3 (heart, lung, and blood).

Clearly, neither NIH nor NHLBI was likely to be endeared to the process by the PHS staff's authoritative stance. In addition, one could argue, as the NHLBI director did, that "ZBB makes no sense for biomedical research institutes." PHS could in the future be persuaded to accommodate the needs of its agencies; other research agencies with constraints not unlike those facing NIH have managed to accommodate themselves to the requirements of ZBB. Improvement is unlikely, however, in the absence of any incentive for NIH to make ZBB work. NIH is unique within the federal government in that many of its programs are viewed as invulnerable by Congress, which frequently gives NIH more money than requested. Noted one official:

> The maintenance level for FY 1979 was based on the President's budget for FY 1978, but we know that we'll have a budget in excess of the President's budget. Eighty percent has no meaning. What the Administration knocks out, Congress adds back. Why did we have to spend a lot of time for nothing, getting the Institutes angry?

Why indeed? It makes little sense, for example, to press the National Cancer Institute for a 20 percent cut, or for greater efficiency, in a political environment traumatized by the disease. On the other hand, in an environment that tends to overfund these programs, obtaining a thoughtful, articulate ranking of the *improvement* budget would have been a helpful part of the ZBB process. The potential for meaningful ranking of the improvement budget was lost in the hostility generated by the process.

The Bureau of Community Health Services (BCHS) also reacted negatively to the ZBB process. BCHS funds a number of programs, including maternal and child health, neighborhood health centers, and health formula grants—the 314[d] monies. BCHS allocated these funds to individual programs within HEW's ten regions using an elaborate management information system. Many observers believed that BCHS had a stronger emphasis on management than any other PHS bureau.

BCHS had begun to prepare for ZBB by January 1977, although it had not yet received guidelines. The agency decided to organize decision packages around functional areas, such as capacity building, health services, prevention, and research and training. A senior official explained:

> We approached the process with great enthusiasm. It was a challenge. When the PHS guidelines arrived, however, we found we had to use the traditional budget structure for the decision packages. We appealed to the Office of the Assistant Secretary for Health, arguing that we could prepare the President's submission to Congress along categorical authority lines, but believed that articulation of the decision packages around functional priorities would facilitate understanding by newly arrived policy makers. PHS would not accept those arguments.

A member of the PHS staff explained why BCHS had been overruled: "Organizations produce budgets. If you choose an alternative budget structure, who will prepare the budget? We have to delegate budget responsibility to line management, and that's difficult to do by function." However, the functional structure chosen by BCHS was almost identical to the ranking criteria later selected by the Acting Assistant Secretary.

BCHS officials also argued that mandating specified levels for each decision package was inconsistent with the ZBB philosophy. For example, the 80 percent level was far too high for a low priority program such as 314[d], but not high enough for others. As with NHLBI, the rigidity of the guidelines concerning decision units and budgetary levels converted potential allies—managers who were generally interested in the resource allocation process—into individuals who were, at best, neutral to the process.

The National Institute of Dental Research (NIDR) of the NIH had one of the few positive responses to ZBB. Dr. David Scott, who was appointed director of the NIDR in 1976, called together all of his program directors and executive and budget officers to plan for ZBB. His attitude was explained as follows:

> I suggested we look at our budget as though we were starting all over again and ask: should we keep the same priorities? We tried hard to take a new look at all our programs. As an example, we had total agreement that, over the years, one particular program had been growing at a rate that was not commensurate with some of the others. We spent four afternoons on setting priorities, then experimented with the numbers several times to see where we came out, taking into account our actual commitments, which limited our flexibility.

The ranking of NIDR programs was to be decided by consensus among Scott and his associate directors. When finished, NIDR submitted thirty-five decision packages to PHS, which later consolidated them into six. Said Scott: "In consolidation, much of the analysis lost visibility." Despite this, it was clear that NIDR had a positive experience with the ZBB process, largely because of Dr. Scott's decision to involve key personnel at all stages. As a result, resources *were* reallocated, and in a style appropriate to the situation.

Conclusions

Implementation of ZBB in the Public Health Service resulted in a few fundamental changes in the distribution of the budget and no discernible change from its normal rate of growth. Of the few changes made by the agencies, many (e.g., the cuts in the Public Health hospitals) were rescinded either by PHS or the Office of the Secretary for political reasons, not as a result of the ZBB process.

Procedure and purpose became inverted in importance; ZBB drove out the analysis and substituted the mechanics. Further, the analysis did not truly evolve from a "zero-base." Few programs were analyzed from the ground up, and minimum decision packages were analyzed in a perfunctory manner. Because of the time spent on the mechanics of ZBB, even the usually thorough analysis of increments to the base budget (the improvement budget in ZBB terminology) was performed in a cursory manner. If every program is to be analyzed every year, without an increase in staff, the results obtained in 1977–78 will likely be repeated in future budgetary periods. Also, conflicts over assigned ranks exacerbated the already strained relationships between PHS and its component agencies, often for little purpose, since the favorable congressional attitude toward health programs guaranteed adequate funding for all.

The only positive response to ZBB was the repeated citation by the agencies, PHS, and the Secretary's staff that ZBB served as a vehicle for presenting data in a clear and informative manner and enabled a new administration to become more familiar with HEW's programs. On the other hand, if better information is ZBB's sole benefit, there are less costly ways of providing it; two or three man-months of work by budget analysts could have generated the same information.

What Went Wrong?

A budgeting failure is frequently a signal of far more significant and deep-rooted managerial problems, and this case is no exception. The problems inherent in the ZBB process were clearly overshadowed by the problems in its manner of implementation. ZBB was a bitter pill for the corps of budgeteers to swallow; it was the Carter medicine, as PPBS was the Johnson cure. The budgeteers did not believe the body was diseased, however, and their resistance to treatment was not overcome by careful co-option from the Carter camp.

ZBB was implemented in a slovenly and indifferent manner that guaranteed its failure. Little thought was given to the technical parts of the process: the definition of decision units; the method of consolidation; the levels of minimum, maintenance, and improvement budgets; and the criteria to be used for ranking. Even less thought was given to the management of the process. The timetable was impossible, no staff additions were made, training was minimal, and no motivation (other than a presidential directive) was offered. It appears that a simple extrapolation was made from the State of Georgia, but the difference in scale was not adequately considered. The NIH, by itself, has a budget double that of the state.

It is facile to enumerate these failures and join the corps of doomsayers who, as Pogo would have put it, are living off the fad of the land by predicting ZBB's failure and eventual demise. The ZBB concept is an intriguing and potentially useful one. ZBB may be hopelessly ill-suited as a budgeting technique in an organization the size of the federal government, and its virtues better realized through an informal zero-base review of selected programs every few years. It is worthwhile, though, to understand how the problems encountered thus far might have been overcome, so that the full benefits of ZBB might be reaped.

TECHNICAL PROBLEMS accounted for a number of difficulties encountered and are relatively easy to address:

Decision Unit selection was handled as an accounting problem rather than as a budgeting exercise. The decision units chosen by PHS, while easing the mechanics of budgeting, were too large for analytic or information purposes; they made the ranking process (particularly in NIH) extremely difficult. Furthermore, unit selections were made without considering that many activities are politically mandatory and, therefore, not likely to be subject to a serious, zero-base review.

The problem could have been overcome by assigning the task of decision unit selection to the manager and budgeteers who would be using the data (not accounting personnel). It would have been preferable to form a task force to define decision units for which a thorough ZBB analysis could be meaningful (because it is indeed politically viable to change them) and desirable (because these are important, controversial, or suspicious programs). This process would result in a much smaller set of decision units to be analyzed usefully with the present level of resources.

In addition, since the decision units were defined as organizational entities, not programs, it was difficult to keep track of programmatic priorities. The Environmental Protection Agency solved this problem by creating three sets of task forces: one for ranking decision units, one for ranking programs, and a third for merging both sets of rankings.

Decision Packages were created through the imposition of uniform minimum, maintenance, and improvement guidelines on the decision units. That policy, while once again easing the mechanics of ZBB, failed to recognize that not all decision packages were created equal. If deviations from the 80 percent, 100 percent, and 120 percent funding levels were allowed, an essentially meaningless and pro forma analytic exercise would have been enlivened.

Criteria for ranking were established by PHS *after* the agencies had submitted their budgets and by the Office of the Secretary *after* PHS had submitted its budget. Both the agencies and PHS were chagrined at this peculiar timing.

Further, the nature of the criteria was unclear. Almost all criteria were intended to measure the congruence between the activity and HEW's goals, which may be an important question but is not necessarily a budgetary concern. The role of the budget is not to make fundamental resource allocation decisions, but to examine the success of a program in meeting predetermined goals, to ascertain how marginal changes in funding will affect that success, to probe for efficiency, and to audit the quality of administration.

Ranking and Reranking were not encouraged by PHS. Allowing lower-level managers to participate in a number of rerankings would have made ZBB more realistic and encouraged the involvement and goodwill of the very people who would be the key to its success.

Consolidation decisions are certainly difficult, but when 108 decision packages are melded into 3 — Heart, Lung, and Blood — the consolidation limit has certainly been exceeded. The Heart package, for example, includes hundreds of millions of dollars and ranges from complex engineering experiments in creating artificial hearts to the subtle biochemistry of plasmas. It is doubtful that a one-page description of all these programs would be of any purpose.

MANAGERIAL PROBLEMS in the implementation of the ZBB process are much harder to address. Their solution first requires that the executive branch's traditional obsession with programs and public policy is subordinated to the less glamorous and visible concerns of administration.

The Timetable was indicative of these problems. The entire ZBB process was condensed into a period of three to five weeks at the PHS agencies, four weeks at PHS, and only slightly longer at the Office of the Secretary. Because ZBB is supposed to benefit primarily low- and middle-level managers, the timing at various levels is inverted; much more time should have been spent at the agency level than at the upper levels of HEW.

In addition, a sensible timetable would ensure that ZBB procedures are *preceded* by the planning of priorities and resource allocation, and *followed* by an evaluation of the effectiveness and efficiency with which the budget is executed. The OS spent the summer on fundamental resource allocation decisions that should have been made before the budgeting cycle began, not at its tail end. Further, although HEW does have an elaborate planning mechanism, only the most cursory linkage between the planning and budgeting systems was evident. If such a linkage had existed, only one set of criteria (not three) would have been articulated.

Finally, while evaluation was handsomely funded, there was no linkage at all between the copious reports and findings of the evaluators, who are primarily outside contractors, and any other part of the financial management process. Further evidence of the absence of evaluation is that the Manpower System, another evaluative device, was found to have the unreliable data characteristic of an information system without a serious, useful purpose.

At no time during the process were the fundamental questions of effectiveness and efficiency addressed. The criteria for ranking addressed basic *policy* questions (e.g., is this activity consistent with our goals?), but not *evaluative* questions (e.g., is this activity successful in carrying out our goals? is it efficient?).

A chief executive officer who understands the benefits of an integrated fiscal management process and is willing to support the tedious and onerous procedures needed to effect it may be able to circumvent this problem. However, the traditionally powerful Assistant Secretaries for Planning have little incentive to work with the Assistant Secretaries for Management and Budget, and in the absence of a top manager to insist upon it, the desired merger between planning and budgeting will not take place in any agency.

The Workforce for ZBB was not increased at all in HEW and was increased by only one person in OMB, in spite of the fact that ZBB was intended to supplement, not supplant, the traditional budgeting process. Given its large organizational resources, PHS could deal with this increased workload relatively easily, but the Office of the Secretary had only four analysts, working for one month each, on a $7 billion budget and 421 decision packages. However able and conscientious, it is difficult for anyone to do a thorough analysis under these circumstances. The lack of manpower at OMB resulted in an equally cursory and superficial analysis by people suddenly overwhelmed by a mountain of paper.

Training and Motivation were given almost no formal attention. The PHS managers were either self-taught in ZBB or else had attended one of the numerous training seminars held by various consulting firms. As a result, there was substantial heterogeneity in expectations and knowledge among the managers, a situation aggravated by the inconsistent and belated guidelines issued by OMB, PHS, and HEW.

A more serious difficulty was the total absence of motivation for cooperation. No one involved in ZBB had a stake in fulfilling anything more than the letter of President Carter's directive; their violation of its spirit is obvious, for example, in PHS's preemptory reranking of its agencies' submissions with little opportunity given for rebuttal. In fact, PHS's actions may have had little to do with ZBB. As one official at NIH commented, "Traditionally, PHS is antagonistic to NIH because of its independence." PHS managers, after years of reorganizations and controversies, may have seized ZBB as an opportunity to dramatize their contribution to the goal of integrating their six agencies: that only they had a sufficiently broad perspective to overcome the provincial concerns of each agency and the technical knowledge necessary for a detailed analysis of these programs. It is unclear what the role of PHS should be and whether there is any point to integrating its six diverse agencies under one umbrella, but many other coordinating agencies have the same shaky organizational legitimacy. Careless implementation of ZBB may well permit them to use the process not for fiscal management but to legitimize and institutionalize their power.

OMB was also indifferent to the process. It is a small, elite, professional agency, staffed at its upper levels by men and women who have spent the bulk of their careers there and who, justifiably, felt they were already experts in the budgets of their particular areas without the help of ZBB. They see themselves as the President's policy analysts hired to answer questions of resource allocation, not budget analysts hired to examine the more mundane questions of relative efficiency. It is difficult to think of a worse choice for the centralized guidance of the process.

Finally, the managers who were to derive maximum benefits from the process were rebuffed for their efforts. Their rankings were ignored, their analyses consolidated, and their desire to be involved rejected. As a result, the managers who were to be trained and motivated by ZBB not only did not benefit, but became, many of them, hostile, sullen, budgetary game players. Again, Dr. Scott's useful experience with ZBB indicated the possibilities offered by a consensus style of management.

The Potential Area for the application of ZBB was incorrectly estimated. It is neither feasible nor desirable to implement this process for the budget of an entire agency. It should be performed only for those programs where a review seems desirable (when those programs are anachronistic or inefficiently administered) and feasible (i.e., without inherent legal or moral commitments). The ZBB process, when expanded to the entire budget as in this case, can only serve to dilute the caliber of the analysis normally performed.

Summary

The PHS experience could just as easily be extended to many other governmental agencies which do not have integrated systems for planning, resource allocation, budgeting, and evaluation. ZBB will only diminish, not extend, their capacity to deal meaningfully with budgetary issues. These agencies also do not have any genuine motivation to participate in the ZBB process. For most government agencies, the bulk of the budget is fixed, and ZBB serves no purpose.

If the technical and managerial problems discussed above were addressed, not only would ZBB become a meaningful process, but also, and more importantly, the entire fiscal management process of the government would improve substantially. It is most unlikely, though, that such changes will be implemented. Budgetary problems are usually addressed as if they existed in isolation. They do not. They are part of deeply rooted managerial problems. The top layers of the federal government are bedeviled by controversies, obsessed by policy issues, and bored by administrative concerns. Very few officials have the interest or experience to take on the painstaking effort required to install a sound budgeting system. Without their willing participation, ZBB will not live up to its potential and will continue to be, at best, a neutral and, at worst, a destructive force in any public organization which undertakes it.

Notes

1. R. N. Anthony, "Zero-Base Budgeting Is a Fraud," *Wall Street Journal*, April 27, 1977.
2. For example, see L. M. Cheek, *Zero-Base Budgeting Comes of Age* (New York: AMA-COM, 1977); J. L. Herbert, ed., *Experiences in Zero-Base Budgeting* (New York: PBI —Petrocelli Books, 1977); and J. W. Pattillo, *Zero-Base Budgeting: A Planning, Resource Allocation and Control Tool* (New York: National Association of Accountants, 1977).
3. A. E. Buck, *The Budget in Governments of Today* (New York: Macmillan, 1934), p. 172; as cited by L. A. Austin, *Zero-Base Budgeting: Organizational Impact and Effects* (New York: AMACOM, 1978).
4. A. Wildavsky and A. Hammond, "Comprehensive versus Incremental Budgeting in the Department of Agriculture," *Administrative Sciences Quarterly* 10 (December 1965): 321–46.
5. P. A. Phyrr, "Zero-Base Budgeting," *Harvard Business Review*, November-December 1970, pp. 111–21; P. A. Phyrr, *Zero-Base Budgeting* (New York: Wiley, 1973); and P. A. Phyrr, "The Zero-Base Budgeting Process," in *How to Improve Profit-Ability through More Effective Planning*, ed. T. S. Dudick (New York: Wiley, 1975).
6. G. M. Taylor, "Introduction to Zero-Base Budgeting," *The Bureaucrat*, Spring 1977, pp. 47–48.
7. G. S. Minmier, "An Evaluation of Zero-Base Budgeting as a Tool for Planning and Control of Discretionary Costs in Government Institutions" (Ph.D. diss., University of Arkansas, 1974); and G. S. Minmier and R. H. Hermanson, "A Look at Zero-Base Budgeting—The Georgia Experience," *Atlanta Economic Review*, July–August 1976, pp. 5–12.
8. See *Science*, May 6, 1977, p. 635.

PART FOUR

Resources

David B. Walker

12. The New System of Intergovernmental Relations: More Fiscal Relief and More Governmental Intrusions

The pattern of governance below the state level in the American federal system has experienced significant fiscal, functional, administrative, and institutional changes during the past decade and a half. The dominant themes that emerge from even a cursory comparison of the condition of American localities in the early 1960s with that of the late 1970s include

1. Continuing local jurisdictional fragmentation and only a handful of formal reorganizations, but also steady federal and, to a lesser extent, state efforts to establish coordinative planning and development units at the multicounty level
2. Significant, but unsystematic, shifts in servicing arrangements with both upward and downward assignments occurring
3. Continuing socioeconomic and fiscal disparities between a majority of the central cities and their respective suburbs, with growing contrasts between central cities as well as their metropolitan areas in the Northeast and Great Lakes regions and those elsewhere
4. Rising fiscal pressures on local governments generally and on those in the Northeast Quadrant especially, coupled with a dramatic hike in intergovernmental fiscal transfers—particularly from the federal government—as the primary response to these pressures.

These are the basic trends in local government and in the system as a whole. They suggest basic changes on certain fronts, significant continuity on others, and above all they combine to confront American federalism with some fundamental structural challenges. The system, after all, has never been as "intergovernmentalized" (marbleized, if you will) as it is now.

The Primacy of the Fiscal Challenge and Responses to It

Significant shifts as well as some continuing changes are reflected in jurisdictional developments, the patterns of local functional assignments (and reassignments), and interlocal disparities, and most of these underscore the mounting pressures to which local public finances have been subjected over the past decade and a half.

213

This, in turn, has produced various intergovernmental fiscal initiatives, and these have been the prime response of the system to the plight of the localities.

The fundamental problem on the fiscal front is that the chief revenue source historically of American local governments has been the property tax and that this levy, generally, has been incapable—for a variety of fiscal, administrative, and political reasons—of meeting the mounting demands for more and better local services.

Beginning in the late 1960s amid the growing realization that dual federalism was an inappropriate principle to apply to state-local finances, various shifts began to transpire. One was a series of efforts to reform the property tax. Over one-third of the states reorganized or strengthened their property tax supervisory units over the past decade. Four states joined Hawaii in centralizing assessment; fifteen established or beefed up assessor-training programs; fourteen launched or revamped their assessment ratio studies; and more than a dozen adopted full-disclosure policies regarding the average level of assessment in a community.

Another move was enactment of various property tax relief measures. Between 1970 and 1975, the number of state-financed relief enactments jumped from twelve to thirty-three. Twenty-five of these were of the "circuit breaker" type, which like its counterpart in an electrical system cuts in when there is an "overload" (i.e., when the property tax reaches a percent of individual income that the state deems oppressive).

Still other changes are reflected in the growing reliance on interlocal contracting and servicing shifts and in the increasing tendency of some states to assume direct responsibility for certain exclusive or shared local functions.

A fourth trend in this broad effort to reduce the dependency on the local property tax was some increase in the number of states authorizing some or all of their cities and/or counties to levy nonproperty taxes. As of 1976, twenty-six states had taken such action in the local sales tax and eleven in the local income tax areas. One state—Minnesota—had sanctioned a modest "share for growth" regional tax arrangement for the seven-county "Twin Cities" region.

Of far greater fiscal significance than any of the above has been the expansion of intergovernmental fiscal transfers. State and federal aid more than tripled between 1967 and 1975 (see table 12.1). And this drastic downward, vertical fiscal response with all of its attendant byproducts has served as the primary conditioner of the super-intergovernmentalized system that at present prevails at the local level.

The cumulative effect of these various fiscal or fiscally related developments has been the emergence of a much more diversified, and some would say, "balanced" local revenue system. As a proportion of both local and state-local revenue systems, the property tax has declined significantly (to 33 percent of the former and 18 percent of the latter, as of 1976). The lesser share in the overall state-local revenue pie, of course, relates directly to the fact that since 1970 the states have assumed the senior partner role in this system, thanks to the fact that thirty-seven states now have broad sales and income taxes (and only one has neither). (See figure 12.1.)

Above and beyond the growing state role here is that of the federal government. Despite a gradual decline in the federal share of own-source general revenues (see figure 12.2), federal domestic expenditures have soared during this decade. Most of these outlays have gone for aid programs to state and local governments (see figure 12.3). Moreover, since 1966 with the advent of the first block grant, the Partnership for Health Program, a tripartite federal aid package has emerged with categorical grants accounting for 79 percent of the 1977 total, five block grants for 12 percent and general revenue sharing for 9 percent. Finally, over 30 percent of the 1977 aid package ($78 billion) was channeled directly to local governments, not through or to states—a marked hike over the 10 percent (of $11 billion) that bypassed the states at the beginning of the Johnson administration.

In general, most of these general trends would seem to bode well for the condition of local public finances. Yet, these fairly salutory cumulative statistics tend to conceal many differences, difficulties, and defects. They focus, after all, too heavily on fiscal figures.

Turning first to the states, their aid packages, overall, more than doubled between 1969 and 1975 (reaching the $50.5 billion mark). Yet, these packages reflect wide interstate variations and are channeled chiefly into four functional areas (education, welfare, highways, and health-hospitals, accounting for 87 percent of the total aid outlays in 1972). The bulk of these conditional aids, then, goes to school districts and counties, not to cities. Ten percent of total state assistance in any recent fiscal year is allocated for general support payments, and this usually favors cities. Yet, only eight states utilize formulas here that reflect any real attempt at equalization. Regarding revenue efforts, seven states in 1975 still were junior partners to their localities. Moreover, only a little more than one-fifth (eleven) of the fifty are making fairly "heavy" use of the income tax, while thirteen are exerting a "moderate" effort and nineteen a "low" one (with nine making no effort at all). In supervising local financial management practices—a matter of more than a little concern of late—only about eight states can be given a good to excellent rating. Overall, then, the state fiscal role, while markedly better than that of a decade ago, still falls short of the normative role many would prefer them to assume.

With the quadrupling of federal aid amounts between 1968 and FY 1978, the nearly 50 percent hike in the number of programs, and the extraordinary increase in the variety of aid programs, more federal dollars have been provided, but several problems have arisen:

1. In terms of participation, practically all local jurisdictions, as well as the fifty states, are direct recipients, thanks to general revenue sharing, CETA, and CDBG—to mention only the more obvious new programs of the early 1970s.
2. Accompanying the heavy bypassing of state governments, local governmental lobbies have assumed a more powerful stance in Washington, raising basic questions about the future of the state as authoritative middlemen in the system.

TABLE 12.1. LOCAL GOVERNMENTS ARE MOVING TOWARD MORE BALANCED REVENUE SYSTEMS, SELECTED YEARS 1942–75

Fiscal Year	All Local Governments		Percent Distribution by Type of Government			
	Amount* (millions)	Percent Distribution by Source	Cities	School Districts	Counties	Townships and Special Districts
		Total General Revenue (local revenue and federal-state aid)				
1942	$ 7,071	100.0%	37.0%	33.7	22.0%	7.3%
1952	16,952	100.0	32.0	38.4	20.7	8.9
1957	25,916	100.0	30.3	41.9	19.5	8.3
1967	59,383	100.0	26.8	47.0	17.8	8.5
1971	93,868	100.0	27.1	46.4	18.4	8.2
1974	133,994	100.0	28.2	43.5	19.3	9.0
1975 est.	147,700	100.0	28.4	42.9	19.5	9.1
		Intergovernmental Revenue (federal and state aid)				
1942	1,785	25.2	24.0	43.8	27.8	4.5
1952	5,281	31.2	18.7	49.9	26.2	5.2
1957	8,049	31.1	17.6	53.6	23.5	5.3
1967	21,338	35.9	17.7	58.2	18.5	5.5
1971	36,375	38.8	21.1	55.1	18.6	5.2
1974	57,253	42.7	24.0	49.6	19.6	6.7
1975 est.	64,000	43.3	24.2	49.0	18.9	7.0

General Revenue From Local Sources (taxes and charges)

1942	$ 5,286	74.8%	41.4%	30.3	20.0%	8.3%
1952	11,671	68.8	38.0	33.3	18.3	10.5
1957	17,866	68.9	36.1	36.6	17.7	9.6
1967	38,045	64.1	32.0	40.5	17.4	10.1
1971	57,491	61.2	30.9	40.8	18.2	10.1
1974	76,742	57.3	31.3	38.9	19.1	10.8
1975 est.	83,700	56.7	31.6	38.3	19.3	10.8

Local Property Taxes

1942	4,344	61.4	39.0	32.9	20.1	8.0
1952	8,282	48.9	32.7	39.2	19.8	8.3
1957	12,385	47.8	29.7	42.8	19.2	8.3
1967	25,186	42.4	24.8	48.9	18.5	7.8
1971	36,726	39.1	23.3	50.3	18.3	8.0
1974	46,452	34.7	23.0	50.0	18.4	8.6
1975 est.	49,220	33.3	22.7	50.1	18.5	8.7

*ACIR Staff Tabulation

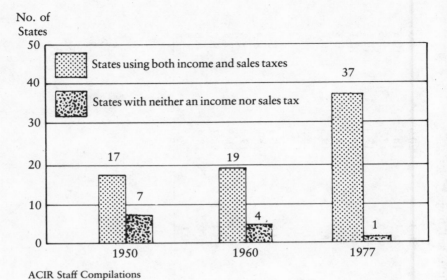

ACIR Staff Compilations

Figure 12.1. Number of States With
General Sales and Broad-Based Personal
Income Taxes As of January 1, 1950, 1960, and 1977

3. With the growing reliance on allocating grant funds by formula (up to 75 percent of the total, compared to 66 percent in the mid-1960s), a new form of grantsmanship (and conflict among the public interest groups) has emerged that focuses not on administrators as much as on Congress and the need to fashion the formulas (and eligibility provisions) to their liking.

4. In terms of services aided, all the big efforts of intergovernmental and national import (like welfare, health, hospitals, transportation, and education) are federally aided with social programs experiencing the greatest dollar and proportionate gains since 1965, but so are a range of activities that not so long ago were deemed wholly state-local responsibilities (like rural fire protection, libraries, jellyfish control, police, and historical preservation).

5. The forms of federal assistance, at least outwardly, have changed drastically since 1966, but with all the traditional types of categorical grants (project, project/formula, formula, and open ended) still in use, along with at least five block grants and general revenue sharing.

6. Conditions now are attached to all forms of federal aid; the procedural strings (civil rights, citizen participation, and auditing requirements) added to GRS in 1976 and the hybrid nature of most of the block grants, along with the tendency to pick up program and other con-

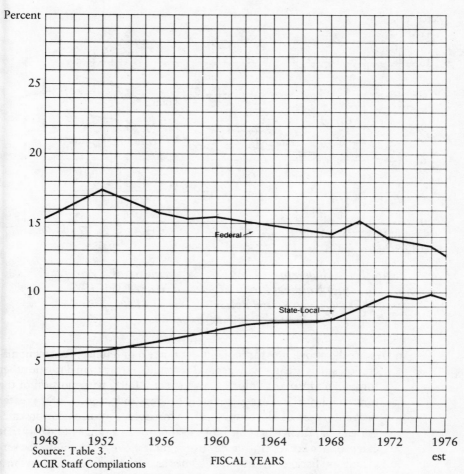

Figure 12.2. The Relative Growth in Federal Taxes
Lags the State-Local Sector, Selected Years 1948–1976.
(Federal, State and Local Taxes as a Percent of GNP)

straints over time, render inaccurate the older description of these
two forms of aid as essentially "no strings" and "few strings"
assistance programs, respectively. Moreover, the emergence of a range
of across-the-board requirements in the environmental, equal rights,
relocation, historic preservation, and personnel areas only underscores the fact that the conditions now attached to practically all federal assistance are infinitely more complex, more controversial (with
more judicial decision making), more pervasive (in terms of the focus
of some on the internal operations of whole governmental jurisdictions)
than their largely program-oriented predecessors of the mid-1960s.

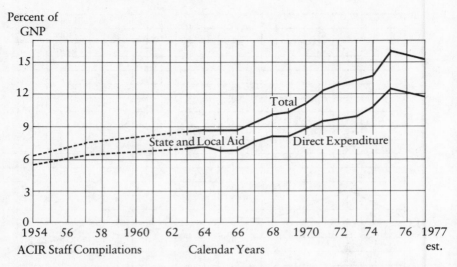

Percent of
GNP

ACIR Staff Compilations   Calendar Years   est.

*Figure 12.3. Government Domestic Expenditures as a Percentage
of Gross National Product. Selected Years 1954–1977
[The Dominant Federal Role in the Domestic Public Sector]
Federal Domestic Expenditure*

7. Despite the above, the form of aid can make a difference. Recipient discretion still is greater with general revenue sharing than with the other
forms, and insofar as block grants cover a fairly wide portion of the
functional turf and are adequately funded, they, too, confer greater
discretion than do the categoricals. Moreover, certain ostensible categoricals in practice become block grants due to a range of factors that
can produce lax federal agency oversight. Above all, perhaps, the servicing and fiscal discretion that comes as a consequence of receiving a
number of federal grants—whether categorical, block or GRS—must
not be discounted at this point in time. Put differently, and relating
this discretionary theme with the previous one, increasing conditions
characterize the recent evolution of all federal assistance and some of
these conditions are more intrusive in a procedural and systematic sense
than the old-style categorical strings, but the practical effect now on
those localities that receive a large and mixed package of federal aid is
potentially, if not actually, to expand their fiscal and program options.
8. Paralleling the above, the fiscal impact of federal aid is more difficult to
gauge now than ever before. Earlier studies tended to agree that its impact was chiefly stimulative of greater state and/or local outlays, either
in the aided area or aggregately. Random evidence and impressions,
along with a Brookings' assessment of CETA and an unpublished Treasury study of the impact of aid on certain hard pressed cities suggests

more of an additive, if not a substitutive, effect. This seems to be especially true with the newer forms of aid and with larger urban jurisdictions that participate in several big money, federal programs. In this connection, the no-match feature of the community development and manpower programs (as well as general revenue sharing, of course) should not be overlooked. And, while "maintenance of effort" and other nonsubstitutive provisions are cited by some as real constraints, others feel they are merely "paper" conditions. A forthcoming GAO report on the subject may shed more light on the real character of their impact.

9. Finally, with the enactment of the countercyclical programs in 1976–77, direct federal aid to cities soared, with the figure for those of more than 500,000 in population zooming from 28 percent of their own-source revenues in 1976 to an estimated 50 percent in 1978; few can argue the need here, but some have questioned the growing degree of fiscal dependence that these figures suggest; the real long-term effects of these recent federal efforts, of course, depend on how "permanent" the programs become (the prospective renewal of CETA, though with many more conditions and constraints, suggests a partial answer to this question), the aggregative impact of these diverse assistance undertakings on the very diverse localities that partake of them (a subject yet to be researched authoritatively) and what the essential nature of dependency really is. Dependency, after all, has more than fiscal connotations to it; administrative, political and even psychological factors also come into play and each of these combine in differing ways in each of the many recipient cities and counties. Needless to say, this topic, too, has received meager attention from the researchers.

Conclusion

The recent rapid hike in federal and state aid, then, has been the basic response to the manifold challenges confronting America's localities. Yet, it has not been an unmixed blessing for the cities, counties, and towns of the nation. Heavily intergovernmentalized local programs, budgets and bureaucracies raise major questions regarding accountability, administrative effectiveness, not to mention economic efficiency. They pose a challenge to how the ideal of strong local government can be made a reality in the years ahead. This growing tendency to focus almost exclusively on intergovernmental fiscal transfers as a means of resolving local governmental difficulties and generally to ignore the fiscal and functional defects of present local institutional arrangements suggests the need for a much more balanced approach — one that recognizes the linkages between and among the functional, institutional, and fiscal factors that shape America's local governments.

Selma J. Mushkin and Charles L. Vehorn

13.User Fees and Charges

Recent years have seen a widespread discussion of various methods to finance municipal services. One method of generating revenue, which is strongly favored by most economists, places public prices on public products.[1] Establishing user fees and charges not only provides an additional revenue source but also provides the opportunity for a more efficient allocation and a more equitable distribution of public services. The twofold purpose of this article is first to present current data on the growth of user fees and charges and then to discuss reasons why further extension of public pricing is desirable.

In the United States, total charge revenues in the cities have increased 308 percent between 1957 and 1975. During this period, the average annual growth rate of revenue from total charges was greater than the growth rate of revenue from taxes, 8.1 percent compared to 7.3 percent. Revenues from the operation of city-owned utilities alone almost quadrupled, amounting to $8.2 billion in 1975 (see table 13.1). This figure includes amounts received from the operation of such utilities as water, gas, electricity, and transit systems. City governments are, in effect, selling their services to the users or customers.

The U.S. Bureau of the Census, in its compilations, defines as "current charges" only those amounts that a government receives from the public for its performance of specific services benefiting the person charged and from the sales of commodities and services. It thus includes fees, assessments, rents, and sales

TABLE 13.1. User Charges in City Finances,
Selected Years (in millions of dollars)

	1975	1973	1971	1968	1963	1957
Charges (total)	$13,852	$11,316	$ 9,307	$ 6,900	$ 5,315	$ 3,392
Current charges	5,443	4,533	3,579	2,418	1,720	954
Utility revenue	8,217	6,619	5,578	4,361	3,513	2,378
Liquor store revenue	192	164	150	121	82	60
Taxes	21,135	18,477	15,090	11,291	8,309	5,908
Ratio: Charges to $1 of taxes	.66	.61	.62	.61	.64	.57

Source: U.S. Bureau of Census, *City Government Finances* (annual issues for the given year).

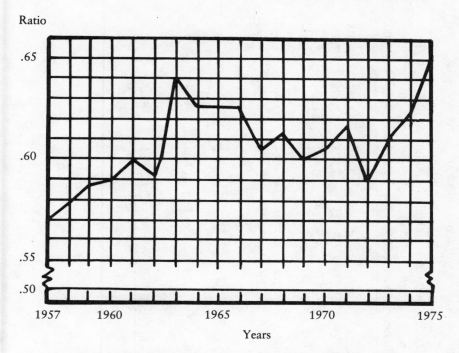

Ratio

.65

.60

.55

.50

1957   1960   1965   1970   1975

Years

Source: U.S. Bureau of Census, *City Government Finances* (annual issues).

Figure 13.1. Ratio Charges to $1 of Taxes, 1957–75

derived from commodities or services furnished incident to the performance of particular functions, but excludes charges related to regulatory activities and privileges granted by the government in connection with such regulations. Thus, license charges and fees in connection with filing for licenses are excluded.

Bureau of the Census data show that by 1975, 65¢ in total charges (current charges plus utility and liquor store revenues) was collected by the nation's cities for each $1 of taxes. This ratio has fluctuated widely since 1957, showing a general increase during the 1957–63 period, a leveling off or decline during the 1963–72 period, and a rapid rise since 1972 (see figure 13.1).

Cities have uneven access to fees and charges because, among other things, they provide different services. And the feasibility of raising revenue through charges is determined in part by the nature of the services the city provides. Fees and charges are customary for some services, but difficult to impose for others either because the benefits of the service are not clearly identifiable or because nonpayers cannot be excluded.[2]

Variations among cities in the functions performed result in wide differences in their fee intensity — the ratio of fees and charges to taxes. Large cities provide a wider range of services than do smaller cities, but not all those added ser-

TABLE 13.2. AMOUNTS OF MUNICIPALITIES' OWN REVENUE (BY SOURCE AND RATIOS OF CHARGES TO TAXES, 1974–75)

City size	All Muni-cipalities	1,000,000 or More	500,000 to 999,999	300,000 to 499,999	200,000 to 299,999	100,000 to 199,999	50,000 to 99,999	Less than 50,000
$ in millions								
General revenue from own sources	30,205	8,773	3,959	1,975	1,076	2,859	3,145	8,418
Taxes	21,135	6,848	2,785	1,235	715	2,003	2,199	5,502
Current charges	5,443	1,153	714	429	206	524	591	1,826
Other revenue	3,628	772	460	312	155	332	355	1,242
Water and utility revenue	8,217	1,576	1,007	342	224	909	739	3,420
Water supply revenue	3,266	479	356	206	118	304	354	1,448
Other utility revenue	4,951	1,097	651	136	106	605	385	1,972
ratios in percentages								
Current charges to taxes	25.8	16.8	25.6	34.7	28.8	26.2	26.9	33.2
Current charges plus water and utility revenue to taxes	64.6	39.9	61.8	62.4	60.1	71.5	60.5	95.3
Current charges to own revenue	18.0	13.1	18.0	21.7	19.1	18.3	18.8	21.7
Current charges plus water and utility revenue to own revenue	45.2	31.1	43.5	39.0	40.0	50.1	42.3	62.3

SOURCE: U.S. Bureau of Census, *City Government Finances in 1974–75*, p. 7.

vices lend themselves to pricing. At the same time, smaller cities may provide mainly utility services and, accordingly, report a large share of revenues from fees and charges. In 1974–75 the fee intensity for cities with a population of less than 50,000 was 95.3 percent, while the fee intensity for cities with a population of more than one million was only 39.9 percent (see table 13.2).

Table 13.3 presents 1975 data for a selection of 104 cities with populations over 100,000. This exhibit groups the cities into three categories: those with current charges only, those with current charges plus water supply revenue, and those with current charges plus water and "other" utility revenue. For purposes of comparison, the most relevant columns are the fee intensity rate (5), per capita expenditures (6), and percent change in fee intensity between 1967 and 1975 (7).

The fee intensity rate for the first group is smaller than that for the second, which, in turn, is smaller than that for the third. A fairly strong regional pattern emerges with northeastern cities posting, in general, low fee intensity rates and high per capita expenditures. In Group 2, only one northeastern city, Erie, has a fee intensity rate greater than .45. During the 1967–75 period, over one-half of the selected cities responded to the problem of pressing financial needs with a larger percentage increase in fees than in taxes (see column 7).

In addition to presenting current data on the growth and implementation of user fees and charges, the second purpose of this article is to clarify the reasons why extended use of prices for public products has been repeatedly recommended by economists as a viable means of generating revenue.

Rationale for User Fees and Charges

Three major reasons why professional opinion has long been in favor of giving greater emphasis to user fees and charges are the following:

> They can greatly improve the public allocation of resources.
> They can be more fair than taxation, in certain cases.
> They can correct private market signals.

Under present public resource allocation practices, the wrong product is sometimes produced in the wrong quantity, and with no, or inappropriate, quality differentiation. "Wrong" is used here with the special meaning of "different" in type, quantity, and quality from that which would be produced if rigorous analysis was made of comparative effectiveness at the given budget level. It is also being used to describe the volume of production that is "lower" than it would be at market prices under competitive conditions.

Analysis of a public service or activity may give new emphasis to uncertainty about the consumer or voter response to the public product being produced. If the government would set a price on the product—thereby opening up a market through which consumers could register their vote for or against by paying the price or by not consuming—this could help guide the city in the production of its services.

TABLE 13.3. FEES, CHARGES, AND SELECTED FISCAL CHARACTERISTICS OF CITIES, 1975*
(AGGREGATE DOLLAR AMOUNTS IN MILLIONS)

Cities	(1) Estimated Population (thousands) 1973	(2) General Expenditures	(3) General Revenue from Taxes	(4) Fees and Charges	(5) Fee Intensity (4) ÷ (3)	(6) Per Capita Expenditures (2) ÷ (1)	(7) Percent Change in Fee Intensity 1967–75
Group 1 (current charges only)							
Patterson, N.J.	143.4	$ 73.0	$ 32.2	$ .9	.03	$ 509	50
Hartford, Conn.	148.5	154.9	74.1	3.2	.04	1,043	– 50
Peoria, Ill.	127.9	27.4	16.5	.7	.04	214	0
New Haven, Conn.	131.3	77.2	51.5	2.9	.06	588	20
Miami, Fla.	354.0	81.7	50.8	4.6	.09	231	– 78
Kansas City, Kan.	172.9	37.4	22.2	3.0	.14	216	– 26
Bridgeport, Conn.	148.3	84.6	44.8	6.5	.15	570	50
Omaha, Neb.	377.3	135.4	45.1	9.4	.21	359	24
Las Vegas, Nev.	144.3	33.4	13.6	3.2	.24	231	20
Indianapolis, Ind.	728.3	237.1	87.7	32.4	.37	326	208
Berkeley, Calif.	111.6	33.2	14.6	5.8	.40	297	29
Oakland, Calif.	345.9	126.0	56.7	27.6	.49	364	63
Group 2 (current charges plus water supply revenue)							
New Bedford, Mass.	98.8	52.5	27.7	2.9	.10	531	– 33
Newark, N.J.	367.7	314.2	115.4	12.1	.10	855	– 9
Washington, D.C.	733.8	1,438.6	543.6	55.5	.10	1,960	– 17
Waterbury, Conn.	110.7	71.2	31.5	3.1	.10	643	– 23
Yonkers, N.Y.	195.5	136.8	71.7	8.6	.12	700	– 33

City							
Providence, R.I.	169.9	80.2	45.6	7.2	.16	472	— 23
Springfield, Mass.	160.4	118.0	50.8	8.7	.17	736	13
Pittsburgh, Pa.	479.3	120.1	63.2	12.2	.19	251	— 9
Rochester, N.Y.	276.8	190.5	80.9	15.8	.20	688	— 38
Rockford, Ill.	142.2	30.2	15.7	3.6	.23	212	— 28
Worcester, Mass.	170.7	123.3	90.9	21.3	.23	722	— 15
Boston, Mass.	618.3	672.4	328.7	79.3	.24	1,087	41
Buffalo, N.Y.	425.1	308.6	95.4	22.5	.24	726	9
Hammond, Ind.	106.4	21.5	11.5	2.8	.24	202	— 17
Philadelphia, Pa.	1,861.7	929.1	451.3	107.0	.24	499	14
Honolulu, Hawaii	685.7	220.5	122.0	31.3	.26	322	37
Dearborn, Mich.	100.8	33.6	23.0	6.1	.27	333	23
Baltimore, Md.	877.8	917.1	266.3	75.8	.28	1,045	33
St. Louis, Mo.	558.0	213.3	140.2	40.7	.29	382	4
Chicago, Ill.	3,172.9	984.2	595.1	176.4	.30	310	— 3
Jersey City, N.J.	255.0	153.6	68.9	21.5	.31	602	94
Trenton, N.J.	104.2	33.0	17.4	5.6	.32	317	52
Camden, N.J.	100.2	27.6	13.3	4.9	.37	275	0
Syracuse, N.Y.	184.7	102.3	28.1	10.7	.38	554	52
San Jose, Calif.	523.1	119.7	55.0	22.1	.40	229	90
Milwaukee, Wisc.	690.7	199.6	79.8	32.8	.41	289	5
Montgomery, Ala.	153.0	31.2	17.5	7.1	.41	204	— 37
Allentown, Pa.	108.7	21.3	9.8	4.3	.44	196	5
Kansas City, Mo.	487.8	193.1	102.5	45.5	.44	396	5
Youngstown, Ohio	133.5	31.3	15.8	7.1	.45	234	7
Dayton, Ohio	214.4	81.0	30.1	14.2	.47	378	52
Birmingham, Ala.	295.7	99.3	44.5	21.5	.48	336	— 25
Canton, Ohio	106.9	25.2	12.0	5.8	.48	236	— 8
Minneapolis, Minn.	382.4	155.8	55.1	27.0	.49	407	17
Greensboro, N.C.	155.5	45.5	18.7	9.3	.50	293	— 9
Sacramento, Calif.	267.5	72.7	35.2	18.3	.52	272	— 20

New Orleans, La.	573.5	197.4	82.9	45.1	.54	344	4
Akron, Ohio	261.5	69.8	33.9	20.4	.60	267	− 19
Topeka, Kan.	136.1	29.0	13.3	8.3	.62	213	− 18
Phoenix, Ariz.	637.1	198.8	67.3	43.3	.64	312	6
Tucson, Ariz.	307.6	101.2	35.3	22.7	.64	329	− 9
Portland, Oreg.	375.9	109.9	46.5	30.0	.65	292	8
Toledo, Ohio	337.4	109.7	39.1	25.5	.65	325	− 24
St. Paul, Minn.	287.3	99.0	36.5	24.0	.66	345	89
Des Moines, Iowa	199.1	64.9	22.3	15.0	.67	326	34
Salt Lake City, Utah	169.2	39.1	19.4	13.4	.69	231	47
South Bend, Ind.	122.0	25.5	9.8	6.8	.69	209	82
El Paso, Tex.	353.2	50.8	29.0	20.2	.70	144	− 8
Denver, Col.	515.6	299.7	118.6	86.0	.73	581	22
Erie, Pa.	130.1	25.2	10.0	7.7	.77	194	93
Louisville, Ky.	335.7	144.1	46.7	38.5	.82	429	− 10
Atlanta, Ga.	451.1	190.2	73.2	66.9	.91	422	40
Cincinnati, Ohio	426.2	364.9	88.6	109.5	1.24	856	35
Group 3 (current charges plus water supply and "other" utility revenue)							
New York, N.Y.	7,646.8	11,641.3	4,852.7	1,580.5	.33	1,522	− 3
Charlotte, N.C.	284.7	90.5	37.9	15.4	.41	318	− 9
Shreveport, La.	184.0	36.4	21.0	8.6	.41	198	− 13
Norfolk, Va.	283.1	190.2	71.4	33.4	.47	672	0
Detroit, Mich.	1,386.8	622.4	287.9	152.0	.53	449	− 13
Houston, Tex.	1,320.0	296.2	180.8	99.2	.55	224	57
Dallas, Tex.	815.9	245.3	143.9	81.0	.56	301	− 15
Mobile, Ala.	188.5	41.8	21.7	12.2	.56	222	− 13
Richmond, Va.	238.1	213.4	93.6	53.9	.58	896	9
Amarillo, Tex.	129.8	20.3	13.3	9.1	.68	156	− 20
Fresno, Calif.	174.9	64.2	25.0	16.9	.68	367	5
San Francisco, Calif.	687.5	586.2	267.0	181.6	.68	853	31

City							
Tulsa, Okla.	335.4	103.6	39.5	27.2	.69	309	— 39
San Diego, Calif.	757.1	176.4	75.8	53.4	.70	233	3
Columbus, Ohio	540.9	140.9	62.5	44.4	.71	260	— 14
Winston-Salem, N.C.	139.7	44.5	14.6	10.4	.71	319	1
Fort Worth, Tex.	359.5	76.1	41.6	29.9	.72	212	— 3
Oklahoma City, Okla.	373.7	96.1	38.0	30.1	.79	257	— 13
Spokane, Wash.	174.0	38.2	18.2	14.3	.79	220	— 13
Wichita, Kan.	261.2	98.4	24.2	19.2	.79	377	— 5
Tampa, Fla.	275.6	86.4	31.3	25.5	.81	313	40
Evansville, Ind.	136.2	30.0	11.4	10.3	.90	220	45
Corpus Christi, Tex.	212.4	33.1	18.8	17.9	.95	156	— 34
Albuquerque, N.M.	273.9	78.6	17.6	20.2	1.15	287	83
Lubbock, Tex.	153.8	36.4	15.1	17.4	1.15	237	21
Nashville, Tenn.	427.1	258.8	124.0	144.8	1.17	606	23
Cleveland, Ohio	678.6	245.5	90.8	110.1	1.21	362	— 2
Los Angeles, Calif.	2,746.9	840.9	479.9	615.3	1.28	306	13
Little Rock, Ark.	142.1	26.3	9.8	12.7	1.30	185	— 7
Seattle, Wash.	503.1	196.2	78.0	107.2	1.37	390	41
Columbus, Ga.	160.4	48.2	20.0	30.8	1.54	300	19
Pasadena, Calif.	109.2	41.5	20.9	36.5	1.75	380	14
Fort Wayne, Ind.	185.5	35.4	13.2	23.3	1.77	191	39
Lincoln, Neb.	163.4	63.7	17.7	41.5	2.34	390	57
Tacoma, Wash.	149.4	54.0	20.9	53.6	2.56	361	— 16
Memphis, Tenn.	658.9	318.3	72.5	211.4	2.92	483	— 7
Lansing, Mich.	129.2	52.3	14.9	55.5	3.72	405	6
Knoxville, Tenn.	182.3	82.6	20.6	77.1	3.74	453	58
Jacksonville, Fla.	522.0	199.1	51.9	195.4	3.76	381	0

SOURCE: U.S. Bureau of the Census, *City Government Finances in 1974–75*, and Selma J. Mushkin, "Public Prices for Public Products," *The Municipal Yearbook, 1971* (Washington, D.C.: International City Management Association, 1971).

*Cities in each group are listed in order of lowest to highest fee intensity.

It would be possible to consider more frequent trash collection, for those who want it, with the additional days of collection offered at a price. In the same manner, extra police patrol services could be purchased from public sources, just as those extra services in some instances are now purchased from private sources. Similarly, there might be a market for more frequent street cleaning, more street lighting, more public snow removal, more public off-street parking, or more public health surveillance of neighborhood restaurants. If public prices for added public services were set to cover the incremental costs of the additional volume of services, and if the demand registered by payment of the price suggested expansion of city services, city administrators would have both a guide to decisions on added services and at least some of the funds for their production.

In addition to meeting some voters' demands for more frequent services, pricing signals offer a method for trying out and responding to quality changes in public services. Again, if the new quality is intended to be financed by fees and charges and not out of general revenue, the consumer who desires not to pay and not to receive has that option. And, at least for some services, he or she can be excluded from the direct benefits that flow from the provision of higher-quality services.

One obstacle to extending user changes in the areas mentioned is that "pricing policies used by municipal governments are often fairly unsophisticated, perhaps understandably so in light of the difficulty of determining price elasticities, marginal costs, distribution of benefits, and other things that enter into economic models of optimal pricing."[3] When a price less than the appropriate price is charged, a subsidy is given to the person purchasing the service. The Advisory Commission on Intergovernmental Relations has suggested that states provide local governments with consultants and technical assistance to determine the appropriate price to charge; however, many states currently do not possess such a capability to offer soundly based advice on the pricing of public services.[4]

Tax resistance to further public sector growth has contributed to a reexamination of the public charge/general taxation issues and to a more realistic assessment of who pays for and who gets the public service, particularly at the municipal level of government. One question to be considered in determining the relative fairness between the present system of financing and a system that employs more extensive use of public prices is whether, for the lower income groups, such prices would be more or less advantageous than the property tax.

Some claim that a drawback of user fees is the regressivity of the charge.[5] It requires a higher percentage of income from poorer families, so the charge could possibly exclude some needy families. But a complete answer to the regressivity question demands knowledge of tax incidence and service benefits by income class.

The property tax is, in fact, many taxes and not a single tax; it works differently under different conditions of housing demand and supply, and is variously affected, in turn, by interest rates, construction prices, and local economic developments. A fee or public price could be a fairer source of revenue than the property tax, since it may be that poor families now pay more through the economic effects of the property tax than under some alternative arrangement. If prices were used instead of the tax, some poor families might choose not to have the priced service, and those who did presumably would benefit in proportion to the prices.

On the benefits side, analysis of "use" by income class or age may disclose a heavy concentration among middle-income individuals rather than poor individuals. In this case, the low-income families would be partially subsidizing the middle-income families through the present financing system. Relative income effects are at issue, as well as the distribution of benefits among age groups.

Prices for services may achieve greater fairness, in that payment would be made only by those who benefit. Prices can be used to discourage some users and encourage others, for example, by negative prices. They also can be used to stimulate more effective provision of public services. The services, the classes of customary users, and the methods of pricing all have a policy effect on fairness.

Even where uniform charges would be more regressive than an alternative revenue system, it is possible to devise a fair pricing method by use of eligibility tests to determine "payability." This method is used typically in financing health-care services, in certain welfare services such as family counseling, and in school meal programs. Such a technique gives the subsidy to those who need it, while making the benefits of the service available to all those who desire to purchase it.

Another case where fairness is an issue involves public services available in small amounts relative to the potential market. An assessment of any of these services usually indicates that it is sustained in its current size by lack of information of many members of the public and that it is then used by those with access to the information, usually those with more education and more awareness of the range of public-service activity. At present, many activities are a charge on general taxation even though a user fee would be fairer.

An important factor contributing to more use of charges by government is the keener awareness of the incentives that current methods of carrying out the public business generate for private market decision. Air, water, and the landscape have been viewed historically as free goods, available to all without cost or charge. Thus, producers have an incentive to use the free resource "waste discharge" in place of more costly methods of production. Given present practices, there is little reason, apart from government regulation, for industry to adopt new production processes that call for less noise or for lower emissions of pollutants; nor is there an incentive to apply practices that will clean the water or the air. And there is often no incentive for the producer to keep his solid wastes down through recycling.

The costs of industrial wastes and the amount of waste vary not only from industry to industry but also among plants and firms within an industry. The damage done varies also with the physical characteristics of the plants' location. The concept of an effluent charge, in principle, calls for setting the amount of the charge in relation to the amount of the damage. An effluent charge that reflects damage costs would vary from industry to industry and from place to place, and it would be different for competing firms.

The effluent charge as an explicit price for the use of the waste assimilative and transport capacities of waterways, for example, would encourage industry to adjust waste discharges in relation to the added cost and the specific circumstances. If the price were set at the correct amount for the damage done, then adjustments in processes, in production inputs of materials, and in energy sources could be expected. Those adjustments would achieve the greatest effluent-charge reduction and thus gain the lowest costs to the plant. But the competitive market forces would work to the advantage of some firms and to the disadvantage of others and to localities in which they are located. How does a municipality impose effluent charges on a firm if the new charges would adversely alter competitive relationships?

The above question highlights one drawback that many fiscal officers are strongly aware of. Is it politically feasible to extend user charges?[6] With the rise of the taxpayer's revolt, it now may be more feasible to meet pressing financial needs through user charges than through increases in local taxes. Of course, any change in the present revenue structure will generate a new set of gainers and losers. But we argue that there is a wide range of services that can be financed through user fees that place the costs and benefits directly on those who desire the public service.

Examples of Services That Can Be Priced

Several examples of public products that can be priced already have been mentioned. Figure 13.2 illustrates the wide variety of fees, charges, and licenses currently existing in various cities. On the average, revenues from utility charges are almost one-and-a-half times the size of those from all other charges. Besides utility operations, other functions that have a high fee potential (i.e., high ratio of charges to expenditures) are special forms of police protection; transportation facilities and services, including harbors and airports; health and hospitals; educational services; recreation; and neighborhood development.

How successful have cities been in establishing user charges? Oakland, California, for example, has reviewed and, in many instances, increased user fees and charges.[7] The bulk of Oakland's receipts from charges comes from sewer services and recreational services, so the city has the potential to extend public pricing into several other areas. But the philosophy of the city has been to support from general revenue sources many activities that could be priced. Nevertheless, where fees have been imposed, the prices have been generally accepted and supported by both local officials and members of the community.

Another example is Omaha, Nebraska, which charges private individuals for use of public space both above and below the ground.[8] Although such a charge program may appear complicated at first glance, Omaha has found that

Police protection
  special patrol service fees
  parking fees and charges
  fees for fingerprints, copies
  payments for extra police
    service at stadiums, thea-
    ters, circuses
Transportation
  subway and bus fares
  bridge tolls
  landing and departure fees
  hangar rentals
  concession rentals
  parking meter receipts
Health and hospitals
  inoculation charges
  X-ray charges
  hospital charges, including
    per diem rates and
    service charges
  ambulance charges
  concession rentals
Education
  charges for books
  charges for gymnasium uni-
    forms or special equipment
  concession rentals
Recreation
  greens fees
  parking charges
  concession rentals
  admission fees or charges
  permit charges for tennis
    courts, etc.
  charges for services
  picnic stove fees
  stadium gate tickets

stadium club fees
park development charges
Sanitation
  domestic and commercial
    trash collection fees
  industrial waste charges
Sewerage
  sewerage system fees
Other public utility
    Operations
  water meter permits
  water services charges
  electricity rates
  telephone booth rentals
Housing, neighborhood and
    commercial development
  street tree fees
  tract map filing fees
  street-lighting installations
  convention center revenues
    event charges
    scoreboard fees
    hall, meeting room leases
    concessions
Commodity sales
  salvage materials
  sales of maps
  sales of codes
Licenses and fees
  advertising vehicle
  amusements (ferris
    wheels, etc.)
  billiards and pool
  bowling alley
  circus and carnival
  coal dealers
  commercial combustion

dances
dog tags
duplicate dog tags
electrician—1st class
electrician—2nd class
film storage
foot peddler
hucksters, itinerant peddlers
heating contractors
junk dealer
loading zone permit
lumber dealer
pawnbrokers
plumbers—1st class
plumbers—2nd class
pest eradicator
poultry dealer
produce dealer—itinerant
pushcart
rooming house and hotel
secondhand dealer
secondhand auto dealer
sign inspection
solicitation
shooting gallery
taxi
taxi transfer license
taxi driver
theaters
trees—Christmas
vending—coin
vault cleaners
sound truck
refuse hauler
land fill
sightseeing bus
wrecking license

Figure 13.2. Types of Fees, Charges, and Licenses

once established, the annual billings are almost self-perpetuating with minimal expenditure in bill preparation and collection. This case illustrates the successful implementation of a user fee that corrects private market signals.

Pricing of public products has a series of objectives—some related to revenues, others to efficiency, and still others to gaining greater equity. Public prices can be used in larger amounts than they are today and for an extended range of public services. Clearly, the way to ascertain whether persons are willing to pay for some public services is to ask them to pay for the services. Without a pricing system, it becomes both difficult and costly to make estimates of consumer preferences. The margin for feasible use of market demand to guide public production is larger than has been realized in many cities.

As cities begin their inquiries into the purposes and results of public programs, they also begin to inquire about the basis of their current user charge practices and about the economic incentives for use of public resources, such as air, water, and land. And consequently, extended use of public prices can be expected.

Notes

1. Selma J. Mushkin, ed., *Public Prices for Public Products* (Washington, D.C.: Urban Institute, 1972); Selma J. Mushkin, "Public Prices for Public Products," *The Municipal Yearbook, 1971* (Washington, D.C.: International City Managers Association, 1971); and James A. Maxwell and J. Richard Aronson, *Financing State and Local Governments* (3rd ed.; Washington, D.C.: Brookings Institution, 1977).
2. For a more detailed discussion of this point, see Calvin A. Kent, "Users' Fees for Municipalities," *Governmental Finance*, February 1972, p. 5.
3. Frederick D. Stocker, "Diversification of the Local Revenue System: Income and Sales Taxes, User Charges, Federal Grants," *National Tax Journal* 29 (September 1976): 320.
4. Advisory Commission on Intergovernmental Relations, *Local Revenue Diversification: Income, Sales Taxes and User Charges* (Report A-47), Washington, D.C., 1974.
5. See Willard Price, "The Case Against the Imposition of a Sewer Use Tax," *Governmental Finance*, May 1975, pp. 38–41.
6. See the findings of a survey conducted by the NTA Committee on Local Nonproperty Taxation in *Proceedings of the Sixty-Seventh Annual Conference*, NTA-TIA, 1974, pp. 398–423.
7. Robert M. Odell, Jr., "Use of Recreation Service Changes," *Governmental Finance*, February 1972, pp. 15–19.
8. E. J. Hewitt, "Areaway and Subway Charges," *Governmental Finance*, February 1972, pp. 12–14.

CHARLES A. MORRISON

14. Identifying Alternative Resources for Local Government

New York City's trip to the brink of bankruptcy beginning in 1974 is by no means typical—but that city's distress has dramatized to most cities the necessity of calling a halt to the headlong expansion of city budgets.

George Peterson of the Urban Institute, writing in *The Urban Predicament*,[1] reminds us that "1975 will be remembered for its rediscovery of the budget constraint. Where once the budget messages of mayors were crowded with promises of new programs and announcements of pay raises for public employees, in 1975 they carried the more somber theme that resources had given out, leaving no option but retrenchment." Expansion of resources at the 1947 to 1970 rates is a thing of the past, and we now face management of "steady state" resources while pressures to increase and add public services continue to mount.

Impressive economic growth is predicted for the U.S. in the years ahead, but the tax revenues generated by this growth are already committed to existing programs. A Brookings Institution study suggests that acute social needs cannot be met without either raising taxes or cutting lower-priority government programs. But there are strongly entrenched interests ready to defend every part of the budget—and to fight for more.

The economic recession of 1974–75 squeezed municipal revenues as receipts from municipal tax sources reflected the reduction of business activity and consumer spending, for social and other public programs. The accompanying inflation increased the pressure from municipal workers for wage increases and raised other costs of government, especially energy costs. In the three years, 1972 to 1974, inflation alone raised state and local government expenditures by 25 percent while increasing revenues by only 15 percent, thus creating a 10 percent gap and loss of purchasing power established at nearly $5 billion annually.

In the absence of greatly increased federal or state help, most cities have been forced to respond with such measures as raising taxes and reducing services. These steps exacerbate the underlying trends that account for most cities' *long-term* fiscal problems—the loss of higher income residents and job-creating enterprises.

Inflation also puts local governments in a financial squeeze. Property taxes lag inflation, and resistance to increased taxes (of all kinds) mounts. The public

235

demands more and increased services and public employees demand higher wages and fringe benefits.

Cost-cutting alone cannot be the answer. It can be counterproductive. It is too simple a response. Rather, there is need for increased productivity in the use and application of the resources which we have, and intensive study into the identification of new resources to assist in meeting the continued demands for public programs. This resource identification activity is the subject of this report.

Resources will be divided into two categories, financial and nonfinancial. Under financial resources, we will look at a process for examining local revenues and identify ways to seek out nonlocal revenues, both governmental and nongovernmental.

Nonfinancial resources are less traditionally examined as ways to assist in the budget crunch. Local employees are a major resource, and we will outline a process for involving employees at all levels of the organization in efforts to meet the challenge. We will also look at potential intergovernmental resources and how they are being effectively used in a number of cities. Finally, we will explore nonservice approaches to the solution of local governmental problems.

Financial Resources: Raising Local Revenues

Many municipalities systematically review their revenue structures annually or every few years as a prelude to identifying new local sources of revenue either in the form of new (or increased) taxes or in new (or increased) charges for service. Douglas Ayres,[2] former city manager of Inglewood, California, has put together a helpful checklist to consider when thinking about raising local revenues. This is a most comprehensive approach, but many of the factors taken alone or in concert with a few others will provide significant information about the viability of new local revenue sources.

The Principles of Local Revenue Raising

1. Be sure the tax/charge legally can be imposed.
2. Prepare an estimate of revenues to be raised by each new/increased source.
3. Estimate the costs of collection and enforcement.
4. Anticipate the difficulties of enforcement.
    a. Who will collect?
    b. Who will pay?
    c. Who will oppose?
    d. Who will favor?
    e. Who will oppose on general philosophical bases?
5. Secure advance clearance.
    a. From elected officials.
    b. From those who will collect.
    c. From those who will pay.

6. Think through the timing of the move.
   a. When broached privately.
   b. When broached publicly.
   c. When legally introduced.
   d. When passed into law.
   e. When effective.
   f. When to start collecting.
   g. When to initiate enforcement.
7. Conduct periodic needs and capacity studies.
   a. Catalogue needs.
   b. Separate out the "necessary projects" from the pious wishes.
   c. Cost each project.
   d. Develop a community goals process to prioritize needs.
   e. Inform the public of the resultant prioritized needs.
   f. Analyze revenue sources to most nearly match benefits with revenue sources.
   g. Extend economic base studies to determine financial capacity of the community.
   h. Develop a source-by-source, month-by-month ten-year revenue analysis.
   i. Project revenues and project costs for ten years.
   j. Match tax/charge, community, financial capacity with needs.
   k. Determine willingness to utilize capacity to meet prioritized needs.
   l. Decide operating expense emphasis.
   m. Decide on pay-as-you-go versus bond issuance for capital projects.
   n. Determine strategies to tap or assess willingness to pay.

Specific Revenue Sources

1. Taxes
   a. Property taxes
      (1) within limits allowed by state law.
      (2) outside levy limits.
      (3) specific levy linkages.
      (4) foreign trade goods are now taxable.
   b. Other taxes
      (1) services taxable by cities.
      (2) utilities users taxes.
      (3) review laws for other taxes and/or consult the state municipal association.
2. Licenses and Permits
   a. Permit fees can reflect and recoup *all* costs of permit investigation.
   b. Shift from flat rate to gross receipts for business and occupation taxes.

        (1) by business category.

        (2) by gross receipts brackets.

   c. Fire inspection permit charges.

   d. Review all permit fees annually for adequacy.

3. Fines, Forfeitures, and Penalties

   a. Negotiate revised bail schedules with the judges.

   b. Consider assumption of parking ticket collection.

   c. Renegotiate county-city percentage split of court fines.

   d. Review parking fine adequacy in view of parking charges.

   e. Review library book fine procedures and rates.

4. From Use of Money and Property

   a. Review cash collection and timing for guide deposit.

   b. Review cash balance reporting procedures to minimize free balances.

   c. Review vacant property for usage and rental level.

   d. Consider use of redevelopment and housing authorities to secure financing flexibility.

   e. Overbuild city hall or other municipal buildings and rent extra space held in future need.

   f. Review rental parking spaces for parity with private lot charges.

   g. Review parks and facilities for concessions possibilities and revenue levels.

5. Service Charges

   a. Review parking meter rates.

        (1) eliminate the penny.

        (2) install electronic flag droppers.

        (3) determine if off-street lots are competitive with meters and/or potential assessment district charges.

        (4) review beach and park parking fees.

   b. Implement a tennis reservation fee.

   c. Create a nonresident recreation facility use card for a fee.

   d. Equate special recreation programs with cost-based fees.

        (1) art classes.

        (2) ceramics classes.

        (3) leagues and teams.

        (4) teen clubs.

        (5) *ad infinitum.*

   e. Rent recreation facilities for receptions, bar mitzvahs, weddings, etc.

   f. Charge for police accident report copies and fingerprint service.

   g. Review xerox charges and add in hook-up costs.

   h. Establish sanitation service on a full-cost monthly fee basis.

   i. Rent police and fire personnel for special private usages.

   j. Divide recreational classes with school district to specialize and eliminate intergovernmental competition.

k. Charge medical insurance for ambulance fees.

l. Find a service that can be restricted in usage, create a fee structure, and control. For example, charge full costs for reports and other written material provided to the public.

m. Review marina and launching ramp cost/fee relationship.

n. Review airport fuel, tie-down, space, and building rental rates.

o. Review special expertise and equipment and rent to other jurisdictions.

p. Keep attuned to recreational needs and respond, on a fee basis.
   (1) skateboard courses.
   (2) dirt bike trails.
   (3) bike trails.

q. Light the golf course and/or employ golf rangers to expedite play.

r. Review animal control costs and fees.

7. From Utilities and Enterprises

a. Acquire water districts or companies to secure the economies of scale.

b. Institute double charges for outside city limits customers.

c. Repair water meters more often—old meters run slow.

d. Review potentialities for pyrolysis refuse reduction/gas/power production facilities.

e. Review sewer service charge under federal water pollution control law guidelines.

f. Impose sanitation charge.
   (1) sewer.
   (2) refuse collection.
   (3) refuse disposal.
   (4) street sweeping.

g. Contributions to construction by developers.

8. Other Revenues

a. Review all special assessment district possibilities.
   (1) streets.
   (2) sewers.
   (3) landscaping.
   (4) street tree maintenance.
   (5) park acquisition/maintenance.
   (6) business development.
   (7) parking.

b. Review surplus real and personal property for sale.

c. Establish policies governing in-lieu transfers from revenue-producing funds.

d. Borrowing
   (1) consider bond anticipation notes to time market entry.
   (2) consider general obligation bonds for interest savings.

  (3) nonprofit corporations.
  (4) joint powers agreements.
  (5) lease notes.
 e. Surplus from discontinued funds.

Interfund and Internal Charging

1. Create intragovernmental funds for:
 a. Equipment rental/replacement.
 b. Office equipment rental/replacement.
 c. Stores/warehousing.
 d. Data processing.
 e. Mail service.
 f. Communications.
 g. Duplication services.
2. Utilize interfund transfers to accumulate and distribute full costs.
 a. For program costing.
 b. For full cost public disclosure purposes.
 c. For depreciation accumulation for replacement reserve creation.
3. Rent services to other jurisdictions.

Implementation and Strategy to Keep Current

1. Package revenue raising measures early in year to achieve maximum interest capability.
2. Change fiscal year to achieve maximum interest benefits.
3. "Index" revenue sources to the *Consumer Price Index:*
 a. For automatic increases.
 b. To relieve annual review burden.
4. Program long-term increases into ordinances.
5. Have fees tied to national actions.
6. Institute automatic rate reviews, based on actual cost accumulation data.

Financial Resources: Seeking Out Nonlocal Revenues

The budget crunch on local governments has forced more and more cities and counties to turn to outside forces for financial aid. The federal government has been the primary source of funds since the mid-1950s with various forms of aid. In recent years state governments have become a second major source of outside funding for local governments.

Federal Aid to Local Governments

The federal government uses a variety of methods to dispense funds to local governments. *Grants for specific projects*[3] are one way. These are competitive by their very nature with funds awarded generally coming from discretionary sources, i.e., the funding agency decides the worth of each proposal and awards the grant(s) to those local governments evaluated as proposing the best projects (within the constraints of legislation and regulations). The competition for a fairly limited amount of funds is fierce. Generally, the funding agency decides on the basis of a grading system that considers the following factors:

1. Does the project meet the goals of the legislation?
2. Is the project within restrictions of legislation?
3. Does the proposer demonstrate the capacity to implement?
4. Does the project address a significant problem area?
5. Does the project demonstrate creativity?
6. Does the project have results which are transferable to other local governments?

Project grant information is generally set forth in the *Federal Register* through which the funding agency notifies all prospective applicants of upcoming grant competitions. Generally, a specific deadline and other application requirements are set forth in the *Register* and applicants should be particularly careful that all requirements are met. One current example of project grants are the community development discretionary grants.

Formula grants do not imply the same competition characteristic of project grants because these funds are allocated to specified units of government (state, counties, or cities) according to a preset formula (usually set forth in the authorizing legislation). Factors include population, income levels, and urbanization. Examples of formula grants include CETA grants for sewage facility construction and community development block grants.

The federal government also dispenses funds to local governments through *contracts* under which the government desires to receive a specific product. A federal agency advertises its intent to contract in the *Commerce Business Daily*, which lists all federal procurement announcements. Organizations wishing to bid contact the federal agency to receive a formal request for proposal (RFP) which outlines all the specific details of the prospective contract.

The government also awards *sole source* contracts where a contract is made with a particular organization without competition. There are, however, few sole source contracts awarded because the issuing agency must follow strict guidelines including the following:

1. Demonstrate the unique capability of the contractor.
2. Is such a tight time schedule dictated so that no other organization could do the project?
3. Are there no financial benefits (i.e., lower costs) that would accrue from competition?

Finally, *unsolicited proposals*, whether for project grants or contracts, sound promising and attractive as sources of government funding. Here, too, there is a caveat. While policy may vary from one agency to another and often within the same agency, it is extremely difficult to obtain funding through this procedure. The ideas behind the proposal must be truly unique and widely beneficial. Furthermore, the bidder must be uniquely well-qualified to do the work. Unless the bidder is confident to the point of not having any doubts whatsoever about the caliber of its ideas, personnel, expertise and ability to complete the task, it is much wiser to try another avenue. Particularly in times of tight federal budgets, funds that have been set aside for unsolicited proposals are the most expendable and the first to be cut.

Suggestions for Applying for Federal Funds[4]

There is no simple way to get federal funds. It requires a mixture of hard work, initiative, perseverance, creativity, timing and a touch of luck. Several factors can be isolated as reasons for success in federal grantsmanship.

1. *Gravity of Problem(s).* A city or county is nationally recognized as having a particular problem—which often times may result from some form of disaster (natural or man-made).
2. *High Recognition within funding agency.* Some jurisdictions have cultivated "patron saints" within various federal funding agencies and have convinced those officials that their city or county are worthy places for many forms of experimental assistance programs.
3. *Political Clout.* While the support of the home district representative or senator no longer carries the weight it once did, such support cannot be ignored (and worthy proposals with such support are all the stronger).
4. *Creative Grantsmanship.* This is the combination of hard work, imagination, dedication, initiative, and energy that are the hallmark of the successful grantsperson.

Government Information Services has compiled the case study below of Peekskill, New York which they consider to be one of the most successful communities in the federal grantsmanship area.

The most successful community in the nation is getting federal dollars is Peekskill, New York, a community of just 20,000 people about 40 miles north of New York City on the Hudson River.

Since 1968, Peekskill has secured nearly $35 million in state and federal aid largely through the efforts of its energetic city planner—David Ornstein. When Mr. Ornstein came to Peekskill in 1968 he set out to get massive portions of state and federal aid.

As *Newsweek* magazine reported he "succeeded beyond anyone's dreams" in shaking the money tree and getting Peekskill "more money per capita than any other city in the country."

"Part of the secret of getting government money," Mr. Ornstein said, "is to know more about the program than the agencies that fund them.

Then you can show them what pigeonhole you belong in." An example of this was Mr. Ornstein's success in getting funds from the state's Open Space Program. Until Peekskill did it, no other city in New York had tried to get money from this program for clearing slum land. Peekskill got $170,000 toward the cost of a 2.2 acre inner city park.

Until then "they had only given out the money to purchase swamps, mountains and stream valleys," Mr. Ornstein said.

Another use of imagination and initiative turned up in Peekskill's request for $30,000 for a planning grant to study the problem of the disposal of the hot water that was used to cool a nuclear power plant. The plant was located on the outskirts of Peekskill on the Hudson River.

You would expect such a request to be made to the National Science Foundation or the old Atomic Energy Commission. But the request was made to the National Endowment for the Arts (NEA). Peekskill got the money.

It applied under the NEA's City Options program whose purpose was "to improve the looks and livability of our communities." Most of the $3,000,000 allocated under the City Options program by NEA went for projects such as urban design and planning studies or historic preservation.

Other communities show the same "imagination and initiative" of creative grantsmanship in applying for NEA's City Options funds. The city of Pawtucket (Rhode Island) got $30,000 to study and plan for the rehabilitation of the city zoo while Princeton (New Jersey) got $8,900 for a study to convert a railroad station into a community transportation center.

NEA's program also showed that smaller communities are given their share. Of the 148 grants made by the NEA, 24 dealt with towns and rural areas of 25,000 people or less.

GET THE INFORMATION. A key initial step in the grants process is the gathering of appropriate information. It is information that gives you the competitive edge in getting a share of the dollars which are granted to local and state governments. Key sources of information are the following:

Catalog of Federal Domestic Assistance published by the U.S. Government Printing Office is very useful although generally somewhat out of date.

Publications and services of the National League of Cities.

ICMA Newsletter, particularly inserts which present "updates" on federal developments.

Publications and services of Government Information Services.

Publications of the National Council for Urban Economic Development.

Commerce Clearinghouse publications on federal assistance.

Other federal publications that also may be of assistance include the following:

Congressional Record
Commerce Business Daily

Federal Register
ETA Interchange (Department of Labor)
HUD Challenge
HUD Newsletter
LEAA Newsletter
LEAA Guide for Discretionary Grant Programs
National Endowment for the Arts Guide to Programs
National Endowment for the Humanities Program Announcement

It cannot be overemphasized that this basic information is critical to the federal fund search because of the large number of federal agencies and departments which give support to local government.

INITIATE INTEREST. Once a program *and a fund appropriation* passes the Congress it is time to act to initiate your interest in a particular program. At that preliminary state there are several key steps a city or county can take.

1. Read the legislation. Rules and regulations will not significantly change the specific language of Congress.
2. Assess local needs to determine what kinds of programs will meet particular local needs. *This is critical*, because federal funds which do not meet local needs pose an unnecessary burden on a locality.
3. Contact the specific program office which will be (or is) administering the program. Get the name of the program officer and begin discussing with that person your ideas about a project in your community. These discussions should seek to determine the limitations of the program.
4. Conceptualize the project and set up a local planning mechanism which includes key people—staff, citizens, and regional agency (if applicable).

Once regulations are published you can begin the formal application process, which will include the following steps:

1. Carefully analyze the regulations and/or guidelines and determine (*a*) does the proposed project fit within the eligibility requirements? and (*b*) does the federal agency plan to spend funds on projects like the one you propose? If the answers to both questions are positive, it is possible to proceed.
2. Draft preliminary proposal and have it reviewed by all key local people.
3. Meet with the agency program office and review the preliminary draft with them. Seek their comments and opinions.
4. Revise the draft into the the formal application.
5. Submit the *complete* application prior to the deadline.

In summary, there are five key points to keep in mind about seeking federal grants:

1. Grants must support local needs to be cost-effective for a community.
2. You can't receive a grant unless you apply for it.
3. Know your chances of success before you apply.
4. Maintain constant contact with the federal agency program office.
5. Hard work, perseverance, and creativity pay off.

Seeking State Aid

In recent years, a larger number of states have been providing increased aid to their local governments.

The process for identifying state resources is not drastically different than that for obtaining federal funds. Again, information is the key. At the state level the key sources of information are as follows:

1. State municipal leagues are usually on top of the state legislative processes and thus have good information about those state departments and programs which provide support to local governments.
2. State departments of community affairs are relatively recent creations. One of their major missions is to provide assistance to local governments and assist local governments to more fully utilize state resources.
3. State budget offices are occasionally helpful in assisting local governments in identifying sources of state funds for cities and providing technical assistance to cities with financial difficulties.

Once the base information has been gathered, the application process is similar to that in applying for federal funds. In the case of state grant programs, it is even more important to maintain the informal contact with the funding agency because they are generally willing and able to provide assistance to the local government in the application process.

County/City Financial Relationships

The perplexing problem of appropriately allocating costs of services among units of government in the same area is one being wrestled with by many local governments. The following paragraphs are excerpted from a presentation made by the city of Grants Pass, Oregon, to the county:

In all of our recent meetings, we have discussed common problems, and each of you have told us on many occasions two important points: (1) that the people who live in the city are county residents, and (2) that the county is prohibited from providing unequal levels of service by spending money to support one area when you are not supporting the entire population. Unfortunately, it is our opinion, that just exactly that is the situation here in Josephine County. We have based our statements on what you have told us…that the board of county commissioners is something more than the city council for the unincorporated areas. We believe that they represent the entire county, including the city residents. This simple premise is the basis for our requests. These requests will basically fall into two categories: the first of which will be for base levels of support and will cover the areas of law enforcement, paving assessments, road maintenance, recreation services and sewer system capital facilities. The other requests will involve payments for fire protection to unincorporated areas already being serviced by the city, and capital projects for use by all city residents.

The County has provided 100% of the recreation costs associated with unincorporated county residents who utilize the city's recreational program. Last year that amounted to $56,583. The City is requesting, however, a change in philosophy. We believe that city residents are just as much county residents as those residing in the unincorporated area. Therefore, incorporated county residents should be eligible for the same benefits as unincorporated county residents. Consequently, the city is requesting the cost of recreation services for both the in-city as well as out-of-city county residents.

The City currently provides fire protection services on a no-cost basis to several public facilities in the unincorporated area of the county. These costs are paid by the city residents. Therefore, we are requesting the County to pay its fair share for the protection of these public facilities.

The problem of overlapping jurisdictional authority is a major characteristic of the U.S. governmental system. The challenge to local governments—counties, cities, and townships (where they exist)—is to ensure that all taxpayers in a given local service area pay equitably for equal service.

Financial Resources: Nongovernmental Sources of Funds

The local government manager who achieves success in getting funding from nongovernmental sources has reached a higher level in the grantsmanship business. These are the less traditional sources of funds for support of local activities. Two potential sources have netted considerable success for local governments: foundations and local private sector sources.

Foundation Funding

Did you know that there are over 2,500 private foundations in the United States with assets in excess of $1,000,000 and who annually give grants totalling more than $400,000? These foundations are located in every state and have purposes ranging from very broad national issues to very specific state problems. Many have stated purposes that include activities central to the missions of local governments. The highest percentage of foundation grants go for educational purposes (broadly defined) followed by health, welfare, and sciences as other principal areas of foundation interest.

As with federal and state grants, the key to seeking foundation support is information. The best source of this information is *The Foundation Directory*[5] published by The Foundation Center. Not only does the directory provide capsulized profiles on the 2,500 largest foundations, but it also tells how to get more detailed information.

The directory also recommends four general rules for grant applicants:

1. Do your homework. Know the foundation's areas of interest and objectives and its potential for support.
2. Submit only those proposals which fall within the foundation's areas of interest and within its means.
3. Clear with the foundation before you prepare and submit lengthy proposals.
4. If you receive a grant, make regular evaluation and progress reports with a sufficiently detailed accounting of expenditures of foundation funds.

Other Private Funding Sources

Local businesses, industries, and chambers of commerce are vitally interested in the activities of their local governments and very frequently are willing to give "grants" to those local governments to facilitate new or ongoing activities. Particularly in such areas as park facilities, recreation programs and other youth activities, and industrial and commercial development, local private sources have a vital interest.

The process utilized in these cases is much more informal than those previously described. Contact is made with the local business (usually at the executive level or through the public affairs department of a large corporation) and the proposal is presented. Discussions continue with further meetings and perhaps the establishment of a local citizens committee. Sometimes a fund-raising drive results, in others a single source may decide to fund the proposal. Two examples of different approaches to private involvement are described in the following paragraphs.

In 1967, Des Moines, Iowa, experienced some minor civil disturbances, and prominent leaders in the community decided that some action need be taken to generate employment opportunities for disadvantaged youth in the Des Moines area. Community Improvement, Inc. was formed. With staff assistance from the chamber of commerce and the city, and with support from the governor, a major local fund-raising campaign was put together. It produced over $200,000 to pay salaries for youth to be employed in public and quasi-public agencies. This program dramatically expanded the existing youth employment program funded by the federal government (via Neighborhood Youth Corps) and provided greater flexibility—because there didn't have to be a strict adherence to eligibility criteria. (In 1972 Iowa began providing financial support to Des Moines and other Iowa cities for youth employment efforts.)

In 1974, Benton Harbor, Michigan, set as two of its priorities the establishment of two new departments: Economic Development, and Human Resource Development. After exploring several funding options the mayor and city manager decided to approach a local industry and seek its support. The government and public affairs department of the industry responded favorably to the idea and asked the city to draft a formal proposal for funding, stating the objectives to be pursued and the expected outcomes. With a minimum of red tape (none) and maximum speed (two months), the industry approved the proposal for full funding for one year on the condition that the city would continue the new departments in the second year if they proved to be successful. No paperwork was required during the grant year, and the city had only to submit a summary report at the end of the grant year.

Nonfinancial Resources: Local Employees

It is popular to match federal grants with "in-kind" contributions from the recipient government. Each organization has a wealth of its own resources, which, if better utilized, can produce more effective organizations. It seems appropriate here to remember Peter Drucker's words of wisdom—that of all the resources at management's command, only our human resources are capable of enlargement.

Developing Local Employees as Resources

How can local employee resources be developed? By utilizing them in a process which involves them more deeply in their jobs and the organization. The following is a brief overview of this process.

There are no constraints on the motivation of employees and their capabilities to work effectively and productively—*if* the organizational environment is conducive to stimulating employee effectiveness. Hours, job classifications, pay, and workloads may be fixed; but there is still room for working both better and smarter—from top management on down throughout the organization. This may be encouraged by inspiring individuals, by adjusting the organizational framework, or both. Obviously, anything done to personally stimulate individuals also affects the organization; and anything done to create a more effective organizational framework affects the individuals in it. The more that can be done on both fronts at once, the better.

WHAT CAN YOU DO? Any program aimed at increasing human effectiveness will need to be specially tailored to each organization. In the continuing absence of pat, universal principles, each organization has to diagnose its own problems and opportunities to develop its own activities and programs.

Because programs to increase employee effectiveness call for activities specially designed for the situation and changes that will have long-term and ongoing impact, the effort needs a great deal of creativity and flexibility. It places responsibility for this on top management in two ways: by being creative in its work and thinking, and by developing an environment to inspire and encourage creativity at all levels. Only through creative thinking can local governments discover ways to work within constraints and to develop and test new methods for stimulating employee effectiveness.

THE ANSWER IS IN THE PROCESS. The emphasis must be on "process" rather than "product." Research, meetings with practitioners, and examinations of successful programs to improve local government employee effectiveness have proven that good "products" can best be discovered, tested and implemented through a deliberate "process" of research and planning. It is not enough to say, "A city or county up the road has done great things through job rotation; I think I'll try it." Or, "Participatory management in their personnel department worked; let's plug it in here." Your county or city is different and may or may not be able to transfer a good program that worked elsewhere. It may require a new program that has never been tried anywhere else, or a tried and true strategy greatly refined for local use.

The *process* that can guide your decisions about what strategies to test and refine for greater employee effectiveness starts when you ask, "Where are we now?" By *diagnosing* what is happening in the organization, how work is getting done, and what individuals feel about their roles, you can begin to define specific problems and opportunities for solving them and, listening to the thoughts, feelings, and suggestions of the people who work in the organization is imperative with this program. Only by recognizing the current situation can you measure future results and accomplishments against it.

From diagnosis, you can move to *identifying problems* and *opportunities for change.* For example, if a survey of employees and their work told you that morale among people handling citizen complaints adversely affects their work, you will need to define exactly what the problem is. Is there a need for increased training of people answering complaints, for a new system of processing complaints, for increased autonomy of the complaint response staff? If you can determine the problem accurately, you can move toward greater effectiveness and productivity of the people handling complaints. There are numerous strategies for this problem definition stage—from forming a task force of employees involved to conducting more specific surveys that dig into the question at hand.

With problems defined, what do you do about them? The *planning for action* phase should be a coordinated planning process for making decisions about new experiments to solve problems. Commitment and initiative from the top is essential, but the people most affected by changes should have some input in planning them. These employees often are in the best position to offer creative ideas, and they certainly are in the right spot to sabotage any changes they do not like. During this planning stage it also will be necessary to identify resources for implementing new programs. ("Do we have the money and people to train our complaint staff?"); to establish goals and measurements ("How will we know when the new complaint response system is successful?"); and to assess the possibility of short-term pilot experiments ("Can we test the idea of increased decision making authority of the complaint staff for a few months and see how it goes?")

Planning for action also calls for being aware of substantive alternatives to increase employee effectiveness—such as incentive and reward systems, fringe benefits, job rotation, job redesign, new physical environments, group decision making, increased autonomy, and career development.

What happens during *implementation* and how to refine and plan future strategies to increase employee effectiveness also are included. Emphasis is on keeping channels of communication open, checking for changes, evaluating results, and maintaining a favorable organizational climate. The implementation phase is at the heart of establishing programs to increase employee effectiveness as ongoing processes for organizational improvement. Continual planning, *testing, evaluating, refining, and retesting* is essential. Organizations and their environments change, but a process of ongoing problem solving can help you keep apace with that change.

Nonlocal Government Resources

Looking outside the confines of your local government, you can also find a variety of nonfinancial resources. First, other governments perform similar functions and a wide array of intergovernmental sharing efforts are being implemented. Several efforts result in a pooling of resources. They include

> Personal contacts or informal cooperation
> Parallel action
> Joint agencies
> Service contracts
> Conferences and informational activities
> Financial cooperation
> Easements
> Regional associations of local governments
> Cooperative authorities
> Compulsory joint cooperation (requirements in some states that local governments act together, usually regional review of plans)

Service contracts will be dealt with at some length below. Personal contacts or informal cooperation are worthy of some explanation. This cooperation is generally in the form of voluntary aid or mutual-aid exchange by informal agreement. Such cooperation has produced some admirable results, and many communities have out of custom or neighborliness rendered mutual aid, but it has a serious drawback.

Where mutual aid has been rendered without formal agreement, the municipal employees performing extraterritorial functions may not be protected by immunity from liability or by pensions, disability, or workmen's compensation; they may not be entitled to other rights and benefits that normally apply when functions are performed within their own municipal limits. Accordingly, it seems more appropriate that formal written agreements (including contracts) be entered into whenever practicable when a decision is made to perform or exchange services beyond specific municipal boundaries.

AGREEMENT OR CONTRACT. Agreements or joint agreements differ from contracts for service. An agreement provides for the joint exercise of powers and is generally used when all the cooperating units participate in the activity. Program development and policy matters such as planning, urban renewal, and recreation are covered agreements.

The contract method is recommended as an approach to be explored seriously by local government officials. Contract agreements differ from joint cooperative efforts in that one municipality provides and administers the services without participation on the part of the municipality to whom the services are furnished. Under the service contract, a political subdivision simply purchases a service from another unit of government. Although the terms of the contract must be agreeable to both parties, the supplier usually has complete control over the administration of the service.

INTERLOCAL COOPERATION THROUGH CONTRACTING. The possibilities as to service and cooperation between levels of government are endless. Almost all local government services can potentially be administered jointly by one or more units of government. Usually an intermunicipal contract is between a larger unit and a smaller one. Whenever local government units are about equal in size and importance, the form of their cooperation is generally through a joint agreement where participation is on a more comparable level. Counties probably provide the greatest number of services to local units of government under contract. Yet the combinations through intermunicipal contracting are many—cities, municipalities, towns, boroughs, townships, and villages can contract with one another or with special districts (schools, water, sewer, etc.).

TRANSFER OF FUNCTIONS. An offshoot of the intergovernmental sharing relationships is the transfer of functions to other levels of government. There is considerable thought that administration of the welfare system should be a national effort and that delivery of education services should be the sole function of states (at least in terms of financial burden). Further, many areas now have county-administered parks and recreation systems that include all facilities within incorporated cities. The process of achieving a transfer of functions involves joint effort, cities, counties, and states working together to logically determine what level of government should administer the various services.

ASSISTANCE FROM OTHER GOVERNMENTAL LEVELS. Another source of nonlocal government resources is the receipt of technical assistance from regional associations, state governments or federal agencies. It is very common for regional planning agencies and councils of government to have as a major function the provision of technical assistance to local governments in their region. This is most common in the planning, transportation, and sewer service areas where the regional entity can afford to employ technical specialists in each area to assist local governments in the development of specific plans.

State departments or agencies of community affairs also provide such services on a statewide basis—as do municipal and county associations. Both the state and the associations have the ability to observe local governments on a broad scale and serve as a mechanism for the transfer of good ideas and projects from one jurisdiction to another.

COLLEGES AND UNIVERSITIES. Institutions of higher education provide an excellent resource in several ways. First, they have facilities for research. Second, students provide a good source of free or reduced price labor for work on projects designed by a local government. Third, universities often act as "think tanks" to develop new approaches to the delivery of local government services.

PERSONNEL TRANSFER. Transfer from one government to another is a possible resource. Under the Intergovernmental Personnel Act, federal personnel can be assigned to local governments for a one-year period at only the cost that a normal employee would have cost. Several states have begun similar transfer programs through their departments of community affairs. Local governments also receive student interns from colleges and universities. In many cases students work at no cost on projects that further their academic goals. For example, one city used a group of business students to make a study of the city's purchasing system and make recommendations for improvement. In other cases, a significant portion of students salary is paid under a work-study program.

Private Resources

A second major nonlocal government resources is private resources, using people and facilities available in the community. Examples in this area could range from simple use of conference or meeting-room facilities at a local business or utility to complex volunteer programs.

Involving citizens in the functions of government is one way to utilize the people resources of communities. Greatly different examples are provided below in cases in Arlington, Massachusetts and Des Moines, Iowa.

Arlington, Massachusetts — Citizens' Involvement Committee

Arlington, Massachusetts, a fairly homogeneous town of 53,000 in the Metropolitan Boston area, suffers many of the difficulties that plague other metropolitan communities: deteriorating housing stock, rising demand for social services for the poor and elderly, and inadequate public transportation. Since 1969, the per capita tax levy has risen an average of thirty-five dollars per person per year and Arlington is looking for new ways of raising revenue and enhancing the efficiency of its public services. Recent comprehensive planning reports show that the local economy is in some trouble. Even with the expansion and further professionalization of Arlington's planning and development activities over the past few years, serious problems still arise when it comes to setting priorities for community development and actually fashioning development policies that can achieve widespread popular support. There are 252 town meeting members representing 21 precincts, and this group makes many of the key decisions. At present, the town meeting structure does not appear to be working very effectively. Specifically, the town meeting members appear to be significantly out of touch with the opinions of their constituencies. Recently, a school bond issue was defeated (twice!) at the polls, after having been endorsed by both the Board of Selectmen and the town meeting members.

In an attempt to deal with these issues, the Arlington Board of Selectmen, some town meeting members, and the Department of Community Development (with the aid of Massachusetts Institute of Technology's (MIT) Department of Urban Studies and Planning) have been working to initiate a citizens' planning process. The key to this process is a nonpartisan organization called the Citizens Involvement Committee (CIC). The CIC's goals are

1. To discover, define, and document the fundamental issues and priorities in Arlington
2. To provide a vehicle for interested citizens, particularly town meeting members, to assist in improving town policies in these areas
3. To interest a wider range of citizens in town affairs and to aid them in becoming more directly involved in town government

In recent months the program has matured in significant ways. The CIC has completed the administering and analysis of several town-wide surveys to document citizen attitudes and priorities and has instituted six task forces, each of which may involve as many as twenty to thirty participants on a regular basis. The group has garnered substantial financial support ($10,000 from the Town of Arlington and $30,000 from foundation sources) as well as donations of student and staff time from MIT. In addition, the project has begun to attract considerable interest in Massachusetts; a town-wide conference, held in January, was attended by representatives of a dozen communities, interested in learning more about this citizen involvement project. Through *FEEDBACK*, the project newsletter, CIC has begun to build ties to other communities which may be interested in instituting a similar program in their locales.

Des Moines, Iowa — Citizen Budget Study Committee
Another approach to the problem was initiated in Des Moines, Iowa, in 1971, when the council, recognizing that growth in resources was not keeping pace with perceived community needs created a "Citizen Budget Study Committee" to make recommendations which will provide the maximum necessary service to the public at the least dollar expenditure. The committee was composed of concerned citizens from the business community and from the city as a whole. This committee acted as a policy board for "loaned" staff contributed by several major firms in the city — staff chosen on the basis of experience in management operations analysis. This "full-time" staff undertook a detailed review of city operationsnand recommended changes to the Committee who reviewed the staff input and prepared a report to the city council and city manager.

What Resulted? 163 recommendations for changes in operations resulting in a net gain to the city of $500,000 (city staff analysis). The city manager concurred in 128 of the 163 recommendations as being feasible for implementation within two years. The committee pointed up areas where the city had not implemented previous reports—and some bold areas where great savings could be achieved.

The city manager was slightly skeptical of the study at its inception—thinking that it would be a hatchet job by people who didn't know anything about government. Results proved the skepticism unwarranted as the study turned out to be a healthy, relatively unbiased view of government operations—one that pointed up the overall good management of the city and at the same time recommended a significant number of improvement areas.

Volunteers are also used more directly in the provision of services. Montgomery County, Maryland, makes extensive use of volunteers to the point of having a separate office to coordinate volunteer services. In Madison, New Jersey, a mayor's talent bank lists citizens who are willing to volunteer time on municipal projects. The volunteers have helped the town with projects involving space allocation in the town hall, pension plans, health-benefit plans, wage negotiations, and personnel policies. The volunteers work alone and in groups depending on their area of expertise. In this way, the town has been able to call on expert advice and assistance without paying for it.

Nonservice Approaches to Municipal Services

In identifying new resources in the manners described thus far, we assume that the solution to municipal problems is the delivery of services. A new trend, developing policy alternatives to service delivery, in government may be emerging. Steven Waldhorn, senior political analyst at the Stanford Research Institute, has described such an approach in a paper entitled *Nonservice Approaches to Social Welfare and Community Development Problems.*[6]

The difference between "service" and "nonservice" approaches to problems rests on the distinction between government, itself, meeting a need by providing a service as opposed to government having others meet a need by changing incentives or requirements. "Service" approaches involve solving problems through such actions as providing social services, new houses, or training to those "in need." "Nonservice" solutions try to solve problems by changing incentives or regulating behavior; this may involve trying to halt housing deterioration by changing codes, restructuring job markets to increase opportunity, or reducing social service costs by eliminating "credentialism" in staffs.

Nonservice approaches focus on using local, state, and federal governments' power *to govern* rather than *spend* to achieve public objectives. Housing nonservice approaches include down-zoning residential areas, thereby reducing incentives for speculators to replace sound low- and moderate-income dwellings with high-rise apartments or offices; and barring arbitrary "redlining" practices by banks to ensure that loans for rehabilitation are available in neighborhoods most in need. Similarly, manpower nonservice approaches include the establishment of new career patterns, such as teacher aides, which offer new opportunities to minorities; and developing affirmative action programs to ensure that low- and moderate-income city residents get jobs in expanding sectors of a city's economy.

The Potential Role of Nonservice Approaches

Distinguishing between service and nonservice planning can be a way to improve public planning at the local level in the future. Planners are already beginning to focus on nonservice issues in the new policy planning movement taking place at local, state, and federal levels. Local policy-planning units, in cities such as San Jose and Cleveland and counties such as San Diego, are beginning to investigate the forces that cause problems and develop improvement strategies that encompass nonservice approaches. Departments of community affairs in New Jersey, Connecticut, and Pennsylvania are attempting to use state power more effectively to "make the rules that shape the communities." However, information about how to develop such nonservice approaches is lacking.

There is a growing awareness that nonservice approach experiments are essential. The trend has been little studied, however. State and local governments are emerging from the service-oriented decade of the 1960s isolated from developments in other places.

What Nonservice Approaches Exist?

Nonservice approaches can be defined as interventions designed to solve public policy problems by requiring, inducing, or encouraging changes in private or public action, as opposed to approaches that seek solutions to problems primarily through direct spending or income transfer. A variety of approaches fit this definition, including

1. *Changing tax policies:* disallowing accelerated depreciation on below code dwellings in order to encourage maintenance; offering tax abatement to labor intensive industries willing to hire hard-core unemployed; offering tax incentives to businesses located near their employees' homes; forbidding hospitals not serving the poor from using the nonprofit charitable exemption.
2. *Regulation:* down-zoning to discourage standard low- and moderate-income housing from being torn down; requiring firms using urban renewal land to comply with broad affirmative action programs covering city residents; allowing jitneys and other innovative forms of transit on city streets; ensuring health maintenance organizations are eligible for reimbursement under government-sponsored health insurance programs such as Medicare.
3. *Stimulation of the private sector:* promoting historic preservation to encourage rehabilitation of architecturally interesting neighborhoods; promoting new job classifications to replace secondary jobs.

These approaches are similar because they attempt to *change the incentives structure* faced by public or private agencies to affect a social welfare or community development problem. They need to be classified and defined more clearly.

Summary

Cities and counties have identified many different types of resources to meet the challenges of "managing in a tight economy." As important, many jurisdictions are using a systematic process for identifying potential new resources including

Examining local taxes, charges, and fees and the local financial management system to determine if other local sources of finance are possible

Exploring intergovernmental sources of revenue, not only from the federal government but also at the state and local level

Uncovering private financial resources, both from foundations in the grant-making business and from local businesses and industries

Developing local government employees as resources

Developing intergovernmental contracts (or other arrangements) for sharing of service delivery burdens

Utilizing people and facilities available in the local community

Examining policy alternatives to the actual delivery of services

Utilizing this process separately or in a brainstorming session with other jurisdictions, cities, and counties has developed ideas for significant new resources.

Notes

1. William Gorham and Nathan Glazer, eds., *The Urban Predicament* (Washington, D.C.: Urban Institute, 1976).
2. Douglas W. Ayres, "Practical Tips to Raising Governmental Revenues" (Center for Public Policy and Administration, California State University, Long Beach, March 1977).
3. Government Information Services, *1976 Federal Funding Guide* (Washington, D.C.: 1976).
4. Ibid.
5. The Foundation Center, *The Foundation Directory* (New York: Columbia University Press, 1975).
6. Steve Waldhorn, "Non-Service Approaches to Social Welfare and Community Development Problems" (Stanford Research Institute, March 1977).

PART FIVE

Productivity

Nancy S. Hayward

15. The Productivity Challenge

For every public official who strives to meet the needs of the public within available revenues, improved governmental productivity is a necessity. For every citizen who expects more public services without increased taxation, productivity improvement must become a priority concern. For every public employee whose job depends upon the continuation of public services despite the pressures of inflation and tax reductions, governmental productivity increases must be realized. For every business that must minimize costs to remain competitive, governmental productivity growth is a significant factor.

The extent to which the public sector has heretofore recognized and addressed the importance of productivity improvement cannot be documented. We lack, in the aggregate, adequate data to determine at what rate productivity is changing—up or down—relative to government's historical pattern, to other sectors of the economy, or to other countries. We do know from studies of certain public functions that differences of up to 500 percent exist in productivity rates between jurisdictions with similar demographic characteristics, service variables, and wage levels. Therefore, it is evident to us that, within the constraints of current knowledge, technology, and legislation, the productivity of public service delivery can be increased. Even those skeptical of this conclusion will agree that, under the demands for more public services, higher wages, and lower taxes, methods for improving governmental productivity must be identified and implemented.

Despite the benefits of increased productivity—higher standards of living, increased real wages, less costly goods and services—the governmental process inherently neither provokes nor supports productivity improvement. The challenge of increasing governmental productivity is not limited to the most progressive public officials and students of government. The targets of opportunity are different in each community, as are the barriers to implementation and the alternative methods of resolution. Yet, while the parameters of the challenge are unique to each jurisdiction, productivity improvement is for every public official not merely an opportunity but a necessity.

What Is Public Sector Productivity?

Governmental productivity is the efficiency with which resources are consumed in the effective delivery of public services. The definition implies not only quantity but quality. It negates the value of efficiency, if the product or service itself lacks value. It relates the value of all resources consumed—human, capital, and technological—to the output of public services or results achieved. Improved productivity results in

> More and/or better services for the same unit cost
> The same quantity and quality of services at less unit cost

The inadequacy of the industrial definition (productivity = output/input) to account for effectiveness and quality in the absence of a competitive market is reflected in the breadth of the public sector definition. Parenthetically it is important to note that private industry feels the traditional output per manhour measure of productivity used by the Bureau of Labor Statistics is also inadequate in that it excludes the cost of other such resources as energy, which are gaining relative value. To this end, the private sector is developing indicators of total factor productivity that would, as does the public sector definition, reflect the contribution of capital and technology in addition to manpower.

Governmental productivity increases most frequently result from

Optimum utilization of manpower, equipment, and capital
Better trained, equipped, and motivated employees
Higher-quality raw materials
Improved technology
Substitution of capital and technology for manpower
Elimination of ineffective laws, regulations, and standards
More precise identification of needs and users
Better design of services to meet constituent needs

Measurement is the yardstick by which the value of productivity improvements can be quantified and assessed. Productivity measures at a single point in time can be used to compare the efficiency and effectiveness of similar operations in different jurisdictions or among sectors of the economy. Productivity data collected over time can be used to monitor performance, identify problem areas, establish standards for improved performance, evaluate the benefits of alternative improvement strategies, and refine resource needs relative to estimated demands. For citizens, productivity data provide a means for holding governmental officials accountable for public resources.

Productivity measures are only one source of information. They must be reviewed in conjunction with organizational objectives and other existing sources of management data. Although the mere existence of a measurement system may temporarily motivate performance improvements, meaningful productivity increases will not be achieved without analysis of the data and implementation of policy or operational changes.

Washington State's Experience

The variety of techniques and approaches through which governmental productivity can be improved is exemplified by efforts in the State of Washington. Individually each improvement project addresses the need for increased productivity, and in most cases the benefits can be at least partially quantified. What cannot be fully accounted for is the value of the added benefits derived from a broad-based approach of simultaneously addressing different types of productivity problems. Subjectively, it appears that the full benefits of each individual effort would not have been attained had the Washington program not tried to address related and contributory problems as well. Psychologically, it makes all levels and functions of the government feel a part of the process and avoids creating the impression that any one area has been singled out for poor performance.

ADVISORY COUNCIL. Building on the resources available within the state, and in recognition of the importance of developing a broad-based consensus for choosing among difficult alternatives, a 28-member Advisory Council was established. Members include business executives, state management and employees, union officials, legislators, local government officials, and representatives of higher education and civic organizations. The council designed and conducted some of the individual improvement efforts; others have been identified and implemented by state staff under the council's guidance. The council has brought to the state government the best ideas, experiences, and resources of the organizations which its members represent; the members have also effectively communicated back to their colleagues the needs and accomplishments of the state.

ORGANIZATIONAL RESTRUCTURING. The council identified as primary to institutionalizing the productivity concern a need to establish clear lines of accountability and eliminate organizational redundancy. They have concluded that the state's organizational structure adversely affects productivity and are currently reviewing alternative mechanisms for reorganization.

HUMAN RESOURCES. As a result of a survey of state employees, deficiencies in communications between management and employees have been identified, which, according to the employees, directly affects their productivity and job satisfaction. Through analysis of the responses the committee will prepare recommendations on how communications can be improved for the purpose of enhancing employee and organizational productivity.

An analysis of the Employee Suggestion Award System indicated that neither the process for making awards nor the value of the award functioned as an incentive for generating employee recommendations. The system has been strengthened by legislation that increases the maximum award from $300 to $1,000; expanding coverage to all state employees, including those working in higher education; and providing for post-auditing of suggestions. This project is an example of the benefits that can be achieved through executive and legislative branch cooperation in improving productivity.

In recognition of the need to emphasize employee understanding and co-operation in productivity improvement efforts, a state labor relations assistant in the Office of the Governor is working with agencies and employee organizations on labor relations issues. As a result of a practice by which each agency bargains independently with either of the two employee unions, significant disparities in labor relations policy have developed among bargaining units. To increase communications between agencies and to enhance the state's labor-management environment, an interagency Labor Relations Task Force has been created. The task force is reviewing problems of consistency in interpreting and implementing executive labor relations policy, adequacy of negotiating data, and deficiencies in managerial labor relations training. In addition to facilitating better communication between agencies, the task force is expected to identify legislative and executive policy needs in this area.

Since the productivity of all organizations reflects to a large extent the capabilities of an organization's employees, the Advisory Council encouraged the creation of a comprehensive training and career development program. Legislation creating this program was proposed by the Advisory Council. It will expand programs for developing skill levels of employees and establish a special system for the selection, advancement, and promotion of managers on the basis of proven managerial ability.

At the same time, the Department of Personnel is proposing a new "General Manager" category within the merit system which would consolidate numerous managerial classifications into meaningful management groups. The proposal also calls for the establishment of a Management Assessment Center to identify and develop managerial skills.

TECHNOLOGY. A Technology Transfer Center has been established in the Office of the Governor to increase the use of technology in the state government. The center is concerned with both "hard" (such as computers or word processing) and "soft" (such as parole guidelines) technology. Washington is also considering the creation of a "technology bank" to identify resources in the public and private sectors that can assist government to implement technological advances.

TOOLS AND MEASUREMENT. A number of analytical tools are being introduced into all levels of government, including operational auditing, value engineering, and quality assurance. In addition, the state is working from several different perspectives to improve their productivity measurement capability, including, with the help of the National Science Foundation, a study of techniques and indicators in two of the less tangible service areas, foster care and nursing homes.

The need for more precise knowledge of the time and resource requirements of specific tasks has resulted in the establishment of a work measurement program. Orientation for all agency managers on the meaning and importance of work measurement has been conducted. Twenty percent (11,000) of the employment force, including higher education, were covered by engineered work standards.

To increase the usefulness to managers of existing measurement data, there has been introduced, on a pilot basis, a Total Performance Measurement System in the Department of General Administration. This integrates efficiency measures with employee and customer attitude surveys, to relate not only efficiency and effectiveness but also point out specific causes of problems reflected in performance variations.

The Washington State program endeavors to realize potential improvements through technology, labor, management, and structure. The effort has the governor's full commitment. It has the support of management, labor, and the citizenry. It depends on the ingenuity of all state employees.

Improvement Strategy

No one model exists, nor, if it did, would it be applicable to every state or local government that wanted to establish a broad-based productivity improvement program. Few governments have been able to muster the executive and legislative commitment, along with the internal staff and financial resources, to initiate an organization-wide productivity improvement program. While the highly publicized problems of some prominent American cities have drawn attention to the need for efficiency and effectiveness, public pressures for increased services have forced allocation of all available resources to service products instead of improved service administration. At the same time every governmental unit *does* improve the productivity of certain functions in the course of its daily "firefighting," for the solution to many public administration problems usually results, as a side benefit, in some percentage increase in efficiency and effectiveness. A broad-based continuing program provides additional benefits. These include

> Avoidance of potential problems
> Increased benefits as a result of better designed improvement strategies
> Better reallocation of savings achieved
> Increased support by all employees as a result of incorporating employee ideas and accommodating employee needs in designing and implementing improvements
> Increased transfer of improvement strategiesnamong functions
> Departmentally shared responsibilities and costs for mutually beneficial improvements.

Jurisdictions face a number of problems when trying to increase productivity. In overcoming these constraints the most successful efforts have pointed out key elements of productivity improvement programs. These are

> To ensure implementation of improvement recommendations, full commitment of the chief executive officer and senior management is necessary.

To minimize politically motivated rejections of improvement recommendations and to encourage appropriate statutory revisions, support by the legislative body is desirable.

To sustain the program's momentum despite limited staff resources, designate a dedicated analytic capability resident in the chief executive's office, or the budget office, or, increasingly, within the departments themselves.

To avoid reinventing the wheel at great cost and to minimize risk, ensure cognizance of methods used by other jurisdictions or other departments within a jurisdiction to effect improvements.

To gain agreement on areas of deficiency and to justify results, establish or incorporate in existing mechanisms a measurement system to monitor ongoing governmental performance and supply baseline data for assessing improvements.

To instill managerial accountability and motivation, link improvement projects to the budget process for reallocating cost savings, but not to be used automatically to justify budget cutting when improvements are achieved.

To dispel the myth that productivity means harder work and to gain labor support for changes, involve all employees by considering employee suggestions, retraining where necessary, and explaining all changes in advance of and during transition.

To maintain job security to the extent possible, effect necessary employment reductions through attrition.

To anticipate citizen reactions toward service changes, use techniques to identify more precisely citizen needs, desired service levels, and satisfaction with service quality.

To minimize union opposition and ensure a smooth transition, communicate with labor unions on proposed changes, methods of labor force reduction, training, safety, quality of work environment.

In essence, the most successful efforts require not only the involvement of all segments of the community but also an understanding that all government employees have a responsibility for improving productivity.

Sources of Productivity Gains

A sampling of the improvements being effected will illustrate typical targets of opportunity:[1]

TECHNOLOGY. While the federal government and private suppliers account for most of the development of new or improved technology, some jurisdictions are designing their own improvements or working closely with equipment manufacturers. Examples, all of which have been well publicized, include automated garbage collection equipment, mini-fire pumpers, automated fire nozzles, longer-lasting road patching materials, and multiuse chassis for heavy equipment.

While new technology offers great potential for future productivity gains, many jurisdictions are attempting to make better use of the equipment on hand. Greater value from investments previously incurred is being realized by increasing the availability of equipment through more efficient repair, more extensive preventive maintenance, and cost-effective replacement policies. By sharing expensive, low-demand equipment among departments or jurisdictions, high initial investments are prevented and flexibility is provided in adapting to new technologies. Further advances in technological innovation and adoption will require both a better articulation of needs and revised financing practices to minimize the single-year impact of large investments that provide multiyear benefits.

HUMAN RESOURCES.[2] Since human resources represent the largest and most valuable resource available to government, the utilization, development and motivation of employees may be our greatest target of opportunity. Improved employee utilization is being achieved through demand-oriented deployment plans, better equipped and supplied employees, reassignment of personnel to backlogged functions, redesign of inefficient tasks, reduced nonwork time (especially in functions that include travel time), and reclassification of underutilized positions.

The most deficient area of governmental management is in the development of human resources. Only a few jurisdictions provide adequate career development paths for skilled and unskilled employees or management. Programs in existence are usually limited to job rotation at the managerial level, although one jurisdiction does provide career development opportunities for unskilled employees. Similarly, training—internal or external—for all employees is very limited, especially managerial training for supervisory personnel.

Increased attention is being given to motivating employees. Where financial incentives are precluded, innovative methods are being developed. These include greater public recognition, competition, support of professional dues, and increased employee autonomy including flextime and floating holidays. Where financial rewards are permissible, innovations include sharing cost savings with employees, piecework incentive programs, and improved suggestion systems. Despite these innovations the most powerful motivation for improved employee performance appears to be a meaningful, well-designed job with fair and competent supervision, performance feedback, equitable compensation, and recognition. These are a management responsibility that must be given higher priority if productivitynis to be increased.

FINANCIAL RESOURCES. Many opportunities for improvement exist through better use of financial resources. Some of those being pursued include better cash and debt management, consolidated purchasing, streamlined payment practices to gain purchase discounts, and development of capital operating plans.

ALTERNATIVE DELIVERY OPTIONS. When considering alternatives for achieving improved productivity, some jurisdictions have included options for service delivery by organizations outside the governmental unit directly responsible for rendering a service. In some cases, contracting with private organizations occurs; this can allow for reduced investments in expensive equipment, access to new technology, greater flexibility in employee utilization, service redesign, and program elimination.

In other cases, service delivery can be contracted with government — either with other jurisdictions or higher levels of government. This usually permits greater economies of scale and better utilization of equipment; it also often provides improved service coverage for the citizens. However, contracts with either private industry or other governments must incorporate performance standards. Consideration must be given to employees affected by transfer of responsibility.

The National Perspective

While specific improvement opportunities vary from jurisdiction to jurisdiction, certain targets of opportunity are felt to be common across the nation. To identify these opportunities, the National Center for Productivity and Quality of Working Life established a committee of appointed and elected local, state, and federal officials, which also includes representatives of labor, citizens, industry, and higher education. From deliberations over the past year this committee has concluded that individually and as a nation we must improve the management of state and local government and strengthen the financing of their operations.

The committee is persuaded that improved management of the delivery of services in state and local government is vital to improving productivity. The committee's research has demonstrated that while important, the traditional approaches to improving management — training, technology transfer, imposition of management and budgetary techniques — are not sufficient to develop strong and lasting productive management in state and local governments. Rather, good government performance results from a strong local commitment to manage services better with lines of accountability drawn more clearly. Encouraging a greater commitment to manage is derived from a clear understanding by public officials of:

> What services are being delivered at what cost
> The manner in which public services meet citizen needs
> and expectations
> Recognition of the importance of employee participation
> Comparison of performance with similar jurisdictions

In order for elected officials, citizens, and higher levels of government to hold public managers accountable for the delivery of services, a better definition of what government produces is required, as well as performance indicators to measure progress toward clearly stated objectives. In the opinion of the committee, emphasis should be placed on broader utilization of existing management tools and techniques for the purpose of raising all governmental performance to the level of the best known. Increased sharing of information and expertise among governmental units could facilitate the adoption of these practices.

The committee has identified two areas that may require further development of managerial tools—citizen involvement and finance. The perceived and actual effectiveness of public programs would be increased by more precise identification of citizen needs and methods of designing public services in response to these needs. This can be achieved by wider application of marketing and citizen involvement tools in the design and implementation of public services. In emphasizing the need for better financial management tools the committee cited opportunities in both cash management and cost accounting procedures.

The committee especially underlined the importance of improved labor relations practices and capabilities. In the opinion of the members, the problem lies not with the worker per se, but in the employee-management relationship. Research and experimentation is necessary in the areas, at the very least, of workforce planning; employee development and training; pension funding, design, and portability; lateral entry positions; performance evaluation; data on employment; and compensation at national and regional levels. In addition, both labor and management negotiators require additional skills and information. It is suggested that labor-management committees may offer potential for addressing a number of employee and productivity concerns.

Within the intergovernmental system, burdensome administrative regulations and reporting requirements significantly increase the cost of public service delivery. In some cases, regulatory requirements actually force resources to be used inefficiently. In many cases, they thwart the more efficient use of resources to achieve the same end. Regulations that prescribe methods of delivery to ensure maintenance of service quality should be replaced by standards of performance developed between governmental units. Transfer of funds programs between levels of government that provide for administrative reimbursements should comprehend incentives for productivity improvement. Such incentives include support of costs for analysis and new equipment that will result in savings to the funding and administering governments as well a shared savings mechanism.

Despite myths that suggest productivity improvement is motivated by economic declines, real productivity growth stems from a healthy economy. It is crucial to the success of productivity improvement that state and local governments function from a sound financial base. To the extent that recent indicators of financial insolvency are proved accurate, corrections in our tax policy and pension funds must be made.

In addition, governmental units must have access to sufficient capital for support of productivity-enhancing improvements. Public use of capital to improve productivity must be accorded higher priority by public administrators, the citizenry, and investors. It is felt that undercapitalization in the public sector may be leading to higher operating costs. In addition "capital improvement" decisions must be based on better estimates of resulting increases in operating costs in the event that design modifications can be made in advance.

In order to address this broad agenda, the committee is working to gain consensus among all affected parties on the importance of these topics. From the committee's perspective, many improvements are directly under the control of state and local officials. In some cases, support and assistance is required from the federal government, the research community, and private industry. To achieve any improvements constituent support is essential.

Conclusion

As has been previously suggested by others, productivity improvement in government represents a need whose time has come. Drawing on the capabilities of their own organizations, many are already responding to this challenge. Every public-interest organization has addressed the topic during its annual conference. Some federal agencies have initiated governmental productivity studies within their research and demonstration programs. The League of Women Voters has been engaged in a productivity project during the past year. Several public-employee unions have participated in either national or local productivity improvement projects. An increasing number of governmental units are incorporating productivity data into the budget or institutionalizing the consideration of productivity implications in the regular policy-making process. The research community is turning its resources toward issues of governmental productivity improvement. Graduate degree programs are revising curricula to equip the new public administrators with the tools and techniques for effecting productivity improvements.

Continued pursuit of these efforts will enable practitioners to build on the experiences of their peers and to develop, as quickly as possible, the capabilities and techniques necessary for increased productivity growth. The real bottom line is, however, the commitment of every public official — federal, state, and local — to manage public resources better. While improved management of capital and technological resources offers significant promise, the greatest untapped potential lies in the management of human resources.

Notes

1. Descriptions of current projects in state and local governments are available from several sources: (a) newsletters and reports of the Public Interest Groups, Public Technology Inc., Labor-Management Relations Service, National Training and Development Service; (b) *Guide to Productivity Improvement Projects*, National Center for Productivity and Quality of Working Life; and (c) *Public Productivity Review*, published by Center for Productive Public Management, John Jay College of Criminal Justice, City University of New York, which published a bibliography in the August 1976 edition.

2. For a broader discussion of this area, see *Employee Incentives to Improve State and Local Government Productivity* (Washington, D.C.: National Center for Productivity and Quality of Working Life, n.d.).

Harry P. Hatry

16. Current State of the Art of State and Local Government Productivity Improvement — and Potential Federal Roles

The following are one person's perspectives on the current state of the art of productivity improvement in state and local government. Six topics are discussed: productivity measurement, improving technology, improving operating procedures, improving employee motivation, various organizational approaches (including joint arrangements and contracting-out), and institutionalizing productivity improvement.

An additional subject that will not be addressed here is that of modifying the federal grant process both (1) to remove numerous inefficiencies caused by federal grant practices and (2) to use the grant system in a positive way to encourage improved productivity. Clearly, however, these are both strategies the federal government should give considerable attention.

To cover such a broad subject in a single chapter, it is necessary to be highly selective. There is a large variety of things being tried somewhere or other in the United States. Unfortunately, there is little comprehensive, objective evaluative evidence on the results of most of these trials. For the most part, available information on such improvements has been information describing the initial implementation. Where evaluative information has been provided, it has generally been highly limited as to scope and comprehensiveness, often coming from the agency undertaking the innovation. Much of the information has had a public relations and promotive focus with the data often primarily impressionistic. And, most often, the findings presented are those from early in the life of the innovation.

The federal government is probably the only level of government that has the resources and capability to provide for comprehensive and systematic evaluations. This particularly applies to innovations that need trials at multiple sites so that generalizations can better be made as to the impacts and conditions under which an innovation is likely to be successful. Partly because of this gap in evaluative information, it is difficult to judge which, if any, of the approaches that follow has the most potential for improving productivity.

Productivity Measurement

Productivity measurement as encouraged by the National Center for Productivity has generally come to include both effectiveness and efficiency. Adequate measurement procedures are needed to permit individual governments to measure their own productivity on each service and assess their progress in improving productivity. Measurement can also be used to provide nationwide, or at least regional, comparative measurement that would permit individual governments to compare their performance against those of similar jurisdictions. Comparative measurements would also be useful for identifying nationwide trends about the productivity of individual services. Such information would be useful, especially to the federal government, for guiding national policy.

There is considerable difficulty with productivity measurement. The most readily available output data are workload data, but unfortunately such data have at least three drawbacks: (1) most often measures of workload accomplished say little about whether the service is producing anything useful; (2) there are seldom quality controls on the outputs, meaning that differences in outputs can, in fact, be due to different quality of output rather than improved productivity; and (3) to date, there has been little attempt to differentiate the incoming workload by degree of difficulty. The incoming work in almost all (if not all) government services usually is more heterogeneous than homogeneous (whether the workload is different types of clients, different types of crimes, or more difficult terrain or weather conditions for making road maintenance repairs). If the data are not classified by difficulty, the aggregate data stand as good a chance of representing different workload mix as they do different productivity levels. The federal government since about 1974 has been providing productivity indices on federal employees —and with these same problems.

There have been numerous attempts in recent years, often sponsored by the federal government, to improve the state of the art of productivity measurement in various state and local services—both the measurement of effectiveness and efficiency. This work has produced what probably should be labeled as *modest* advances.

Much additional work to improve them is still needed; however, the advances are sufficient enough that many, including myself, believe that the state of the measurement art has moved ahead of its utilization. Thus, attention to improving the ability of state and local governments to *utilize* the productivity measurement procedures and the resulting data seems a relatively high priority.

The state of the measurement art differs by functional area. It is generally agreed that such services as solid-waste collection and disposal, waste-water treatment, and water supply are the most readily measurable, although even in these cases, measurement of service quality leaves much to be desired. I am probably in the minority in believing that the next easiest services to measure are a number of the "human services," such as vocational rehabilitation, employment and training programs, mental and physical health programs, and social services. The principal hangup is that measurement procedures for these services involve relatively costly approaches. My personal perception as to the most difficult measurement areas are those that have *prevention* as a major government objective; these include fire and police protection. Some outputs of these services can be measured more readily, but meaningful measurement of the number of crimes or fires *prevented* seems currently impractical.

For comparative, cross-jurisdiction measurements, there are all of these problems, plus the additional one of obtaining comparable data on both outputs and inputs. Each state and local government in each service area seems to use somewhat different data collection procedures and definitions even on measures that are currently in widespread use. There currently are some data series collected nationally, such as data on reported crimes and arrests, fires, traffic accidents, various measures of health such as infant mortality rates, unemployment rates, air- and water-quality data, and so on. But often the national data series are provided only for large geographical areas, not for individual local or even state governments. Some attention to making such data series more useful to individual local and state governments is desirable.

There have been a few recent tests of comparative measurements. The National Science Foundation sponsored efforts on solid-waste collection and fire, and the National Center for Productivity (and now the Office of Personnel Management) has sponsored three regional studies on local services such as fire, police, and solid-waste collection. Most of these projects have encountered major difficulties in solving the productivity measurement problem. However, the presentation format used in the solid-waste collection study undertaken by Columbia University and the International City Management Association illustrates what can emerge. It developed ranges of "costs per household" for solid-waste collection, broken out by such factors as backdoor or curbside collection, frequency of collection, amounts of waste generated, number of households served by the jurisdiction, monthly wage rates, and collection arrangement (i.e., whether by government employees, by contract, or by private collection).

Although there are many good reasons for undertaking such comparative measurement at the regional or state level, there also is considerable reason for attempting at least some national collection so that all organizations do not have to develop their own procedures. The most practical approach might be for a federal agency annually or biennially to survey the larger jurisdictions and a sample of the smaller ones, collecting data in a common format, perhaps through onsite visits to alleviate the burden on the jurisdictions. State and local agency participation is needed to help identify and classify key service characteristics by jurisdictions in order to permit proper disaggregation of the data by groups of jurisdictions, so that fair comparisons among governments can be made (e.g., collection location for refuse collection).

In terms of overall priorities, a first order of business would seem to be to encourage increased utilization of the current state of the art of productivity measurement by individual governments. To encourage utilization, HUD has recently sponsored a project in which Public Technology, Inc., and the Urban Consortium is undertaking a series of workshops on performance measurement. The need here is to assemble the state of the art on the various measurement approaches and present it thoroughly to local governments. At the state government level, no comparable effort has been undertaken yet.

Improving Technology

Recent findings, such as those of Irving Feller of Penn State University and Bob Yin of Rand Corporation, have indicated that the pace of technology transfer in state and local governments may not be substantially different from that in the private sector. Furthermore, there is no real evidence that there is a major performance gap from nonuse of currently available technology. This implies that state and local government officials may actually be making rational decisions in not jumping into new technology faster than they have been. Seldom are technological products adequately evaluated as to their full performance capability and costs under actual operating conditions. Thus there may be what Feller has labeled "a pro-innovation bias," particularly by a federal agency that wants to push technology it has sponsored.

Probably a major potential federal role is that of attempting to develop "breakthrough" technology. There are likely to be at least a few areas where major federal research and development activity could provide major improvements, though perhaps requiring many years and large sums of money. The federal government already exercises this role in a few areas, such as in health.

For existing technological advances, a relevant federal role is to provide for comprehensive multisite testing of technology products, perhaps by supporting what might be called a "consumers' union" for state and local governments. Such an operation should provide estimates of the full costs, benefits, and limiting conditions for potentially important new technological products.

Dissemination efforts, which with federal funding have been relatively strong recently, could then focus on those products for which there is substantial evidence of significant payoff. It is my impression that the federal government has recently tended to focus too much on dissemination issues and too little on the systematic identification of major R&D opportunities.

The federal government has also sponsored a number of efforts to build science and technology capability in state and local governments. Thus far, there has been limited evaluation of these efforts to determine whether major payoffs have been obtained over and above their costs (but more extensive evaluation is currently under way by NSF). It is likely to be most usefOl if such support for improved government capability is explicitly encouraged to cover the range of approaches for productivity improvements and not emphasize technology.

Capital Investment

Capital investments provide some special problems for state and local governments, such as their vulnerability at budget time. Capital-budgeting analysis in state and local governments is rudimentary compared with the private sector. There is seldom significant provision for such techniques as "make or buy" analysis or "optimal equipment replacement" analysis. A federal government role would be to support the development of such techniques and tests of their use, for state and local governments.

A related proposal has been to use "capital investment productivity improvement funds." These would provide front-end funds to encourage efforts to improve productivity. They would recapture at least part of the savings from previous investments to fund capital improvements for future investments. The only instance that I know of where this is currently being tried in state or local government is in New Jersey. That trial has only recently begun with $400,000 appropriated by the legislature for allocation among promising capital investment proposals. Large savings have been projected for the proposals that have thus far been funded. There clearly are major problems that are yet to be worked out, such as how to recapture part of the savings to return to the fund and how to validate the savings so as to maintain credibility.

The support of such experiments and their independent evaluation by the federal government would be helpful.

Improving Operating Procedures

This is a catch-all covering a wide variety of things that can be done to improve any particular service. A few of the major approaches that seem applicable to many services, and that recently have begun to receive a number of trials in state and local governments, are discussed below. The basic procedures are not new; some governments have used them for a while.

1. *Use of work measurement and work standards.* These are being applied to many different government activities—sometimes questionably. In some instances, sizable savings have been reported by the using governments. But there have been few occasions when these savings have been validated as real and not paper savings. Work measurement and work standards are used to assess performance, to provide incentives to employees, and to help with planning and scheduling. These procedures have not seemed to be used adequately for identifying improved procedures, one of the major purposes of work measurement.

2. *Resource allocation models:* to permit better matching of government resources to demand, such as the allocation of police and fire fighters as to location, time of day, and day of the week. Variations of this technique can be applied to many other services.

3. *Scheduling techniques:* to better schedule materials and labor and so have less delay time, for example, in street maintenance.

4. *Routing models:* for example, to better route solid-waste collection vehicles and building inspectors so as to reduce travel time and travel costs.

5. *Location models:* to identify optimal locations of equipment and facilities, such as fire stations and other emergency vehicles, to reduce travel times and perhaps reduce the need for additional facilities.

An appropriate federal role here is to sponsor multisite trials and evaluation of such efforts.

In addition, the federal government might undertake a series of *in-depth* examinations into the productivity improvement possibilities for individual service areas. The National Center for Productivity undertook three service examinations (police, solid-waste collection, and building inspection), but these were primarily small, low-keyed studies involving the solicitation of ideas from a number of experts and the convening of conferences on the subject. Those were useful procedures, but a much more in-depth approach, including the use of analytical tools, could be added. The work begun in those studies and that of the National Academy of Public Administration in its forthcoming state and local government productivity handbook might represent an excellent starting point for such in-depth analyses. The analysis could also have the function of identifying potential key areas where federal government R&D could have major payoffs.

Improving Employee Motivation

There are numerous theories here, and numerous approaches have been attempted. Approaches include (1) providing monetary incentives, including the use of performance bonuses and savings-sharing plans; (2) the use of performance targets (such as in management-by-objectives systems); (3) the use of a more effective process for employee performance appraisal; and (4) a variety of "job enrichment" approaches, such as the use of work teams, increased worker participation in decisions concerning their jobs (perhaps through labor-management committees), and the redesign of jobs to give employees either more variety or more responsibility in their jobs.

There is remarkably little evidence as to the effects of such approaches in state and local government on either productivity or job satisfaction. More experimentation has been done in the private sector, but systematic evaluation has been surprisingly sparse there also. The following summarizes the very limited evidence available to date.

Despite the many problems and controversies surrounding *monetary incentives* for government employees, the evidence suggests that monetary incentives, linked to objective performance criteria that focus on job outcomes and productivity, seem to have had significant positive effects on productivity, at least in the short run (one or two years after introduction). These successes, however, have been confined largely to services where objective information on performance has been fairly readily available, such as in sanitation, vehicle maintenance, water-meter repair, and data processing. On the other hand, there seems to be no evidence that the traditional *merit-increase procedures* now used by many if not most state and local governments serve as a significant incentive.

Performance targeting, especially MBO, has thus far not demonstrated substantial evidence of improving productivity in the public sector. This seems to be due in part to the prevalent use of objectives that are primarily process-oriented rather than focused on efficiency or effectiveness. However, recently a number of state and local governments have begun to introduce more output/outcome-oriented measurement.

Most current *performance appraisal* processes seem to have questionable motivational value and may, in fact, be counterproductive. More often than not, these have focused on purely subjective assessments, often of personal traits. We are beginning to see the use of behavior-based scales tailored to specific jobs and based on observable behavior, and appraisal by objectives (ABO). ABO focuses on achievement of prespecified goals set jointly by the employee and supervisor. These appear to have promise, but there has been only a small amount of testing and evaluation thus far. An additional major problem with performance appraisals seems to be the lack of adequate training of supervisors delivering the appraisals.

Four major conditions appear to be prerequisite for productivity improvement in these approaches:

1. The performance of individuals should be assessed in a valid, objective manner, emphasizing the public purposes of services provided by those employees.
2. Such assessments should be closely linked to some type of reward or penalty, whether monetary or nonmonetary.
3. There should be early, meaningful involvement by employees such as in goal-setting.
4. There should be adequate training for those affected, including supervisory employees.

Almost all existing attempts to use performance appraisals, performance targeting, and merit increases seem to have major defects regarding one or more elements.

The fourth employee-motivation approach, *job enrichment,* is attractive to many, but again the evidence of substantial beneficial effects on productivity in the state and local sector is so limited that the value of this approach must still, for the most part, be taken on faith. Probably the most common examples of job enrichment have been (1) the use of teams, such as team policing; (2) the combining of related jobs, such as various types of inspections so that one building inspector can handle many types of inspections; and (3) the use of joint labor-management committees to identify improvements.

Clearly the introduction of these various forms of employee motivation approaches needs to be done voluntarily by individual state and local governments and not by the federal government. Nevertheless, there are at least two potentially important roles here for the federal government:

1. Support tests and evaluation of particular approaches, particularly (*a*) to improve performance appraisal systems; (*b*) to examine the

potential of various monetary incentive approaches both for managerial and nonmanagerial employees (probably with an emphasis on group rather than individual incentive systems) and including such approaches as performance bonuses and savings-sharing plans; and (*c*) to examine the potential of various job-enrichment approaches, particularly those involving major efforts at job redesign and worker participation.

2. Support the investigation of ways to restructure civil service systems so as to reduce obstacles to these innovations.

Various Organizational Approaches

A number of productivity improvement approaches that can be labeled "organizational" have been tried at some time or other by various state and local governments. These include such approaches as the following:

Joint service-delivery arrangements by more than one government, including joint purchasing and joint data-processing arrangements

Contracting out to another government or to the private sector for service delivery

Decentralization of activities to smaller geographical areas, such as neighborhood service units

Increased use of volunteers, rather than government employees, or otherwise switching the burden for a service to citizens (e.g., use of volunteers for some recreation and library activities, switching from backdoor to curb refuse collection, use of citizen patrols in high-crime neighborhoods, and citizen groups arranging for private bus service between major origin-destination points)

Consolidation of small governments into larger ones (such as Jacksonville, Nashville, and Indianapolis)

The last approach, *consolidation,* has been the subject of debate for many years. The issues are certainly complex, and the effect of such consolidations on productivity to my knowledge is unclear. This approach and the *joint service-delivery* approach are based on the theory that governments can achieve economies of scale through consolidation and joint agreements. Joint purchasing arrangements, for example, seem to have considerable potential, particularly for smaller governments, both to take advantage of lower unit costs from larger procurement quantities and to take advantage of more highly specialized personnel.

Decentralization approaches, such as providing neighborhood service centers, have not, to my knowledge, demonstrated, or even had as a major objective, significant productivity improvements (as distinguished from the objective of better matching services to citizen desires). At least I have not seen any studies that indicate a major potential for reducing unit costs.

Whether the use of *volunteers* represents a true productivity improvement can be debated, at least in those instances where the volunteers are merely substitutes for government employees.

Major government interest and controversy exists over *contracting out* to private enterprises for public services—where the service is currently being undertaken by government employees. The underlying theory here is that enterprises are more efficient when they face competition and that the private sector is able to avoid bureaucratic red tape such as government regulations. The principal analyses that have been done here have been primarily in solid-waste collection. These studies have generally involved cross-sectional analysis in which unit costs, such as "costs per household," are compared for governments that use public employees versus those that contract out. These studies for the most part have indicated somewhat smaller unit costs for governments that contract for collection.

Other studies have been more cautious, finding that it is often difficult for a government, over the long run, to maintain competition among potential suppliers, so that the competitive aspect of contracting out may be lost after the initial contractor obtains a competitive advantage. And there seems to be some evidence, though limited, that when a government switches *either* from private to public or from public to private that productivity improvements result. One hypothesis is that when conditions are so bad in a government that it makes a radical shift, almost anything would work. This suggests that an approach that might have considerable potential value is for governments to review their agencies' productivity every few years. If an agency's performance appears to be lower than that achievable through other arrangements, such as contracting out, the government agency should be given a year or two to "shape up or ship out." This, hopefully, would introduce a constructive, competitive element. A major problem with this idea is the current lack of satisfactory productivity measures and standards.

Other disadvantages of contracting out, such as the potential for graft, have been well argued by public-employee labor unions. The federal government's role here would seem to be primarily one of supporting comprehensive and objective experiments and evaluations of these various arrangements.

Institutionalizing Productivity Improvement

Thus far, we have been discussing a piecemeal approach to productivity improvement. Another strategy, of course, is to try to strengthen state and local government capacity to make productivity improvements on a regular basis—"capacity building."

With the demise of the National Center for Productivity, there was a substantial reduction in the explicit attention among governments to the need for productivity improvement. The perception by many governments that productivity was no longer a priority for the new federal administration and was out of favor probably contributed to this. Proposition 13 has been a cause for rejuvenated interest, and now the federal government again seems to be concerned with this issue (though its full support is yet to be seen). Unfortunately, Proposition 13 has probably led to cutbacks in some productivity-improvement-related activities (such as cutbacks in program evaluation staffs in California), where the pressure is primarily to cut costs rather than to improve productivity.

The following are some possible federal (and state) strategies that can be followed to develop an ongoing, continuous, and explicit effort at productivity improvement:

1. Provide a *central coordination activity* to focus attention nationwide on the need for and desirability of productivity improvement efforts in state and local governments, and to provide at least some limited assistance and information dissemination to state and local governments interested in pursuing productivity improvement. This would not be unlike past efforts of the National Center for Productivity. Some of this attention should be directed at legislators, not just the executive branch.

2. Support *training* in productivity-improvement-related subjects. There have been some efforts, such as that of the HUD–National Training and Development Service curriculum development program, which, with the University of California at Riverside, produced a two-semester course in Productivity Improvement and Measurement. Though aimed at university students, such courses can be adopted for inservice training programs.

   Many believe that continuing training in management for government managerial and supervisory employees is a first priority. My personal observation is that the most undertrained group of state and local employees are the lower levels of supervision, which have persons that often have come up through the ranks and have had little exposure to supervisory or work-improvement principles.

   Some of the technology-diffusion research has begun to make the case for focusing major attention on individual *operating* agencies as being major innovators and not only on central staff offices. This indicates that major staff development work should be aimed at personnel in operating agencies.

   As part of the training of managers and supervisors, there also seems to be a need for training in the *utilization* of analytical data that would be forthcoming from productivity improvement and analysis efforts.

   It must be pointed out, however, that there is little information available on the extent to which such training has led to better productivity. Most of us take it on faith that more, and continued, exposure to basic management and productivity improvement princi-

ples are likely to be constructive. One reservation: unless such training is linked to improved incentives for improving productivity, the
training is likely to have little significant long-run effect.

3. Support the expansion of productivity improvement *analysis staffs* in
   state and local governments. Some believe that such staffs are a central
   feature of many successful productivity improvement efforts. It seems
   clear today that there are few governments that have analytical staffs
   of any size that have productivity improvement as a major function.

   The federal government's role in supporting efforts to get science
   and technology applied in state and local governments is probably
   the major effort by the federal government in this regard. As indicated earlier, this support may be quite appropriate if these "technology
   agents" are encouraged to aim at all approaches to productivity improvement and not merely those involving "science and technology."

4. Develop improved *productivity analysis methods and procedures*. The
   assumption here is that improved analysis, in turn, leads to improved
   productivity. Again there is little evidence in regard to this, and such
   evidence would be difficult to collect. Some items that fall into this
   area are improved budgetary practices (for capital as well as operating budgeting); program evaluation techniques; improved cost-anal-
   ysis methods; better productivity measurement; and use of employee
   attitude surveys, especially surveys that identify obstacles to productivity improvement (such surveys are included in the "Total Performance Measurement System," TPMS, efforts, whose testing has been
   sponsored by GAO and HUD, and in other recent efforts).

Summary of Federal Roles

With the current lack of information on the inputs of the various individual productivity approaches, it is impossible to be very definite about choices among the
various options or their relative priority. At this stage, a multipronged approach
seems appropriate. Here are my opinions as to the six most attractive roles for the
federal government:

1. Provide a central source of stimulation, encouragement, coordination,
   and dissemination of productivity improvement efforts for state and
   local governments nationally.

2. Undertake an examination of the needs and potential for major breakthrough R&D for specific service areas and fund the R&D that has particular promise.

3. Provide for multisite testing and evaluation of productivity improvement
   approaches that have major potential—in any and all the approaches, such as technology, improved operating procedures, improved employee motivation, and various organizational approaches.

Provide objective, comprehensive information on the effects on efficiency and effectiveness and on job satisfaction after the programs have been in place for a reasonable period of time.

4. Support efforts at development of training and training materials for both current and future state and local government employees at various levels of state and local government.

5. Provide encouragement for the development of analytical skills to permit better productivity improvement analysis within governments.

6. Encourage efforts to improve state and local government awareness and utilization of the current state of the art of productivity measurement. As a secondary step, test national productivity measurement for selected services, both to provide time trends nationwide and to provide norms against which individual government can compare their own performance. But great care in developing meaningful procedures is needed.

Two Final Comments

It seems important that expectations be kept reasonable. Most of these productivity improvement endeavors are likely to lead only to small-scale improvements. But with the total dollars involved in state and local services being so large, accumulating many small-scale improvements can lead to long-term major effects.

And, finally, it seems clear that sustained, long-term effort by the federal government is needed. The more typical short-term, politically oriented federal approach, which changes directions as frequently as the political winds change, should be avoided.

E. S. Savas*

17. Policy Analysis for Local Government: Public vs. Private Refuse Collection

Government in this country is big business. There are almost 80,000 governments in the United States, and their combined revenues in 1974 amounted to one-third of the gross national product. Contrary to popular impression, state and local governments in the aggregate are much larger than the federal government, by two important measures. First, most of the money spent by government for goods and services is spent by state and local governments, not the federal government: the former spent $192 billion in 1974; the latter, $116 billion. Second, state and local governments employ 11.5 million people, about one-seventh of the civilian workforce and four times the federal nonmilitary workforce. Between 1953 and 1973, the number of state and local government employees nearly tripled—and the payroll increased sevenfold.

Not surprisingly, then, productivity has emerged as a dominant problem in managing local government. Many Americans feel that government—particularly local government, which is responsible for the daily delivery of highly visible services—is inefficient and ineffective: the disparity between what local government takes and what it gives looms large in the public eye, as manifested by the annual taxpayers' revolt.

There is a growing belief that significant and enduring increases in the efficiency and effectiveness of local government can be achieved only by recognizing the institutional nature of the basic problems, designing management strategies to overcome them, and building the political support to do so.

One strategic approach to improving the performance of local government deals with the institutional arrangement by which municipal services are delivered. Municipal agencies and workers can and do provide services, but many alternatives are to be found, as governments contract with each other and with

*I am grateful to Professor Barbara Stevens, Ms. Eileen Brettler Berenyi, Mr. Daniel Baumol, and the many other members of the project whose efforts contributed to the work reported in this article. The support of the National Science Foundation, Research Applied to National Needs Division, under contract NO. SSH 74-02061 AOI, is gratefully acknowledged. Any opinions, findings, conclusions, or recommendations are my own and do not necessarily reflect the views of the National Science Foundation.

private firms,[1] for example, and as citizens retain the responsibility of making private and voluntary cooperative arrangements for certain services.

For an illustration of the range of alternatives, consider that health services, social services, and education are provided under contract, as are installation and maintenance of street lights and traffic lights, animal pounds, water supply, street cleaning and maintenance, refuse collection and disposal, snow removal, tax assessment and collection, vehicle maintenance, inspection services of various kinds, emergency ambulance service, and police services, to name but a few. Less well known is that fire protection is purchased by some communities from private firms, reportedly at a lower cost than cities can provide it.[2] In Minneapolis, a major civic effort is under way to examine systematically the public services that might better be provided by the private sector;[3] and in California, the widespread "Lakewood Plan" has created a competitive marketplace for municipal services, with both public and private providers.[4] Interest in the subject of alternative service arrangements can be intense, as evidenced by the strong reactions in various quarters that greeted my own report comparing the efficiency of public and private service in one large city:[5] two city agencies disagreed vociferously about the findings, newspaper editorials warmly endorsed the recommendations, the affected union attacked the study, and enterprising journalists and good-government groups conducted their own analyses and corroborated the findings.

An enlarged role for the private sector in delivering public services has been advocated.[6] Furthermore, it has been pointed out that government agencies can and do behave in monopolistic fashion,[7] and strategies for introducing and establishing competition—from both public and private organizations—have been identified.[8] However, while there have been many individual studies of particular services in specific localities, and while much has been written in the way of ideological bombast, polemic tracts, and unsubstantiated assertions, there has been little in the way of definitive research. The basic policy questions remain unanswered:

1. How does the organizational structure of municipal services affect their efficiency and effectiveness?
2. How do publicly and privately provided services compare?
3. What accounts for any differences?
4. What policies and actions in this area should be followed by governments and by private industry?
5. How can the public interest best be protected if vital public services are provided by the private sector?

Solid Waste Collection

The Center for Government Studies at Columbia University has been examining these policy issues in a nationwide study of refuse collection. This article examines the findings of that study.

TABLE 17.1. RESIDENTIAL SOLID-WASTE GENERATION IN THE UNITED STATES

Type of Waste	Millions of Tons per Year	Pounds per Person per Day
Garbage (i.e., food wastes)	17.8	0.47
Rubbish (excluding yard waste)	48.0	1.27
Yard waste (grass, clippings, twigs, leaves, etc.)	18.1	0.48
Bulky waste (large appliances, furniture, etc.)	6.4	0.17
TOTAL	90.3	2.39

SOURCE: Data are for 1971 and are derived from F. A. Smith, *Comparative Estimates of Post-Consumer Solid Waste*, SW-148 (Washington, D.C.: U.S. Environmental Protection Agency, 1975).

Because of its impact on public health, refuse collection is a concern of government, particularly local government. Although this service does not share the life-saving characteristics of the local emergency services—police, fire, ambulance—it has higher political visibility: garbage requires conscious action every day by every family, and if service is unsatisfactory, the fact is quickly evident. The importance of this subject is demonstrated by a recent survey in which elected local officials named solid waste management most frequently as a problem, ranking it ahead of crime, housing, and addiction.[9]

Refuse collection has been studied extensively with respect to its technical aspects,[10] including the technical factors that affect productivity.[11] However, it has not been studied closely in terms of the fundamental policy issues addressed here, despite its eminent suitability for the purpose: both the public and the private sectors provide the service, under a variety of institutional forms, thereby affording an excellent opportunity for drawing comparisons. For these reasons —namely, a vital service, high visibility, and delivery by both public and private sectors—as well as the relative ease of measurement (compared to measuring education services, for instance), refuse collection provides a superb focus for studying the basic policy questions listed above.

Solid waste, or refuse (I use the terms interchangeably), is defined as discarded solid materials resulting from domestic and community activities and from industrial, commercial, and agricultural operations. This analysis centers on residential refuse, that portion of solid waste originating in residences. The amount of such refuse generated annually in the United States—some 90 million tons, or 2.39 pounds per person per day—is shown by type in table 17.1.

In the following pages I identify the organizational arrangements employed in residential solid-waste collection and discuss the extent to which each arrangement is used. Then I compare the relative efficiencies of the major alternative arrangements and, finally, analyze disparities in relative efficiencies.

Extent of Use of Alternative Arrangements for Residential Refuse Collection

Residential refuse collection is carried out in the United States under many different organizational structures. A full discussion is available elsewhere,[12] but for this report it is sufficient to identify only the most common arrangements: municipal, contract, franchise, private, and self-service. Under municipal collection, a unit of the local government performs the service. In contract collection, the local government hires and pays a private firm to do the work. In franchise collection, a private firm is granted the exclusive right to provide refuse-collection services in an area, and the firm charges the customers it serves. Under private collection, as defined here, the household arranges for service by any private firm and, as in franchise collection, pays the firm directly. Under self-service, a household brings its own refuse to a disposal site. Note that a particular city may utilize more than one of these arrangements.

Between 1902 and 1974, no less than eleven major surveys attempted to determine the prevalence of the different arrangements in American cities. In the aggregate, however, these surveys suffered from a variety of defects that made it difficult to interpret and compare the findings and to detect changes in the utilization of alternative arrangements. The prior surveys were weakened principally by—

Absence of a clear and coherent framework defining the organizational arrangements

Low response rates to survey questionnaires, with unknown biases in the returns

Use of mail surveys in all but one case, with ambiguous responses

Inclusion or exclusion of various types of solid waste

Varying limits on the size of cities included in the surveys

Presentation of data in ways that defied comparison

Failure to distinguish clearly between residential collection and collection from commercial establishments and from institutions such as schools and hospitals.

Columbia University Survey

The Columbia survey, conducted in 1975, was designed to avoid the defects of the earlier efforts. It was carried out by telephone instead of mail for (a) rapid completion; (b) a high response rate (to minimize error due to bias in responses); (c) accuracy, through verbal discussion and clarification where necessary; and (d) firsthand impressions, by interviewers experienced in local government, as to the reliability of the data.

It is important to describe the data base used for this study. The primary basis for including a given governmental jurisdiction in the sample is its location in any Standard Metropolitan Statistical Area (SMSA) lying entirely within a single state and having a total population of less than 1.5 million. (These restrictions were imposed by the National Science Foundation, which supported the research.) Two hundred of the 243 SMSAs (according to the 1970 Census) were eligible. Within these SMSAs, all incorporated municipalities with populations of more than 2,500 were eligible. The largest eligible city had a population of 750,000. In addition, any township was eligible if authorized by its state to collect or arrange for the collection of solid waste, as long as the population for which it had such authority was 2,500 or more. Altogether, 2,060 communities proved eligible and con- stituted the statistical universe for the survey; 252 were central cities in the SMSAs, and 1,808 were satellite cities or townships. All eligible communities in 41 of the 200 eligible SMSAs were included in the sample. From the remaining 159 SMSAs, all central cities but only one-half of the satellite cities (randomly selected) were in- cluded. The latter were then double counted to create the complete data file upon which the analysis was based.

The total sample, then, consisted of 1,378 communities, and responses were obtained from 1,377 (one community could not be reached by telephone, despite repeated attempts); because of the nature of the statistical sample, it can be stated with confidence that the results describe the entire universe of 2,060 com- munities. This universe is analyzed and described below. (Note that the terms "city," "municipality," and "community" are used interchangeably and should be under- stood as meaning both the cities and the townships already described.)

Because of the size of the sample, the way it was selected, the high response rate, and the conduct of the survey by telephone, I believe that the findings presented here are the most authoritative to date.

Altogether, the 200 SMSAs in the sample have a total population of 76.5 mil- lion, or 33.3 percent of the 1970 U.S. population; the 2,060 communities have a population of 52 million. The sample is intentionally biased toward metropolitan areas, ignoring rural areas and small communities with populations of less than 2,500. This bias reflects the study's focus on policy: refuse collection is a more significant problem in urban than in rural areas.

Survey Findings

A detailed presentation of survey results appears elsewhere,[13] but the key findings relevant to our purpose are summarized here. Table 17.2 shows the distribution of cities according to the identity of the collector of mixed residential refuse. Totals are over 100 percent in all cases because in some cities more than one kind of refuse collector is available, though not necessarily to a given household.

It is clear that collection by private firms is commonplace. Indeed, the number of cities that have private firms collecting at least some of the residential refuse is almost twice as large (66.7 percent) as the number that have municipal agencies collecting at least some (37.4 percent).

TABLE 17.2. COLLECTION OF MIXED RESIDENTIAL REFUSE

Refuse Collector	Number of Cities	Percentage of Cities	Number of Cities With Only One Kind of Collector	Percentage of Cities With Only One Kind of Collector	Percentage of 2,052 Cities
Municipality	768	37.4	668	41.6	32.6
Private Firm	1,368	66.7*	929	57.8	45.3
Self-Service	376	18.3	10	0.6	0.5
Other	19	0.9	N.A.	N.A.	N.A.
Column Sum	2,531	123.3	1,607	100.0	78.3
Total No. of Cities	2,052	100.0	—	—	—

NOTES: Because many cities have more than one kind of refuse collector, the number of types of collectors is greater than the number of cities.

The total number of cities reported in this table is only 2,052, because 8 of the 2,060 cities have collection systems only for *separated* residential refuse, not for *mixed* residential refuse.

*That is, private firms collect at least some of the mixed residential refuse in 66.7% of the 2,052 cities.

Furthermore, if we restrict our attention to those cities that have *either* municipal collection *or* collection by one or more private firms (but not both), as shown in table 17.2, we find that substantially more communities rely entirely on private firms (45.3 percent) than on municipal agencies (32.6 percent).

A rather different pattern emerges, however, by looking not at the number of cities serviced by private firms but at the number of people serviced by them. Because large cities are more likely to have municipal collection, the fraction of the *population* serviced by municipal agencies is significantly higher than the fraction of *cities* with municipal collection. We find 61.3 percent of the population in this sample receiving municipal service, 36 percent receiving service from private firms, and 1.2 percent practicing self-service. These figures must be used with caution, however: the data for the fraction of a community's population serviced by a given arrangement may be biased, since the information was obtained from municipal employees, whose estimates of the magnitude of private-sector operations may be in error. A 1973 study that relied on private firms for its data concluded that 50 percent of the population was serviced by the private sector.[14] For our sample communities, it seems safe to conclude that 36 to 50 percent of the population has its refuse collected by private firms.

Private firms, as noted earlier, collect refuse under several different arrangements, the observed distribution of which is shown in table 17.3. Private collection is found (to a greater or lesser extent) in 38.1 percent of the cities, contract collection in 20.5 percent, and franchise collection in 8.0 percent. Table 17.4 shows that the distribution of arrangements differs significantly by city size and by region: larger cities are more likely to have municipal service; franchise arrangements are more common in the West than elsewhere; southern cities are more likely to utilize municipal collection than other arrangements, while northern cities in the East and Midwest favor private collection. Municipal collection is used to the same extent by mayor-council and council-manager cities.

TABLE 17.3. SERVICE ARRANGEMENTS FOR THE COLLECTION OF
MIXED RESIDENTIAL REFUSE

Arrangement	Number of Cities	Percentage of Cities*	Percentage of Arrangements**
Municipal	768	37.4	30.3
Contract	421	20.5	16.6
Franchise	165	8.0	6.5
Private	782	38.1	30.9
Self-service	376	18.3	14.9
Other	19	0.9	0.8
COLUMN SUM	2,531	123.3	100.0

*Based on 2,052 cities.
**Based on 2,531 arrangements in 2,052 cities.

TABLE 17.4. SERVICE ARRANGEMENTS FOR THE COLLECTION OF MIXED RESIDENTIAL REFUSE, BY CITY SIZE, REGION, AND FORM OF GOVERNMENT

	Total	Municipal		Contract		Franchise		Private		Self-Service		Other	
		#	%	#	%	#	%	#	%	#	%	#	%
Total	2,531	768	30.3	420	16.6	166	6.5	782	30.9	376	14.9	19	0.8
Population Group	2,531												
≥250,000	37	27	73.0	4	10.8	0	0	4	10.8	1	2.7	1	2.7
50,000–249,999	268	149	55.6	25	9.3	22	8.2	41	15.3	28	10.4	3	1.1
10,000–49,999	706	242	34.3	152	21.5	59	8.4	170	24.1	81	11.5	2	0.3
2,500–9,999	1,520	350	23.0	239	15.7	85	5.6	567	37.3	266	17.5	13	0.9
Geographic Region	2,531												
Northeast	981	186	19.0	213	21.7	22	2.2	382	38.9	176	17.9	2	0.2
North Central	715	143	20.0	111	15.5	16	2.2	330	46.2	107	15.0	8	1.1
South	469	341	72.7	28	6.0	34	7.2	33	7.0	27	5.8	6	1.3
West	366	98	26.8	69	18.9	93	25.4	37	10.1	66	18.0	3	0.8
Form of Government	1,799*												
Mayor-council	876	374	42.7	214	24.4	42	4.8	178	20.3	64	7.3	4	0.4
Council-manager	724	319	44.1	109	15.1	103	14.2	100	13.8	87	12.0	6	0.8
Other	199	54	27.1	32	16.1	5	2.5	60	30.2	45	22.6	3	1.5'

NOTE: This table shows the distribution of *arrangements*, not the distribution of *cities*. There are a total of 2,531 arrangements in the 2,052 cities.
*Information on form of government was not available for some cities.

Relative Efficiency of Alternative Arrangements

The survey shows extensive use of several principal organizational arrangements: municipal, contract, franchise, and private. Three key issues emerge for public policy at the local government level: Do the alternative arrangements differ significantly in efficiency? Under what circumstances? Why?

Efficiency was defined solely in terms of cost to the household. For municipal collection, this was the cost of municipal service, regardless of the means used to finance the service—taxes or user charges. For collection by private firms, it was the price of service, again without regard to the means of financing. The cost to the household represented the cost of collection only; disposal costs were not included. The cost of collection was defined to include the cost of transporting the wastes to a disposal site or transfer station, excluding all handling costs beyond that point.

Procedures for Collecting Data

By defining efficiency as the cost to the household, the researchers avoided a major obstacle: it was not necessary to obtain the *costs* to private firms, but only the *prices* they charged. The latter differ from the former in that they include profits.

Even so, collecting the necessary data was no trivial undertaking. A different method was employed for each of the major arrangements studied.

MUNICIPAL COLLECTION. Many comparative studies of municipal services utilize cost data reported in the municipality's published budget. While such an approach has the advantage of ease and simplicity, it is hopelessly inadequate in a study of efficiency, because budgetary and accounting practices differ greatly among cities. The following problems are anticipated:

1. Capital costs of vehicles do not always appear in the budget of the department using the vehicles.
2. The cost of fuel and oil and other operating costs of vehicles are often missing from the budget of the refuse-collection agency.
3. Labor costs for vehicle repair often appear elsewhere in the budget, depending on how vehicle maintenance is carried out.
4. The cost of fringe benefits (including pension contributions) may or may not be allocated to the department where a worker is assigned.
5. The cost of supplementary workers "borrowed" from other departments to fill in during absences and vacations of regular workers is sometimes overlooked.
6. The costs of constructing, maintaining, and operating garages and offices may not be included in departmental budgets.
7. The cost of the property used by the agency, in the form of property taxes that would be collected if the property were privately owned, is rarely treated as a cost of the service.
8. Overhead costs often are similarly ignored.

9. If the municipality is self-insured, the cost of liability claims paid should be included in the cost of the service. This cost, as well as the cost of insurance premiums (for vehicle and personal liability, for instance), is often excluded from departmental budgets.

The magnitude of the costs that are properly attributed to the service — but not explicitly allocated to it — can be large. A study of New York City's refuse-collection service showed that vehicle-purchase costs, fringe benefits, liability expenses, and overhead were not included in the budget but added 44.2 percent to the cost.[15] If the value of property taxes foregone on Sanitation Department property had been included, the figure would have been 48.4 percent. In other words, the full cost of collection for New York City was 44.2 to 48.4 percent greater than the cost reported in the budget.

The methodology used in the New York study was subsequently applied to a study of municipal refuse collection in five cities in New Jersey.[16] It was found that total costs were from 3 percent to 44 percent greater than the costs reported in the budgets of those cities. (The average was 22 percent.) Because of such unsatisfactory accounting practices, cities are often unaware of their true costs of refuse collection and are therefore unable to make valid cost comparisons between their current municipal operations and alternative arrangements.

To avoid these problems, the Columbia researchers gathered all the cost data on municipal refuse collection by conducting on-site interviews. On the basis of preliminary visits to cities and in-depth conversations with finance officers, public works officials, and accountants, they developed a detailed form that included all the relevant cost items. Two-person teams then visited the selected cities and spent one to three days obtaining detailed cost information.

Note also that many municipalities levied a user charge for the refuse-collection service. The amount of any such charge was recorded but was *not* used to determine the cost of municipal collection; that cost, as explained earlier, was determined by examining expenditures, not revenues.

The total cost of municipal collection was determined in this manner for 102 cities. The cities were randomly selected, after stratifying by population size and region, from SMSAs that were themselves randomly selected. (Only cities with municipal collection were eligible, of course.) The sample chosen was small enough to be economically feasible to study but large enough to offer a high probability of finding significant results.

CONTRACT COLLECTION. Determining the cost to the household of contract collection was relatively straightforward. The reseachers selected a sample of 165 cities at random (after stratifying by city size and region) from the cities identified in the telephone survey as having this arrangement. They determined prices by obtaining and examining the contract documents, by verifying the basic facts (price, service level, type of service, number of households served) with city officials by mail and telephone, and by conducting telephone interviews with the private contractors. The response rate was 79 percent for the cities and 80 percent for the contractors (99 and 100 cities, respectively, but the two sets of cities did not completely overlap).

In many cases the contract provided for no-cost disposal by the contractor at a municipal disposal facility or for separate payment of a disposal fee by the municipality. In other cases the contractor had to pay for disposal, and in still others he had to dispose of the waste at his own site. In the latter two cases the disposal fee paid at the relevant site was determined in telephone interviews with the contractor, and the contract price was adjusted to reflect the price of collection alone. This figure was then converted to a per-household price.

FRANCHISE COLLECTION. The Columbia team drew a random, stratified sample of 65 cities at random, telephoned them at random, and asked the price they paid, the name of the firm providing the service, and the level of service received (that is, the frequency and location of pickup). Then they called the firm and asked about its rate structure (price for a given level of service), disposal costs, and operating characteristics, such as crew size, salaries, and type of vehicle used. (The prices quoted by the household and by the firm were virtually identical, differing by an average of only 1 percent.) In addition, mail questionnaires were sent to the city government to learn about the procedures for awarding franchises and setting rates.

PRIVATE COLLECTION. The term "private collection," it will be recalled, describes the arrangement whereby an individual household contracts directly with a firm that has no exclusive franchise to provide service. Data were gathered as in the case of franchise collection, except that no contact with the local governmental unit was necessary beyond the initial determination that private service was the dominant method of collection in that community. A sample of 125 such cities was drawn at random after stratification by size and region.

Biases in the Data

Despite the care exercised in collecting the data, certain biases were unavoidable: there was a tendency to underestimate the cost of municipal collection and, to a lesser extent, contract collection.

MUNICIPAL COLLECTION. First, data on the cost of the buildings used by municipal agencies and on the taxes the property would yield if not owned by the municipality were generally not available and could not be estimated with any confidence. Therefore, these costs were usually not included in the cost of municipal collection.

The second cause of the understatement is more complicated. The service that was examined was the collection of mixed residential refuse. The separate collection of bulky waste, leaves, commercial refuse, street litter, and so on, was carefully omitted from the cost analysis. An examination of operating procedures, however, revealed the occasional existence of practices illustrated by the following example: In one southern city, the municipal agency operated five days a week. It provided twice-a-week collection service: on Mondays and Thursdays on half the routes, and on Tuesdays and Fridays on the remaining routes. What happened on Wednesdays? Wednesday was deliberately designed as a light-duty day for the men. Bulk collections were made on that day, but that took rather little time; the rest of the day was spent on minor clean-up work and on various chores in and around the garage. Because Wednesday was formally earmarked for bulk collection, the labor costs for that day were not assigned to residential mixed-refuse collection in the cost analysis. In essence, then only 80 percent of the department's labor costs were assigned to mixed-refuse collection, although one could argue with considerable justification that 90 percent or more of the costs are properly attributable to this service. Nevertheless, this cost-accounting procedure was employed, because a sound alternative treatment of the costs would have demanded something approaching a time study in each city.

Third, the cost of municipal collection may be understated to the extent that the city's pension fund is underfunded. That is, the city may be incurring a greater liability for pensions than its current payments into the pension fund will cover. This problem has arisen in a number of cities, because unsound actuarial assumptions are used to calculate the city's contribution to the pension fund.

CONTRACT COLLECTION. The full cost to the household under contract collection is somewhat understated. The municipality incurs some costs when collecting taxes or billing its residents for the service, and these costs are not included in this calculaton. They are usually quite small. In the case of tax-financed refuse collection, the proportion of taxes allocated to refuse collection is generally minor, and tax-collection costs are themselves rather modest on a per-household basis. If the community bills its residents for service, it is often as part of a joint bill for several services—for example, water, sewer, electricity, gas, and refuse collection. Only under separate billing for refuse service does this cost become an appreciable fraction of the total collection cost. In cities that billed their residents for this service, either jointly or separately, the average billing cost amounted to 3 percent of the total cost of municipal refuse collection; the highest billing cost was 8 percent.

Additionally, it does cost something, after all, for the city to prepare and execute the contract, handle citizens' complaints about the service, and otherwise monitor the performance of the contractor. These marginal costs, although probably small, were not determined and are excluded from the calculation.

Findings: Economies of Scale

Before examining the relative efficiency of different organizational arrangements, we must isolate certain other factors that may affect efficiency. Foremost is the matter of city size and the scale of the service-producing organization.

Stevens studied this issue and concluded that, for cities with populations of up to 20,000, the cost per household decreases as city size increases, and that there are small additional economies of scale up to a city size of about 50,000 in population. Furthermore, she found that these economies of scale, where they do exist, are passed along to the households—by both municipal agencies and private firms. For cities with populations of 50,000 to 720,000 neither economies nor diseconomies of scale were found with increasing city size. No larger cities were studied.[17]

Findings: Efficiency

The findings of the in-depth study, for 315 cities, are shown in table 17.5. Contract collection is the least costly service arrangement ($27.82 per household per year). It is followed by franchise and municipal collection and, finally, by private collection, the most costly at $44.67 per household per year. In the key comparison of the public and private sectors, municipal collection turned out to cost 15 percent more per household than contract collection.

TABLE 17.5. ANNUAL COST PER HOUSEHOLD, BY SERVICE ARRANGEMENT

	Mean	Maximum	Minimum	Ratio of Mean to Contract Mean	Number of Cities
Municipal	$32.08	$71.12	$13.96	1.15	102
Contract	27.82	89.00	11.73	1.00	68
Franchise	29.74	50.28	12.00	1.07	59
Private	44.67	92.04	22.14	1.61	86
TOTAL	$34.16	$92.04	$11.73	—	315

However, the situation is complex. First, the range of costs within any arrangement was quite broad: service in the most expensive city cost four to almost eight times more than service in the least expensive city with the same arrangement. Second, there were certain systematic differences. In particular, the service level provided by cities with municipal collection was somewhat higher than that provided in contract cities; the frequency of collection in the former averaged 1.59 times per week, compared to 1.52 in the latter. Furthermore, 30 percent of the cities with municipal collection provided backyard service, while only 13 percent of the contract cities did. It is not surprising, then, that municipal collection is more costly than contract collection.

The data were therefore analyzed more closely by holding the level of service constant. The results for 206 cities are shown in table 17.6. (Fewer cities are included here than in table 17.5, because cities with different collection frequencies in different areas of the city were excluded.)

For once-a-week curbside service, contract collection again emerges as the least costly, at $22.42, followed by municipal collection, at $24.41. Private collec-

Table 17.6. Annual Cost per Household, by Service Arrangement and Service Level

| | Service Level | | | | | | | | | Weighted Total | |
| | Once-a-week Curbside | | | Twice-a-week Curbside | | | Once-a-week Backyard | | | | |
	Mean	Std. Dev.	No. of Cities	Mean	Std. Dev.	No. of Cities	Mean	Std. Dev.	No. of Cities	Mean Cost	No. of Cities
Municipal	$24.41	$ 8.86	26	$28.83	$ 8.22	31	$38.71	$11.42	8	$28.28	65
Contract	22.42	8.98	30	29.14	10.79	23	31.63	20.39	4	25.78	57
Franchise	27.94	10.23	22	29.85	8.57	8	27.48	10.50	9	28.23	39
Private	35.91	7.96	27	38.71	12.32	9	46.24	10.87	9	38.54	45
TOTAL	$27.54	$ 9.95	105	$30.30	$10.04	71	$36.66	$14.03	30	$29.82	206

tion is most costly ($35.91). For once-a-week backyard service, both franchise and contract collection ($27.48 and $31.63, respectively), cost less than municipal collection, which is $38.71 annually per household. Only for twice-a-week curbside service is municipal collection slightly less costly than contract collection ($28.83 compared to $29.14).

But even though service level was held constant in this analysis, the standard deviations shown in table 17.6 are quite large, and the differences in means are not statistically significant. Part of the reason for the large standard deviations is that certain factors could not be held constant and tend to obscure the relationship between collection arrangement and efficiency. For example, there are regional differences in collection frequency, with higher frequency of service more common in the South, as one would expect in an area where both plant growth and putrefaction of food waste occur rapidly. Also, labor costs in the South are lower than elsewhere. Finally, contract and franchise collection are relatively uncommon in the South, and the sample could not be stratified simultaneously by size and by region. As a result of these three interrelated factors, the cost of high-frequency service in table 17.6 is biased on the high side for nonmunicipal collection.

ECONOMETRIC ANALYSIS. Because not all variables could be held constant in this manner, Stevens constructed an econometric model and fitted it by regression analysis in order to isolate the independent effects of the multiple variables.[18] Briefly, the model employs a Cobb-Douglas production function to relate the total cost of refuse collection in a community to the following independent variables: total quantity of refuse, quantity of refuse per household per year, wage rate, density (households per square mile), temperature variation, frequency of collection, and location of pickup point.

For purposes of this analysis, cities with franchise collection were divided into two categories: those with mandatory service (where all residents are required to purchase the service) and those with nonmandatory service (where the resident has a choice of purchasing service from the single, franchised firm or else hauling his own refuse to a disposal site). Mandatory franchised collection is structurally equivalent to contract collection, in that one firm services every residence in the area; the only structural difference is that the franchised firm incurs billing costs that the contract firm, which is paid by the city, does not. Nonmandatory franchised collection, on the other hand, is structurally equivalent to private collection, in that the firm faces competition either from other firms or from self-service households and in general does not service every residence. The franchise category was therefore eliminated, and the cities with franchise collection were included within the contract or private category, depending on whether service was mandatory or not.

Stevens estimated her model in two ways: by using weight as a measure for 177 cities (including 91 with municipal collection, 34 with contract or mandatory franchise collection, and 52 with private collection); and by using volume as a measure of refuse quantity for 262 cities (92 municipal, 79 contract or mandatory franchise, and 91 private). The two approaches yielded mutually consistent results.

In terms of cost to the household, Stevens found that private collection was significantly more costly than contract collection. No significant difference was found between municipal and private collection for cities with less than 20,000 or more than 50,000 in population, nor between municipal and contract collection for cities with less than 50,000. But for cities of more than 50,000, contract collection was significantly less expensive than municipal collection: the cost per household for municipal collection in such cities was found to be 29 percent (or 37 percent) greater than the corresponding cost of contract collection, on the basis of refuse data in terms of tons (or cubic yards). This was significant at the 99 percent level.

Table 17.7 illustrates the effect of arrangement on cost, using the indicated values for the independent variables. Details concerning the theoretical derivation and empirical estimation of the model are given in Stevens's research paper cited above.

Discussion

The significantly lower cost of contract collection compared to municipal collection firmly discredits the popular but simplistic assertion that "government can do it cheaper because it doesn't make a profit." Government clearly cannot do it

TABLE 17.7. ANNUAL COST, BY SERVICE ARRANGEMENT,
FOR A CITY OF 60,000 IN POPULATION

	Cost per Household	Ratios of Costs per Household	Estimated Ratios of Cost per Households before Taxes and Profits
Municipal	$23.77	1.29	1.61
Contract and Mandatory Franchise	18.40	1.00	1.00
Private and Nonmandatory Franchise	24.10	1.31	1.31

NOTE: Entries in the first column were calculated using the following reasonable values of the independent variables:

    Total amount of refuse: 30,000 tons per year
    Amount of refuse per household: 1.5 tons per year
    Wage rate: $600 per month
    Density: 600 households per square mile
    Temperature variation: 15°C.
    Frequency of collection: once a week
    Point of pickup: curbside
The final column is discussed in the text.

cheaper, at least in the case of residential refuse collections in cities with more than 50,000 people. Private firms under contract are less expensive than municipal agencies in providing this public service.

Furthermore, remember that the price charged by private firms includes three factors: the pretax cost of providing the service; the cost of taxes and fees paid to local, state, and federal governments; and profits. From the point of view of the ultimate consumer of service, the household, the price it must pay is the relevant figure. Whether the price is paid by taxes or by fees, and whether the government retains the money and provides the service directly or retains a private firm and pays the latter for providing the service, appear to be irrelevant, at least at first glance. In fact, the American Public Works Association, the professional society of municipal officials responsible for refuse collection, cites as an advantage that, since municipal operations "are not subject to state or federal taxes,... these costs are not passed on to the citizens."[19] However, this issue bears closer examination. Private firms pay various fees and taxes that governments generally do not: they may pay for a local business license, a state fee for vehicle registration, property taxes, fuel taxes, sales taxes, corporate income taxes, and so forth. Industry sources estimate that the sum of all the fees and taxes paid to governments by private refuse-collection firms amounts to 15 percent of revenues. The cost of these taxes is, of course, included in the price charged by the firm. Therefore, when customers pay government $100 for municipal refuse-collection service, they receive only refuse-collection service. But when they pay $100, directly or indirectly, to private firms for the service (by municipal contract or otherwise), *they receive not only refuse-collection service but also a bonus of $15 worth of other, unidentifiable government services* (wanted or unwanted) that the firm, in effect, rebates to consumers via its taxes. This important factor must be kept in mind when efficiency is measured narrowly, as it is here, in terms of the price paid by the household for refuse collection.

If we look at the question of efficiency not with the consumer's concern for his own direct, visible, out-of-pocket expenses but with the policy analyst's desire to examine, on a strictly equivalent basis, the relative productivity of the municipal and private sectors in delivering comparable services, the relevant comparison changes. It is not the *cost* of municipal service and the *price* of service charged by a private firm, but the *cost* of the former and the *cost* of the latter, for, again, the price charged by the firm includes pretax production costs, taxes, and profits.

Industrywide data on profits are not available, but the published annual reports of several publicly owned firms report net profits after taxes that average 5.9 percent of sales. Assuming that profits amount to only 5 percent of sales, and that taxes represent 15 percent of sales (see above), then the cost of collection by a private firm is only 80 percent of the price it charges, and the price is 25 percent greater than the cost. In other words, if refuse collection by a public agency and by a private firm were equal in terms of *cost to the household*, then in terms of *cost of production*, the public agency would be 25 percent more costly (less efficient) than the private firm. (It must be emphasized, however, that the level of taxes and the assumed profit rate have not been studied here in depth; therefore, this illustrative computation cannot be said to reflect carefully established empirical data.)

This analysis can be applied to the data in the first column of table 17.7 to generate the last column. On this basis (cost of production rather than cost to the household), it costs the average municipal agency an estimated 61 percent (71 percent if based on cubic yards) more than it costs the average contract firm (before taxes and profits) to provide the refuse-collection service.

A small portion of the difference in efficiency between municipal and contract collection is due to the (relatively minor) costs of billing and tax collection incurred by the municipality but not by the private firm under contract. Furthermore, as noted above, the full cost of contract collection is slightly understated because the contract cost does not reflect the costs incurred by the city to prepare and execute the contracts, handle citizens' complaints, and monitor the contractor's performance. Nevertheless, these factors cannot explain the observed difference. Instead, the high cost of municipal collection compared with contract collection is apparently due to what some might call "bureaucratic inefficiency" or "governmental inefficiency": compared to private firms with contracts in cities of over 50,000, municipal refuse-collection agencies in such cities have higher employee absentee rates (12 percent vs. 6.5 percent, significant at the 99 percent level); employ larger crews (3.26 men vs. 2.15, significant at the 99.9 percent level); serve fewer households per shift (632 vs. 686, not significant at the 95 percent level); spend more time servicing each household (4.35 man-hours per year vs. 2.37, significant at the 99.9 percent level); and are less likely to utilize labor-incentive systems (80 percent vs. 89 percent, not significant at the 95 percent level).

For cities in the size range where service under private arrangement is more costly than service under contract or mandatory franchise arrangement, the difference is due partly to the overlapping of collection routes: an arrangement that allows only one organization to collect refuse from every residence in an area is more efficient for areas of up to 50,000 in population, because at constant population density there are more customers per route-mile. In addition, arrangements that require private firms to bill their customers (franchise and private arrangements) are generally more costly than contract arrangements, where no billing expense is incurred by the firm. Payment by taxes rather than by a special fee is expected to yield lower ultimate costs per household, because billing expenses are reduced and also because taxes — but not fees — are deductible on federal income tax returns.

Limitations of the Findings

Keep in mind that this analysis studied only efficiency, and that it measured efficiency narrowly as the cost to the household for collection service, excluding the cost of disposal. It was demonstrated that private firms under contract to cities are significantly more *efficient* than municipal agencies in providing this service. However, the *effectiveness* of the different arrangements was not studied in detail. A devil's advocate could take the position that private firms are of course more efficient, but only because they do a hasty and sloppy job, providing service that is irregular, unreliable, and unresponsive: they show up hours later than they are supposed to—if they show up at all—and make excessive noise, spill half the garbage in the street, damage the containers, kick the dog, are surly and mean to residents, and either lack an office telephone (so that you cannot reach them to register complaints) or, if they have a phone and answer it, are abrupt and abusive to the caller and ignore the complaint. Indeed, the American Public Works Association makes the following assertions:

> Because of their direct responsibility to the people, municipal employees often provide numerous extra services and exercise greater care in handling and loading than is expected or realized from contractors or private collectors.[20]

> Under municipal operation it is much easier for city officials to respond to legitimate requests of citizens for improved community appearance.[21]

> Courteous and prompt response to citizen complaints is one of the outstanding characteristics of municipal service.[22]

The assertions are unsubstantiated, however, and are offered without supporting evidence. Still, these elements of effective service were not examined completely in the analysis reported here. Recipients of *private* collection reported very satisfactory service, in a special survey, but from the work done so far we cannot tell whether *contract* collection is less effective, as effective, or more effective than municipal collection. We *can* say, however, that it is more efficient.

Remember also that this analysis was restricted to residential solid-waste collection. The devil's advocate could argue that, although contract collection results in the lowest direct cost to the household, its comparative cheapness is illusory: If a contract firm also collects commercial refuse in the community and charges a relatively high price for that service, the commercial service may be subsidizing the residential service; meanwhile, the high price charged to the city's commercial establishments—restaurants, drug stores, supermarkets—is passed on to the city's residents in the form of higher prices for the establishments' goods and services. Hence, the devil's advocate might conclude that the true total cost of residential collection is greater than indicated by the cost-measuring procedure used in this analysis, and that contract collection may be even costlier than municipal collection.

This hypothesis, that residential service by contract is subsidized by commercial service, cannot be rejected on the basis of work to date. Like the effectiveness hypothesis, it remains to be tested in subsequent research. It seems at least as likely, however, for reasons stated above, that municipal refuse-collection service is "subsidized" by other municipal activities.

Finally, from the broadest viewpoint of social costs and benefits, it should be recognized that a change from municipal to contract refuse collection may reduce the service's direct cost to the household. But if this is achieved by increasing the number of unemployed residents, whether or not they receive unemployment or welfare benefits, the net costs to society and to taxpayers across the nation may outweigh the direct savings to local households.

Policy Recommendations

The implications of these findings for improving the productivity of this service in American cities are clear, subject to the qualifications noted above. Cities of less than 20,000 in population are likely to lower their per-household cost of collection if they form larger markets, of up to 50,000 in size, to be serviced by a single organization—public or private. The cost will be even lower if the service is paid for by taxes.

Cities with private collection, whatever their size, are likely to have lower costs if they use contract collection. The average city of over 50,000 can expect to achieve significantly lower costs by contracting with a private firm for service, provided that its procedures for awarding contracts or franchises are at least of average effectiveness, and provided that the local refuse-collection industry is at least as competitive as it is in the average community. (Of course, not every city larger than 50,000 will achieve a lower cost if it changes from municipal to contract collection.)

For cities larger than 100,000 in population, pragmatic considerations suggest that the best approach may be to divide the city into two or more districts, each with at least 50,000 in population (this procedure results in no appreciable loss of economies of scale) and to have a municipal agency service one or more of the districts while the city contracts with one or more private firms to service the remaining districts. By doing this, a large city might best assure a continued competitive environment and protect itself against possible collusion by its contractors or coercion by its employees. Such an arrangement might also be expected to reduce the city's risk of service disruptions due to strikes or business failures.

The important strategic point is that a city should, if at all possible, retain some options in service delivery and some standard for measuring and comparing performance. While this door-to-door service industry does not lend itself to continuous competition—there are economies in providing exclusive service to all customers in an area—it does lend itself, in many cases, to periodic competition in the form of bidding for exclusive contracts or franchises of several years' duration.

Although the difference in cost between municipal and contract collection is substantial for cities of more than 50,000, the observed ranve is large enough for considerable overlap: in many otherwise similar cities, municipal collection is more efficient than contract collection.

Therefore, the first step for a city is to determine the true total costs paid by its residents for service, distinguishing between collection and disposal costs and being careful to include all cost elements. The feasibility and cost of alternative local arrangements can then be explored. If the community is small, there should be discussions and joint studies with adjacent communities to explore the possibility of achieving economies of scale by forming a more populous service area.

There is no danger that cities will plunge headlong into a change from their current service arrangements. There are many barriers to changing either from or toward municipal collection. But, at the very least, an objective and thorough examination of alternatives can help management-minded local officials make their current arrangements more efficient.

The basic issues in this study of one municipal service area, and the principles that emerged, would seem to have major policy import for many other government services. The analysis should provide support for public officials and citizens who are seeking ways to improve the productivity of local government.

Notes

1. International City Management Association, *Contracting for Municipal Services*, Management Information Service Report 240 (Washington, D.C., 1964); Herbert Kiesling and Donald Fisk, *Local Government Privatization/Competition Innovations* (Washington, D.C.: Urban Institute, 1973).
2. Roger S. Ahlbrandt, Jr., *Municipal Fire Protection Services: Comparison of Alternative Organizational Forms* (Beverly Hills, Calif.: Sage Publications, 1973).
3. Citizens League, *Why Not Buy Service?* (Minneapolis, Minn., 1972).
4. Robert O. Warren, *Government in Metropolitan Regions* (Davis: University of California, Institute of Governmental Affairs, 1966).
5. E. S. Savas et al., *Refuse Collection: Department of Sanitation vs. Private Carting* (New York: Office of the Mayor, City of New York, 1970).
6. Peter F. Drucker, *The Age of Discontinuity* (New York: Harper & Row, 1968); Lyle C. Fitch, "Increasing the Role of the Private Sector in Providing Public Services," in *Improving the Quality of Urban Management,* ed. W. D. Hawley and D. Rogers (Beverly Hills, Calif.: Sage Publications, 1974).
7. Anthony Downs, *Urban Problems and Prospects* (Chicago: Markham, 1970); E. S. Savas, "Municipal Monopoly," *Harper's,* December, 1971, pp. 55-60; William A. Niskanen, *Bureaucracy and Representative Government* (Chicago: Aldine, 1971).
8. Savas, "Municipal Monopoly"; E. S. Savas, "Municipal Monopolies versus Competition in Delivering Urban Services," in Hawley and Rogers, *Improving the Quality of Urban Management.*
9. National League of Cities, *America's Mayors and Councilmen: Their Problems and Frustrations* (Washington, D.C., 1974).
10. See, for example, American Public Works Association, *Solid Waste Collection Practices* (Chicago, 1975); and Ralph Stone and Co., Inc., *A Study of Solid Waste Collection Systems Comparing One-Man with Multi-Man Crews,* Public Health Service Publication NO. 1892 (Washington, D.C.: U.S. Government Printing Office, 1969).
11. Harry P. Hatry et al., *The Challenge of Productivity Diversity, Part II: Solid Waste Collection* (Washington, D.C.: Urban Institute, 1972).
12. E. S. Savas, "Solid Waste Collection in Metropolitan Areas," in *The Delivery of Urban Services,* ed. E. Ostrom (Beverly Hills, Calif.: Sage Publications, 1976), p. 207.
13. Savas, "Solid Waste Collection," in *Delivery of Urban Services,* p. 218.

14. Applied Management Sciences, Inc., *The Private Sector in Solid Waste Management: A Profile of Its Resources and Contribution to Collection and Disposal* (Washington, D.C.: U.S. Environmental Protection Agency, 1973).
15. Savas, *Refuse Collection*, p. 44.
16. Seton Hall University, *Comparative Estimates of Post-Consumer Solid Waste*, sw-148 (Washington, D.C.: U.S. Environmental Protection Agency, 1972).
17. Barbara J. Stevens, "Scale, Market Structure, and the Cost of Refuse Collection," Research Paper NO. 107 (New York: Graduate School of Business, Columbia University, 1976), p. 22.
18. Stevens, "Scale, Market Structure, and Cost of Refuse Collection," p. 13.
19. American Public Works Association, *Solid Waste Collection Practices*, p. 244.
20. Ibid., p. 241.
21. Ibid., p. 242.
22. Ibid.

PART SIX

Cutbacks

CHARLES H. LEVINE

18. More on Cutback Management: Hard Questions for Hard Times

We are entering a new era of public budgeting, personnel, and program management. It is an era dominated by resource scarcity. It will be a period of hard times for government managers that will require them to manage cutbacks, tradeoffs, reallocations, organizational contractions, program terminations, sacrifice, and the unfreezing and freeing up of grants and privileges that have come to be regarded as unnegotiable rights, entitlements, and contracts. It will be a period desperately in need of the development of a methodology for what I call "cutback management."[5]

Let me explain why this will not be an easy time to manage government programs. Writing in 1965—in happier times—Robert Lane, in an article entitled "The Politics of Consensus in an Age of Affluence," observed that support for government and political tolerance was promoted by economic growth and government expansion: "Since everyone is 'doing better' year by year, although with different rates of improvement, the stakes are not so much in terms of gain or loss, but in terms of size of gain—giving government more clearly the image of a rewarding rather than a punishing instrument."[2] In 1969, Allen Schick added to this with an observation of his own: "If there were losers in American politics, there was no need for concern, for they, too, could look to a better tomorrow when they would share in the political bargains [and benefits]."[3]

Cast against these observations, the challenge of *scarcity* and public sector *contraction* to the viability of our political and administrative systems should be obvious. Growth slowdowns, zero growth, and absolute declines—at least in some sectors, communities, regions, and organizations—will increase the probability of rancorous conflict, decrease the prospects for innovation by consensus, and complicate the processes for building and maintaining support for administrative systems and democratic processes. In this potentially turbulent environment the dominant management imperatives will likely involve a search for new ways of maintaining *credibility, civility,* and *consensus*; that is, in an era of scarcity, we will need new solutions to problems of how to manage public organizations and maintain the viability of democratic processes.

I have no ready solutions for these hard questions. I do not know of anyone else with solutions either. For now, I can only pose some questions which may point the way to the development of a methodology for cutback management:

1. What is cutback management? Why is it different and difficult?
2. What are the unique problems and paradoxes of cutback situations?
3. What strategic choices must managers make in cutting back?
4. What do these questions and problems suggest as directions for future research?

What Is Cutback Management? Why Is It Different?

Cutback management means managing organizational change toward lower levels of resource consumption and organizational activity. Cutting back an organization involves making hard decisions about who will be let go, what programs will be scaled down or terminated, and what clients will be asked to make sacrifices. These are tough problems compounded by four aspects of resource scarcity. First, behavioral scientists have demonstrated that change is most easily accomplished when the people affected have something to gain, but under conditions of austerity the acceptance of change will be unlikely because the rewards required to gain cooperation and build consensus will be unavailable. Second, public organizations are confronted with professional norms, civil service procedures, veteran's preference, affirmative action commitments, and collective bargaining agreements, which constrain the ability of management to target cuts. Third, organizational contraction produces some serious morale and job satisfaction problems which make it difficult to increase productivity to make up for the cuts. Fourth, cutbacks reduce the enjoyment of working and managing in an organization because nearly everyone is forced into a position of having to do with less. Under these conditions, creativity diminishes, innovation and risk taking decline, and the sense of excitement that comes from doing new things disappears. Simply put, it just is not as much fun working and managing in a contracting organization as it is in an expanding one.

A declining organization confronts its management with several unique problems. The first problem I call *The Paradox of Irreducible Wholes*. This problem refers to the fact that an organization cannot be reduced piece-by-piece by simply reversing the sequence of activities and resources by which it was built. The "lumpiness" of public organizations stems from the growth process in which critical masses of expertise, political support, facilities and equipment, and resources are assembled. Taking a living thing like an organization apart is no easy matter; a cut may reverberate throughout a whole organization in a way no one could predict by just analyzing its growth and pattern of development.

The criminal justice system provides one example of the complexity of scaling down public services. Over time, the criminal justice system has become increasingly interpenetrated and interdependent so that functional agencies like police, courts, parole, corrections, and juvenile services continually interact and depend on one another. Yet each of these units is usually controlled and funded by different decision-making bodies—local governments, state and federal agencies, independent boards. If a cut is made in one function or funding source, it will likely impact on the other units in the system; but because of the fragmentation of political and managerial decision making, coordinating and planning these cuts on a multiunit basis will likely be extremely difficult, if not impossible.

The second problem is *The Management Science Paradox*. This problem is caused by the way public organizations invest in and use their data systems and analytic capacity. When organizations have slack resources, they often develop analysis capabilities, and hardware and software systems. But, when resources abound, this capacity is rarely used because public agencies usually prefer to spend slack resources building and maintaining political constituencies. In a decline situation, on the other hand, maintaining and using this analytic capacity often becomes impossible for a number of reasons. The scenario goes something like this: First, the most capable analysts are lured away by better opportunities; then, freezes cripple the agency's ability to hire replacements; and finally, the remaining staff is cut in order to avoid making cuts in personnel with direct service responsibility. All the while, organizational decisions on where to take cuts will be made on political grounds with important constituencies fully mobilized to protect their favorite programs. Therefore, in brief, the management science paradox means that when you have analytic capacity you do not need it; when you need it, you do not have it and *cannot* use it anyway.

The third quandary is *The Free Exiter Problem*. Economists have identified what they call "free riders"; i.e., people who take advantage of an organization's collective goods without contributing their share to achieving the organization's goals. When an organization is growing, the problem for management is how to prevent (exclude) free riders from enjoying the fruits of growth such as promotions, travel, training opportunities, and other available slack resources. During contraction, however, organizations must find ways to limit (include) "free exiters", i.e., people who seek to avoid sharing the "collective bads" produced by the necessity to make sacrifices by either leaving the organization or avoiding its sacrifices. Some potential free exiters, like skilled technical people and talented managers, are vitally needed if the organization is to function well through a contraction. Yet, these people have the greatest employment mobility, and their replacements are usually the hardest to attract to a declining organization. The problem declining organizations have to solve is how to design mechanisms to limit free exiters and reward valuable people for remaining in the organization through its difficult times.

The fourth problem is *The Tooth Fairy Syndrome*.[4] In the initial stages of contractions few people are willing to believe that the talk of cuts is for real or that the cuts will be permanent. The initial prevailing attitude in the organization will usually be optimistic, i.e., that the decline is temporary and the cuts will be restored soon by someone—in some cases as remote as the tooth fairy. Under these conditions, management's credibility suffers, and resistance, cynicism, and sarcasm tend to dominate responses to calls for voluntary budget cutting. Top management appeals for voluntary sacrifice tend to be met with a "you first, then me" response from middle and lower levels in the organization. The preferred tactical response for nearly everyone is to delay taking action while waiting for someone else to volunteer cuts or for a bailout from a third party.

The fifth problem is *The Participation Paradox*. The field of organization development teaches that the best way to manage change is to encourage the maximum amount of participation by all affected parties. But, a rational cutback process will require that some people and programs be asked to take greater cuts than others. By encouraging participation, management also encourages protective behavior by those most likely to be hurt the most. The participation paradox confronts management with a nearly insoluble problem: How does one single out units for large sacrifices who have people participating in the cut process? The usual answer is to avoid deadlocks or rancorous conflict and allocate cuts across-the-board.

The Forgotten Deal Paradox is the sixth problem. Ideally an organization or unit should be able to plan cuts and attrition on a multiyear basis. Such an optimum arrangement would allow an organization to plan its cuts so that six months, two years, or further on it will be allowed to fill *some* vacancies, replace some equipment, or restore some services when needed. In the private sector it is possible to make bargains for restoring some cuts later on knowing that they will likely be honored by the management team in the future. This kind of arrangement is much less likely in the public sector because the top management team usually lacks the continuity required to make and keep bargains with a long time frame. Most managers will resist multiyear bargaining if they fear that the other party to the bargain will not be around when the cuts are to be partially restored.

The seventh problem is *The Productivity Paradox*. Briefly stated, when dealing with productivity, it takes money to save money. Productivity improvement requires up front costs incurred by training and equipment expenses. Under conditions of austerity, it is very difficult to find and justify funds to invest in productivity improvement, especially if these funds can only be made available by laying off employees or failing to fill vacancies.

The eighth problem is the *Mandates Without Money Dilemma*. This problem stems from the practice of legislative bodies and courts passing laws and issuing court orders without providing funds to offset the additional expense incurred by compliance. These mandates without accompanying financial assistance, ranging from occupational health and safety standards in public works to minimum education and social service requirements in correctional facilities, have had the effect of committing absolute levels of local resources to programs that sometimes have low local priority or are already overfunded relative to other programs. Since these mandates rarely take into consideration the financial health of the government units affected, they can force managers and public officials into the uncomfortable position of choosing between responding to local public service preferences and retaining their flexibility to target cuts or noncompliance and the possibility of indictment and jail. In most cases, managers and public officials have chosen grudging acquiescence and exempted mandated programs from absorbing cuts. In some rare cases, however, where prevailing public sentiment is strongly on their side, officials have been willing to risk indictment rather than sacrifice local autonomy.

The ninth problem, *The Efficiency Paradox*, is perhaps the most important and most troublesome to public managers. This paradox stems from two ironies of public management. First, it is one of the hard realities of cutback management that it is easier to cut inefficient and poorly managed organizations than those that are efficient and well run. Inefficiency creates slack and waste that can be easily identified for cuts. Efficiency, on the other hand, tends to enmesh slack resources in the organization's core tasks by encouraging the commitment of spare resources to long-term planning and capacity-building activities. When cuts are to be taken across the board, efficient organizations are likely to be penalized more than their poorly performing peers because they will be forced to make much tougher decisions about who, what, and how cuts will be distributed. Also, efficient organizations have a difficult search for more productivity gains because they are likely to have already exhausted most of the easy and obvious productivity improvement strategies. For poorly performing organizations the task is much simpler: to achieve higher performance, all they have to do is borrow the management practices and productivity ideas already employed by high performing agencies.

Second, there are few rewards for conserving resources in public management. Too often, to conserve is to be irrational. In many agencies there are substantial *dis*incentives against saving or underspending resources. Early in their careers, most government managers learn that frugality will usually not bring them personal rewards or more resources for their programs. Instead, more often than not, they will be *indirectly penalized* for their frugality because the resources they save will likely be used to make up deficits incurred by other less efficient and self-sacrificing units and managers. To change this attitude, *managers will have to be shown that saving has rewards. In most government organizations this will require fundamental reforms in budgeting and personnel practices.*

These nine problems are illustrative of the difficulty involved in managing cutbacks. They tend to force management to rethink the process of organizational development and growth; and they force managers to make new kinds of strategic choices.

At the present stage of our knowledge about cutback management, strategies are easier to describe than prescribe. So at this point, we need to be satisfied to raise appropriate questions and hope that later their answers can help managers cope with austerity. A proper start, therefore, is to investigate the major steps in the cutback process; that is, the strategic choices that an organization must make about confronting, planning, targeting, and distributing cuts.

Resist or Smooth Cuts?

When confronting possible cuts, managers and political leaders will have to choose between resisting these cuts or smoothing them out by limiting their impact on the organization's most important functions, procedures and long-term capacity. Since no organization accedes to cuts with enthusiasm, some initial resistance is likely. But resistance is risky because "stonewalling" financial stress may ultimately force the need to make cataclysmic cuts like massive layoffs; missed paydays; defaults on loans, bonds, and notes; and the selling off of physical facilities and equipment. No responsible manager or public official wants to be caught in that kind of situation with its unpredictable long-term consequences and embarrassing short-term implications. At some time, usually early in the planning process, an organization's or government's leadership will have to make the choice between struggling to resist cuts or struggling to minimize their negative effects.

Deep Gouge or Small Decrements?

This choice is affected by The Forgotten Deal Paradox; that is, the utility of taking deep cuts initially in order to rebuild the organization later is limited by the risk that the resources needed to build back capacity later will not be available. The alternative strategy is to take the cuts year by year in small decrements to minimize their impact in the hope that public support of the agency will increase and the cuts will stop. NASA, an agency that has had eleven consecutive years of budget cuts in real dollar terms, chose to follow the "small decrement strategy." People familiar with NASA in the late 1970s and who know something about the agency during the 1960s often comment about the detrimental effect the "small-decrement strategy" has had on the organization's management systems including some of the management innovations it pioneered, like project management. The deep-gouge strategy tends to make the most rational *management* strategy, but, the small-decrement strategy *may* make the only rational *political* strategy.

Share the Pain or Target the Cuts?

Sharing the pain of cuts by allocating them across the board to all units may minimize pain, help maintain morale, and build a good team spirit in the organization; but it is not responsible management. Not every unit in an organization or every agency in a government contributes equally to the goals, purposes, and basic functions of that organization or government. In the initial stages of austerity, however, the preference of public officials will be to avoid conflict by asking for across-the-board cuts from every unit—usually to be absorbed by vacancies and voluntary attrition. Eventually, however, if an austerity situation gets bad enough, some leadership will emerge to identify and rank priorities and allocate cuts to units based on them. These hard choices will be accompanied by intense debates over such matters as the importance of different services, the method of ranking priorities, and the difficulty of maintaining excellence in an organization when it is declining. Targeting cuts is a difficult job that tends to be avoided by all but the most brave or foolhardy public officials. But, if things get bad enough, and the across-the-board strategy is no longer feasible, somewhere along the path of decline, top management will have to switch from across the board to targeted cuts.

Efficiency or Equity?

Perhaps the most difficult strategic choice to make in the cutback process involves the tradeoff between efficiency and equity. This dilemma stems from both the cost of delivering services to different populations and the composition of the public workforce. The most dependent parts of our population—minorities, the poor, the handicapped, and the aged—are often the most costly to serve. Blind cost-cutting calculated on narrow productivity criteria could do grave harm to them. The dilemma is also compounded by the recent rises in minority public employment and the salience of seniority criteria in laying off public employees; last-in, first-out criteria for layoffs usually means that minorities and women will be differentially hurt—*irrespective of their productivity*. Since there will always be a tendency to allocate cuts disproportionately to the politically weak, and productivity criteria *could* be used to disguise such an intent, we can expect cutbacks to spark much litigation as they become more widespread. The outcome of this litigation will, of course, greatly constrain but never completely eclipse managerial and political discretion over the locus and extent of the cuts.

Directions for Future Research

To begin to answer these hard questions, a commitment must be made to develop a research program on the management of fiscally stressed public organizations. We know almost nothing about what works best under different cutback conditions. So, the first thing we need to develop is a baseline inventory of tools and techniques for managing cutbacks along with case studies of their application. With this information we can begin to sort out methods for scaling down public organizations and make some judgments about their appropriateness to solve cutback problems of different types and severity.

Second, we need to find methods for solving the credibility, civility, and consensus problems that plague organizations and governments during periods of large-scale cutbacks. We need to invent and perfect democratic processes for allocating cuts which will make cuts effective yet equitable.

Third, we need to devote a great deal of thought to the ethical dimensions of cutbacks. We need to ask, for example, what the ethical responsibility of an organization is to its terminated employees and decoupled clients. No one to my knowledge has systematically struggled with this problem yet.

Finally, we need to understand how cuts affect public expectations and support for government, i.e., whether expectations about government performance will be lowered and toleration for poor services will be increased. If the post–World War II era has been until recently characterized by rising expectations and optimism about an active public sector's ability to solve public problems, will this new era produce a downward spiral of expectations and a pessimism about the efficacy of government to help create a better society?

On a similar but more narrow note, how long and to what depths will Americans tolerate the effects of reduced public services on their lives? For example, how much will roads have to deteriorate from deferred maintenance before potholes become more than a minor irritation? At what point will drivers abandon poorly maintained highways and roads? How irregular and undependable will services become before there develops a movement in the citizenry to reorganize and reassign functions or refund and rebuild public services and facilities. In other words, if support for government services swings back and forth like a pendulum, how poor will services have to become before support for their improvement begins to build?

These are some hard questions we need to worry about. These, I predict, will be some of the dominant issues of public management in the decade ahead.

Notes

1. For another explication of this theme see Charles H. Levine, "Organizational Decline and Cutback Management," *Public Administration Review*, July/August 1978, pp. 316–25.
2. Robert E. Lane, "The Politics of Consensus in an Age of Affluence," *American Political Science Review*, December 1965, p. 893.
3. Allen Schick, "Systems Politics and Systems Budgeting," *Public Administration Review*, March/April 1969, p. 142.
4. I credit Robert W. Wilson, Chief Administrative Officer, Montgomery County (Maryland) Government, for first labeling this phenomenon for me.

Leonard Greenhalgh and Robert B. McKersie

19. Reduction in Force: Cost Effectiveness of Alternative Strategies

Change is a constant aspect of public employment. As government adapts to emerging needs and shifting budgets, some programs grow and others decline. The workforce needs to be adjusted to changing program needs, and such adjustments can be taken in stride by governmental organizations as long as the changes are gradual, and overall patterns of governmental employment are stable. Recently, however, many public-sector organizations have undergone short-term, system-wide, major changes that have exceeded the organizations' coping ability. Within New York State, for instance, the 1970s saw the highly publicized New York City fiscal crisis lead to layoffs of more than 10,000 municipal employees, followed by a general statewide retrenchment resulting in the layoff of more than 10,000 state employees. The fallout from California's Proposition 13 has made large-scale public sector retrenchments a nationwide phenomenon.

In reflecting on organizations' inability to cope with major changes affecting the workforce, it becomes apparent that while a great deal of research attention has been given to organizational change, little of it has specifically addressed cutbacks.[1] As a result, techniques of planning for and dealing with a workforce surplus are poorly developed. The literature on workforce planning, for instance, consists mainly of mathematical models devoid of a history and context, and provides little guidance in dealing with problems of application; the literature on workforce readjustment consists mostly of case studies that are devoid of analytical techniques and tend to have limited generalizability. There is little integration between the two approaches.

These shortcomings of the state of the art have contributed to the tendency for public administrators, faced with a workforce surplus, to resort to the simple expedient of layoffs.[2] In fact, our experience with one state government undergoing a series of organizational retrenchments during this era suggested that public administrators had come to rely on layoffs virtually as a standard operating procedure for accomplishing reductions in force, or worse, had come to equate the concepts of reduction in force and layoff, and as a consequence, did not even consider alternative strategies.

This chapter compares the cost effectiveness of the two principal strategies — layoff and attrition — for accomplishing a reduction in force. The data presented were gathered as part of a research program supporting the work of a state-level, labor-management committee[3] created to develop and implement alternatives for accomplishing future workforce reductions, and to develop action programs to restore previously laid-off employees to suitable jobs.

Reduction in Force Is an Outcome

Layoffs have been used extensively as a cost-saving strategy, partly because the benefits are easy to measure, the state's rule of thumb being "If you lay off a hundred workers, you save a million dollars." This point merits closer investigation, since the state decision-makers' rule of thumb blurs the distinction between *outcomes* and the *processes* by which they occur. A reduction in force is an outcome, and a layoff is just one process by which that reduction can be accomplished.

The hypothesis of this study is that in typical situations where workforce reductions are desired, planned attrition programs are more cost-effective than layoffs. It is not hypothesized that in *every* situation where a workforce reduction is necessary, an attrition program will be more cost-effective than layoffs.[4] Nonetheless, some important principles developed in this research can be applied to most situations, and it would be appropriate for decision makers to take these principles into account when planning reductions in force.

Calculation of the Cost-Benefit Balance Sheet[5]

This study is organized in a balance-sheet format. That is, the costs of the layoff strategy and the attrition strategy are assessed and then subtracted from the savings of each program. It is important to bear in mind that this study focuses on the costs and benefits of the alternative reduction strategies that accrue to the state as a governmental unit and is not limited to those costs and benefits that are borne by an individual state agency. This distinction is important because state policy should be evaluated on a state level, and an analysis performed at this level may differ from one performed with an agency's costs as the focus.

A state institution will be simulated in this study to illustrate the balance sheet's costs and benefits. Specific cost items will be discussed as they apply to this average or typical site, as data from actual state agencies are applied to the generic case to test the cost effectiveness hypothesis.

The institution simulated in this study employs 2,100 individuals at the point in time when a decision needs to be made as to how to reduce its workforce to 2,000 workers.[6] If the fiscal year is used as our unit of analysis, the 100-worker adjustment (a 5 percent reduction) can be made immediately through layoff or throughout the fiscal year using an attrition program.

Table 19.1 shows the summary cost-benefit balance sheet; each of the figures is briefly explained below. Figures have been adjusted in the conservative direction throughout the analysis.

TABLE 19.1. A COMPARISON OF THE TOTAL SAVINGS DURING THE FIRST YEAR OF TWO ALTERNATIVE STRATEGIES FOR ACCOMPLISHING THE 100-WORKER REDUCTION IN FORCE*

	Layoff	Attrition
Gross Savings:		
Payroll reduction	$1,000,000	$1,000,000
Costs:		
Holding costs	—	$ 500,000
Losses due to voluntary quits	142,000	—
Lost productivity	252,000	—
Unemployment Insurance chargebacks	167,000	—
Lost state income tax revenues	9,000	—
Cost of preferred hiring system	10,000	—
Losses due to increased alcohol abuse	7,000	—
Total Costs	587,000	$ 500,000
Net Savings	$ 413,000	$ 500,000

*Beyond the first year, there would be a constant savings of $1 million per year resulting from either strategy, for as long as the workforce remained reduced.

Gross Savings

The balance sheet shows a payroll savings of $1 million for each strategy. It is being assumed that at the start of the fiscal year when the 100 positions are identified as being redundant, the workers are removed from the regular payroll. In the case of layoffs, one can assume that dismissal is instantaneous. This can be seen graphically in figure 19.1.

Where an attrition program is being used, workers are assumed to be paid out of a special account until they quit or retire, so that *holding costs* can be calculated. Thus for the purpose of cost comparison, the payroll savings of $1 million[7] can be posited for both strategies.

Holding Costs

As noted, holding costs are the wages paid to workers until they leave the organization of their own accord. Figure 19.2 illustrates these costs, showing the calculation of the holding costs on the assumption that the workforce in the simulated institution drops steadily, such that 100 workers leave by the end of the year. For the sake of conservatism, the assumption is made that no productive services are contributed by employees who remain on the payroll. It should be noted that if there is any useful output, this would reduce the net cost of holding the hundred workers.

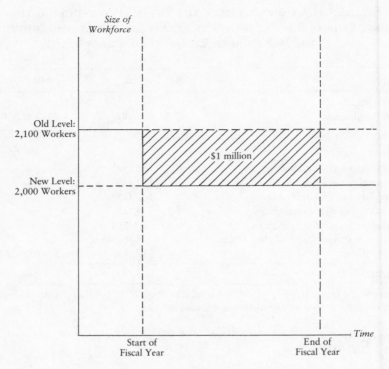

Figure 19.1. Payroll Savings to the State
Resulting from a Layoff of 100 State Workers

In the case of the attrition strategy, the savings would amount to $1 million per year *after* the transition year, the same as in the immediate layoff approach, since by the end of the year, the 100 positions would have been eliminated either way. The issue is thus a short-run decision between the two strategies to minimize net total costs during a transition period.

The 100-worker workforce reduction would be accomplished in the simulated institution if the natural attrition rate amounted to only 5 percent per year, or 100 workers out of 2,000. State records show that the average rate for the state studied is almost double this figure, therefore a calculation of holding costs based on this rate is conservative.

Of course, attritions cannot be expected to be perfectly uniform across titles or throughout a time period. As a result of random variation, there will be little or no attrition in some titles.[8] Thus administrators trying to accomplish a reduction in force through attritions might have to use some mechanism, such as a transfer program coupled with retraining, whereby these fluctuations would not interfere with the achievement of reduction quotas in each title. Additional costs of managing such an attrition program are specifically provided for in the next section, and certainly accommodated within the margin of conservatism already built into the holding-cost estimate. The above comments do not represent an attempt to gloss over the serious problem of differential attrition rates. It is likely that skills that are valuable to the employer contemplating a reduction in force will be valuable to other employers, while skills that are of limited use to the employer are likely to be of limited use throughout the labor market.[9]

As a final note before proceeding with the analysis, it is recognized that any substantial reduction in force requires administative effort, which can be viewed as lost productivity in that the effort directly contributes nothing to the delivery of state services. Interviews of state officials revealed a consensus that layoffs tend to require more administrative effort than attrition programs; thus it was concluded that equating the administrative costs of the two strategies would not violate the principle of conservatism. To simplify the balance sheet, administrative costs are excluded from the calculations for both strategies;[10] since all the conclusions drawn from the analysis involve *relative* costs, this omission does not bias the study's implications.

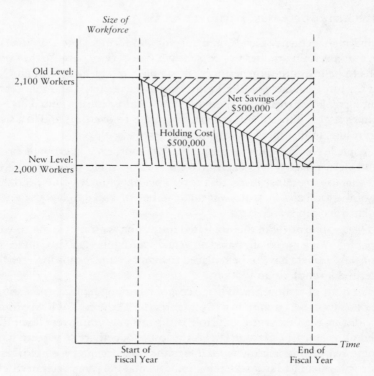

Figure 19.2. Holding Costs to the State where there is Attrition throughout the year of 100 Workers in the Simulated Institution

Incremental Costs of the Layoff Strategy

The remaining costs that appear on the balance sheet are incremental costs of the layoff strategy. Layoff costs accrue to the state in two ways. First, there are costs to a particular state institution, as the immediate employer. For example, turnover and lost productivity would affect each state facility, and these costs can be aggregated as costs to the state as a whole. Most of the institution-level costs result from the *threat* of layoff.

The depressed organizational climate that results from the actual or rumored use of the layoff strategy generates a feeling of employment insecurity, which affects employees' work, their relationship with management, and their commitment to continue working for the organization.[11] By contrast, actual layoffs lead to costs that accrue more directly to the state in its role as a governing and taxing body and provider of services. Examples include lost state income tax revenues and increases in unemployment insurance chargebacks.

Job Insecurity Increases Turnover Costs

Union and management officials, and current and former state employees, tend to agree that a certain number of people leave state service because they perceive their jobs to be insecure. Furthermore, it has been established through research that it is the more valuable workers who tend to leave first,[12] and that recruiting and training replacements is costly, so that the state loses a substantial investment in human capital.[13] Subsequent understaffing leads to overtime and lost services, and also results in disrupted teamwork and poor morale.

People leave their jobs for a variety of reasons, even in growing organizations, and all turnover generates costs to the employer. However, there is strong evidence that job insecurity increases the number of voluntary quits, and the proportion of the total costs of turnover that can be attributed to layoff anxiety can be calculated from research data.

The total turnover in the simulated institution is estimated at 210 workers in the year following the layoff, based on actual state figures gathered under similar conditions. All leavers have to be replaced to maintain the institution's workforce at the desired level of 2,000 workers.

The costs of turnover include the cost of recruiting replacements, estimated by state officials to be a minimun of $50 per recruit;[14] the cost of lower total productivity during the first year on the job as the 210 new employees learn the job, estimated to be at least 5 percent;[15] plus the lost productivity of veteran workers' taking time away from their own jobs due to the presence of new employees. This last figure was calculated from data that indicate that the 1,790 veteran employees would be expected to spend 6 percent of their time neglecting their primary functions.[16] The total cost of replacing *all* voluntary leavers can be summarized as follows:

Recruiting cost (210 recruits × $50)	$ 10,000
Down-time of new recruits (210 recruits × 5 percent of their time × $10,000 per year)	105,000
Down-time of veteran workforce (1,790 experienced workers × 6 percent of their time × $10,000 per year)	1,074,000
	$1,189,000

It was pointed out earlier that people leave their jobs for a variety of reasons, only one of them being job insecurity. The proportion of leavers whose exits can be attributed to layoff anxiety was estimated at 12 percent (or 25 leavers out of the 210) through regression analysis; the figure was corroborated by two independent sets of findings.[17] The 25 quits attributable to job insecurity would cost the state $142,000.[18]

Job Insecurity Leads to Lost Productivity

The interviews also revealed that when workers feel the threat of losing their jobs, they do not work as hard. They pointed out that the lower productivity of troubled workers would likely occur in areas that are not readily measurable (such as quality of care in state hospitals) since an already insecure employee would be unlikely to further risk his or her job by highly *visible* nonperformance. Wages are paid at the same rate even though less state services are being delivered, which raises unit costs.

A survey instrument was constructed to measure the lower worker effort. The survey was filled out by 149 randomly selected employees at a state hospital system where small layoff had caused job insecurity during a merger. Regression analysis shows that the greater the feeling of threat, the lower the productivity of at *least* 1.5 percent attributable to insecurity that would not be expected in a secure workforce.[19] It will be assumed that the simulated institution could lay off the 100 workers (a much larger proportion than at the research site) with only this drop in productivity of 1.5 percent.

Double-counting has been carefully avoided in calculating the cost of lost productivity.[20] First, there is a diffrence between the loss of productive services due to reduced effort and the loss due to veteran workers' being away from their own jobs for 6 percent of their time, compensating for the presence of new recruits and (informally) training them. The socialization/support costs have already been included as turnover costs. Costs of lost productivity through reduced effort apply only to veteran employees and only for the 94 percent of the time they spend doing their regular jobs. The cost of lost productivity is $252,000 (1,790 veteran workers × 94 percent of their time × 1.5 percent lost productivity due to reduced effort × $10,000 per year).

Cost of Unemployment Compensation Chargebacks

People who leave the organization voluntarily are usually ineligible for unemployment compensation; thus it can be assumed that attritions do not normally result in unemployment insurance claims. By contrast, many laid-off employees, not finding immediate substitute employment, collect unemployment insurance benefits. The state typically is charged the entire cost of unemployment insurance benefits for the first 26 weeks and 50 percent of extended benefits for an additional 13 weeks.

The length of the average claim period was computed from actual state unemployment history records. The average unemployment insurance claim period for state workers proved to be 23 weeks (24 weeks minus a one-week waiting period) for 1975–76 data. Using a chargeback cost of $95 per week for each of the first 26 weeks, $47.50 per week for each of the next 13 weeks, and zero thereafter, the average chargeback cost per hundred workers was $167,000.

Cost of Foregone State Income Tax Revenues

One effect of layoffs is that many employees, in effect, are removed from the state taxpayer rolls and transferred to tax-free unemployment rolls. The loss of state tax revenues is thus an incremental cost of the layoff strategy, since it is reasonable to assume that under an attrition strategy, voluntary leavers would normally find alternative employment before resigning.

State workers remain unemployed for an average of 24 weeks after layoff, as noted in the previous section. A family of four is taxed $206 per year for an annual income of $10,000, or $4 per week. Thus the foregone state tax revenue for each 100 laid-off workers is $9,600 (100 workers × $4 per week × 24 weeks).

Cost of the State's Preferred Hiring System

The sole purpose of the state's civil service preferred hiring system is to administer the legal rights of laid-off employees; thus maintenance of the system represents an incremental cost of layoffs. It should be noted that this item is a state-level cost; thus the expense arises in addition to the agency-level administrative costs of accomplishing reductions in force, already factored in.

State records show that the state's preferred list system currently serves approximately 3,000 employees, at an annual maintenance cost of $300,000. The average cost per person is thus $100, and the cost per hundred layoffs, $10,000.

Cost of Increased Alcohol Abuse

There is a strong relationship between a rise in unemployment and the subsequent increase in deaths due to cirrhosis of the liver.[21] Data from research conducted by the authors show an increase in drinking by laid-off employees. It is known from state records that 71 percent of all state layoffs reenter state service; therefore it is reasonable to expect subsequent on-the-job alcohol-abuse problems.

A survey of closedowns of the state's urban drug-abuse agencies showed the increased drinking of workers affected by the closings to be 2.6 times the rate for a control population whose continuity of employment was unthreatened. A study of the federal civil service reported that between 4 and 8 percent of the workforce are problem drinkers, with a cost to the system estimated at 25 percent of the average annual salary.[22] One would expect that the rate of alcoholism of employees laid off and recalled to state service would shift at least from the lower end of the established range to the upper end (i.e., from 4 to 8 percent). The costs to the state of their alcohol problems can be considered to have accrued during the layoff year for the 71 percent of laid-off employees who are recalled. Just one year of losses will be assumed, even though in actuality one would anticipate a stream of losses over several years, which would also include a greater incidence of alcoholism among workers who have not actually been laid off but have been traumatized by the threat of layoff.

Alcohol abuse resulting from layoffs would thus cost the state an estimated $7,100 per 100 workers laid off (4 percent increase in alcoholism × 71 reinstated workers × 25 percent loss in productivity × $10,000 per year), exclusive of state-funded treatment costs.

Further Costs of the Layoff Strategy

Several additional costs should be recognized. Thus far, consequences were considered only if costs could be attached fairly confidently. Other major costs of layoffs exist that were not factored into the balance sheet because accurate estimation of their magnitudes is difficult. However, it is important for policy makers to take into account these additional costs when considering the economic wisdom of the layoff as a means of accomplishing a reduction in force. Such additional costs should at the least be considered as additional evidence of the conservatism of the analysis.

Costs of a Damaged Employer Image

Lower job security tends to require a tradeoff in higher pay, since risk is associated with higher rates of return. Such would be the expected value of outcomes of collective bargaining, as union officials seek a settlement that the disenchanted membership will ratify. While the tradeoff may not be apparent in a particular case, in the short run, across state employment and in the longer run, the effect will materialize. In addition, lower-quality workers will tend to permeate state service because the better workers will tend to doubt their future career stability in state service and more carefully explore their labor-market alternatives.

A damaged security image thus creates real costs for the state. When labor contracts are settled higher, the unit cost of state services will rise. If the pay rate can be held constant, then lower-productivity workers will tend to displace better workers, and unit costs of public services will likewise increase. At the least, the state would have to compensate for its tarnished image through increased recruiting investment, which also raises unit costs.

Costs of Resistance to Change

The prerogative to effectuate budget and program changes has been jealously guarded by state policy makers. Ironically, however, the means by which recent changes have been brought about tends to increase the difficulty of successfully introducing changes, because job insecurity resulting from the threat of layoff engenders resistance to change.[23] In practical terms, this means that insecure employees are likely to fight any changes that management tries to introduce. Workers will tend to cling to whatever stability they have, losing their identification with the broader mission of state government and a willingness to adapt to changing mandates. As a result, changes will be accomplished *in spite* of the workers rather than through their cooperation, and will likely last only as long as pressure and surveillance are applied.

Costs of Increased Grievances

Organizational decline creates an environment that tends to foster grievances. Union and management officials confirmed the suspicion that many grievances were engendered (or at least aggravated) by worker malaise about job security, even when the layoff issue was absent from the substance of the grievances.[24]

Each grievance represents a cost to the state, since a grievance involves down-time during which the worker and the supervisor (and, typically, also the union representative) are not contributing any productive services to the state, even when settled at the lowest level. For higher-level settlements, the costs increase, since down-time is cumulative at each level, and higher-level managers are paid more. When an arbitrator is called in at the final step, there is an additional cost, half of which is paid by the state.

The Social Costs of Layoffs

In a national study, Harvey Brenner[25] found relationships between increases in job loss and other sources of unemployment, and increases in mortality, homicide, suicide, cardiovascular-renal disease mortality, cirrhosis of the liver mortality, imprisonment, and mental hospital admissions. Each of these effects imposes costs upon the state, since the state has to maintain a police force and a corrections system to deal with deviancy, clinics and a health insurance system to deal with health problems, and a welfare system to deal with survivors.

Findings and Specific Implications for Policy

The relative cost effectiveness of the two alternative strategies for accomplishing the reduction in force has been explored. It has been shown that a decision to effectuate a reduction in force as of a particular moment in time has certain transition costs that will be incurred with either strategy, so that the state cannot hope to save the entire labor expense in *the short run*.

Thus the choice between the two alternative strategies involves an analysis of costs that are contingent on each alternative to minimize transition costs. In this regard, it has been demonstrated that in the average situation, *the layoff strategy is not cost-effective*, as compared with a planned attrition strategy. For the simulated institution, transition costs using layoffs are estimated to be at least $87,000 higher than the transition costs involved in an attrition program.

The first implication of the study is that government as employer should seriously consider prohibiting the use of layoffs as a standard operating procedure, to help restore the civil servant's confidence in continuity of employment.

Administrators could be discouraged from considering layoffs as the primary strategy to effectuate a reduction in force either through legislation or by requiring a "workforce impact statement" (analagous to an environmental impact statement) that identified the alternatives and enumerated the costs and benefits of each.

Implementing an attrition strategy is not a simple matter, but is enhanced by some of the following techniques: instituting expanded comparability of titles, to facilitate transfers, expansion of administrative support to manage the reduction in force, encouraging (i.e., putting pressure on) other agencies to hire surplus employees before new workers are brought in off the street; creating a high-level task force to arrange interagency cooperation; providing for early retirement; granting retraining or moving allowances; providing outplacement assistance; and offering severance pay to encourage voluntary resignations.

A second implication is that from an economic viewpoint, since layoffs cost $87,000 per 100 workers more than attritions, the government (in this case the state) should be indifferent between incurring the cost of layoffs and investing an additional $87,000 per hundred workers to facilitate attritions where necessary. This amounts to an average allocation of $870 per worker, which could be used to fund some of the techniques listed above.

General Implications for Government

Having tested and confirmed the hypothesis that layoffs would not be cost-effective in the simulated institution, it is necessary to assess the generalizability of this conclusion. Specifically, we must ask whether the conclusion applies to all state organizations, and whether the conclusion applies to other levels of government, such as the municipal and federal levels.

Attention must be focused on both the savings and cost sides of the balance sheet, in deciding whether the conclusions apply to a specific state organization where a reduction in force is contemplated. First, it must be determined whether there is anything unique about the attrition rates of the titles to be reduced, since such peculiarities might affect the calculation of holding costs. Questions about specificity of skills, condition of the labor market for these skills, and the number of workers thus skilled are relevant in determining whether the attrition rate is adequate or whether action is needed to influence it. Finally, it must be determined whether the specific circumstances of the organization would alter any of the cost items. It is expected that some adjustments of the figures would be necessary depending on the particular agency involved, but that very few of these adjustments are likely to call into question the conclusion—that in the long run, attritions are more cost-effective than layoffs in the typical situation.

When the municipality is the level of analysis, some of the cost items become invalid (such as state income tax receipts). This cost item would be partly offset, however, by the loss of other revenues to the municipality (such as sales tax receipts) resulting from the multiplier effect of the sudden loss of income one would expect upon layoff that would not be expected if workers left of their own accord upon finding replacement employment. In any case, the loss of state income tax revenue is a sufficiently small cost item so that the bottom line would still favor the attrition strategy even if there were no compensating costs. Each cost that accrues at the state level is also relevant at the federal level; some costs (particularly lost tax revenues) become even more pronounced. Furthermore, the federal government must underwrite the costs of many ripple effects of layoffs, ranging from costs of individual and family support to costs of aiding depressed communities, occupational groupings, and social classes. Thus the conclusions drawn in this study are probably more conservative if data are calculated at the federal level of analysis.

Summary

Decision makers have apparently been utilizing the layoff strategy based on the partly false premise that "if you lay off a hundred workers, you save a million dollars." The rule of thumb has proved to be misleading because it does not count all the costs, and is of limited heuristic value because it does not encourage the consideration of alternative courses of action. The research data presented in this study indicate that even with the most conservative assumptions and calculations, in the average situation the layoff strategy cannot be demonstrated to be cost-effective as compared to the attrition strategy, so that it is well worth while for the public administrator to grapple with the knotty problems of attrition programs.

Notes

1. See William G. Scott, "Organization Theory: A Reassessment," *Academy of Management Journal* 17 (June 1974): 242–54; Charles H. Levine, "Organizational Decline and Cutback Management," *Public Administration Review* 38 (July/August 1978): 316–25; and Charles H. Levine, "More on Cutback Management: Hard Questions for Hard Times," *Public Administration Review* 39 (March/April 1979): 179–83.

2. The impoverished state of the art is only one factor contributing to administrators' reliance on layoffs as a primary means of accomplishing reductions in force. Other factors include the following: (1) politicians may see an apparent political advantage in highly visible layoffs as evidence that "something is being done" to save taxpayers' money; (2) legislation may *require* at least "technical" layoffs in order to activate employees' bumping and transfer rights, so that layoff automatically becomes part of the process; (3) unions sometimes constrain informal redeployment of a workforce, with the intention of protecting members from punitive reassignment; and (4) layoff can become what Graham Allison, in *Essence of Decision* (Boston: Little, Brown, 1971), calls "standard operating procedures," whereby events trigger a routine response from administrators (rather than a response tailored to the needs of the situation).

3. Robert B. McKersie was selected as the impartial chairman of the labor-management committee, which was named the Continuity of Employment Committee. The four management representatives were drawn from different agencies. Each union representative was a regional president of the union. All committee decisions were reached by consensus, steering clear of policy-formulation issues and focusing the committee's energy on policy implementation. The committee's full-time research staff was directed by Leonard Greenhalgh.

4. For example, if the need suddenly materialized to eliminate an entire function of government, then attritions might not prove more cost effective, at least in the short run. Even this exception might be questioned: does the need for a major cutback suddenly materialize, or do administrators suddenly turn their attention to a situation that has been developing over a period of time? Leaving this issue aside, there is no pretense that the results of this study can be generalized to *all* organizations.

5. A more complete account of the research underlying this study is presented in Leonard Greenhalgh, *A Cost-Benefit Balance Sheet for Evaluating Layoffs as a Policy Strategy* (Ithaca: New York State School of Industrial and Labor Relations, Cornell University, 1978). Note that the term "balance sheet" is used colloquially rather than in a strict accounting sense.

6. Officials of the state's most vulnerable agency picked ten sites spanning the range of security. The mean size of this set of institutions was 2,000 employees. This figure was used in determining what was "the most typical" institution.

7. Although the $10,000 pay figure used in the "rule of thumb" is not accurate to the dollar, even large discrepancies would not invalidate the overall conclusion because the figure is used on both the cost and savings sides of the balance sheet. Fringe benefits were likewise omitted from the calculations, to avoid unnecessary complexity.

8. See David J. Noonan, "The Role of Organizational Simulation in Work Force Planning" (Master thesis, Cornell University, 1980).

9. See, for example, John F. Burton and John E. Parker, "Interindustry Variations in Voluntary Labor Mobility," *Industrial and Labor Relations Review* 22 (January 1969): 199–216.

10. A figure of $10,000 per hundred workers — for both strategies — was used in the original study. See Greenhalgh, *Cost-Benefit Balance Sheet*, pp. 14–15.

11. Empirical evidence to support these points can be found in Leonard Greenhalgh, "Job Insecurity and the Disinvolvement Syndrome: An Exploration of Patterns of Worker Behavior Under Conditions of Anticipatory Grieving Over Job Loss" (Ph.D. dissertation, Cornell University, 1979).

12. Leonard Greenhalgh and Todd D. Jick, "The Relationship Between Job Insecurity and Turnover, and Its Differential Effects on Employee Quality Level" (paper presented at the annual meeting of the Academy of Management, Atlanta, 1979).

13. Levine recognized the seriousness of this exodus problem, noting the need to "penalize and constrain '*free exiters*' and cheap exits at the convenience of the employees while still allowing managers to cut and induce into retirement marginally performing

and unneeded employees." Levine, "Organizational Decline and Cutback Management," p. 317.

14. Recruiting cost proved to be difficult to estimate, since no cost records were kept for this functional area. Another difficulty arises in the fact that there is little general consistency in the methods of estimating recruiting costs. The estimate of $50 per recruit that will be used in this analysis was supplied by a personnel official in a very large state agency.

15. See Greenhalgh, *Cost-Benefit Balance Sheet*, pp. 43–45.

16. This estimate was based on empirical data from two surveys. For further details, see ibid., pp. 40–42.

17. Ibid., pp. 31–51.

18. Once the workforce has reached 2,000 workers—by either the layoff or the attrition strategy—185 people would leave each year and have to be replaced; such is the nature of employee attrition. The research data indicate that in the wake of the layoff strategy, 25 *additional* employees would quit and have to be replaced, a marginal cost of the layoff strategy. The figure of 1.5 percent is very conservative, having been calculated by rotating the regression line to the most conservative position within the confidence interval. The best estimate of lost productivity is close to 9 percent.

19. A full explanation of how the cost estimate was calculated from regression equations is presented in Greenhalgh, *Cost-Benefit Balance Sheet*, pp. 52–61. Since that manuscript was published, the findings have been supported by two further studies.

20. The figures used in this section are slightly more conservative than those appearing in ibid., pp. 52–61. A full explanation of how double counting was avoided appears in that study.

21. Harvey Brenner, "Estimating the Social Costs of National Economic Policy: Implications for Mental and Physical Health, and Criminal Aggression," Paper NO. 4, Joint Economic Committee, Congress of the U.S. (Washington D.C., U.S. Government Printing Office, 1976).

22. Comptroller General of the U.S., *Report to the Special Subcommittee on Labor and Public Welfare, United States Senate; Substantial Cost Savings from Establishment of Alcoholism Program for Federal Civilian Employees* (Washington, D.C.: U.S. General Accounting Office, 1970), p. 9.

23. See Greenhalgh, "Job Insecurity and the Disinvolvement Syndrome," p. 222.

24. See Sumner H. Slichter, James J. Healy, and E. Robert Livernash, *The Impact of Collective Bargaining on Management* (Washington, D.C.: Brookings Institution, 1960), p. 699.

25. Brenner, "Estimating Social Costs."

Robert D. Behn

20. How to Terminate a Public Policy: A Dozen Hints for the Would-Be Terminator

So you want to terminate a public policy? Think again! It is not likely to be a rewarding undertaking. Your chances of succeeding are poor, and even if you prevail, you will not make many friends doing so.

Indeed, you are embarking on a long and perhaps brutal political fight that will earn you some very hostile and very dedicated enemies. As one senator commented about President Carter's efforts in early 1977 to terminate thirty water projects: "What's he saving? Two or three hundred million in next year's budget? And for that, he's willing to spoil his relations with Congress for four years?"[1] Senate majority leader Robert C. Byrd told the President: "It's a battle you don't need. It will cost you on other, more important battles."[2] What about *your* termination target? Aren't there some more useful and satisfying undertakings in which you can invest your political resources?

Okay. You're stubborn. You think the policy is really bad and ought to go. In that case, think carefully about how to achieve your goal. The following "hints" are not rules; rather they reflect educated speculation about some general political tactics that may help terminate a variety of public policies, programs, projects, and organizations. Not all these suggestions will be appropriate for every termination effort, nor will they guarantee termination; but for any specific public policy some of these hints may be quite central to an effective termination strategy.

Hint 1: Don't Float Trial Balloons

In January 1975, President Ford was considering eliminating the Office of Telecommunications Policy (OTP), an agency within the Executive Office of the President, and transferring its responsibilities to the Office of Telecommunications in the U.S. Department of Commerce. The formal announcement was to be contained in the President's Budget for fiscal year 1976, which was to be sent to Congress in February. On Thursday, January 16, the decision was reported in the *New York Times*.[3] Opposition immediately mobilized; congressmen called the

White House and Howard H. Baker, Jr., senator from Tennessee, announced that he was drafting legislation to prevent the termination. The next day, Friday, January 17, the President reversed his decision.[4]

The trial balloon is a valuable political tactic for testing what political winds will buffet a new policy idea and how hard each will blow. The objective is to generate public discussion, to elicit views and arguments pro and con, to see who supports and who opposes the proposal, and how impassioned the two sides become. Weaknesses in the proposal can be revealed, and, if the opposition is too great, the idea can be quietly discarded. A trial balloon can save a political leader from the unnecessary embarrassment and antagonism that can result from advocating a new, untested policy that will never generate enough support to be adopted.

But a termination trial balloon will produce no real test. The results are predestined. Those who benefit from the policy and those ideologically committed to it will complain—immediately and loudly. This constituency is (almost always) well organized; it can and will quickly mobilize opposition. People will write letters, send telegrams, make phone calls, deliver speeches, and draft legislation to block the termination. All this is easy to forecast.

Equally predictable is that few individuals or groups will come forth to support the termination suggestion. Only those already opposed to the policy, because of ideology or self-interest, are likely to embrace so noncommittal a proposition. In part this is because the trial balloon is necessarily tentative and incomplete; it does not contain the full case for termination. And in part this is because of the "entitlement ethic": once the government establishes a policy, people accept that those who receive benefits from that policy are "entitled" to them.[5] An established policy is presumed necessary until the case is made against it; yet a trial balloon, by definition, cannot contain such a detailed and comprehensive case. Finally, as Bauer, Pool, and Dexter discovered in their study of the politics of foreign trade, "fear of loss is a more powerful stimulus than prospect of gain."[6] Little wonder that, shortly after its release, any termination trial balloon will be shot full of holes and fall rapidly.

Actually, the report in the *Times* about Ford's decision to close the OTP was not necessarily a trial balloon. More likely, the decision, which had already been made by Ford, was leaked by one of the OTP's staff or supporters. But the result was the same. Thus, a corollary to this first hint is, Prevent leaks.

For example, when Secretary of Health, Education, and Welfare Joseph A. Califano, Jr., undertook in March 1977 to reorganize his department, and to abolish the Social and Rehabilitation Service, he was extremely concerned about the impact of leaks. An aide who worked on the reorganization commented, "To be brutally frank, if you let it seep out on you you'll never get it done."[7] Consequently, only five people in HEW knew what was proposed. Moreover, to prevent leaks while the reorganization documents were being printed, Califano called upon his old friend Harold Brown, the new secretary of defense. Brown had the HEW reorganization materials printed at the Pentagon.[8]

When termination is first publicly proposed, the rationale for it should be thorough and complete. Otherwise the announcement (or trial balloon or leak) will serve chiefly to mobilize opposition to the termination. In his February 21, 1977, one-page letter to Congress "announcing his review of water resource projects," President Carter merely stated, "I have identified 19 projects which now appear unsupportable on economic, environmental, and/or safety grounds."[9] That was not very convincing. Did those projects merely *appear* unsupportable? Much opposition and little support quickly materialized, and the President was forced to "revise" his plan twice within two months.

Ideally, the complete justification for termination should be widely publicized before termination itself is even suggested. This tactic forces the policy's supporters to refute such substantive attacks while denying them the advantage of a specific threat of termination that can rally sympathy and support. Before Dr. Jerome G. Miller, as commissioner of the Massachusetts Department of Youth Services (DYS), attempted to close that state's public training (i.e., "reform") schools, he focused public attention on the evils of those institutions. Miller placed the supporters of the training schools on the defensive and created a political climate in which termination could occur.[10]

The case against termination is easy to make. The case *for* termination is much more difficult. As Biller observes, "Persons arguing draw-down or demise are always arguing a *general* benefits case...while proponents of the status quo are always arguing a *'particular'* benefits case..."[11] Terminators put themselves at a further disadvantage if they do not make a complete and detailed argument for termination before opponents can mobilize opposition.

Hint 2: Enlarge the Policy's Constituency

Rarely will the proposed termination of any policy, program, project, or agency become such an open and dominant issue that general public opinion will determine the outcome. More likely, the question of continuation or termination will be decided by the policy's attentive public—its constituency. Most of this constituency benefits, directly and unmistakably, from the policy—the policy's clientele in the form of cash, subsidies, or protection, and government employees in the form of salaries. Moreover, this group will be well organized.

"The behavior of adult institutions can be changed," says Harold Seidman. "But this requires nonorganizational measures which enlarge the agency's constituency...."[12] And, as E. E. Schattschneider points out, "the most important strategy of politics is concerned with the scope of conflict."[13] Unless those advocating termination can attract a group of new, dedicated, and active constituents, the policy's original clientele will control the debate and ensure continuation.

To close the Massachusetts public training schools, DYS Commissioner Miller recruited a number of liberal interest groups that were upset with the treatment of juveniles at the institutions. This new constituency broadened the scope of the conflict and was able to defeat the coalition of state legislators, county office-holders, and employees of the institutions that had quietly controlled the training schools in the past.[14]

The scientists who undertook to terminate the beach erosion control policy of the National Park Service (NPS) at the Cape Hatteras National Seashore also enlarged this policy's constituency. The policy had been designed to protect North Carolina's Outer Banks from erosion, and to most inhabitants of those barrier islands erosion control meant the protection of private property. The policy was perpetuated by the quiet pressure of the local residents with the active support of their congressman. But the scientists, who were convinced that erosion control was destroying the ecology of the Outer Banks, enlarged the policy's constituency by attracting the interest of environmentalists—and of newspaper editorial writers across the country.[15]

All citizens share a common interest in the termination of ineffective, inefficient, duplicative, and obsolete public policies. But this public concern is of low intensity and little salience—a classic case of an unorganized interest.

At some time in the future, the growing public concern about governmental inefficiency and ineffectiveness may be transformed into an organized termination interest similar to the health and safety, consumer protection, and environmental interests.[16] Currently, however, political leaders have a far greater propensity to talk about the need for termination in general than to undertake the distasteful task of terminating anything in particular. Consequently, would-be terminators had best not rely upon such an amorphous interest, but instead should seek support from those with specific concerns about the policy targeted for termination. Broadening the policy's constituency and enlarging the political arena in which the policy's fate is debated can most directly alter the balance of influence upon those who will make the termination/continuation decision.

Hint 3: Focus Attention on the Policy's Harm

The best way to attract constituents who will vigorously support termination is to focus attention on actual harm caused by the policy. The elimination of inefficient, ineffective, obsolete, or duplicative policies produces only *general benefits*; such issues usually generate little political activity. The termination of harmful policy, however, produces *particular benefits*. If it can be demonstrated that a governmental activity is positively harmful, specific, organized interests can be aroused.

To close the Massachusetts public training schools, DYS Commissioner Miller directed attention to the poor conditions of the institutions. He actually invited the press in to see the training schools—to create scandal. As a result, Miller was able to change the political question from "What do we do with these bad kids?" to "What do we do with these bad institutions?" Although in his speeches Miller often observed that it cost more to send a youth to training school than to

Harvard, the harm caused by the institutions, not their expense, motivated this termination coalition.[17] Similarly, the harm to the environment, not the expense, of the NPS beach erosion control program forced the program's termination. The scientists were able to convince NPS officials that "erosion control" actually contributed to erosion of the barrier islands.[18]

Ineffective policies can be revised, inefficient policies can be rejuvenated, obsolete policies can be modernized, and duplicative policies can be combined. A variety of remedies exist for such deficiences: better management, new approaches, better-trained personnel, more legislative oversight, and—always—increased funding. Termination will often be considered only after these less extreme alternatives have been tried and have failed.

If a policy is harmful, however, there is only one cure: the policy must be eliminated. If some demonstrable harm exists (which obviously is not always the case) it can serve to mobilize new, active, and dedicated constituents, and can provide the best justification for termination.

Hint 4: Take Advantage of Ideological Shifts to Demonstrate Harm

In Massachusetts, the harm caused by the training schools was exposed in two forms, physical and ideological. Commissioner Miller created a general public awareness that youths were being physically harmed at these institutions. In addition, he took advantage of what David Rothman describes as "the steady loss of legitimacy of incarcerating institutions in our society" to mobilize a group of dedicated and organized opponents.[19] This new ideology of "deinstitutionalization" reflects the belief that institutions such as juvenile training schools and mental hospitals are inherently harmful precisely because they are incarcerating institutions. It is not necessary to demonstrate that a specific institution is psychologically (or physically) destructive to those incarcerated there. It is presumed. Miller had little difficulty recruiting what Rothman calls the "general anti-institutional movement" in support of his efforts to close the reform schools.[20]

Similarly, an ideological shift provided support for the closing of mental hospitals. James Cameron writes that the new "ideology of community mental health proved to be a potent impetus for terminating mental health policy in California."[21] As for beach erosion control, the scientists who were advocating termination emphasized that active erosion control was more ecologically harmful to North Carolina's Outer Banks than a passive policy of doing nothing. Yet this harm would have had little public or political salience had it not been for the emergence of the new ecological ideology.[22]

Ideology establishes the central premise for evaluating all policy ideas within the ideology's purview. Individual policies are good or evil depending upon the ideological framework from which they are viewed, and a shift in ideology can make a once beneficial policy appear quite injurious. Thus, a would-be policy terminator may find it helpful to take advantage of—or create—ideological shifts that provide a new perspective from which it is "obvious" that the policy to be terminated is harmful.

Hint 5: Inhibit Compromise

Demonstrating that a policy is harmful does not ensure termination, however. Not everyone will accept that this harm has been proven. Others will consider the harm a necessary cost of the policy's even greater benefits. And still others will propose modifications of the policy to eliminate the harmful while maintaining the beneficial.

As with every other type of political conflict, compromise is the most likely resolution of any termination battle. Indeed, compromise is one of what Simon, Smithburg, and Thompson describe as the five "tactics of survival."[23] Political leaders dedicated to a policy or an organization will invariably make those compromises necessary to ensure its continuation.

In some situations, however, a reasonable compromise may be impossible to devise. For example, no natural compromise existed for the policy of erosion control at the Cape Hatteras National Seashore. The NPS concluded that it must either spend millions of dollars controlling erosion or spend nothing.[24] Modest expenditures made little sense, for anything less than a massive effort would be swept away by the waves and the winds. The difficulty of constructing a logical compromise between extensive erosion control and complete termination ensured that the latter alternative would be seriously considered.[25]

Such was not the situation in the case of the Massachusetts public training schools. A variety of obvious ways to attempt to alleviate the institutions' problems was possible. That was not the political perception of the alternatives, however. Commissioner Miller so polarized the public debate that everyone was forced to choose between unequivocal support of the training schools and advocating their complete abolition. Taking an intermediate position became impossible.[26]

If compromise is somehow precluded, the supporters of a policy are denied one of the basic tactics of survival, and the terminators (who presumably will be satisfied only with complete termination) can gain a significant advantage. They can emphasize the harm caused by the policy, thereby placing its supporters on the defensive. A stand-up fight ensues, and the terminators have a chance for a clean knockout.

Hint 6: Recruit an Outsider as Administrator/Terminator

Termination occurs only after a political struggle. Thus the termination coalition needs political leadership—a "terminator"—to dramatize the policy's harm, to mobilize new constituencies, and to manage the administrative details. Clearly, a terminator who is also the policy's administrator will have the most control and influence. An administrator/terminator will not only speak with authority about the policy but will have access to critical political intelligence and be able to guide the process of the termination.

Termination of a policy requires that the responsible agency divorce its past—that it must renounce its programmatic philosophy and disrupt its administrative procedures. Thus Eugene Bardach suggests that a "change in administrations" facilitates termination.[27] A new leader may not always feel compelled to justify an agency's past behavior. Still, an administrator who has worked thus far within the agency that administers the policy—and who expects to remain there—may be reluctant to criticize, even implicitly, a predecessor, or to antagonize present or future colleagues. Consequently, the ideal candidate to implement the termination is an outsider who intends to leave the agency in the future.

The most obvious example of an outsider as administrator/terminator is Howard J. Phillips, who, in January 1973, became acting director of the U.S. Office of Economic Opportunity (OEO) for the sole purpose of dismantling that agency. Phillips fired existing personnel and hired a complete staff of other outsiders as fellow administrator/terminators.[28]

Jerome Miller of the Massachusetts DYS was also an outsider. He came from an academic position in Ohio and planned to stay only a few years, correctly anticipating that he would make so many enemies that he would be forced to leave. Miller was commissioner of youth services for a little over three years; had he attempted to make a career in the state government, rather than leaving it when he did, his reforms could have been reversed.[29] Indeed, Miller's reputation followed him to similar positions in Illinois and Pennsylvania and created problems for him in both states.

Similarly, the decision to terminate erosion control at Cape Hatteras was officially made and publicly justified by an outsider. In 1973, after the Nixon re-election landslide, Ronald H. Walker (like a number of other White House aides who were given key administrative assignments in various agencies) was appointed director of the NPS.[30] Walker, who came to the agency without any prior experience in conservation or similar issues and left it after two years to return to private business, was the only director of the NPS who did not rise through the agency's ranks. In the summer of 1973, Walker recommended to his superiors in the U.S. Department of the Interior that erosion control be ended, and his recommendation was accepted. Several weeks later, when the decision was accidentally revealed to the press, Walker acknowledged and defended the decision. Those inside and outside the NPS who were primarily concerned about the erosion control policy were pleased with Walker's performance—with his willingness to state personally and publicly that erosion control was ending and to explain why. But those more concerned about the organization itself than about any specific policy, including erosion control, believed that Walker's blunt statements were detrimental to the NPS.[31]

Clearly, as terminator, an outsider will be much more willing to make the unpopular statements and issue the discomforting directives that may be necessary to ensure termination.

Hint 7: Avoid Legislative Votes

Termination is more likely to result from executive than from legislative action, for two reasons. First, the leaders of the termination coalition within the legislature cannot, almost by definition, be influential outsiders. Indeed, for legislatures that assign key responsibilities by seniority, the opposite will be true. Any termination decision will be controlled by the policy's oversight committee and appropriations subcommittee, and such committees are most likely to be dominated by ranking members who are closely associated with the policy's past. Perhaps, as junior members of these committees, they even proposed or developed the policy.[32] A committee chairman who is about to retire may be willing to make the enemies necessary to force through a termination bill, but those who aspire to a career of legislative influence will seek friends, not enemies.

Second, legislative bodies are designed to facilitate compromise. Thus, the most likely result of any termination legislation will be modification, reorganization, revision—perhaps not unchanged continuation, but certainly not complete termination. Consequently, the terminator should develop a decision-making procedure that avoids requiring the legislature to vote, consciously and publicly, on a specific termination bill. Informal approval from key legislative leaders—as DYS Commissioner Miller had from the Speaker of the Massachusetts House of Representatives and the NPS had from its House appropriations subcommittee—is the best way to obtain legislative support.[33]

Hint 8: Do Not Encroach on Legislative Prerogatives

Often, informal agreements between legislative and executive branch leaders will not be sufficient to terminate a policy. Formal legislative action may be required. In such cases, executive branch terminators can avoid turning potential supporters into opponents by not attempting to usurp the prerogatives of the legislative branch —or even appearing to do so. An executive branch memo, prepared while Phillips was acting director of OEO, listed as one element of a successful congressional (termination) strategy "Avoid confrontation between the Constitutional powers of the President and the Congress."[34] Yet Phillips did not follow this advice. President Nixon never submitted Phillips's name to the Senate for confirmation as OEO's director—"I'd have to spend all my time up there getting confirmed, and I'd never get the place dismantled," Phillips explained[35]—and in June 1973 a district court judge, ruling on a suit brought by four Democratic senators, found that Phillips had been working as director "unlawfully and illegally."[36]

The second Nixon administration undertook other termination efforts with similar disregard for congressional prerogatives. In December 1972 it announced that it was terminating the Rural Environmental Assistance Program (REAP) by impounding its funds. This program under the U.S. Department of Agriculture (USDA) subsidized farm owners who construct dams and other soil conservation facilities, even though many of these "environmental" projects need to be built in the normal course of farming. Urban congressmen had long been apathetic if not hostile to REAP, and the Nixon administration might well have won their support for terminating the program. But neither the White House nor the USDA made any real effort to explain or to publicize the evils or inefficiencies of the program. The USDA merely issued a statement announcing that the funds appropriated by Congress had been impounded.[37]

As a result, the major issue became not the merits of REAP but the President's authority to impound funds and to terminate a program without congressional approval. By permitting the central issue of the debate to be congressional prerogatives rather than the policy itself, the Nixon administration turned REAP's urban opponents into supporters. The view of W. R. Poage, chairman of the House Agriculture Committee, that "the authority of Congress as a separate branch of government has been harshly challenged," was echoed by Phillip Burton, rep-. resentative from San Francisco: "It is in the best interest of all of us, from the cities and suburbs as well as from the rural areas, to reaffirm the congressional will."[38]

Moreover, the controversy over legislative prerogatives ensured that any termination would require a legislative vote. In February 1973, the House passed a bill (251 to 142) that required the President to spend the REAP funds appropriated by Congress, and the Senate passed similar legislation (71 to 10) in March. Fearing that a veto would be sustained in the House, congressional leaders did not send the legislation to the President; instead a revised REAP (called the Rural Environmental Conservation Program) was included in the omnibus farm bill passed in August 1973. Today, farmers still receive subsidies for undertaking soil conservation projects.[39]

Any policy action involves a variety of different issues, both substantive and procedural, and any one (or several) of these issues can dominate the political debate. For any policy entrepreneur the obvious strategy is to emphasize those issues that will mobilize the largest supporting coalition and will give the opposition little opportunity to raise issues that may cause desertions from that coalition. For a terminator from the executive branch this usually means focusing attention on the substantive issues—the harm caused by the policy, or at least the policy's inadequacies—and avoiding a confrontation over constitutional prerogatives.

Hint 9: Accept Short-Term Cost Increases

"City Defense Office Costs More to Shut Than Run for Year," announced a headline in the *Washington Post*. The accompanying story reported that it would cost the District of Columbia $134,000 to operate the mayor's civil defense office for fiscal year 1977, but $313,000 to close it.[40]

In fact, terminating a public policy often costs more in the short run than continuing it. While Massachusetts was in the process of closing its public training schools and replacing them with a collection of privately operated group homes,

ROBERT D. BEHN

the state was forced to pay for both systems.[41] And when the U.S. Navy decided in early 1977 to "disestablish" the Naval Electronic Systems Engineering Center in Washington, D.C., it calculated that this would result in an annual cost savings of $47,000 and an annual manpower savings of $450,000, but that "anticipated one-time costs" were $818,000.[42]

Terminating a public policy may not save money during the next fiscal year. Severance payments and the costs of initiating a replacement policy (and, for a period of time, a redundant policy) may make termination a poor tactic for achieving short-term economies. Termination may require a temporary rise in costs to gain long-term savings.

Hint 10: Buy Off the Beneficiaries

Such short-term increases may result, in part, from attempts to mollify those opposed to the termination. Complete appeasement will not be possible, but some form of severance payment may mitigate the consequences of termination for some of the beneficiaries.

The government employees who administer the policy will be the easiest to placate; they can be offered new jobs. Yet even such a guarantee will not completely assuage them. The professional uncertainties and the personal inconveniences will be disruptive. Any public program is administered, in part at least, by people dedicated to the policy, and it may simply be impossible to buy them off.

To a policy's clientele, termination for any reason looks like discrimination — "Why my policy? Why not that guy's policy?" Consequently, the clientele may not consider any severance payment an equitable settlement. If the case for termination is strong, however, the political leaders of the constituency may accept the severance payment offered as the best deal that can be made in a nearly hopeless situation. Moreover, a severance payment may help convince the general public that the termination is not discriminatory.

Hint 11: Advocate Adoption, Not Termination

Political leaders do not like to terminate policies. As Peter deLeon explains, there are too many "strong negative connotations" associated with such undertakings.[43] Political leaders do, however, like to initiate new and better policies. Consequently, the termination of policy A may be best realized through the adoption of policy B, when the selection of B necessitates the elimination of A. Most policy innovations can be viewed from several perspectives, and it is most effective to present any change in a manner that focuses attention on the issues that have the most political support and deemphasize those aspects that will generate opposition.

This appears to be what happened in the closing of California's mental hospitals—though not because of any conscious strategy—for the debate was over whether the state should involuntarily commit individuals to these institutions, not whether to close them. Cameron notes, however, that rewriting the involuntary commitment laws "would achieve essentially the same purpose since the hospital clientele was predominately this category of patient." Selecting involuntary commitment as the policy to be changed made the central issue a moral one—individual liberty—and rallied support from civil libertarians. Yet if the legislature "had centered its attention upon termination of the state hospitals," writes Cameron, "it would have faced considerable resistance." Cameron concludes that "the question of the eventual termination of state hospitals was never addressed during the policy adoption phase, nor do the designers of the legislation acknowledge it as their intention."[44]

Unfortunately, this approach can lead to some difficulties at the implementation state. Since no one recognizes or acknowledges that policy A will have to be terminated, such consequences of adopting policy B will be ignored. And this too, reports Cameron, happened in California: "Because policy makers failed to address the termination aspects of the new mental health law, they were unable to project the consequences of putting the plan into operation....Termination of hospital programs for the mentally ill proceeded with little planning and less coordination."[45] Obfuscating the termination aspects of an innovation may be politically expedient to achieve policy adoption; but, at the implementation stage, this may appear to have been a deleterious strategy that also obscured some critical problems that could have been resolved when the policy was designed and adopted. As Pressman and Wildavsky emphasize, political leaders need to identify and deal with the various tasks of implementation from the earliest stages of the policy process.[46]

Hint 12: Terminate Only What Is Necessary

Given the variety of reasons for terminating a policy, terminators should be conscious of their own motivation. "Opponents" seek to terminate a policy because it is wrong. "Economizers" seek to terminate a policy because it is inefficient, ineffective, or expensive. "Reformers" seek to terminate a policy because doing so is a prerequisite to the institution of a better, replacement policy.[47]

The motivation of the terminators and their principal allies will indicate precisely what aspects of the policy are the most important to eliminate and what aspects it is acceptable to retain. Opponents may settle for the termination of merely the one component of a large policy that they consider wrong, even if this does not save the government any money. Economizers may settle for reorganization or modification rather than complete termination, if this produces significant savings. (Indeed, since economizers, unlike opponents or reformers, may be able to achieve their objectives without complete termination, they may find compromise quite acceptable.) The less terminated, the fewer the people threatened by the termination, and thus the smaller and less energetic the antitermination coalition.

When Commissioner Miller closed the Massachusetts public training schools, he understood that what he really wanted to terminate was the policy of incarcerating juvenile offenders in state-operated institutions. In the short run, at least, he was much less concerned about terminating the policy of paying state employees to operate and maintain these institutions. Terminating the salaries of the institutions' employees was necessary only to ensure that the policy of housing youths in those institutions could not be reinstated.

This distinction gave Miller an extra degree of strategic flexibility. He simply removed the youths from the institutions. He retained the staffs of the training schools, but without any youths to supervise. Three years after the institutions were closed, some state employees were still "working" in them.[48] Miller's willingness to keep unproductive employees on the payroll, while the institutions were closed and his policy changes consolidated, was essential to neutralizing the resistance of the employees to termination. Miller in effect provided them with a significant severance payment.

The distinction between a policy and the agency that administers it is important. Is the policy to be terminated because it is harmful or needs to be reformed, or is the agency to be eliminated because it is too expensive? The policy can be terminated and the agency maintained, or the agency can be terminated and the policy transferred to another department. To concentrate their energies, terminators must understand precisely what is their target.

Some Thoughts on the Research Base

These hints are clearly designed to facilitate termination that results from a relatively brief but very visible political struggle rather than from a slow process of attrition. This bias in favor of the "big-bang" rather than the "long-whimper" mode of termination reflects the practicalities of both policy research and political action.[49]

Because the conflict generated by big-bang termination efforts is more public and intense, examples of this process (both successful and unsuccessful) are easier to identify and more interesting to study. Indeed, how do you even distinguish a serious but unsuccessful attempt to achieve termination through decremental budgeting from the normal fluctuations in the policy's budget?[50] There is no empirical evidence to suggest that termination occurs more frequently or more successfully as a result of sudden and vigorous efforts than as a result of prolonged and subtle ones. The big-bang mode is simply easier to identify and study.

Furthermore, the outcome of a big-bang termination effort is more easily affected by any individual terminator's strategic thinking and political action. Long-whimper termination may require a decade or more to implement, and a political leader may not hold a position of influence long enough to initiate and complete such an effort. Consequently, anyone seeking assistance about how to terminate a public policy is probably, if unconsciously, asking for suggestions about how to achieve a big-bang success. Thus, the orientation of these suggestions also reflects the interests of termination activists.

338

It should be obvious that the research base from which these hints are drawn (a few quite detailed, termination case studies, plus numerous, less formal, observations of a variety of termination efforts, both successful and unsuccessful) is uncomfortably narrow. As Bardach has noted, problems are inherent in any attempt to analyze the termination process.

> A...reason for the scholarly neglect of this subject is that it is hard to study such an infrequent phenomenon as policy termination. One always suspects that each instance of the phenomenon is bound to be so idiosyncratic that no interesting generalizations will be possible. Since social science—and social scientists—thrive on generalizations rather than idiosyncracies, termination has never become "hot" as a topic of academic interest.[51]

These hints are an attempt to sort the general from the idiosyncratic. They are presented not as a final guide to planning termination strategies—not as "Ironclad Laws that Guarantee Termination"—but with the hope that they will provoke debate, new thinking, and new research. The field of policy termination clearly needs a set of hypotheses with which to experiment and an expanded base of case studies—cases that explicitly address and attempt to test these hypotheses.

The Ethics of Policy Termination

The difficulty of terminating a public policy can easily entice terminators into flagrant and excessive manipulations of the political process. Frustrated by the ease with which a policy's supporters can thwart them, terminators may quickly conclude that success simply cannot be achieved by traditional and legitimate political activity. Thus there is a clear need to examine the ethics of policy termination. Both Howard Phillips at OEO and Jerome Miller at Massachusetts DYS generated serious debate about the legality and morality of their tactics.

If termination is more likely to result from executive rather than legislative action, how legitimate is it to ignore the legislature? What is an acceptable exercise of executive discretion and what is a violation of the legislature's constitutional responsibilities? Both Phillips and Miller clearly considered it their duty to be decisive and manipulative. Neither sought formal legislative approval for his decision to close down statutorily established governmental activities. Yet Miller, an appointee of a Republican governor, had the support of the Democratic Speaker of the Massachusetts House of Representatives for his policy objectives. Although he permitted House members to hold hearings and make noise about the issue, the Speaker privately let it be known that Miller was not to be stopped.[52] Phillips, in contrast, had no such support from the leadership of Congress. Is this difference significant? Can we define Miller's actions as within his administrative discretion, but Phillips's as unethical?

Further, if termination is more likely to result from a situation in which compromise appears impossible, how legitimate is polarizing debate so that an appropriate compromise cannot be achieved? Reasoned, informed, and intelligent political debate is a central value of democratic government. When is an effort to promote termination by inhibiting compromise a legitimate political activity, and when is it a violent disregard of the fundamental necessity of democratic debate?

These twelve hints have been presented starkly—as commandments. In some situations, they will be clearly acceptable. In others, they will be obviously unethical. The hard questions concern the ambiguous cases. Careful thinking about the ethics of termination tactics is necessary.

Policy entrepreneurs have a responsibility not only to the integrity of the political process, however, but also to the policy consequences of their actions, an obligation to see that ineffective and inefficient policies are either changed or eliminated. This points to another aspect of the ethics of termination—the need to specify conditions that justify termination as well as those that mandate it.

Finally, a special problem is posed by the beneficiaries of an established policy. Since the objective of termination is to deny people existing benefits, any attempt at termination will arouse some who believe that the termination itself is unethical. This view is clearly unacceptable; every government activity should be subject to evaluation, modification, and the possibility of termination. As implied by the "entitlement ethic," public obligation to the beneficiaries of a policy marked for termination does exist, however. Individuals and organizations make plans and commitments based on the assumption that the policy will continue. If the termination of a public policy involves the abrogation of a government commitment—a commitment either expressly stated or merely implied—the terminators have an obligation to provide the policy's constituency a smooth transition to a benefitless future.

Termination is difficult, in part, because we are so ignorant about how it can be achieved. It is clearly the neglected butt of the policy process. Of Harold D. Lasswell's seven categories of functional analysis, we know the least about termination.[53] Moreover, as Biller observes, "when resources are insufficient to afford new ventures without ending old ones, a situation increasingly recognizable in most contexts, the strategies of facilitating termination take on major importance."[54] A better understanding of the termination process would not only be intellectually welcome, but also could have significant practical consequences.

Notes

1. The (anonymous) senator is quoted by Tom Braden in "Scraping the Pork Barrel," *Washington Post*, April 23, 1977.
2. Senator Byrd is quoted by Adam Clymer in "President, in Shift, Favors Some Funds for Water Projects," *New York Times*, April 16, 1977.
3. Les Brown, "Ford Weighs Shift of Telecommunications Office," *New York Times*, January 16, 1975.
4. See Les Brown, "President to Retain Communications Policy Office," *New York Times*, January 18, 1975; and John Carmody, "TV Oversight Unit Gets Ford Reprieve," *Washington Post*, January 18, 1975.
5. For a discussion of the "entitlement ethic," see Robert D. Behn, "Policy Termination and

the Sunset Laws," prepared statement in *Sunset Act of 1977, Hearings on S.2 before the Subcommittee on Intergovernmental Relations of the Committee on Governmental Affairs, United States Senate, 95th Cong., 1st sess.* (Washington, D.C.: U.S. Government Printing Office, 1977), p. 349.

6. Raymond A. Bauer, Ithiel de Sola Pool, and Lewis Anthony Dexter, *American Business and Public Policy* (Cambridge, Mass.: MIT, 1963), p. 142.

7. The aide is quoted by Haynes Johnson, "Government Gone Awry," *Washington Post*, March 29, 1977.

8. For a discussion of this maneuver, see ibid.

9. White House press release, February 21, 1977.

10. See Robert D. Behn, "Termination: How Massachusetts Department of Youth Services Closed the Public Training Schools" (Duke University, Institute of Policy Sciences Working Paper 5752, May 1975), pp. 38–46; and Robert D. Behn, "Closing the Massachusetts Public Training Schools," *Policy Sciences* 7 (June 1976): 156–58.

11. Robert P. Biller, "Prepared Statement" in *Sunset Act of 1977*, p. 341.

12. Harold Seidman, *Politics, Position, and Power* (2nd ed.; New York: Oxford University Press, 1975), p. 157.

13. E. E. Schattschneider, *The Semisovereign People* (Hinsdale, Ill.: Dryden, 1975), p. 3.

14. See Behn, "Termination," pp. 20–27; and Behn, "Closing Massachusetts Training Schools," pp. 152–54.

15. See Robert D. Behn and Martha A. Clark, "Termination II: How the National Park Service Annulled Its 'Commitment' to a Beach Erosion Control Policy at the Cape Hatteras National Seashore" (Duke University, Institute of Policy Sciences Working Paper 1176, November 1976), pp. 60–69.

16. For a discussion of how these "unorganized interests" are represented, see Mark V. Nadel, "Unorganized Interests and the Politics of Consumer Protection," in *Politics in America: Studies in Policy Analysis*, ed. Michael P. Smith and Associates (New York: Random House, 1974), pp. 148–68.

17. See Behn, "Termination," pp. 38–46; and Behn, "Closing Massachusetts Training Schools," pp. 156–58.

18. See Behn and Clark, "Termination II," pp. 37–59.

19. David J. Rothman, "Prisons, Asylums, and Other Decaying Institutions," *The Public Interest* 26 (Winter 1972): 15.

20. Ibid., p. 3.

21. James M. Cameron, "Restructuring California's Mental Health System: The Role of Ideology in Policy Termination" (paper presented at the 1977 annual meeting of the American Political Science Association, Washington, D.C., 3 September 1977), p. 24.

22. See Behn and Clark, "Termination II," pp. 37–59.

23. Herbert A. Simon, Donald W. Smithburg, and Victor A. Thompson, *Public Administration* (New York: Knopf, 1950), pp. 410–12.

24. The U.S. Army Corps of Engineers estimated in 1972 that to stabilize the entire seventy-five miles of the national seashore would cost an initial $50 million, plus $2.5 million in annual maintenance.

25. See Behn and Clark, "Termination II," pp. 70–78.

26. See Behn, "Termination," pp. 38–46 and 77–78; and Behn, "Closing Massachusetts Training Schools," pp. 156–58 and 166.

27. Eugene Bardach, "Policy Termination as a Political Process," *Policy Sciences* 7 (June 1976): 130.

28. See Richard E. Cohen, "Congress Report/Courts act as ally to Congress in battle with President over spending," *National Journal* 5 (April 21, 1973): 571–73.

29. See Behn, "Termination," pp. 71–75; and Behn, "Closing Massachusetts Training Schools," pp. 164–65.

30. See Richard P. Nathan, *The Plot That Failed: Nixon and the Administrative Presidency* (New York: Wiley, 1975), esp. p. 68.

31. See Behn and Clark, "Termination II," pp. 99–101.

32. Since these "hints" are not rules, each has its counterexample. The bill that resulted in the termination of the Bay Area Sewer Services Agency (BASSA) in California was introduced in 1976 by state Assemblyman John T. Knox, who had first proposed the agency in 1971. Moreover, BASSA was terminated because it was ineffective and expensive; it had not in fact been creating any harm (such as increasing the sewage dumped into San Francisco Bay.) See Lee Fremstad, "Hallelujah! The Death of a Public Agency (almost)," *California Journal* 3 (January 1977): 21–22.

33. See Behn, "Termination," pp. 28–35; and Behn, "Closing Massachusetts Training Schools," pp. 154–55.

34. This undated, unsigned memorandum was excerpted in *Congressional Quarterly Weekly Report* 31 (March 3, 1973): 432–43.

35. Ibid., p. 431.

36. *National Journal* 5 (June 16, 1973): 882. The third component of the OEO termination strategy, as outlined in the memo—"Present the Congress with a fait accompli"— did, however, ensure that judicial interference came too late to reverse much of Phillips's work. OEO was dismantled, although community action, the OEO program marked for termination rather than transfer, lives on in the Community Services Administration.

37. The USDA issued a one-page press release on December 26, 1972 headlined "Activities Under REAP and Water Bank Programs Terminated."

38. U.S., Congress, *Congressional Quarterly Almanac*, 93rd Cong., 1st sess. 1973, 29, pp. 308–9.

39. Ibid., pp. 307–10. See also Louis Fisher, *Presidential Spending Power* (Princeton, N.J.: Princeton University Press, 1975), pp. 177–79.

40. Paul W. Valentine, "City Defense Office Costs More to Shut Than Run for Year," *Washington Post*, March 5, 1976.

41. Behn, "Termination," pp. 32–33; and Behn, "Closing Massachusetts Training Schools," p. 195.

42. From an undated "Briefing Sheet" provided by the Office of the Chief of Naval Operations, U.S. Department of Defense.

43. Peter deLeon, "A Theory of Termination in the Policy Process: Roles, Rhymes, and Reasons," *Policy Analysis* 3 (Summer 1978): 369–92.

44. Cameron, "Restructuring Mental Health," pp. 24, 25, and 26.

45. Ibid., pp. 26–27.

46. Jeffrey L. Pressman and Aaron B. Wildavsky, *Implementation* (Berkeley and Los Angeles: University of California Press, 1973).

47. For a discussion of the different motives for termination see Behn, "Termination," pp. 9–14; and Bardach, "Policy Termination," pp. 126–27.

48. See Behn, "Termination," pp. 24–27; and Behn, "Closing Massachusetts Training Schools," pp. 153–54.

49. For a discussion of "how termination occurs," see Bardach, "Policy Termination," pp. 125–26.

50. For a discussion of decremental budgeting, see W. Henry Lambright and Harvey M. Sapolsky, "Terminating Federal Research and Development Programs," *Policy Sciences* 7 (June 1976): 203.

51. Bardach, "Policy Termination," p. 123.

52. See Behn, "Termination," pp. 25–28; and Behn, "Closing Massachusetts Training Schools," pp. 154–55.

53. Lasswell's seven categories of functional analysis are intelligence, recommendation, prescription, invocation, application, appraisal, and termination. See Harold D. Lasswell, "The Decision Process: Seven Categories of Functional Analysis," in *Politics and Social Life*, ed. Nelson W. Polsby et al. (Boston: Houghton Mifflin, 1963), pp. 93–105.

54. Robert P. Biller, "On Tolerating Policy and Organizational Termination: Some Design Considerations," *Policy Sciences* 7 (June 1976): 134.

About the Contributors

Robert D. Behn is an associate professor at the Institute of Policy Sciences and Public Affairs, Duke University.

James R. Cleaveland is a vice president of Management Analysis Center, Inc., Washington, D.C.

Leonard Greenhalgh is an assistant professor at the Amos Tuck School of Business Administration, Dartmouth College.

Edward K. Hamilton is president of Hamilton, Rabinovitz & Szanton, Inc., and adjunct professor in public management, University of California—Los Angeles.

Harry P. Hatry is director of the State and Local Government Research Program at the Urban Institute, Washington, D.C.

Nancy S. Hayward is an independent consultant. She has served as assistant director for the National Center for Productivity and Quality of Working Life.

Regina E. Herzlinger is an associate professor of business administration at the Harvard Business School.

Charles H. Levine is director of the Institute for Urban Studies and the Bureau of Governmental Research, University of Maryland.

Richard L. Lucier is an associate professor of economics at Denison University.

Robert B. McKersie is a professor and former dean of the New York State School of Industrial and Labor Relations at Cornell University.

Charles A. Morrison is city manager of Auburn, Maine. His essay in this book was written while he was an associate of the National Training and Development Service.

Selma J. Mushkin was a professor of economics and formerly director of the Public Services Laboratory at Georgetown University.

B. Guy Peters is a professor of political science and director of the Center for Policy Studies, Tulane University.

Richard Rose is director of the Centre for the Study of Public Policy, University of Strathclyde, Great Britain.

Irene Rubin is an assistant professor at the Institute for Urban Studies, University of Maryland.

E. S. Savas is a professor of public systems management and director of the Center for Government Studies in the Graduate School of Business at Columbia University.

Paul R. Schulman is an assistant professor of political science at Mills College.

Martin Shefter is an associate professor of government at Cornell University.

David W. Singleton is an administrative assistant to the mayor of Wilmington, Delaware.

Bruce A. Smith is a special assistant to the mayor of Wilmington, Delaware.

David T. Stanley is an independent consultant. He is a retired senior fellow of the Brookings Institution.

Charles L. Vehorn is a staff economist at the U.S. General Accounting Office.

David B. Walker is assistant director of the Advisory Commission on Inter-governmental Relations for governmental structures and functions.